The Martin Luther Quincentennial

Martin Luther.   Woodcut by Lucas Cranach the Elder

THE MARTIN LUTHER QUINCENTENNIAL

edited by
Gerhard Dünnhaupt
UNIVERSITY OF MICHIGAN

Published by Wayne State University Press
for *Michigan Germanic Studies,*
Detroit   1985

Library of Congress Cataloging in Publication Data

Martin Luther Quincentennial Conference (1983 :
  University of Michigan)
  The Martin Luther quincentennial.

  "These studies were presented at the Martin Luther
Quincentennial Conference held at the University of
Michigan, Ann Arbor, September 26-29, 1983. They are
reprinted from Michigan Germanic studies, volume 10,
numbers 1 and 2, spring/fall 1984."
  Includes index.
  1. Luther, Martin, 1483-1546—Congresses.
2. Reformation—Congresses. 3. Germany—History—1517-
1648—Congresses. 4. German Literature—History and
criticism—Congresses. I. Dünnhaupt, Gerhard.
II. Michigan Germanic studies. III. Title.
BR323.7.M36   1983   943'.03'0924   84-15239
ISBN 0-8143-1774-X

Published by Wayne State University Press, Detroit, Michigan 48202.

These studies were presented at the Martin Luther Quincentennial Conference held at the
University of Michigan, Ann Arbor, September 26-29, 1983. They are reprinted from
Michigan Germanic Studies, volume 10, numbers 1 and 2, Spring/Fall 1984.

TABLE OF CONTENTS

THE MARTIN LUTHER QUINCENTENNIAL

THE RHETORIC OF REFORMATION: LUTHER AND HIS TEXTS

THE HISTORICAL CONTEXT: LUTHER AND HIS CONTEMPORARIES

v

TABLE OF STANDARD ABBREVIATIONS
USED THROUGHOUT THIS VOLUME

AAS   *Acta Apostolica Sedis.*

CL   *Luthers Werke in Auswahl,* ed. Otto Clemen. 6 vols. Berlin: Walter de Gruyter, 1960.

LW   *Luther's Works, American Edition,* ed. Helmut T. Lehmann et al. 54 vols. Philadelphia and St. Louis, 1955 ff.

WA   *D. Martin Luthers Werke,* Kritische Gesamtausgabe. Weimar, 1883-1983.—Quotes refer to volume, page, and where necessary, line.

WA Br   *D. Martin Luthers Werke, Briefwechsel.* Weimar, 1930-1948.

WA TR   *D. Martin Luthers Werke, Tischreden.* Weimar, 1912-1921.

FOREWORD: LUTHER'S LITERARY LEGACY

Gerhard Dünnhaupt

The forty-two-line Bible was the publishing project that brought world renown and lasting fame to Johann Gutenberg of Mainz. Yet years earlier, he had been busily putting his new moveable type to good use by printing certain small items much in demand by his contemporaries: letters of indulgence! Printers continued to enrich themselves supplying this market for several generations after Gutenberg, until 1517, when Martin Luther first tried to express his indignance about the practice of indulgence sales. That he directed his complaints to Albrecht, the youthful Cardinal of Mainz, who had a strong financial interest in these sales, may be attributable to his guilelessness or inexperience in business matters.

Luther's struggles thus commenced with a skirmish over the products of the printing press, that infernal yet divine instrument to which his Reformation may well have owed its ultimate success. Indeed, some scholars have noted that earlier reformers who had expressed views not unlike those of Luther were not blessed with similar success because they had no way of communicating them to the public. Luther was well aware of the debt owed to the new medium at his disposal. Firmly convinced that the end of the world was close at hand, he called printing "God's last and greatest gift to mankind...the final flame before the extinction of the world."[1]

As the historian Elizabeth Eisenstein has pointed out, the power of the printing press, "often overlooked in the discussions of the Renaissance, is less likely to go unnoticed in Reformation studies."[2] Even Luther's earliest pamphlets from 1517 to 1520, the fledgling years of the Reformation—only thirty in number—probably sold well over 300,000 copies.[3] During the next couple of decades, however, when publications started to flow from his pen *en masse,* the total number of printed copies certainly ran into the millions, representing an ever-increasing percentage of the total production of German printers, especially if one considers that Luther's own texts stimulated a river of argument both *pro* and *con.* Though Luther steadfastly maintained his policy of never accepting money for his writings, his printers grew rich by producing a flood of reprints, both authorized and unauthorized.[4]

ix

After 1520, Luther provided his publishers with opportunities hitherto undreamed-of. From then until his death twenty-six years later, he produced no less than 1,250 different titles, ranging from broadsheets to huge folio tomes. Bibliographers have counted some 3,700 separate editions of these works issued before he died in 1546, and a total of some 9,000 before the end of his century. Moreover, the profitable "Luther business" of course encompassed works by his contemporaries, with praise and comment, criticism and condemnation of his writings. Martin Brecht counts no less than nineteen printers in the little town of Wittenberg alone, who—more or less on a full-time basis—were engaged in printing and reprinting Luther's works. Printers in other towns were no less active: at Strassburg there were 24 of them, and 22 at Nürnberg. Augsburg had 20, Basel 13, Antwerp 12, and Erfurt 10 printers spreading Luther's word, to say nothing of foreign-language translations now appearing with increasing frequency in England, Sweden, Poland, Bohemia, Hungary, Italy, France, and the Netherlands.[5]

Subsequent centuries saw the violent polemics between Luther's followers and their enemies gradually give way to a more detached, scholarly approach, but the flow of secondary literature never diminished. Even today, in an average year some six hundred to one thousand new scholarly treatises on Luther and his Reformation appear, and no doubt the Quincentennial will provide another banner year for the world's publishing trade. In the face of such overwhelming evidence of continued scholarly interest in Luther and his time, a layman might consider it almost presumptuous to expect new breakthroughs in a field on which such a vast amount of research has already been expended. In reality almost the opposite is true. Scholarly emphasis may have shifted somewhat from the positivistic-biographical toward the socio-historical plane, but so much new information has come to light in recent decades that it becomes increasingly clear that Reformation scholarship still stands at the threshold of new and exciting discoveries.

Notes to Foreword

1. "Die Druckerey ist Summum et postremum donum/ durch welches Gott die sache des Euangelij fort treibt/ es ist die letzte Flamme für dem außleschen der Welt," the closing passage of the second edition of *Der Tischreden D. Mart. Luthers,* ed. Johann Aurifaber (Frankfurt/M., 1567), p. 775.

2. Elizabeth Eisenstein, *The Printing Press as an Agent of Change* (Cambridge, 1979), p. 303.

3. Arthur Geoffrey Dickens, *Reformation and Society in 16th-Century Europe* (New York, 1968), p. 51.

4. Cf. Harry G. Haile, review of Elizabeth Eisenstein, *The Printing Press as Agent of Change,* in *Michigan Germanic Studies,* 6 (1980), 120-129.

5. Martin Brecht, "Gott hat uns die Druckerei dazu geschenkt, um hauptsächlich den Papst zu unterdrücken," in *Börsenblatt für den Deutschen Buchhandel,* Frankfurt ed., 39th year, no. 20 (March 11, 1983), pp. 597-599.

EDITOR'S NOTE

In planning a major interdisciplinary conference in honor of Luther's five-hundredth anniversary, those involved believed that The University of Michigan should refrain from the temptation of organizing a mere media event of the sort being mounted in other places around the world. A major scholarly institution is indeed the proper forum for a group of first-rate North American Luther scholars to present the results of their most recent research. That our conference proved to be such a success in every respect is largely due to the quality of the active participants and to the chance it offered for a meeting of minds. Lively discussions followed the presentation of each paper, and the casual atmosphere of private gatherings provided ample opportunity for a further exchange of ideas. A verbatim transcription of the discussions was not undertaken, as it might have hampered the spontaneity of the proceedings. Instead, the speakers were given an opportunity to review and revise their papers to reflect important points brought out during the discussions.

The Martin Luther Quincentennial Conference of The University of Michigan was made possible by the efforts of V. Charles Hubbs, Co-Chairman for Finance of the Luther Conference, and the generosity of the following corporate and private donors: the Dean's Enrichment Fund, College of Literature, Sciences, and the Arts, The University of Michigan; The Max Kade Foundation; The Bank of Nova Scotia; the Exxon Education Fund; Elaine Adler Bresnick; Ralph P. Fichtner; Mr. and Mrs. Harold K. Jacobson; Stephen W. Shepard; and Richard A. and Barbara J. Wagner.

The editor of this volume wishes to acknowledge here the following individuals who generously contributed their time and personal effort to making this conference the success it has been:

Anne Beebe
Holde E. Borcherts
Paul C. Boylan
Helen S. Butz
Jennifer A. Carlson
Elaine W. Court
David E. Crawford
Garry W. Davis

William N. De Turk
Robert DeWerff
Elizabeth L. Eisenstein
Hans J. Fabian
David Noel Freedman
Peter A. Hess
Robert L. Kyes
Erich H. Markel

Margot Massey
Anne Maycock
Margarete Orlik-Walsh
Robert E. Peel
Henry N. Pollack
Andrew Preis
Jacob M. Price
Tim Slavin
Robert J. Starring
William B. Stegath

Peter O. Steiner
Marsha D. Stuckey
Enid D. Sutherland
Thomas N. Tentler
Charles Trinkaus
James A. Vann III
Martin W. Walsh
Lee Wandel
Charles Witke

This volume collects the papers presented at the Martin Luther Quincentennial Conference held at The University of Michigan on September 27-29, 1983. The publication was made possible by a grant from The Max Kade Foundation. The undersigned editor is especially indebted to his colleagues V. Charles Hubbs and Robert L. Kyes for their help in seeing this volume through the press.

Ann Arbor, Spring 1984   *Gerhard Dünnhaupt*

THE RHETORIC OF REFORMATION
LUTHER AND HIS TEXTS

LUTHER THE PREACHER

John W. O'Malley S.J., *Weston School of Theology, Cambridge MA*

The corpus of Luther's writings that has come down to us contains an immense amount of material that relates directly and obviously to preaching. Many studies have utilized this material for a more accurate understanding of his theology, but examinations of his "art," of his preaching practice, have been few. The treatment of him in general histories of preaching has often been vague and sometimes uncritically encomiastic.

How is this phenomenon to be explained? Part of the explanation surely lies in the fact that the history of rhetoric has only recently begun to be explored by scholars in a technically adequate way and applied to preaching.[1] It is from the viewpoint of this relatively new discipline that I intend to address Luther here. Although I have been interested in him for years, I can make no claim to a comprehensive knowledge of his writings, and I come at him almost as an outsider. However, by looking at Luther with somewhat fresh eyes, from a somewhat different academic perspective, perhaps some light will be thrown on him, and we will be able to assess his place in a different tradition from the doctrinal and institutional ones in which he is commonly studied. I will build upon a few recent studies of Luther that with technical competence have examined his preaching art, especially Ulrich Nembach's *Predigt des Evangeliums,* and try to carry the examination a step further by placing it in a wider context.[2] I must right off apologize for the highly condensed nature of my treatment, which to be done properly would require a full volume.[3]

Surely another reason for the neglect of Luther's preaching art is that, unlike so many of his contemporaries and near-contemporaries, he left us no specific treatise on how to preach. One of the most characteristic features of theology after the first few decades of the sixteenth century was the proliferation, the veritable explosion, of such treatises.[4] This phenomenon was a continuation of the tradition of the scholastic *artes praedicandi* and at the same time a vigorous reaction against it, as preachers searched the classical and Christian traditions for alternatives to the prescriptions of those manuals.

In this search, despite his failure to write a treatise on the subject, Luther was in the forefront. For the moment, however, we must simply be aware that any study of Luther's art of preaching must be done inductively—from the sermons and sermon materials he left us, and from the *obiter dicta* in these and his other writings.[5] Although we know that we do not possess many of his sermons in the form in which they first left Luther's pen or mouth, we have to work with what we have, and trust that the very volume of his *Nachlass* will be to some extent self-correcting.

The classical treatises on rhetoric isolated three general categories that enter into the assessment of any speech: the speaker, the speech-act, and those to whom the speech is directed. Since these treatises professed to be themselves inductive, we can assume that we have here three categories with which to approach any speech situation, including the Christian pulpit. For economy of space in this short essay, I will concentrate on the second category, in which both form and content must be taken into account. For Luther, both are crucial in assessing him. Unfortunately, I will not be able here to enter into the complex subject of Luther's theology of the Word, essential though that theology is for any comprehensive treatment of his preaching.

Let us, therefore, turn our attention to the form of Luther's sermons and postils, to the form of the speech-act, as we now have it. What do we find? As has often been noted, the structure of a few of the early sermons is heavily influenced by the scholastic or "thematic" sermon as delineated in the medieval *artes*. Luther, however, soon moved away from the thematic model. The trained eye will still detect on occasion some features that correlate with scholastic sermons: Luther sometimes retains the *thema* or scriptural quotation at the beginning; proof-texts still play an important part in most of the sermons; the scholastic *quaestio* does not altogether disappear; there is often no clearly discernible conclusion or peroration.

Yet, despite these seemingly scholastic vestiges, the sermons immediately strike the reader with how different they are from those laid down in the *artes*. Most obviously, they are much freer in their structure than thematic sermons were supposed to be. In this regard they evince a certain variety. For the most part, however, they resemble in a generic way the patristic or monastic homilies in that they progress verse-by-verse through a pericope of Scripture. Not the only, but surely the most clearly visible structure undergirding the sermons, therefore, is the course of the biblical text itself.

What influenced Luther to adopt this homiletic form? Here we must to some extent speculate. It is surely tied to his rejection of scholastic theology for a theology more obviously and directly attached to the text of Scripture.[6] This shift in theological method perforce influenced his preaching style. In this shift we find the most profound reason for the change in his art.

He did not have to search far for this new form. His reading of Augustine would easily have inclined him to it. Moreoever, we know from many examples that in his day the rigid structure prescribed or encouraged by the *artes* was as often followed in the breach as in the observance. That structure was too stiff to be used in its rigor outside formal settings like university audiences. If we examine the sermons of some of the famous preachers who were chronologically close to Luther like Nicholas of Cusa and Thomas à Kempis, two preachers who also had misgivings about scholastic theology or innovated within it, we see that their sermons do not conform to the *artes*.[7] They usually retain the *thema,* as many sermons continued to do until quite recently, but they then move into looser forms similar in some respects to Luther's, and they often manifest a clear relationship to the homily.

We tend to forget the continuing influence of the patristic homily all through the Middle Ages and its renewed influence in the sixteenth century.[8] It is my opinion, for instance, that Erasmus, for all that he has to say about the adaption of classical rhetoric to the pulpit in his *Ecclesiastes* of 1535, still in fact preferred the simple verse-by-verse exposition of Scripture.[9]

Luther made some significant modifications within this form, as we shall see. Nonetheless, in so far as he followed this homiletic pattern, he was not unique among his contemporaries. His practice coincided with and promoted the widespread dissatisfaction with scholastic forms of preaching that characterized the late Middle Ages and that continued well into the sixteenth and seventeenth centuries, even in quarters where we would not be inclined to expect it. The *Constitutions* of the Society of Jesus, for instance, while commending the theology of Aquinas, expressly discouraged the use of the "scholastic manner" of preaching.[10] Robert Bellarmine echoed this distaste for scholastic preaching, and expressly commended the homily, the form ratified for him by its use by the Fathers.[11]

In Luther's day, however, the most innovative attempt to displace the thematic sermon of the scholastics took place in Italy in the context of the humanist movement. This was an attempt to apply classical rhetoric to sacred discourse in a way and to a degree that had hitherto in the history of Christianity been practically unknown. Something must be said, therefore, about the relationship of Luther's preaching to the humanistic revival if we are to place him in the context of his times. One of the limitations of Nembach's book is his failure to locate Luther in this larger context, even though he tries to show that Luther was indeed influenced by a Renaissance enthusiasm for Quintilian.

Relating Luther to the humanistic concerns of some of his contemporaries is a difficult task to accomplish, because we now realize more clearly than ever before how complex a movement Humanism was and how terms like "humanistic theology" or "rhetorical theology" must be broken down into component parts. In the interest of clarity, I shall distinguish within the humanistic tradition a "grammatical" and a "rhetorical" component, corresponding to the traditional stages in classical education, and then subdivide both of these categories once.[12]

"Rhetoric," as presented in classical treatises on the subject, meant oratory. Scholars today make a useful distinction, however, and subdivide rhetoric into "primary" and "secondary."[13] Primary rhetoric is the rhetoric described in Aristotle's *Rhetoric*, in Quintilian's *Institutio oratoria,* and in similar treatises. These treatises deal directly with speech-making, the art of oratory. This rhetoric is oral; in itself it has no text, although subsequently an enunciation can be treated as a text. It is directed to public and civic concerns in the law courts, in senates and popular assemblies, and in ceremonial settings like temples and the courts of princes. The single goal of rhetoric understood in this primary sense is the training of the public speaker.

"Secondary rhetoric" derives from primary and is an adaptation of it, as the term itself implies. It consists in the apparatus of rhetorical techniques clustering around discourse when those techniques are not being used for their primary oral purpose. In secondary rhetoric, the speech-act is replaced by the text, as in epistolography, historical narrative, diatribes, and dialogues. A consistent tendency of classical rhetoric has been to move from the speech-act itself to secondary forms like these. This means a tendency to shift from persuasion to narration, from civic to personal and private contexts, and from speech-making to literature, including poetry. It is at this point, at poetry, that secondary rhetoric begins to blur almost imperceptibly into "grammar."

In classical times and in the Renaissance, rhetoric presupposed grammar, but grammar meant much more than the elementary skills of reading and writing correctly. The "grammarian" taught literature, especially poetry, for it was from poetry that the rules of grammar were originally derived. One of the purposes of grammar was, thus, to teach good style, to teach accurate, appropriate, and felicitous expression. In pursuing this purpose, grammar in fact sometimes becomes almost indistinguishable from "secondary rhetoric."

Another purpose, more distinctive, was to teach how to interpret a text that was being studied in class. The grammarian was, indeed, almost myopically attached to his texts. His exposition of them was, in the first instance, philological, and concentrated on a word-by-word or line-by-line reading. When it was necessary to rise above this so-called "atomistic" exegesis to broader meaning, allegory was invoked. Texts were seen as expressions of philosophical or theological doctrines artfully masked "under the poetic veil." Within grammatical exegesis we have, therefore, two different levels or categories of interpretation—the philological, with attention to minute details of usage, syntax, orthography, and similar matters, and the "poetic," which allowed the scribe or teacher to discover truths of broader scope.

We now have our four categories, useful instruments of analysis even though in practice these sometimes blur into one another: rhetoric, subdivided into primary and secondary, and grammar, subdivided into philology and poetry. Because of the stylistic purposes that constituted an important part of the grammarian's task, he borrowed elements from rhetorical treatises. Nonetheless, an altogether fundamental distinction remained between the grammarian and the rhetorician in the strict sense. Grammar was by definition a text-related discipline, and its practitioners were scribes, schoolmasters, and scholars. Primary rhetoric was not text-related. It was action-related, deed-related, and decision-related, and it looked to public issues like war and peace, like the innocence or guilt of the accused. If we imagine at one end of the spectrum a scribe pouring over his text and at the other a statesman pleading before the senate for a declaration of war, we perceive the issues at stake.[14]

When we apply these categories to Christian preaching, we immediately see how complex the problem is. At least since the days of Origen, who was himself a practicing grammarian before he became a Christian preacher, the Christian art of oratory has been an essentially text-related pursuit. It is concerned with the writings of the Bible. As text-related, it almost eschews the life-related immediacy that primary rhetoric envisioned, and evinces an almost natural affinity for the grammarian's techniques in interpreting a text; yet it is public and communitarian discourse, oratory.

Origen's homilies, despite the relationship they might have to similar practices in the Jewish synagogues, are probably best understood as the application of the interpretative techniques of the classical grammarian to the biblical text.[15] Origen's verse-by-verse exegesis in his homilies closely parallels what must have been his techniques as a grammarian, and he left those techniques as his heritage to the Fathers, most of whom would themselves have been trained in the grammarians' classrooms. His homilies are an *explication de texte*.

How does Luther fit into this scheme, and how does he relate to the humanistic revival of his day? I would maintain that he fits, first and foremost, into the tradition of "the Christian grammarian," and that it is in this category that he was most palpably influenced by the patristic and the Renaissance adaptation of the classical tradition. His sermons generally manifest in their form the characteristics of an *explication de texte*. He saw preaching as a text-related art. He sticks to his text, and he lets it guide the movement of his discourse. Luther's appreciation for the simplicity of the Word of God would make him susceptible to the direct and simple form of the grammarian.

Luther makes use of philological methods, sometimes comparing the Latin or German translation with the Greek or Hebrew original, and he does not hesitate to present this scholarly erudition to his simple audiences, just as a patient teacher would. Luther was dependent in this area on the philological researches of Valla and Erasmus, the two greatest humanists of the Renaissance, whose interests, significantly enough, centered on what I have called grammar and secondary rhetoric, not on primary rhetoric, the art of oratory.[16]

Luther also viewed the text of Scripture as essentially a book of doctrine.[17] Early on he abandoned the traditional four-fold sense of Scripture, yet he wanted, especially when commenting on the Gospels, to get under the actions to the teaching the actions signified. This "sacramental," "spiritual," or "mysterious" level of exegesis, to use his terms, corresponds in a generic way to the allegorical level.[18] He despised the fantasies into which the allegorical method had lapsed, but his own method sometimes has an affinity with a purified version of it. Not so much "under the poetic veil" as "under the historical veil," there lay deeper truths—law-gospel, works-faith, wrath-grace.

Perhaps most fundamental of all, the image that he projects of himself is that of teacher.[19] If the bible is a book of teaching, he is its expositor, laying it open for understanding and appropriation by the student. This explains the lecture-like quality of his sermons. It also explains why only a thin, though important, line seems to distinguish them from his written commentaries on Scripture.[20]

Some of this "grammatical," "scribal," "pedagogical" quality Luther surely drew from the reading of Valla and Erasmus, as well as from his reading of Augustine and other Fathers. But it also relates, I believe, to his training as a scholastic. We tend to be unmindful that Scholasticism early incorporated into itself a grammatical, as well as a dialectical, component, and that that component continued to play a part in the scholastic enterprise, though different in its techniques from the "grammar" of the humanists.[21] Most certainly, the scholastics viewed Scripture as a book of doctrine, almost identifiable in its content with the articles of the Creed.

In a famous passage from the *Tischreden,* Luther defined preaching, basing himself on Romans 12:7-8, as teaching and exhortation—*doctrina et exhortatio.*[22] For him teaching was identical with the practice of dialectics. This, it seems to me, is another link with his early scholastic training. He defined *exhortatio* as the practice of rhetoric, an idea he probably derived to some extent from the scholastic tradition, but more directly from the classical, as I hope to show.

What about Luther and the rhetorical component of the classical tradition? If we focus for a moment on "secondary rhetoric," we see immediately that he did not exercise that art in writing dialogues or historical narratives. He did, however, write letters, treatises, and diatribes. Moreover, he is universally acknowledged as possessing a direct and effective style, which pertains to grammar as well as secondary rhetoric. I do not claim, in fact, the competence to enter into a professional assessment of the literary qualities of his style or to try to trace the sources from which he acquired his stylistic skills. Important though such considerations are for any final assessment of him as preacher, we must on this occasion bypass them and move to primary rhetoric, the art of oratory itself.

We all know from Luther's "Appeal to the Nobility" that he was willing to retain even Aristotle's *Rhetoric* if it could be utilized to produce good preachers.[23] Nembach has demonstrated that Luther esteemed Quintilian.[24] In my opinion, Nembach overstates his case that Quintilian directly influenced the style and structure of Luther's sermons.[25] Nonetheless, his arguments that some of Quintilian's precepts concerning the *contio* (III, 8) are in fact verified in Luther's sermons deserve further study. The *contio* (a term sometimes used by Luther himself) was the form of the classical "deliberative speech" addressed to popular assemblies.[26]

More convincing than Nembach, but independently supportive of his thesis, is the article by Birgit Stolt that analyzes in detail Luther's "Predigt, dass man Kinder zur Schulen halten solle" (1530).[27] This "sermon" completely abandons the homiletical form. Stolt concludes that its structure and rhetorical techniques remarkably correspond to what classical theory envisioned for a speech of the *genus deliberativum* when it was addressed to popular audiences—in other words, the *contio.*

Thus, besides relating to the grammatical component in the classical tradition, Luther's sermons may well have a hitherto unexamined relationship to primary rhetoric. This proposition has a prima facie plausibility, despite a common prejudice that Luther disdained classical rhetoric as a human invention that detracted from a pure presentation of the Word of God. He lived in an age in which primary rhetoric emerged in learned circles with a new prominence. He was in contact with colleagues, enemies, and disciples, especially Melanchthon, who would almost force some of the precepts of primary rhetoric upon his awareness, particularly since he seems to have been born with or early acquired some of the natural gifts of a public speaker.[28]

What is significant is not only that he was, in some way or other, almost certainly in touch with the principles of primary rhetoric, but also that he was influenced by them in a specific way, that is, by ideas found in the classical treatises about the *genus deliberativum*. The fact that Melanchthon was at the same time developing his own theories about the applicability to the pulpit of the *genus deliberativum* and inventing his own new *genus* related to dialectics, the *genus didascalicum* or *didacticum,* provides some external confirmation of this thesis; similar adaptations were being undertaken by Veit Dietrich and Johannes Hoeck, as well as by Erasmus.[29] By the middle of the century it seems that in both Protestant and Catholic circles the *genus deliberativum* had assumed a preeminence over the other two classical *genera—judiciale* and *demonstrativum*.[30] Through a curious act of plagarism from Melanchthon, the *genus didascalicum* made its way into the Catholic tradition in 1543.[31] Luther seems to have played a role in these developments, although his importance has yet to be determined. There is no doubt about the importance of Melanchthon—and, of course, of Erasmus.

What we seem to have in Luther's sermons, therefore, is basically a homiletic form, conditioned in part by the classical *contio*. This combination would allow Luther to fashion his sermons as direct exposition of the text of Scripture, yet give him techniques for public address that were lacking in the homily as such. The sermons certainly possess a strongly doctrinal emphasis and a pedagogical intent, which relates to Melanchthon's *genus didascalicum*. To this intent was conjoined an exhortatory component. This component was directed by him to a popular audience—not to the learned, but to ordinary men, women, and youths, who were assumed to be relatively ignorant and in need of clear directives and motivation. This would correspond to the feisty oratory of the popular assembly, as adapted to an exposition of the *doctrina* of sacred Scripture. The incorporation of elements prescribed for the *contio* would also lift the homily out of the privatized issues that the grammatical form tended to promote, and gave it a more public character, suited to a *Gemeinde.*

To understand the emergence of the *genus deliberativum* in these years, we must examine the humanistic sermons that had come into vogue in Italy in the Quattrocento and that I studied in detail as they were practiced at the papal court.[32] Like Luther, the preachers of these sermons were reacting against the scholastic tradition. However, whereas Luther's sermons were most deeply influenced by the grammatical component of the classical tradition and less clearly by primary rhetoric, the opposite was true in Italy. Moreover, the sermons were clearly constructed according to the principles of the *genus demonstrativum,* the *genus* of ceremonial oratory, the art of praise and blame, the art of panegyric.

These sermons have obvious exordia and perorations. They are less closely attached to individual verses and words of the biblical text, and, rather, focus on the totality of the event, deed, or history they portrayed. Whatever teaching underlies the Gospel story tends to be communicated by a retelling of the story and an elaboration on it, rather than immediately extracting from it a doctrinal proposition. They usually relate more directly to the liturgical feast, season, or solemnity than do Luther's. They are thus more notably historical, narrative, and contextual in their approach. They avoid proof-texts, and their purpose is not so much the defining, proving, or driving home of a doctrine as an attempt to enhance appreciation for a belief already operative and for values already shared. The audience, though frequently reproved for its failings, is more frequently congratulated on its Christian status and dignity. The basic purpose, however, was to praise God for His great acts in history, His mighty deeds—especially Creation and the Incarnation. This is ceremonial oratory, in every sense of the word. It is *oratio,* not *contio.* By placing preaching in the *genus demonstrativum* rather than the *genus deliberativum* (or *didascalicum*) a different product is obtained—a product that tends to fit religion into a different frame of reference. It is this consideration that makes a study of the rhetorical *genera* helpful for understanding religious controversies in the sixteenth century.

Until Melanchthon, Erasmus—and, presumably, Luther—began to relate preaching to the *genus deliberativum* (and, for Melanchothon, to the *genus didascalicum*), contemporaries seem to have assumed that the appropriate *genus* for it was the *demonstrativum.* This is an hypothesis that is somewhat difficult to verify, because until Melanchthon, Erasmus, and others began to write their treatises on preaching, published after Luther began to preach, we possess no contemporary works on the subject that deviate from the *artes,* except Reuchlin's brief and confused *Liber congestorum* of 1504. In any case, by mid-century the *genus didascalicum* and especially the *genus deliberativum* had begun to dominate the discussion wherever there was question of an adaptation to preaching of classical rhetoric. Even in Catholic circles the *genus demonstrativum* seems to have become ever more restricted to funeral oratory and to panegyrics of the saints as the century moved on. The implications of this development for the history of preaching are great, I believe, but I have only been able to suggest a few of them here; a more forcefully didactic and exhortatory quality would be the most obvious result.

In the time left to me, however, I want to isolate some other features of Luther's sermons that made them effective forms of public address. These features correlate with some basic principles of primary rhetoric, but in Luther they correlate just as clearly with his personality, his theology, and the existential situation in which he found himself. I will single out three for special mention.

The first is a clear and untiringly repeated doctrine. The message of works-faith, law-gospel, wrath-grace recurs implicitly or explicitly in practically everything he wrote.[33] This was, at least on one level, a simple message, and one that Luther insisted upon in season and out of season. His message, in other words, had a clear center. What came to be distinctive of Lutheran treatises on preaching, in fact, was how prescriptive they were about precise doctrinal content. Catholic treatises tended to be much less so.

In the second place, Luther's preaching isolated some clear enemies. These enemies—the papists and, later, the *Schwärmer*—were well known to Luther's hearers and designated by him in unmistakable terms as evil.[34] "Clear and present danger" characterized the way these enemies were presented. Such a presentation was almost bound by the nature of the case to excite a reaction.

Finally, from both of the above flowed an agenda for the hearers that was specific and immediate, yet fraught with implications for a better order to come. Luther gave his hearers what every orator longs for: something to *do.* His hearers were urged to read their Bibles instead of their lives of the saints. They were encouraged to eat meat on days of abstinence. Those with vows of celibacy were told they could marry. Abstract though the doctrine of justification might be in its slogan-like formulation, it had, as expounded by Luther, an immediate impact on the way those who heard it viewed themselves and acted. It clashed dramatically with received opinions and with what other preachers had been saying. As such, it had to make an impression.

In summary, then, what do we find in Luther, the preacher, when he is placed in the Western tradition of oratory? First of all, he was deeply influenced by the first step in the training of orators—"grammar." He fits into the tradition of the "Christian grammarian" especially in the basic task he undertook, the exposition of a text. The fundamentally homiletic form of his sermons corresponds in a generic way with that tradition.

His relationship to the rhetorical tradition is much more problematic than his relationship to the grammatical tradition, as is true also of Augustine, Erasmus, and most others who have reflected on the art of preaching. In his style he surely utilized some of the most effective stylistic techniques of secondary rhetoric; just how self-consciously he did so, is quite another question. There is evidence today that either formally or informally he appropriated in some of his sermons principles of primary rhetoric as indicated for the *contio,* the form of the *genus deliberativum* addressed to popular audiences. In any case, that *genus,* along with the new *genus didascalicum,* began to emerge in northern Europe during his lifetime with a new importance for preaching, and shifted the purposes and ethos of the sermon from those envisioned by the Italians who had utilized the *genus demonstrativum.*

It is clear, moreover, that Luther understood some of the most fundamental principles of primary rhetoric, whether he acquired this understanding from formal study or from the exercise of his natural gifts. Included in these would be the central role of a predetermined content—of a clear message made relevant to the concerns of his hearers. He also grasped the importance of explicit directives for action, of having a practical agenda that required decision, and that clearly distinguished friends from enemies, good from bad.

Notes

1. See, e.g., James J. Murphy, "One Thousand Neglected Authors: The Scope and Importance of Renaissance Rhetoric," in *Renaissance Eloquence: Studies in the Theory and Practice of Renaissance Rhetoric,* e.g., James J. Murphy (Berkeley, Los Angeles, and London: University of California Press, 1983), pp. 20-36.

2. *Predigt des Evangeliums: Luther als Prediger, Pädagoge und Rhetor* (Neukirchen-Vluyn; Neukirchener Verlag, 1972). See also Yngve Brilioth, *A Brief History of Preaching,* trans. Karl E. Mattson (Philadelphia: Fortress Press, 1965), pp. 103-18; John W. Doberstein, "Introduction to Volume 51," in *Luther's Works,* ed. and trans. John W. Doberstein, vol. 51 (Philadelphia: Muhlenberg Press, 1959), pp. xi-xxi; Emanuel Hirsch, "Luthers Predigtweise,"

Luther: Mitteilungen der Luthergesellschaft, 25 (1954), 1-23; Alfred Niebergall, "Die Geschichte der christlichen Predigt," in *Leiturgia: Handbuch des evangelischen Gottesdienstes,* 4 vols. (Kassel: Johannes Stauda Verlag, 1954-61), vol. II, pp. 181-353, esp. 257-275; *idem,* "Luthers Auffassung von der Predigt nach 'De Servo Arbitrio,'" in the collection of his studies, *Der Dienst der Kirche: Gesammelte Aufsätze 1954-1973,* ed. Rainer Lachmann (Kassel: Johannes Stauda Verlag, 1974), pp. 85-109; Birgit Stolt, *"Docere, delectare,* und *movere* bei Luther," *Deutsche Vierteljahresschrift für Literaturwissenschaft und Geistesgeschichte,* 44 (1970), 433-474. Studies like the following also deserve mention, although they are less technical in their approach: Harold J. Grimm, "The Human Element in Luther's Sermons," *Archive for Reformation History,* 49 (1958), 50-60; *idem, Martin Luther as a Preacher* (Columbus: Lutheran Book Concern, 1929); Elmer Carl Kiessling, *The Early Sermons of Luther and Their Relation to the Pre-Reformation Sermon* (Grand Rapids: Zondervan Publishing House, 1935); Peter Newman Brooks, "Luther the Preacher," *The Expository Times,* 95 (November, 1983), 37-41. Important, but not so directly pertinent to Luther's preaching are Birgit Stolt, *Studien zu Luthers Freiheitstraktat mit besonderer Berücksichtigung der lateinischen und deutschen Fassung zueinander und der Stilmittel der Rhetorik* (Stockholm: Almquist & Wiksell, 1969); Klaus Dockhorn, "Rhetorica movet: Protestantischer Humanismus und karolingische Renaissance" in *Rhetorik: Beiträge zu ihrer Geschichte in Deutschland vom 16.-20. Jahrhundert* (Frankfurt: Athenaion, 1974), pp. 17-42; Heinz Otto Burger, "Luther als Ereignis der Literaturgeschichte," in his *Dasein heisst eine Rolle spielen* (Munich: C. Hanser, 1963), pp. 56-74.

3. For further background and for elaboration of some of the ideas and categories used in this study, see my "Lutheranism in Rome, 1542-43: The Treatise by Alfonso Zorrilla," *Thought,* 54 (1979), 262-273; "Content and Rhetorical Forms in Sixteenth-Century Treatises on Preaching," in *Renaissance Eloquence,* pp. 238-252; "Grammar and Rhetoric in the Theology of Erasmus," *Paideia: Special Renaissance Issue,* ed. George C. Simmons, 3 vols. (forthcoming); "Egidio da Viterbo and Renaissance Rome," in *Egidio da Viterbo e il suo tempo* (Rome: Augustinian Historical Institute, 1983), pp. 67-84; *Praise and Blame in Renaissance Rome: Rhetoric, Doctrine, and Reform in the Sacred Orators of the Papal Court, ca. 1450-1521* (Durham: Duke University Press, 1979).

4. See my "Content and Rhetorical Forms."

5. Many of Luther's statements on preaching have been collected in *Luthers Werke in Auswahl,* ed. Emanuel Hirsch (Berlin: Walter de Gruyter, 1950), vol. VII, pp. 1-38.

6. On this theological shift, see Nembach, *Predigt,* pp. 118-124; Hirsch, "Predigtweise," pp. 3-5; and Leif Grane, *Modus Loquendi Theologicus: Luthers Kampf um die Erneuerung der Theologie (1515-1518)* (Leiden: E.J. Brill, 1975).

7. See my *Praise and Blame,* pp. 94-101, and Thomas à Kempis, *Opera omnia,* ed. M.J. Pohl (Freiburg i/Br.: Herder, 1910), vol. VI, pp. 7-314.

8. See, e.g., André Godin, *L'Homéliaire de Jean Vitrier: Texte, étude thématique et sémantique* (Geneva: Librairie Droz, 1971), esp. pp. 14-18. Jehan Vitrier is the Franciscan friar whom Erasmus first met in 1501 and described at length in his famous letter to Jodocus Jonas, June 13, 1521; *Opus epistolarum Des. Erasmi Roterodami,* ed. P.S. Allen, H.M. Allen, and H.W. Garrod, 12 vols. (Oxford: Clarendon Press, 1906-58), vol. IV, pp. 507-527.

9. See my "Grammar and Rhetoric in Erasmus."

10. Saint Ignatius of Loyola, *The Constitutions of the Society of Jesus,* trans. George E. Ganss (St. Louis: The Institute of Jesuit Sources, 1970), p. 201 (pt. IV, chap. 8 [402]).

11. "De ratione formandae concionis," in *Auctarium Bellarminianum: Supplément aux oeuvres de cardinal Bellarmin,* ed. Xavier-Marie le Bachelet (Paris: G. Beauchesne, 1913), pp. 655-657.

12. See H.I. Marrou, *A History of Education in Antiquity*, trans. George Lamb (New York: The New American Library, 1964), and *idem, Saint Augustin et la fin de la culture antique* (Paris: E. de Boccard, 1958).

13. On this distinction, see George A. Kennedy, *Classical Rhetoric and Its Christian and Secular Tradition from Ancient to Modern Times* (Chapel Hill: University of North Carolina Press, 1980), pp. 3-9.

14. On this issue in the Renaissance, see O.B. Hardison, "The Orator and the Poet: The Dilemma of Humanist Literature," *The Journal of Medieval and Renaissance Studies,* 1 (1971), 33-44, and W. Keith Percival, "Grammar and Rhetoric in the Renaissance," in *Renaissance Eloquence,* pp. 303-30.

15. See Pierre Nautin, "Origène prédicateur," in Origène, *Homélies sur Jérémie,* ed. Pierre Husson and Pierre Nautin (Sources chrétiennes, 232, Paris: Cerf, 1976), pp. 100-191; Howard Marshall, "Palestinian and Hellenistic Christianity: Some Critical Comments," *New Testament Studies,* 19 (1972-73), 271-87; and William S. Kurz, "Hellenistic Rhetoric in the Christological Proof of Luke-Acts," *The Catholic Biblical Quarterly,* 42 (1980), 171-195. See also Hartwig Thyen, *Der Stil der Jüdisch-Hellenistischen Homilie* (Göttingen: Vandenhoeck & Ruprecht, 1955).

16. See my "Grammar and Rhetoric in Erasmus," and Salvatore I. Cámporeale, *Lorenzo Valla: Umanesimo e teologia* (Florence: Istituto Nazionale di Studi sul Rinascimento, 1972).

17. See, e.g., *WA* 10.1.1, 199.

18. See, e.g., *WA* 4, 620; 9, 416-417, 439-442; 10.1.1, 132-136, 382, 384, 391, 422, 619; see also Nembach, *Predigt,* pp. 162-168.

19. See, e.g., *WA* 4, 717; 10.1.1, 75-76, 220, 280, 284; 26, 52; 39.1, 428; *TR* 2199[a], 2216, 4426, 4612, 5082[b]; on the "pedagogical," even catechetical, nature of preaching in Luther, see Nembach, *Predigt,* pp. 13, 25-39, 117, 152.

20. On difference between the two forms, see Nembach, *Predigt,* pp. 175-209, and Doberstein, "Introduction," p. xiii.

21. See, e.g., M.-D. Chenu, *La théologie comme science au XIIIe siècle* (Paris: J. Vrin, 3, 1957), pp. 18-22; *idem, La théologie au douzième siècle* (Paris: J. Vrin, 1957); *idem, Introduction à l'étude de saint Thomas d'Aquin* (Paris: J. Vrin, 1950), p. 67: "Toute la pédagogie médiévale est à base de lecture de textes, et la scholastique universitaire institutionalise et amplifie ce type de travail."

22. *TR* 2199[a]: "Dialectica docet, rhetorica movet. Illa ad intellectum pertinet, haec ad voluntatem. Quas utrasque Paulus complexus est Rom. 12, quando dixit, Qui docet in doctrina, qui exhortatur in exhortando. Et haec duo conficiunt modum praedicandi." See also ibid., 2216, 4426, 5082[b], and Nembach, *Predigt,* 25-39, 120-124.

23. *WA* 6, 458.

24. *Predigt,* pp. 130-135.

25. *Ibid.,* pp. 135-174.

26. See, e.g., *TR* 3494.

27. "*Docere, delectare.*" Further indication that principles of primary rhetoric influenced Luther's sermons comes from the fact that he understood technical terms of rhetoric like *status* and *hypothesis,* and correctly applied them to preaching; see *TR* 3032[b] and 3173[b].

28. See Maria Grossmann, "Humanismus in Wittenberg, 1486-1517," *Luther-Jahrbuch,* 39 (1972), 11-30, and *idem, Humanism in Wittenberg 1485-1517* (Nieuwkoop: B de Graaf, 1975).

29. See my "Content and Rhetorical Forms," pp. 241-244. Uwe Schnell, *Die homiletische Theorie Philipp Melanchthons* (Berlin and Hamburg: Lutherisches Verlagshaus, 1968); and Wilhelm Maurer, *Der junge Melanchthon zwischen Humanismus und Reformation,* 2 vols. (Göttingen: Vandenhoeck und Ruprecht, 1967-69), esp. vol. I, pp. 171-214.

30. See my "Content and Rhetorical Forms," p. 244, and Schnell, *Homiletische Theorie,* pp. 172-176.

31. See my "Lutheranism in Rome."

32. See my *Praise and Blame.*

33. I believe this statement is incontrovertible; see e.g. Niebergall, "Auffassung," pp. 86, 103; Gerhard Heintze, *Luthers Predigt von Gesetz und Evangelium* (Munich: Chr. Kaiser Verlag, 1958); and the recent article by Peter Iver Kaufman, "Luther's 'Scholastic Phase' Revisited: Grace, Works, and Merit in the Earliest Sermons," *Church History,* 51 (1982), 280-289.

34. See Brilioth, *History,* p. 112.

THE CHIMERA AND THE SPIRIT:
LUTHER'S GRAMMAR OF THE WILL*

Marjorie O'Rourke Boyle, *Toronto*

"Free will since the Fall is a reality in title only (*res est de solo titulo*), and when it does what is in it, it sins mortally."[1] Revising this controversial dogma, Luther confessed, "I have poorly stated that free will before grace is a reality in title only. I simply should have said, however, that 'free will is a figment with respect to the realities (*figmentum in rebus*) or a title without a reality (*seu titulus sine re*).'"[2] He emphasized this assertion as "the most excellent of all and the principal subject of our theses."[3] Contrary to the history of doctrine, however, it was not flatly theological. It affirmed rather a logic of the impossible. It articulated, moreover, a grammar which demonstrated Luther's commitment to the correct alignment of word and reality.

Confronting semi-Pelagian initiative in salvation, Augustine had formulated the theology which would be ratified as orthodox. Man assents to his justification, he had taught, by a particular intervention to the will of a grace which heals and liberates the will to do so.[4] Although this proposition that grace operates in man a decision that is man's free choice is theologically a mystery, logically it is nonsense. It predicates pure antinomies. Some definition of terms is required for its intelligibility. Augustine himself proposed such a clarification by distinguishing acquired from natural freedom. Had he clearly and consistently referred to "freed will" (*liberatum arbitrium*) rather than "free will" (*liberum arbitrium*), the science of theology might have escaped the momentous reform which climaxed in that explicit definition by the Formula of Concord.[5] For stopping Ockham's razor on the theory of congruous merit itself, Luther slashed the ambiguity of "free will" to a single and singular sense. "Free will," he pronounced, "is a sacred name for God alone."[6] The implication of Augustine's formula, as Luther astutely perceived, was that prior to its liberation by grace the freedom of the will toward salvation was merely potential. As Peter Lombard had phrased it, free will pertained to future contingents.[7] With scholastic genius Luther transferred the term from the metaphysical category of reality to that of potentiality, and thence argued its unreality. He thus boldly altered the traditional context by subsuming "free will" into the medieval disputes concerning the ontological and logical status of possibles and impossibles.

Pondering things not yet existent and even those which would never realize existence, the masters at Paris in the latter half of the thirteenth century had deliberated whether such possibles enjoyed any reality (*res*) in themselves. Thomas Aquinas concluded no. He argued that a possible, prior to its realization as an existing individual, had no distinctive reality from eternity apart from its existence as a divine idea in the divine intellect. It had, therefore, no reality in itself apart from God. Henry of Ghent, concerned to account for the human knowledge of nonexisting possibles, rejoined that some kind of essential being must be ascribed to them. Because of the real relation from all eternity of creaturely essences to God as their formal exemplar cause, he argued that possibles, prior to their reception of actual existence, could be described as things (*res*). He thus conferred upon possibles what has been described as "a strange and intermediary kind of reality" in a "metaphysical 'no-man's land'" between purely intentional and actually existing being. Alternating between the affirmation and denial of reality to nonexisting possibles, the debate continued among the recruits who routinely considered the problem in commenting on distinction forty-three of the first book of Lombard's *Sententiae.*[8]

In this context Luther's capital assertion was consistent with the consensus that denied ontological status to possibles. His refusal to attribute reality to free will, except as a divine name, resonated with Aquinas' relegation of the possible to the prime intellect. Quoting the devil against himself, Luther exploited this ontological theory to argue the inconsistency of retaining the term "free will." A possible was not a reality (*res*). But prior to grace, free will toward salvation was only a possible. Therefore, free will before grace was not a reality (*res*). Luther thus objected that the term "free will" sophistically violated logic. "Free will," he protested, was "too magnificent, too ample, and full a phrase." It deceived the laity into supposing that it signified a power capable of freely turning itself in either direction, without subjection to anything. If the people should ever discover, he speculated, that the term scarcely signified even "a teeny-weeny spark" of power, and that utterly ineffective in itself, captive to Satan as it was, they would likely stone theologians as sophists. "Since therefore," he pleaded, "we have lost the signification and the reality (*significatio et res*) of this such boastful vocabulary, or rather have never had it, ... why do we so pertinaciously retain such an empty name to the danger and deception of the faithful?"[9] He counselled as the "safest and most religious course" the abolition of the term. Failing such a measure, he suggested that "free will" should at least be used honestly, as a divine name, or as a human attribute before the Fall while restricted to natural power since the Fall.[10]

In stating and deliberating his thesis Luther appropriated the argument on this very question of John Duns Scotus. In his commentary on 1 Sent. d. 43, Scotus considered not only possibles but impossibles. An impossible he defined as a figment (*figmentum*) consisting of two or more positive entities which, although possible separately in themselves, could not by their nature be combined into the unity of a single being. An impossible then was not a true notion but a figment possessing unity in name only. Because it was composed of incompatible parts, it could not be properly defined. And it was impossible in relation to any agent.[11] This text provided the source and sense of Luther's anti-definition of "free will" as "a figment with respect to the realities or a title without a reality." His thesis against free will coincided with Scotus' definition of the impossible.

The ontological debate about such figments was paralleled by a logical controversy. Fascinated with the problem of signifying the impossible, medieval logicians speculated on the propositional status of such terms as "irrational man" and "asinine man." Their favorite example of a figment, as introduced by Jean Buridan's *Sophismata,* was the chimera, that imaginary beast of classical lore which was composed of three disparate parts: a lion's head, a goat's body, and a serpent's tail. Dialecticians pondered the status of the term "chimera" in the proposition, "A chimera is a chimera," as they spun their own fantasies into an elaborate tissue of speculation. The term "chimera," they reasoned, was not nonsensical, as was the syllable "baf." It appeared in dictionaries and sentences concerning it were both uttered and understood. The term thus seemed significative, by definition representing cognitively some thing or things. What "chimera" was said to signify, however, was an impossible object. This quandary bedevilled logicians of the early sixteenth century, as they wondered how "chimera" could signify the impossible, if the impossible could not by definition be signified. Paralleling Henry of Ghent's attribution of quasi-real status to possibles, some logicians argued that impossibles must be impossible objects of some sort, capable of being comprehended. From Aristotle's premise that the impossible could be willed, and Augustine's that nothing could be willed unless it were known, they deduced that the impossible must be known. This was the position on the *complexe significabile* of Marsilius of Inghen, whose two ardent loyalists were: Luther's own teacher of logic, Jodocus Truttvetter, and his acrid polemicist, Johann Maier von Eck. Both had pledged their allegiance to the reality of impossibles in their commentaries on that fundamental scholastic text, the *Summule logicales* of Peter of Spain.[12]

The concise and cogent context of Luther's capital assertion then was not the theology of grace but the logic of signification. His thesis criticized a tradition, sanctioned by Augustine and extending to Eck, of attributing ontological and logical status to possibles. Luther essayed to expose the sophistry of the term "free will" by identifying it as a chimera, a figment constructed of essentially incompatible parts, and therefore an impossible. This was the logical rationale of his antithetical theology. As he expounded his assertion, Is a will free which can do nothing of itself, but of necessity sins gravely? Is it freedom to be able only to sin? Can that faculty which does nothing prepare itself for grace? Does evil dispose itself toward good? When free will exercises its own power all the works it performs are mortal. Does death therefore yield life? enmity toward God, grace? Luther thus concluded his catalogue of oppositions: "Figments (*figmenta*), therefore, are all the items which are treated in so many books concerning the preparation of free will toward grace." From the premise that the spirit and free will are contradictions, he reiterated that "free will is nothing except a reality in title only (*res de solo titulo*)." Again he emphasized, "It is entirely a figment (*figmentum est penitus*)." The pope and his cohorts insanely "imagine" (*fingunt*) "mere figments" (*mera figmenta*).[13]

Luther complained that the papists had so distorted and confused the issue as to introduce "a new language," like the architects of the tower of Babel. He regretted that the term "free will" had ever been invented. While it might be applied to Adam as created sinless, since the Fall man was no longer free but enslaved. Because such captives of sin might become free through grace, they might be termed men of free will, he conceded sarcastically. Analogically he suggested that a beggar might be called rich, because he might become so. "But it is neither right nor good," he insisted, "to bandy words in such gravely important matters. A simpleton is tricked by frivolity, and such teachers are called sophists." Criticizing such odd usage he concluded, "One ought to shun the sophists, and to speak as Scripture does, simply and clearly and openly, especially in discourse on the highest heavenly things." Scripture, he observed, excludes the expression "free will."[14]

With the analogy of the beggar who could be termed "rich" because he might become so, Luther ridiculed the vogue of terming the will "free" because it might be liberated through grace. He argued this most incisively against Erasmus, who solidly in the Augustinian tradition, retained a "something" (*nonnihil*), a "reality" (*res*), minute and impoverished yet stimulated, promoted, and perfected by grace, which the term "free will" signified.[15] Relying on Scotus' definition of the impossible as a nominal unity of contradictions, Luther censured Erasmus for a "plainly unheard-of grammar and dialectic by which nothing is something, which would be an impossible according to logicians, since the terms are contradictory."[16] In the utterance "free will," one word, "will," referred to the thing itself, the reality; the other, "free," to an extrinsic possiblity which might occur to it. Concerning the accidental rather than substantive predication of freedom to the will, as established on Augustine's theory of an acquired rather than natural freedom, Luther criticized "the inverted usage of all language and terminology, so that 'No man is every man,' and 'Nothing is everything.'" Substantively, or naturally, he argued, free will was "an empty name" (*inanis vox*).[17]

This designation of free will as an empty name resonated with a history of argument about signification. From the premise that words were signs, Augustine had stated that a sign could not be a sign unless it signified something. Yet the word "nothing" (*nihil*) was said to signify that which was not. It would appear then that "nothing" could not be a word, since it did not signify something, but rather nothing. As Augustine pondered: Either all words then are not signs or every sign does not signify something. Reflecting that the syllables *ni-hil* did not convey empty sounds, Augustine ventured this resolution: "Instead of saying that *nihil* signifies something which is nothing, shall we say that this word signifies a certain state of mind when, failing to perceive a reality, the mind nevertheless finds, or thinks it finds, that such a reality does not exist?" He thus struggled to extricate himself from the absurd situation in which "nothing" was impeding his apprehension of truth. Boethius, however, subsequently argued that empty names, such as *nihil,* were not really names. "If some utterance designates nothing," he wrote, "it is not a name; hence if it is the name of nothing, it certainly cannot be said to be a name." The question of empty names was also addressed by Anselm. Seeking a resolution to the problems surrounding the word "evil," which he defined as a "nothing," Anselm considered the argument that the word *nihil* was a name and yet did not signify anything. He then postulated a dual significative function: remotively in which *nihil* signified something and constitutively in which it signified nothing. The term thus asserted both by a surface grammar or apparent form (*secundum formam loquendi*) and by a logically correct language of how things actually are (*secundum rem*). This distinction was adopted wholesale by William of Ockham, who extended Anselm's *quasi-aliud* treatment of *nihil* to other empty names, such as chimera. Considering propositions in which figments were posited, as "A chimera is a chimera," he also accepted Boethius' judgment that a proposition which affirms substantively (*secundum se*) is truer than one which affirms accidentally (*secundum accidens*).[18]

Luther also argued the contradiction between the definition respecting the name (*nomen*) and the definition respecting the reality (*res*), since the sound (*vox*) signified one thing while the reality (*res*) another.[19] His insistence on substantive rather than accidental signification as normative for evaluating the term "free will" was indebted to this theorizing by which Boethius, Anselm, and Ockham attempted to resolve Augustine's problem. Luther maintained that, although the will might be posited as "free" accidentally, that is by grace, substantively, by nature, this was to utter an empty name. By sophistical magic[20] it had been inflated into a verbal monstrosity,[21] he complained. It was, however, "a mere dialectical figment" (*merum figmentum dialecticum*),[22] composed like the monstrous chimera of "sheer contradictions."[23] It was "a bald lie,"[24] "a phantom particle of speech,"[25] "a nothing" (*nihil*).[26] Luther banished the term "free will" to the pages of Lucian's *Verae historiae,* where that satirist had admitted his poetic deceit: "I am writing about things ... which, in fact, do not exist at all and, in the nature of things, cannot exist. Therefore my readers should on no account believe in them."[27] Free will, Luther reiterated, was "an empty name (*inanis uocula*) whose reality (*res*) had been lost" in the Fall. "In my grammar," he argued, "lost liberty signifies no liberty; moreover, to attribute the title of liberty to that which has no liberty is to posit an empty name" (*inane vocabulum*).[28]

Luther thus rejected the inflation, initiated by Augustine and perpetuated by scholastics, of a term which signified nothing substantively, only accidentally, into one that signified something. He protested the assertion that man has free will because God grants him by grace his own divine liberty. This was like saying "against universal usage," he argued, that a beggar was rich, not because he possessed wealth, but because some monarch might bestow part of his own treasury on him. Or, it was like stating that a dying man was perfectly healthy because some benefactor might donate his own health to him. Or, he concluded, it was like saying that a basely illiterate man was really the paragon of erudition because some schoolmaster might be able to instill in him his own learning.[29]

This argument replicated the critique of Aristotelian potentiality by Lorenzo Valla, whom Luther praised for his excellence in piety and in literature.[30] In appealing for a functional rather than a speculative norm of speech, Valla had ridiculed as a violation of ordinary language the assertion that a stick was a bow in act. The attribution of potentiality denied that the stick was now a bow, he reasoned. The nominal tag "in act" was therefore superfluous. To posit that a stick was a bow in act because it was convertible into one destroyed the distinction in ordinary language between material and product. If, Valla argued, potentiality were applied to everything that could possibly be converted into something else, then many distinctions would evaporate: hot would be cold, light heavy, small large, all by the magic of potentiality.[31] Potentiality threatened definition, the very foundation of philology. Luther's critique of the accidental supposition of "free will" paralleled this argument. Scholastically the will was termed "free" because it might become liberated by grace. This was an abuse of ordinary language, Luther complained, like calling a beggar rich, or an invalid healthy, or a dunce brilliant because they were potentially so, like the stick that was a bow "in act."

Such reasoning coincided with the nominalist reversal of scholastic logic. In his *Summa logicae* Ockham had appealed consistently to ordinary language (*usus loquentium*),[32] so remarkably so that this has been considered its "most important and significant feature." Since Anselm, scholasticism had situated propriety and intrinsic signification with technical, logical discourse; impropriety and oblique signification with common speech (*usus loquendi*). Ockham, however, essayed to render technical language pointless, or to condemn it as false and senseless. He did this by reference to a standard of propriety which he conversely situated with ordinary language.[33] In demonstrating the function of terms in propositions he cited "the use to which those who speak the language put the expression."[34] In his own logical treatise, *Dialecticae disputationes,* Valla also championed "the common usage of speech" (*communem loquendi consuetudinem*). Judging that housewives understood the meaning of words better than philosophers did, he desired a language that would be "simpler and better accommodated to natural sense and common usage" (*simplicius et ad naturalem sensum usumque communem accommodatius*).[35]

Repudiating the scholastic governance of grammar by a technical logic, Luther defined grammar as the articulated consensus of a native intelligence. This spoken consensus was not the erudite norm of humanists such as Erasmus, however, who also struggled to wrest speech from the scholastic grasp. It was a consensus by popular authority. Luther appealed to what "the crowd (*vulgus*) knows and accordingly confesses sufficiently in proverbs, prayers, devotions, and daily living."[36] Although he cited the practice of poets and grammarians, he accorded their learned texts no more authority than the everyday speech of commoners. His grammatical democracy included street urchins and barbarians, such as himself.[37] He boasted, moreover, that a barbarian could surpass any humanist who babbled a new grammar. Luther's reform redefined eloquence itself. By exalting commoners, as expressing the truth faithfully in their rude prayers and daily conversations, he restored the prescriptive power of popular usage, "in whose hands," as Horace had favorably declared, "lies the judgment, the right, and the rule of speech."[38]

Zealous for correct signification, Luther established his theology of grace on this grammar. His hermeneutics maintained two criteria of interpretation. The interior criterion was the singular gift of the Spirit, by which Christians were affectively grasped by the manifest meaning of the text for them. The exterior criterion was the common property of humanity by which all men intellectually grasped the manifest meaning of the text in itself. This criterion was grammar, defined as the common usage of speech expressing native human intelligence. Since it was this exterior criterion which regulated preachers in their public office of refuting error,[39] Luther's theological reform was necessarily grammatical. Some of his argumentation against the term "free will" was syntactical, as when he stated the rule that the assertion of fact or probability could not be in the subjunctive or imperative moods but only in the indicative.[40] His strategy was essentially semantic, however. Luther consistently appealed to "grammar and the most universal usage of words" for the meaning of terms which needed explanation only to tots who had not yet learned the alphabet.[41] He argued from "words very clearly known even to children."[42] Maintaining that the term "free will" failed this external criterion of grammar, he caricatured his disputant Erasmus as "an importune neologist who against universal usage would attempt to introduce his own manner of speaking."[43] Erasmus, he charged, perpetrated "a new grammar."[44] His argument for free will was "an abuse of speech" which contradicted ordinary language and common usage. Erasmus declaimed in the diction of actors and tricksters, whereas theologians should speak with "words appropriate, plain, sober, and as Paul says, sound and irreproachable."[45]

Luther disclaimed ever having heard such language as Erasmus spoke.[46] He especially condemned his tropological "license of interpretation, so that by a new and unheard grammar everything is confused."[47] Luther pleaded a manifest Scripture whose "words are simple and their meaning simple."[48] Since there was "no inconsistency in the sayings of Scripture," he reasoned, there was "no need of an interpretation to resolve any difficulty."[49] Nevertheless, he complained, Erasmus "invents a new art of eluding the most evident passages" by discovering tropes in the simplest and clearest words.[50] It was from such counterfeit tropes and figures, hatched from the human brain in neglect and even contempt of the simplicity of language, he declared, that all heresies and errors concerning Scripture had arisen.[51]

Tropological exegesis was not licit unless the evident context of the words and the absurdity of the fact exposed so transgressed an article of faith as to compel such a resort.[52] Calling this his "invincible argument," Luther stated, "Vocabulary ought to remain in the usage of natural signification, unless the contrary is demonstrated."[53] Otherwise, he insisted, an interpreter "must always adhere to the simple and plain and natural signification of words that grammar and the habit of speech, which God created in man, maintain." The consequence of violating this rule, he warned, would be a Scripture so flimsy that a trope could sophistically reason away an article of faith, so that ultimately "nothing certain may be determined or proved."[54]

It was an "absolute certainty for establishing consciences"[55] that Luther inexorably demanded. His adherence to the literal sense of the text as interpreted by ordinary usage was a corollary of his epistemological requirement of absolute certitude.[56] Theologians, he argued, should adhere to "the universal usage of the Latin tongue,"[57] that is, "grammar and its ordinary meaning."[58] Only such obedience would guarantee and safeguard the rational certainty which faith demanded. "Wouldn't there otherwise be a Babel of words and language in the world?" he posed.[59] And wouldn't sinners then perish amid the confusion of the truth? Luther thus condemned as promoting uncertainty the tropological demonstration of free will from Scripture. He scorned Erasmus' humanist commitment to achieve an exposition which would serve the commonweal. "Are we to say here, 'A suitable interpretation ought to be essayed'? But there is no heretic for whom his own interpretation is not suitable. Evidently this is the resolution," he addressed Erasmus, "to throw open the window to such license for corrupt minds and deceitful spirits? For you, I believe, who consider the certitude of Scripture indifferent, this license of interpretation will be convenient. But for us, who labor to establish consciences, nothing can be more unsuitable, nothing more harmful, nothing more pestilential than to defile with this accommodation."[60] Luther admonished, "My advice to anyone who cannot firmly hold to the sacred writings in accordance with some definite meaning is to leave them alone. It is safer to be like the laity and not know them, than to be uncertain regarding them."[61] As for himself, he averred, "I want to have the Scripture in the purity of its powers, undefiled by any man, even if he is a saint, and not spiced with anything earthly. . . . Man's word when added to the divine veils the pure truth; nay rather, as I said, it is human dung which covers it . . ."[62] Opposing the confusion of human exegesis with the clarity of divine discourse, he hoped the pious might understand Scripture in unmediated silence. "And so my dear Christians," he urged, "get to it, get to it, and let my exposition be no more than a scaffold, and an aid for the construction of the true building, so that we ourselves grasp and taste the pure and simple word of God and abide by it; for there alone God dwells in Zion."[63]

In this posture Luther was confident that he transmitted the undefiled word of God. His assurance that his own interpretation was not human dung was established on his ecclesiastical appointment to the parish and university of Wittenberg.[64] It was sanctioned, moreover, by the exterior criterion of grammar, to which he was subject in discharging his public office. As a minister, especially in refuting error, he was a grammarian, a custodian of the Word. Since in his understanding each utterance (*verbum*) corresponded to a reality (*res*), the apprehension of the reality depended on the correct definition of the utterance. And since it was the function of grammar to define words, that discipline was essential to the interpretation of Scripture. In this discrete match of word and reality Luther's interpretive task was a literal imitation of the truth, in which mimesis he merely observed, recorded, and transmitted meaning. In meditating on the incarnation of the primordial Word, Luther reflected that it did not pass through its human mother like light penetrating a windowpane, but rather suffered a real birth in which Mary's organs functioned naturally.[65] In considering the perpetual rebirth of that Word in human speech, however, Luther did not allow Christians a participation analogous to Mary's parturition. As he expressed his own pure instrumentality, "I simply taught, preached, and wrote God's Word; otherwise I did nothing.... I let the Word do its work."[66]

Although Luther declared that "among all the sciences humanly invented, the most advantageous for propagating theology is grammar,"[67] grammar remained human invention, not divine grace. It only manifested the objective, literal sense of the text as universally apprehensible. It did not manifest its subjective, affective sense as apprehending Christians. Such interior understanding was the unique gift of the Spirit, who respected no grammar schooling but conferred his grace gratuitously, even rebuffing human effort at comprehension. Grammar, therefore, was not propaedeutic to piety. Just as moral effort in no way prepared for justification, even by congruous merit, so the most assiduous study of language in no way clarified Scripture interiorly. The supernatural and natural orders were discontinuous. In Luther's Stoic slogan, there was "no middle ground."[68] Grammar, as expressing a common and native intelligence, disclosed the sense of Scripture superficially, not salvifically. Grammar was secular, a worldly wisdom, as in the patristic symbiosis of classical and Christian cultures. "Languages in themselves do not make a theologian," Luther stated, "but are an auxiliary. For it is necessary first to know the subject (*res*) which is expressed in languages."[69] As for the subject in dispute, free will, Luther was certain it was no such *res* and deserved therefore no linguistic expression.

As a heuristic, grammar may not resolve the grand historiographical question of distinguishing Renaissance and Reformation pieties. It is, nevertheless, a critical index. As masterminds of those cultures, Luther and Erasmus represented a fundamental contrareity in grammar. They differed concerning its definition as a popular or an erudite consensus, its province as the literal or the tropological sense, its status as a secular or a sacred discipline, and its function as auxiliary to or constitutive of theology.[70] This grammatical conflict informed their dispute importantly. Those reformers were not arguing about whether or not there is free will. As Erasmus stated the case with elegant precision, they were engaged rather in λογομαχία, a war of words.[71] In that verbal strife both professed an orthodox faith in justification as the liberation of the will by a special intervention of healing grace.[72] They contended whether or not the will which only acquired its freedom by the intervention of that grace could legitimately be termed "free." Specifically they disagreed over the validity of accidental supposition, with their controversy recapitulating a history of ontological and logical debates on possibles and impossibles and reflecting their divergent grammars. Appealing to an erudite consensus and tropological signification, Erasmus retained Augustine's major term "free will" (*liberum arbitrium*). Appealing to a popular consensus and literal signification, Luther substituted Augustine's minor term "enslaved will" (*servum arbitrium*). He did so to align terminology and doctrine, language and reality. Augustine's theory that the acquired freedom of the will was nevertheless freedom was consistent with that doctor's concession of reality to empty names. It was justified, moreover, by a logic of accidental supposition. To Luther, however, this resort was sophistical. It gravely endangered faith. Insisting on a clear and cogent term which would manifest the truth with absolute certainty, he rejected the extraordinary usage of freedom for its ordinary sense. Luther posited the term "free will" only substantively, that is, of God himself, of Adam before the Fall, and of his posterity in its natural dominion. And if the criterion for theological discourse is indeed ordinary language—and *that* is the question,—can it be doubted that Luther's is the clear and cogent formulation, surpassing even that of the doctor of grace?

This evidence that Luther's capital thesis was semantic contradicts the ecclesiastical and academic traditions of interpreting his controversy on free will as doctrinal. This proposal that the Church divided historically not over an eternal truth of faith but a disputed question of logic may offend moral sensibilities—it certainly offended Erasmus. The resolution of this research is not sermonic but scholarly, however. In the Reformation of theology the trivium was not trivial. Investigations which analyze Luther's doctrine in disregard of the grammar, or logic, or rhetoric of its discourse are chasing the very chimera. There are no disembodied ideas. Not even the winged thoughts of theologians are pure spirits. The gift of the Holy Spirit, as Luther well knew, was the gift of tongues. And so it was that he wrestled to defeat that tongue-twister, "free will."

Notes

*This and other studies, especially *Rhetoric and Reform,* were sponsored by a Fellowship from the John Simon Guggenheim Memorial Foundation.

1. Luther, *Disputatio Heidelbergae habita:* Ex theologia 13 (1518), in *WA* 1, 353, 5-6.

2. Luther, *Assertio omnium articulorum per bullam Leonis X. novissimam damnatorum* (1520), *WA* 7, 146, 4-6.

3. *WA* 7, 148, 16.

4. For Augustine's mature position see especially *De spiritu et littera* and *De gratia et libero arbitrio,* PL 44, 199-246, 880-912.

5. "Formula of Concord: Solid Declaration" 2.67, in *The Book of Concord: The Confessions of the Evangelical Lutheran Church,* trans. and ed. Theodore G. Tappert (Philadelphia: Fortress, 1959), p. 534. See Augustine, *Contra duas epistolas Pelagianorum* 3.8.24; cf. 1.2.5, 2.5.9; PL 44, 606-607, 522, 577.

6. Luther, *De servo arbitrio* (1525), in: *CL* 4, 127, 38 and 154, 13.

7. Peter Lombard, II *Sent.* d. 25.1.3, in *Sententiae in IV libris distinctae* (2 vols.; Rome: Collegium S. Bonaventurae, 3, 1971-81).

8. John F. Wippel, "The Reality of Nonexisting Possibles according to Thomas Aquinas, Henry of Ghent, and Godfrey of Fontaines," *Review of Metaphysics,* 33 (1981), 729-58.

9. Luther, *De servo arbitrio, CL* 4, 128, 14-17.

10. Ibid., 128, 40-129, 5. For "free will" as descriptive of man's natural powers see also 151, 19-20; 162, 6-15; 251, 6-8; 258, 25-29; and as a divine name, n. 6.

11. Scotus, *Quaestiones in librum primum sententiarum* d. 43, q. 1, nn. 6, 10, in *Opera omnia* (26 vols.; Paris, 1891-95), vol. X, pp. 734-35, 737.

12. See E.J. Ashworth, "Chimeras and Imaginary Objects: A Study in the Post-Medieval Theory of Signification," *Vivarium,* 15 (1977), 57-77.

13. Luther, *Assertio, WA* 7, 142, 25-149, 7.

14. Luther, *Grund und Ursach aller Artikel, so durch römische Bulle unrechtlich verdammt sind* (1521), *WA* 7, 445, 30-450, 7.

15. Erasmus, *De libero arbitrio,* διατριβή *sive collatio* (1524), ed. Johannes von Walter (Quellenschriften zur Geschichte des Protestantismus, 8; Leipzig: A. Deichert, 1910), p. 82, l. 26. See Boyle, "Erasmus and the 'Modern' Question: Was He Semi-Pelagian?," *Archiv für Reformationsgeschichte,* 75 (1984), in press.

16. Luther, *De servo arbitrio, CL* 4, 248, 12-17.

17. 155, 40-156, 7. This technical term also occurs at 135, 30-31; 136, 19-20, 37-38; 150, 23-24; 160, 14, 26-29; 192, 14-15.

18. Augustine, *De magistro* 2.3, cf. 8.21, in *PL* 32, 1196; trans., Robert P. Russell (Washington, D.C.: Catholic University of America Press, 1967), p. 11. Boethius, *In librum Aristotelis de interpretatione* 1, in *PL* 64, 408D. Anselm, *De casu diaboli* 11, in *Opera omnia,* ed. F.S. Schmitt (6 vols.; Segovia: Abbey Press, 1938-40; Edinburgh: T. Nelson, 1946-61), vol. I, 248, 15-22; 249, 6-250, 1; 250, 17-251, 16. William of Ockham, *Summa logicae* 2.14, in *Opera philosophica et theologica,* ed. Philotheus Boehner *et al.* (St. Bonaventure, NY: Franciscan Institute, 1974, vol. I, pp. 286-288; citing Boethius, *De interpretatione* 1a.2, in *PL* 64, 387C-D. D.P. Henry, *The Logic of Saint Anselm* (Oxford: Clarendon, 1967), pp. 207-219.

For Ockham on the question of nonexisting possibles see his *Scriptum in librum primum sententiarum ordinatio* d. 43, in *Opera philosophica et theologica,* vol. IV, pp. 622-650. See also Allan B. Wolter, "Ockham and the Textbooks: On the Origin of Possibility," in *Inquiries into Medieval Philosophy: A Collection in Honor of Francis P. Clarke,* ed. James F. Ross (Westport, Conn.: Greenwood, 1971), pp. 243-273, rpt. from *Franziskanische Studien,* 32 (1950), 70-96; and Gordon Leff, *William of Ockham: The Metamorphosis of Scholastic Discourse* (Manchester: Manchester University Press; Totowa, N.J.: Rowman and Littlefield, 1975), pp. 445-447.

19. Luther, *De servo arbitrio, CL* 4, 151, 27-29.

20. Ibid., 156, 12; 157, 10.

21. Ibid., 160, 34; 151, 34.

22. Ibid., 159, 25.

23. Ibid., 136, 19-20; 181, 17-18.

24. Ibid., 97, 4-5; 136, 2, 36.

25. Ibid., 135, 35-36; cf. 230, 10-11.

26. Ibid., 136, 27, 33; 139, 35; 183, 37-38.

27. Ibid., 150, 33-39. Lucien,'Αληθῶν Διηγμάτων *(Verae historiae)* 1.4, in *Opera,* ed. M.D. Macleod (Oxford: Clarendon, 1972), p. 83; trans., A.M. Harmon, *Lucian* (8 vols.; London: William Heinemann; New York: Macmillan, 1913), vol. I, p. 253.

28. Luther, *De servo arbitrio, CL* 4, 160, 26-29; see also 180, 1.

29. Ibid., 128, 25-34.

30. Luther, *Tischreden, WA Tr* I: 109, 1-4; II: 107, 6-10; V: 333, 5-6. *De servo arbitrio, CL* 4, 130, 14-15.

31. Valla, *Dialecticae disputationes* 1.16, in *Opera omnia,* ed. Eugenio Garin (Basel, 1540; rpt., 2 vols.; Turin: Bottega d'Erasmo, 1962), vol. I, pp. 678-679.

32. Ockham, *Summa logicae,* in *Opera philosophica et theologica,* vol. I, pp. 208, 225-227, 237, etc., as indexed, 885.

33. Henry, *The Logic of Saint Anselm,* pp. 18, 26.

34. Ockham, *Summa logicae* 1.69.15, in *Opera philosophica et theologica,* vol. I, p. 208; trans., Michael J. Loux, *Ockham's Theory of Terms: Part I of the Summa Logicae* (Notre Dame and London: Notre Dame University Press, 1974), p. 199.

35. Valla, *Dialecticae disputationes* 1.16, 1.2, in *Opera omnia,* vol. I, pp. 678-679, 649. See also Richard Waswo, "The 'Ordinary Language Philosophy' of Lorenzo Valla," *Bibliothèque d'humanisme et renaissance,* 41 (1979), 255-271; and Salvatore I. Camporeale, *Lorenzo Valla: Umanesimo e Teologia* (Florence: Istituto Nazionale di Studi sul Rinascimento, 1972), pp. 149-171.

36. Luther, *De servo arbitrio, CL* 4, 287, 37-39.

37. Ibid., 95, 3-4.

38. Horace, *Ars poetica* 72, in *Horace on Poetry: The 'Ars Poetica',* ed. C.O. Brink

(Cambridge: Cambridge University Press, 1971), p. 58; trans., H. Rushton Fairclough, *Satires, Epistles and Ars poetica* (London: William Heinemann; New York: G.P. Putnam's Sons, 1929), p. 457. For Luther's use of Horace in *De servo arbitrio* see Boyle, *Rhetoric and Reform: Erasmus' Civil Dispute with Luther* (Cambridge: Harvard University Press, 1983), pp. 81-82, 85.

For other examples of the classical canon of usage see Varro, *De lingua latina* 10.73; Cicero, *De oratore* 3.170, 1.3. 12; *Rhetorica ad C. Herrenium* 2.28.45.

39. Luther, *De servo arbitrio, CL* 4, 141, 32-142, 11.

40. Ibid., 162, 35-39; 168, 22-29; see also 195, 19-33.

41. Ibid., 180, 1-11, 20.

42. Ibid., 214, 16-17.

43. Ibid., 128, 25-26.

44. Ibid., 173, 21-29; 174, 28-32; 276, 36-37. At Augsburg Luther had complained of hearing "a new Latin language." *Acta F. Martini Lutheri Augustiniani apud D. Legatum Apostolicum Augustae, WA* 2, 6, 23-28.

45. Luther, *De servo arbitrio, CL* 4, 128, 30-39. For Erasmus' abuse of speech as contradicting ordinary usage and the common sensibilities of humanity see also 161, 34-38.

46. Ibid., 250, 4-11.

47. Ibid., 197, 28-29. See also his charge that Jerome applied to Scripture "an inverted grammar," 234, 1-4.

48. Ibid., 229, 11-12.

49. Ibid., 229, 1-3.

50. Ibid., 194, 5-7.

51. Ibid., 195, 9-12.

52. Ibid., 194, 29-32. See also *Rationis Latomianae confutatio* (1521), *WA* 8, 63, 27-30; 64, 8-11.

53. Luther, *De servo arbitrio, CL* 4, 249, 15-17.

54. Ibid., 194, 33-39. See also *Rationis Latomianae confutatio, WA* 8, 83, 31-84, 6; 62, 8-10.

55. Luther, *De servo arbitrio, CL* 4, 195, 40; 248, 1-2.

56. See Boyle, *Rhetoric and Reform,* pp. 47-57; and "Stoic Luther: Paradoxical Sin and Necessity," *Archiv für Reformationsgeschichte,* 73 (1982), 90-91.

57. Luther, *Rationis Latomianae confutatio, WA* 8, 91, 4; trans., George Lindbeck, in: *LW* 32, 206.

58. Ibid., 119, 30; trans., p. 247.

59. Ibid., 63, 31; trans., p. 167.

60. Luther, *De servo arbitrio, CL* 4, 247, 37-248, 3.

61. Luther, *Rationis Latomianae confutatio, WA* 8, 113, 3-5; trans., p. 237.

62. Ibid., 103, 16-19, 26-28; trans., p. 223.

63. Luther, *Kirchenpostille* (1522), *WA* 10.1.1, 728, 18-21; trans., John G. Kunstmann, *LW* 52, 286.

64. See Karl Holl, "Martin Luther on Luther," in *Interpreters of Luther: Essays in Honor of Wilhelm Pauck,* ed. Jaroslav Pelikan (Philadelphia: Fortress, 1968), pp. 17-18; Gerhard Ebeling, *Luther: An Introduction to His Thought* (Philadelphia: Fortress, 1970), pp. 16-17.

65. Luther, *Kirchenpostille, WA* 10.1.1, 66, 8-67, 12; trans., *LW* 52, 12.

66. Luther, *Predigten des Jahres 1522, WA* 10.3, 18, 14-15, 19, 2-3. For other citations of his sense of instrumentality see Holl, "Martin Luther on Luther," p. 19.

67. Luther, *Conclusiones quindecim tractantes, An libri philosophorum sint utiles aut inutiles ad theologiam, WA* 6, 29, 7-8.

68. Luther, *De servo arbitrio, CL* 4, 241, 23-26; 159, 4-6. See Boyle, "Stoic Luther," 71-77, 82-83.

69. Luther, *Tischreden, WA Tr* 2, 639, 27-28; cf. 457, 37-458, 1. See also *WA Tr* 2, 506, 14-27; *WA Tr* 4, 608, 6-8; *Vorlesungen über 1. Mose* (1535-45), *WA* 42, 600, 23-25; *In epistolam S. Pauli ad Galatas commentarius* (1531-35), *WA* 40, 170, 25-28.

70. For Erasmus on grammar see Boyle, *Erasmus on Language and Method in Theology* (Toronto: University of Toronto Press, 1977). For his response to Luther's critique of the nomenclature "free will" see *Hyperaspistes diatribae adversus servum arbitrium Martini Lutheri* (1526-27), in *Opera omnia,* ed. J. Clericus (Leiden, 1703-06), vol. X, especially 1288A-1289D, 1320C-E, 1331F-1332C.

71. Ibid., 1524C-D.

72. Although Luther's orthodoxy has generally been granted, Erasmus' has seemed less certain. For a clarification and analysis see Boyle, "Erasmus and the 'Modern' Question: Was He Semi-Pelagian?," *Archiv für Reformationsgeschichte,* 75 (1984).

LUTHER THE SATIRIST: STRATEGIES AND FUNCTION OF HIS SATIRE

Josef Schmidt, *McGill University*

In his eulogy of 1546, Philipp Melanchthon remarked that occasionally Luther's rough and coarse way of writing had often offended friends and foes alike; he then followed this cautious remark up with what had become the most common apologetic topos for the satirist:[1]

> That difficult times in which enormous ills had been prevailing
> had asked for a doctor with bitter and acerbic medicines.

Some of the administrations of those medicines had indeed left extremely bitter aftertastes, while others—remarks ad hominem and ad rem mostly—reveal a cheerful side of the reformer's character, his refreshing sense of humor. The man who in the midst of controversy reportedly quipped: 'Whenever I fart, the pope in Rome wrinkles his nose' kept his gift for satire and predilection for scatological language right to the end of his life. When one of many false reports announcing his premature demise appeared in 1545, Luther was not in want of the appropriate proverbial comment; he characterized the rumormonger in the following way:[2]

> The author is a poor, miserable and shitty priest who would like
> to relieve himself, but, alas, there is truly nothing in his bowels!

If one takes satire, especially Renaissance satire, for a literary genre, then Luther, in the strict sense, wrote only one work of this kind, the *Mönchskalb* (1523), a mock-exegesis of the apparition of a monster in the previous year. But I should also like to address myself to the numerous remarks and passages where the reformer used satirical style rhetorically, including works where his contribution or tacit approval seem very likely. Let us briefly review and highlight the more notable texts and illustrations in question.

Of the many shorter passages produced between 1521 and 1545 a few are of particular interest with regard to what I intend to develop as Luther's satirical strategies. You will remember Luther's inexhaustible supply of satirical references to his adversaries of the early years of the Reformation: Carlstadt, Eck, Emser, Müntzer, Murner, and above all: Cochlaeus. Contrary to a recent East-German study's claim—namely that Luther rarely used the sermon for polemics and satire—I have found numerous passages where the preacher Luther lashes out in a satirical and polemic manner that reminds one of earlier preachers of the mendicant orders who had mastered the art of delivering their catalogues of the vices in the satirical style.[3] E.g., Luther's *Sermon of the First Sunday of Advent* in 1524 contains many satirical/parodistic attacks on the Catholic liturgy that surfaced again in one of the last treatises, *Against the Papacy . . .* of 1545.[4] Many of the reformer's attacks on Catholic legends—e.g. the pamphlet against Cochlaeus about the legend of St. John Chrysostomus, where he introduces himself with his usual mention of the offices of being an unworthy preacher and doctor of theology—are compilations of satirical side-remarks designed to exaggerate the miraculous features into grotesque lies.[5] But the central text in this domaine is undoubtedly Luther's preface to the second systematic attempt to void the traditional legendaries of any credibility by means of parody and satire, namely Erasmus Alberus' *The Mendicant Monks' Koran* (1542).[6] Luther accuses the Franciscans of having replaced the life of Christ for that of their patron saint; and he distorts some of these suspected aberrations into parodistic features.

This paper will present an inventory of the various satirical strategies which Luther used. I shall not try to systematise that which is not systematic, for it would be a futile exercise. The reformer's style in this respect resembles his theology; many basic notions only emerged in tentative form from specific historical contexts. Satire here will be understood mainly as a stylistic attitude, not as a genre. Surprisingly little research has been done on Luther's satirical and coarse (grobianisch) writings; as to the two most comprehensive bibliographies: Herbert Wolf's *Martin Luther* contains only a small section on the reformer's "Grobianismus"; and Bernhard Lohse's bio-bibliography of 1981 refers to the topic only in a most cursory way.[7] The host of new biographies which publishers have so busily produced for this historical year mostly plod along well-trodden paths.[8] The reformer's boisterous character remains sketched within the confines of the established image of a teutonic choleric given to fits of rage and wit.

This lack of research is surprising. And I should like to develop some of the reasons why this field merits intensive study. Luther's basic attitudes coincide almost perfectly with those of the satirist per se. To understand his frequent use of satire exclusively as a personal trait, is most misleading. His central aim, to reform or recreate evangelical Christianity against an existing institution and tradition fits the satirist's position perfectly, namely to measure perceived deficiency against moral norms.

Before I outline this basic condition of context, let me turn to the attitudes of the satirist and the mechanics of the satirical style.[9] Satire involves a whole range of attitudes, from burlesque, ironical, mocking, sarcastic chastizing to outright invective. Satire is an attack, admittedly often an aesthetically socialized one that expresses collective anger, or at least irritation, but it nevertheless does involve aggression. Historical satire addresses itself to social conditions and institutions, which become objects of ridicule. Because the satirist notes the incongruence of elements of a particular situation, he proceeds to codify what he wants signified into a distorting code. Depending on the degree of aggression, the difference between the code and reality approaches congruence, implicitly setting up a norm through negation. In the extreme case, mockery becomes condemnation, scolding an intentional curse. Reformation satire provides a unique opportunity to analyze the structure of satire, its production and reception. Because it was a dominant form of expression and attitude of the time, there are numerous instances where basic features are accessible to the scholar as model cases.

Let me now introduce the notion of satirical strategies; for satire both as a genre and as an attitude is by definition prone to demand an unusually high degree of correspondence in terms of understanding, between the satirist and his audience, in the production and the reception of a text, play or pictorial design. If this is lacking, the product can literally not be understood as satire. Or if we approach the problem from another perspective: Cognitive dissonance on the part of the producer or the recipient must remain fairly low, for if it becomes excessive, non-understanding or misunderstanding will be the result. Let us consider two illustrations, for this context, with which you are no doubt familiar. The reception of the *Epistolae obscurorum virorum* (1515) is significant in many respects. Firstly, its gradual radicalization and enlargement in the final 1517 version demonstrated how a satirical joke in Maccaronic jargon moved during the course of its immediate reception in 1515 to a more fundamental and programmatic criticism. A second point was the basic misunderstanding that those early disciples of Luther derived from the enlarged version in that they mistook anonymous consent for willingness to actively take sides in the religious controversy; for them, a critical humanist was ipso facto a Lutheran. The historical evidence for this fact is well known; and I do not want to present a simplistic literary interpretation. But cognitive dissonance in determining the degree of satirical attack did bring about a fundamental misunderstanding which, in part, is to be found in the contextual situation of that particular satirical text.

The second example concerns a 20th-century reader of Luther's works, Erik H. Erikson, and his *Young Man Luther. A Study in Psychoanalysis and History.*[10] Throughout the analysis of young Luther's development, Erikson is preoccupied with the reformer's excessive use of scatological and bestial language in denouncing adversaries and temptations. He termed the preoccupation with swinish imagery rather aptly 'porcography'. But Erikson falls prey to a basic misunderstanding when he attributes this type of language mainly to the reformer's personal character. Scatology as well as bestial language and imagery were, at that time, the favorite satirical code of all developed European national literatures. In fact, were one to choose among the German scatologists of the early Reformation years, Thomas Murner's *Vom grossen lutherischen Narren* undoubtedly would win first prize. However, Erikson's contention of individuality cannot be dismissed that easily. For in terms of literary history, the period of the Reformation coincided with a monumental transition in the German literary tradition: the emergence of individual style—also the emergence of individual satire—where collective irritation and unrest surface as satirical attacks by individuals. As I pointed out at the beginning of this paper, contemporaries of Luther felt that his satirical aggression was unique, that it had extraordinary features; to see only the extratextual dimension of the reformer's historic confrontation with the papacy would be too simple if not simplistic.

A few typical instances of satirical strategy from the works mentioned earlier help illustrate the function of Luther's satirical style. The first example will be the *Monk-Calf,* the second example the Sermon for the *First Sunday of Advent* of 1524 and the repeated attack on the papacy *Wider das Pabsttum. . .* (1545); the concluding example is Luther's attitude towards legends, then we will consider both the Catholic anti-hagiography and the condemnation of the reformer after his death.

One of the very early satirical attacks on the papacy, Lucas Cranach's *Passional,* appeared in 1521. The series of woodcuts contrasting excesses of the papal court in Rome with scenes from Christ's life among the poor and destitute was a very powerful attack in more than one sense, for the idea of such an antithesis was firmly rooted in John Wycliffe's *Tractatus de Christo et suo adversario Antichristo!*[11] In fact, some of the pictorial contrasts seem to directly reproduce Wycliffe's *conditiones papae Christo contrariae.* Some of the illustrations for the *New Testament* which came out the following year are also direct attacks on the pope. Most notable are the ones accompanying the *Revelation of St. John,* e.g. chapters X and XIII. The illustration for the latter depicts the seven-headed beast crowned with the appropriate emblems of ecclesiastical dignitaries including that of the pope. [12] These illustrations must have pleased Luther, for in his final edition of the whole Bible (1545) they remained inserted with biting marginal comments alluding directly to the papacy. During that same year Luther's attack *Against the Papacy in Rome Instituted by the Devil* contained a true inventory of the satirical techniques used in the early years of the Reformation; catalogues of invective, parodies of the Catholic liturgy, and lists of the atrocities of the ecclesiastical adversary, all in Luther's inimitable style. [13]

The *Mönchskalb* and the *Papstesel* were produced in collaboration with Melanchthon in 1523 and provoked an immediate response. Cochlaeus felt compelled to reply to them in his latest attack on the reformer of the same year (*Adversus Cucullatum Minotaurum Wittenbergensem*). Whereas the *Passional* had manifestly been written and composed in reference to Wycliffe, the two satirical mock-exegeses had pictorial and textual imitations and allusions to Hus.[14] This reference was already an act of defiance and an acknowledgement of the justified attack on the church of those two earlier heretics. By choosing allegorical and moral exegesis in the vernacular, Luther, who did the major portion of the *Monk-Calf,* fused the method of biblical commentary with that of the satirist who in the literal sense of the word demasks. The whole piece is a denunciation of the orders as typical blatant perversions of the false church. A then established mixture of biblical prefigurations, doctrinal arguments and proverbial expressions from the vernacular bears the now characteristic mark of Luther's style. He attributes the dissolution of the orders to the apparition of this monster; and every part of the body and the dress signifies a particular atrocity of this kind of clergy. In our context, the satirical exaggeration and demasking are of importance, for the reformer turns the image of the monster as a direct sign of God into an explanatory satirical topos:[15]

Auffs erst und zursumma dieses zeychens laß dir das keyn schimpff seyn: Das Gott eym kalb das geystlich kleyd, die heylig kutten hatt angezogen. Damit hatter on zweyffel auff eym hauffen bedeut: das es bald offenbar werden muß, wie die gantze Muncherey und Nonnerey nichts anders sey denn falscher lugenhafftiger scheyn und eußerlich gleyssen eines geystlichen gottlichen lebens.

As a first and comprehensive point: Be not offended that God clothed a calf with a clerical garb, a holy cassock: Through this, He signified many things with one figure, namely that it has to become manifest that all the monks and nuns are nothing but false, deceitful phantoms and secular hypocrites of a spiritual, godly life.

One has to remember at this point that during the early Reformation vitriolic satire had an accepted status as discourse/disagreement; Thomas Murner's *Vom grossen lutherischen Narren* was in its concept an official refutation in the vernacular of Luther's three major treatises of 1520. Luther, in the text quoted above, makes the question of the offensive and vulgar topicality into an argument for his interpretation; throughout the treatise the reformer points out how the monstrosity of the calf (res significans) is nothing but a fitting image of divine intervention for the message (res significata). Even though he affirms that he is no prophet the question of how serious the mock-exegesis was *meant* to be cannot be truly answered. The history of reception seems to indicate that "the text" was understood as a literal warning by both by Catholics and Lutherans.[16] The question to be raised would then be to what extent the satirical offense— reduction of a religious institution to a vulgar and pathetic monstrosity— becomes a truth/lie in the conception of its recipients. The cognitive reduction to a one-dimensional understanding seems, however, to magnify the power of the initial satirical thrust: the attack against clerical authority.

Luther's *Sermon on the first Sunday of Advent* (1524) is a blow by blow refutatio of the canon of the catholic mass:[17]

Ee und wir anfahen zuͦerzelen die erschrockenlichen grewel und allerschendtlichsten Abgöͤtterey des gotß lesterlichen Canon, den die tollen Papisten Mess nennen...	Before I enumerate the terrible abuse and the most horrible idolatry of the blasphemous Canon which the mad papists call their mass . . .

Thus begins the exordium, followed by the inclusion of other forms of Catholic devotion like pilgrimages, indulgences etc. The satirical strategy is simple: Luther comments on a line-by-line basis, showing that not only the whole but also its parts are completely blasphemous. He follows the same technique in his *Against the Papacy in Rome Instituted by the Devil* (1545)[18]—the inspiration was the imminent danger of the Pope agreeing to a political solution by means of a general Church council or an official session at the Diet—, but what a difference in strategy! The now seasoned writer exhorts the blasphemy of his main adversary in cascades of invective and parody, opening his treatise with a pun that can be translated into English:

Der aller Hellischt Vater Sanct Paulus Tertius, als were er ein Bischoff der Römischen Kirchen, hat zwey breve an Carolum Quintum unsern Herrn Keiser geschrieben...	His most hellish father St. Paul the third, as if he were the bishop of Rome, has written two letters to Charles V., our lord emperor...

and comparing the pope's suspected initiatives a few sentences further to a "Fastnach kurtzweil," a shrovetide play. By then the code of Reformation polemics had been firmly established. Luther repeats invective from previous assaults throughout the text; most notable in terms of puns are his variations on the "Papstesel" towards the end. A very short passage from the center piece of argumentation and its analysis should make clear what a complex strategy the refutation of Catholicism had become. The following point is but one of many ridiculing the power of the papacy as an institution, and its practices:[19]

Jtem, das Sacrament wil der Herr hie gegeben haben, zu stercken die armen gewissen durch den Glauben. Nein, sagt Bapst Fartzesel, Man sols opffern für die Todten und Lebendigen, Verkeuffen, eine hantierung und jarmarckt draus machen, das wir den bauch damit weiden und aller Welt gûter fressen.	Ibid. The sacrament that our Lord has given should strengthen the faith of the poor faithful through faith. No, says Pope, farting-donkey, one should bring sacrifices for the living and the dead, make a business and a festival out of it so that we may tend to our belly and eat up everybody's wealth.

Various forms of parody overlay the message. The answer-question pattern is taken from the catechism, the invective follows the established glossary of condemnation, and the mock-decree of the pope, alluding to a formula of the Catholic creed (the living and the dead), blasphemously defends the old practices of selling indulgences. But what begins as satirical invective becomes, towards the conclusion of the whole treatise, an open condemnation of the papacy; the pope *is* the Antichrist for Luther. This raises an important question in the satirical context. For while normally satire distorts reality in order to unmask the discord in a given situation, Luther's treatise, by adding the eschatological dimension, goes full circle: what is presented as a blasphemous deviation and perversion turns out to be the actual state of affairs! Satire changes from an attack into recounting the actual conditions. Satirical imagery is, in Luther's perspective, transformed into depictions of realities. The papacy *is* the devil, distortion *is* description.

Lifting scatology to eschatological proportions, the question arises how Luther the preacher could justify the use of excessive satirical invective. For especially in the early years he was rather self-conscious about his outbursts of vituperation.[20] One of his satirical opponents, Thomas Murner, also reflects in *Vom grossen Lutherischen Narren* (1522):[21]

Ob mir das stand zůn eren an,	Does it infringe on my honor
Das ich so manch schympff red hab than,	That I have produced so many satires?
So ich doch bin ein geistlich man?	I, a man of clerical status?

The question is part of a more complex problem: What place does satire occupy in the transition of the late Medieval 'thematic sermon' to Reformation polemics? The thematic sermon in the vernacular had, after 1500, reached full maturity; in fact, the most telling example, Geiler von Kaisersberg's collection of sermons on Sebastian Brant's *Ship of Fools,* was published in 1520. Scatological humor, rough eroticism and even explicit sexual imagery served to exemplify the traditional condemnation of moral vices for all social classes. But, as James J. Murphy has recently pointed out, very little is known about the rhetorical justification for the choice of thematic sermons over the traditional biblical explication.[22] It goes without saying that these types of sermons were of central importance for Luther who saw in this practice another perversion of the Catholic Church while, at the same time, making full use in the vernacular of this tradition both in his sermons and in his treatises. His appeal to the new lay church was so powerful, among other things, because he employed the strategy of the mendicant preacher who knew how to reach this kind of target audience. Joachim Suchomski has recently done a small study on the use of satire in the late Medieval tradition of preaching. His scant and tentative findings stay within the confines of the predictable.[23] Because the preacher could justify almost anything with the main functions of his office, namely to chastise and better the morals of his audience, he could be

MONSTRVM ROMAE INVENTVM MOR
TVVM IN TIBERI. ANNO 1496.

Was Gott selbst vom Bapstum hell
Zeigt dis schrecklich bild hie gestellt:
Dafür jederman grawen sollt:
Wenn ers zu hertzen nemen wollt.
Mart:Luth:D.

very open-minded in his choice of stratagems to reach a recognizable balance between *utilitas* and *delectatio*. From popular culture we also know that in late Medieval times many sides of life, if verbally or visually expressed, are offensive to a modern recipient, however, for an audience in late Medieval times such manifestations were entirely within the socially tolerable. But just how these two features of the late Medieval satirical sermon aided Luther's appeal when he lashed out with verbal abuse against his adversaries, remains to be explained.

Earlier we saw that some of the functions of satire corresponded to Luther's basic aims in the Reformation. Let us now develop a last point along these lines: Luther's condemnation of legends by means of parody; and the problem of his own Catholic anti-hagiography and the history of its reception.

Luther coined the satirical name for legend ("lügent" = a pun, meaning: lie) fairly early. This very popular form of devotion was anathema to him because from his perspective saintly lives had more and more displaced the passion of Christ; the mendicant orders responsible, above all the Franciscans and the Dominicans, had turned the cult of their patron saints into business ventures. Theologically, however, there was the problem of what the Reformation movement could do in terms of substituting a more suitable form of devotional literature. Luther recommended stories from the *Old Testament,* fables, etc. He made several attempts to create a Lutheran devotional literature that would rival the traditional legend, and he even lamented the fact that, in spite of his objections, some legends had grown very dear to him.[24] This part of the history of the legend during the Reformation is well documented; the same goes for the battle of legends where Erasmus Alberus' parody, declaring the *liber conformitatum* to be the equivalent of the *Koran,* a pagan collection of stories, decisively marks the outbreak of the battle for true evangelical devotional literature.[25] Luther's preface to this collection sketches in a few sentences his basic objections; there is even a bit of earthy humor when he compares marital bliss to St. Francis' castigations in order to ward off temptations of the flesh. The ensuing war of Lutheran parodies and Catholic anti-legendaries reached a climax with the *Quinta Centuria* of Johannes Nas (1570),[26] part five of a collection of satires on the Reformation movement. This fifth volume is an anti-biography of Luther in the vernacular, illustrated with some of the more famous polemical woodcuts which are now, however, interpreted back against the camp which, in the eyes of Nas, was the camp of the heretics. The 30th chapter contains a point-by-point counter-exegesis of Luther's *Monk-Calf* of 1523; the author even reproduces the original woodcut for the instruction of his readers. What strikes us today is the fact that a vast number of documents from the immediate Reformation period were popularized in this battle of legends, for they were apparently very influential and warranted rebuttal and counter-rebuttals. The predilection for detail and the reproductions of the more excessive caricatures of the earlier days are manifest; they are also puzzling, for who would expect, many decades after the outbreak of the movement, such encyclopedias of polemical trivia with a pathological fixation on detail? The historical development is well known—the Catholic tradition of legendaries has lived on—, but the causes for this unsuccessful bid of Lutherans and Protestants to undermine the authority and the popularity of this genre still awaits analysis.[27]

This leads to my final point, a sub-chapter so to speak of the battle of legends, the Catholic anti-hagiography of Luther's life. According to a recent ecumenical evaluation of Luther, edited by Hans F. Geiß et al. (1982), the issue is very much alive as the title of this collection of essays indicates: *Weder Ketzer noch Heiliger. Luthers Bedeutung für den ökumenischen Dialog.*[28] The tradition of the official Catholic image of the reformer has been thoroughly researched and conclusively established. Cochlaeus' *Commentarii de actis et scriptis Martini Luther* (1549) became the almost unquestioned source of generations of Catholic anti-legendaries right down to our days.[29] Satire and invective played a major role in the various compilations of the facts of Luther's life; hate and outrage about what was seen as the great heretic's atrocities turned most of the Reformation criticism into Catholic attacks on the reformer and his descendants. Scorning and scolding, developed during the Reformation, remained for centuries the appropriate style of non-discussion. What then remains to be analyzed? Behind all the vitriolic depictions of the reformer's life there is a true obsession of 16th century Catholic biographers to deny any credibility to the heretic's cause. The means to do this are the ones employed by Cochlaeus: to compile an anthology of Luther's writings and juxtapose them into points that are contradictory, unjustified, or even irrelevant. In true inquisitorial style, the object of scorn should judge himself by offering his own recantations. Therefore, it is important not only to have that heretic, at least posthumously, contradict himself in essential points, but also to have him demonstrate his unworthiness and non-credibility by having led a non-model life. In other words: a satirical technique, parody, is the device by which the rectification is accomplished, and a good measure of vituperation is added. E.g., Luther's condemnations of monkish life are rebutted in that the Catholic biographer wants to show that the reformer's attacks actually applied to problems arising in his own life.

ORTVS ET ORIGO PAPAE.

Hie wird geborn der Widerchrift
Megera fein Seugamme ift:
Alecto fein Kindermeidlin
Tifiphone die gengelt jn.

Mart.Luth.D.

One such collection, aptly written by a lawyer turned priest, was the *Anatomiae Lutheri, Pars I.*[30] "Lege lector et judica" says the title page; the sub-title is rather revealing of the satirical intent of the exercise:

Das ist/auß den Siben bö^esen Geistern des vil Seelen ver- lustigen und also tewren M̧anns D. Martini Lutheri, die Drei erste Geister. I. Der Fleischlich geist. II. Der Lester geist. III. Der Lotter geist.	That is: From the seven evil spirits of Martin Luther who lost so many souls, the dear man. The three first spirits: 1. The spirit of the flesh. 2. The spirit of scorn and satire. 3. The spirit of looseness.

The author, Johannes Pistorius, addresses the tome to all, but especially to those who have been "seduced" by the reformer. The style of juxtaposing has most of Luther's more salty satire in the vernacular played off against excerpts from his writings. The structure of the book is such that it allows easy cross-checking; but most of the time wording is used that indicates very clearly the satirical intent of this mock-refutation of the reformer's life and doctrine. The section on Luther's invective and satire introduces a many-pronged attack: the reformer is simultaneously accused of linguistic inability, of contradiction, self-accusation and, of course, blasphemy. Catalogues of satirical utterances and distorted names are listed and commented upon. Why this display of such enormous, excessive length? Why the urge to turn documentary proof into satirical evidence of its own negligibility, thereby acknowledging its potency?

Clearly, Luther's satirical style merits intensive study. It continues to be intriguing because it's function is inextricably linked to the reformer's central aim: the unmasking and uncovering of the true Christian tradition.

Notes

The criticism of H.W. Frischkopf, J. Hellman and R. Sullivan has greatly aided me in trying to strive for brevity and clarity.

1. Translated from Caspar Creutziger's German rendering of the *Oratio,* in: Josef Schmidt, ed., *Renaissance, Humanismus, Reformation.* Vol. III: *Die deutsche Literatur in Text und Darstellung* (Stuttgart: Reclam,[2] 1983), p. 109.

2. *WA* 54, 188.

3. Bentzinger, Rudolf and Kettmann, Gerhard. "Zu Luthers Stellung im Sprachschaffen seiner Zeit." *Zeitschrift für Phonetik, Sprachwissenschaft und Kommunikationsforschung,* 36.3 (1983), 272-273.

4. *WA* 15 (*Dominica prima Adventus* 1524), pp. 765 passim.

5. *WA* 53, 406 ff.

6. *Der Barfuser Münche Eulenspiegel und Alcoran.*

7. Sub-title: *Eine Einführung in germanistische Luther-Studien* (Stuttgart: Metzler, 1980), p. 50 f.—The sub-title of Lohse's book is *Eine Einführung in sein Leben und Werk* (München: Beck).

8. This, I think, is even true for Peter Manns' *Martin Luther* (Freiburg/B.: Herder/Lahr: Kaufmann, 1982) not to mention the blatantly journalistic 'stories' of Barbara Benys (*Und wenn die Welt voll Teufel wär. Luthers Glaube und seine Erben.* Reinbek b. Hamburg: Rowohlt, 1982), Horst Herrman (*M.L., Ketzer wider Willen.* München: Bertelsmann, 1983), or Hellmut Diwald (*L. Eine Biografie.* Bergisch-Gladbach: Gustav Lübbe, 1982).

9. For information on secondary literature on the topic of Reformation, cf. my book *Lestern, lesen und lesen hören. Kommunikationsstudien zur deutschen Prosasatire der Reformationszeit* (Bern: Peter Lang, 1977), pp. 77-106.—I am indebted to Eva Kushner for letting me read her final draft of "L'ésprit satirique et le développement de la satire" (to be published soon in vol. I as chapter 7 of *Renaissance* which forms part of a large publication project, *Histoire comparée des littératures européennes,* produced under the auspices of the Association Internationale de Littérature Comparée.). Kushner's chapter deals mainly with 15th-century satire.

10. (New York: W.W. Norton, 1962) ([1]1958).

11. Cf. *WA* 9, 677.

12. Cf. the edition of Hans Volz et al. (Darmstadt: Wissenschaftliche Buchgesellschaft, [2]1973). The illustrations alluded to in my text are reproduced in vol. 2, pp. 2491 and 2495.

13. *WA* 54, 195-299.

14. For the authoritative texts (and pictures) cf. *WA* 11, pp. 357 ff. But also Konrad Lange, *Der Papstesel* (Göttingen, 1891); H. Preuss, *Die Vorstellung vom Antichrist im späten Mittelalter, bei Luther und in der konfessionellen Polemik* (Leipzig, 1906) and Josef Schmidt, note 9, pp. 209-238.—For specific examples of satires, cf. John Klassen, "Women and Religious Reform in Late Medieval Bohemia," *Renaissance and Reformation,* New Series, vol. V, no. 4 (1981), pp. 203-221.

15. *WA* 11, 381.

16. "Text" is here understood in the active sense which Roland Barthes has outlined in "From Work to Text," In *Textual Strategies. Perspectives in Post-Structuralist Criticism,* ed. and introd. by Josué V. Harari (Ithaca: Cornell University Press, 1979), pp. 73-81.—Other topoi of the Reformation period, the lecherous/hypocritical nun/monk/pious person as they surface after Reformation polemics in 'high literature' has not really been analysed with regard to its satirical origin: e.g. Alizon in one of the first French renaissance comedies, Jean de la Taille's *Les Corrivaus* (1562), to Molière's *Tartuffe* (1664/67).—It is also puzzling to see that authoritative Marxist research has not developed the concept of satire according to its ideologically fitted position in the field of German Renaissance and Reformation studies. Cf. the conspicuous lack in *Renaissanceliteratur und frühbürgerliche Revolution. Studien zu den sozial- und ideologiegeschichtlichen Grundlagen europäischer Nationalliteraturen,* eds. Robert Weimann, Werner Lenk, and Joachim-Jürgen Slomka (Berlin and Weimar: Aufbau-Verlag, 1976); or Gisela Brandt, "Massenkommunikation während der deutschen frühbürgerlichen Revolution—stimulierendes Moment im sozialen und territorialen

Sprachausgleich des 16. Jh.", in *Zeitschrift für Phonetik, Sprachwissenschaft und Kommunikationsforschung,* 36.3 (1983), 276-286.

17. *WA* 15, 765.
18. *WA* 54, 195-299.
19. Ibid., p. 266.
20. Cf. *WA* 6, 323; 8, 213.
21. Quoted from Jürgen Schutte, *"Schympff red". Frühformen bürgerlicher Agitation in Thomas Murners "Grossem Lutherischen Narren"* (Stuttgart: Metzler, 1973), p. 169.
22. *Rhetoric in the Middle Ages. A History of Rhetorical Theory from Saint Augustine to the Renaissance* (Berkeley/Los Angeles/London: University of California Press, 1974); and more recently in "The Middle Ages," in Winifred Bryan Horner, ed., *The Present State of Scholarship in Historical and Contemporary Rhetoric* (Columbia/London: University of Missouri Press, 1983), pp. 57 ff.; cf. also Rudolf Cruel, *Geschichte der deutschen Predigt im Mittelalter* (Darmstadt: Wissenschaftliche Buchgesellschaft, 1966; (¹1879).
23. *"Delectatio" und "Utilitas". Ein Beitrag zum Verhältnis mittelalterlicher komischer Literatur* (Bern/München: Francke 1975), pp. 76 passim; but also the small appendix on "satira," pp. 249-256.
24. E.g. *WA* 30, 644; 36, 388.
25. Rudolf Schenda, "Hieronymus Rauscher und die protestantisch-katholische Legendenpolemik," in Wolfgang Brückner, ed., *Volkserzählung und Reformation. Ein Handbuch zur Tradierung und Funktion von Erzählstoffen und Erzählliteratur im Protestantismus* (Berlin: Erich Schmidt, 1974), pp. 178-259. For a survey of the tradition: Werner Williams-Krapf, "German and Dutch legendaries of the Middle Ages; a Survey," in Hans Bekker-Nielsen, ed., *Hagiography and Medieval Literature, A Symposium* (Odense: Odense University Press, 1981), pp. 66-75.
26. Johannes Nas: *Quinta Centuria. Das ist Das Fünfft Hundert/der Evangelischen warheit...* Ingolstatt: [Alexander Weissenhorn], 1570.
27. Cf. Adolf Herte, *Das katholische Lutherbild im Banne der Lutherkommentare des Cochlaeus,* 3 vols. (Münster: Aschendorffsche Verlagsbuchhandlung, 1943).
28. Regensburg 1982. Especially Otto Herrman Pesch's "'Ketzerfürst' und 'Vater im Glauben'—Die seltsamen Wege der katholischen 'Lutherrezeption'" (pp. 123-174) gives an up-date of Herte's classic on the topic.
29. Cf. Herte, *Lutherbild,* vol. I, p. IX passim. But also a Catholic study: Remigius Bäumer, ed., *Lutherprozess und Lutherbann. Vorgeschichte, Ergebnis, Nachwirkung* (Münster: Aschendorff, 1972). The editor's own contribution is basically a plea that the trial against Luther up to 1521 was a fair one!—The hagiography on the Lutheran side has been well summarized in: Ruth Kastner, *Geistlicher Raufhandel. Form und Funktion der illustrierten Flugblätter zum Reformationsjubiläum 1617 in ihrem historischen und publizistischen Kontext,* Bern: Peter Lang, 1982 (= Mikrokosmos, 11).
30. (Köln: Arnold Quentel, 1590). The second part is far less satirical, dealing almost exclusively with doctrine.

THE OLDER LUTHER, 1526-1546

Mark U. Edwards, Jr., *Purdue University*

Fully two-thirds of Luther's extant works were produced between 1526 and his death in 1546.[1] Yet less than a third of the publications on Luther deal with these later years, and only a very small percentage concentrate on the years 1531 to 1546. The last critical biography that gives thorough consideration to the later years is the venerable study by Julius Köstlin, revised by Gustav Kawerau, and published in 1903.[2] Since 1903 Heinrich Boehmer and Martin Brecht have given us detailed studies of the early years, to 1521, and Heinrich Bornkamm has examined the middle years, to 1530.[3] The last fifteen years of Luther's life still await their biographer.

I do not expect to see a full critical biography of the older Luther any time soon, for the task is a formidable one. Helmar Junghans has edited a two-volume collection of essays on the older Luther, 1526 to 1546, in which more than forty scholars have pooled their efforts.[4] They are not proceeding chronologically, of course, but even so this works out to more than two scholars per year for the later years, a rough indication of the magnitude of the task. Moreover, although this is a fine collection of individual studies of aspects of the biography of the older Luther, it does not, and by its nature cannot, alleviate the need for a single, comprehensive study of the later years.

In the meantime we do have in English the superbly written study by H.G. Haile, which concentrates on depicting the older Luther's personality as he faced the challenges of the later years and reflected on the events that brought him to his unique position within the history of Christianity.[5] I particularly admire Haile's treatment of Luther's literary gifts, sense of humor, and concern for equity (*epikeia*). Several specialized studies concentrating on the life of the older Luther have also recently appeared. Hermann Kunst examined Luther's advice to rulers, as expressed in his letters.[6] Eike Wolgast, in one of the best recent historical studies of Luther, has examined the formal opinions that Luther and his colleagues at Wittenberg penned for the Saxon princes over the years.[7] Heiko Oberman recently published a study of Luther's writings against the Jews, which rightly insists on the importance of context for understanding Luther's writings.[8] I, too, examine Luther's anti-Jewish writings as part of my study of the polemics of the older Luther.[9] There has also been a number of studies published on aspects of the older Luther's theology.[10]

There is much that can be said about the approach that should be taken to a comprehensive biography of the older Luther. I have my own ideas. Several of the authors who have written on aspects of the older Luther are participating in this conference, and I am sure they have theirs. This conference gives us, thus, an unusual opportunity to share our thoughts, to discuss and debate the most neglected area in Luther research: Luther's later years.

Out of the many possible approaches that could be recommended, I have chosen to argue for two that are not normally considered in studies of Luther, although the principles are regularly applied to other historical figures:

1. The biographer must pay much more attention than is common in Luther studies to external forces that influenced and constrained the older Luther's activities.

2. The biographer must distinguish between the older Luther's intentions and the actual results of his actions, and give proper consideration to both. That is, the biographer must go beyond Luther's stated motives and his theological rationale to ask how Luther was understood by others and what the practical effect of his actions was.

But before we consider these two points, I should like to say a few words about the best point to begin the biography of the older Luther, that is, when does Luther become the "older Luther"?

Beginning the Biography of the Older Luther

In a recent essay entitled "Interpreting the Old Luther (1526-1546)," Helmar Junghans sees the third and last stage of Luther's life as characterized by Luther's personal involvement in attempts to implement the Reformation.[11] This phase began on 9 October 1524 when Luther laid aside his cowl. Soon afterwards he called for the abolition of the mass in the Castle Church and he himself married. Of greater importance still, on May 1525 Elector Friedrich died and was succeeded by Elector Johann. Friedrich had tolerated reforms. Johann actively encouraged them. And the recess of the Diet of Speyer in 1526 gave him and other rulers a legal justification for reform. The publication of the German Mass in 1526 signaled to the wider world that something new was afoot in Wittenberg.

Since I am convinced that we need to approach the biography of the older Luther with a greater awareness of events and forces that defined the boundaries in which Luther was constrained to act, I would add to Junghans' argument that more was involved than just a transition from toleration to encouragement of reform. These years happen to coincide with a transition in the Reformation itself, from a revolutionary movement made up primarily of ideologically committed individuals to a more conservative movement led by rulers of territories and city-states.

This transition was unavoidable if the Reformation was to endure. It is one thing to initiate a revolution; it is quite another to pass it on to your children and your children's children. The former may be accomplished with belief and individual effort; the latter requires institutions and bureaucracy. But these new circumstances imposed new and difficult requirements on Luther. They called for him to react to an agenda set by others, especially by rulers, or dictated by events. They called for a willingness to compromise, to accommodate belief to political necessity, to take sides publicly in disputes where no great principles were at stake and where ideological conviction found itself leagued with political self-interest. Too great a reluctance to make the called-for adjustment would have doomed Luther to ineffectualness. Too great a readiness to compromise or reach accommodation would have opened him to the charge of hypocrisy and insincerity, accusations fatal to his authority. Principles had to bend to necessity, not break.

It is this change in the Reformation movement itself, in external events, that, to my mind, best divides the 'old Luther' from the 'young Luther.' In this contention, I am only slightly modifying Junghans' argument. He states that this third period is characterized by the fact that Luther personally worked to institute the Reformation. I have no quarrel with this, but I would add that during this third period political leaders sometimes took the initiative away from Luther and his fellow theologians. The theologians not infrequently danced to the politicians' tune. This change is very important for our evaluation of the old Luther and his Reformation.

This change occurred gradually. Luther was still able to forestall a "preventive attack" against the Catholics in the so-called Pack Affair of 1528. He was able to postpone for a time the formation of a Protestant League designed to protect Protestants against an imperially led attack. But finally he and his colleagues were prevailed upon, at Torgau in 1530, to leave the question of the propriety of armed resistance to the jurists and politicians. In 1531 the League of Schmalkalden was formed, without Luther's opposition but also without his wholehearted blessing. And then, in 1532, Elector Johann died, and his son Johann Friedrich succeeded.

This transition from Johann to Johann Friedrich may be of even greater significance for Luther's later years than the earlier transition from Friedrich to Johann. For Elector Johann Friedrich was more prone than his predecessors to use Luther to provide sanction and support for policies arrived at independently. "Time and again," Eike Wolgast concludes in his fine monograph *Die Wittenberger Theologie und die Politik der evangelischen Stände,* "there is an obvious effort to commit the theologians to decisions already made, to win their approval for them, and to use them to accomplish the Elector's ends among the other evangelical estates. The original function of the Wittenberg opinion, to advise conscience, was increasingly transformed by Johann Friedrich into the function of relieving consciences, as a religious sanction and reassurance for otherwise autonomous and often previously made decisions of the politicians."[12]

In general, the publications and correspondence of the older Luther were more political. Karl Trudinger has shown that a much larger percentage of Luther's correspondence in these later years was directed to secular authorities.[13] In my recent book, *Luther's Last Battles,* I documented a similar change with his polemics, which in these years were directed largely at convinced Lutherans and were often politically inspired and of direct political significance.[14]

This shift in the character of his polemics and their intended audience is manifest also in the locations where the works were printed and reprinted. In contrast to the earlier years where a number of printing centers throughout Germany accounted for a substantial percentage of works by Luther, the later years saw most of the printings and reprintings coming from Wittenberg, supplemented by the production of a few staunchly Lutheran cities, mostly in central and northern Germany. In the period 1516 to 1530, for example, Wittenberg accounts for only 25 percent of the printings and reprintings of Luther's works, followed by Augsburg with 18 percent, Nuremberg with 9 percent, Strasbourg with 8 percent, and Erfurt with 8 percent. In contrast, in the period 1531 to 1546, Wittenberg accounts for fully 55 percent of the printings and reprintings, followed by Nuremberg with 12 percent, Augsburg with 6 percent, Magdeburg with 6 percent, and Strasbourg with 4 percent. If one examines only the last six years of Luther's life, 1541 to 1546, the new focus of his major audience is even more apparent: Wittenberg does 43 percent, Nuremberg 11 percent, Frankfurt a.M. 9 percent, Augsburg 9 percent, Leipzig 7 percent,

Strasbourg 5 percent, and Magdeburg 5 percent—to list the top seven centers for the printing and reprinting of Luther's works. Luther, these statistics suggest, had become the publicist for an established, territorially defined ideology.[15]

As I have stated, this transition begins in about the mid-1520's, and hence a good case can be made for beginning the biography of the older Luther about this same time. The danger, of course, is that a biographer who begins in, say, 1526, may become so bogged down by the mass of primary and secondary material that he or she will never finish. This is the common fate of most biographies of Luther. Heinrich Bornkamm suggested that the biography of the older Luther should begin in 1532, with the peace the Nuremberg Standstill provided.[16] This year also marked the change in Saxony's rulers from Elector Johann to Elector Johann Friedrich. If one were to begin in the 1530's, I would recommend beginning with 1531, when the League of Schmalkalden was formed. This date would also have the practical value of starting about where Bornkamm leaves off in his *Luther in der Mitte seines Lebens.*

External Pressures and Constraints

Too often biographers attribute to Luther more control over actions than he had. They do this, if not explicitly, at least implicitly by focusing their accounts almost exclusively on Martin Luther himself. Certainly, Luther shaped his choices more than most people ever do, but he too was constrained by the circumstances of his time and particularly by the often unpredictable or uncontrollable dynamics of his own movement. By the late 1520's and early 1530's, as we have just discussed, the Reformation had passed from a revolutionary movement made up primarily of ideologically committed individuals to a more conservative movement led by rulers of territories and city-states. In his later years, therefore, Luther had to confront the problems of institutionalization, including the establishment of doctrinal norms, the development of bureaucracy, and the maintenance of in-group solidarity in the face of external threat. To put this another way, the later years saw Luther significantly constrained by political and social dynamics, often not of his choosing. Let me illustrate this with a summary discussion of a topic I know well, the older Luther's polemical writings.

To avoid misunderstanding, let me state at the outset that the older Luther was no docilely obedient publicist for the League of Schmalkalden or for the Elector of Saxony. When his conscience demanded it, he defied even a direct electoral prohibition and refused to count the political costs of his action. As he saw it, if he did not respond to public attacks on his teachings, it was equivalent to denying and forsaking them. So when, for example, the Catholic Duke Georg of Saxony publicly attacked his 1531 *Warning to His Dear German People* and *Glosses on the Alleged Imperial Edict,* he replied, ignoring his Elector's command that he not publish an attack on the Duke.[17] In the negotiations that followed the public dispute, he stated the limits of his obedience. He would refrain in the future from anti-Catholic polemics, but only, as he put it, "to the extent that it is possible in respect to my conscience and the [Protestant] teachings."[18] Some years later, in his public dispute with Cardinal Albrecht over the death of Hans Schonitz, he once again followed his conscience rather than the dictates of political wisdom. Unable in good conscience to remain silent in the face of the Cardinal's wrongdoing, he did what he could to minimize possible adverse effects on the Protestant cause, but he published his attack nonetheless.[19] Finally he forced the Elector to abandon plans to attack the city of Halle[20] and refused to countenance publicly Landgrave Philipp's bigamy despite threats that the Landgrave would defect to the Catholics or attack him in print.[21]

Having illustrated Luther's independence, let me now sketch some of its limits. Eike Wolgast has noted how Elector Johann Friedrich was prone to solicit advice from Luther and Luther's colleagues only after policy had been set.[22] Much the same thing can be said about the polemics that Elector Johann Friedrich solicited or encouraged in support of his own policies or the policies of the League of Schmalkalden. On several occasions the Elector used Luther's polemical abilities to relieve and reassure Protestant consciences and to provide sanction for what were largely autonomous political decisions. Of course, it did not take much to induce Luther to attack the opponents of the Elector or the League. He was usually quite willing to attack Pope and papists, and many of his published attacks in his later years were unsolicited. Nevertheless, there can be no doubt that these treatises were a support to Elector Johann Friedrich's political goals and to League policy. This was true even in cases where Luther harbored some reservations concerning the politicians' decisions. The question of whether to accept an invitation to a papally convened general council illustrates this point.[23]

The rulers and theologians were of different minds on how best to deal with a papal invitation to a council. Rulers such as Luther's own prince, Elector Johann Friedrich, tended to view the problem as political and legal. The Elector himself saw the papal invitation to a council and the papal council itself as legal snares, set to capture the Protestants. He thus thought it best to protest the papal council and refuse to participate. The Elector's theologians, including Luther, disagreed. They expected nothing good from a papal council, but nonetheless they repeatedly urged their prince and the League not to refuse the invitation. Not surprisingly they lost the argument with the princes, not once but on several occasions. They then acquired the task of justifying the rulers' decision and discrediting the papal council. The numerous attacks on a papal council that flowed from Luther's pen in the 1530's and especially in the months following the League meeting of 1537 were honest expressions of Luther's critical view of a papal council. But by discrediting the papal council in his readers eyes, he also gave tacit support to the politicians' policy of nonattendance.

Political pressures also influenced his publications on the question of resistance to a possible Catholic attack led by the emperor.[24] Under intense pressure from politicians and jurists who were unwilling to accept the theologians' reservations concerning armed defense of the faith, Luther first "allowed" a positive law justification of resistance and finally, much assisted by his apocalyptic expectations, developed the theological argument that if the Emperor attacked the Protestants on account of their faith then he would not be acting in his capacity as a superior secular authority but rather as a servant of the papal antichrist. Similarly, his publication justifying Elector Johann Friedrich's seizure of the bishopric of Naumburg represents an accommodation to the wishes of his prince despite Luther's own misgivings.[25] His two treatises concerning Duke Heinrich of Brunswick-Wolfenbüttel also involved him in what was largely a political affair.[26] Even his "matter of conscience," his *Against the Bishop of Magdeburg, Cardinal Albrecht* (1539), appears to have served his prince's political interests, whatever Luther's own intentions.[27]

In fact, all the major anti-Catholic and anti-Turkish polemics of his last years, save only his *Against the Bishop of Magdeburg, Cardinal Albrecht,* were written at the instigation of the Elector.[28] Even *Against the Papacy at Rome* (1545), the most violent and vulgar treatise to issue from Luther's pen, was written at the behest of Elector Johann Friedrich.[29] The conclusion seems inescapable that the Elector was using Luther's extraordinary polemical abilities as one more weapon in the ongoing struggle between Protestant and Catholic forces. Luther's implicit task was to exhort Protestants to stand fast in the face of the Catholic (and also the Turkish) threat and to reassure them that God and right was on their side. The Elector encouraged and commended Luther's vehemence and even vulgarity, and this encouragement was given not only for works that he himself had commissioned but also for works such as Luther's attacks on the Jews and on the Sacramentarians, which Luther himself had initiated.[30]

Another manifestation of the changed historical circumstances of the

1530's and 1540's was that most of Luther's polemics during this period were addressed to his own supporters. The polemics of the previous decade or so included a significant number of treatises that were directed towards the unconverted, at open-minded Catholics, and were dedicated to the exposition of Protestant faith. In contrast, the polemics of these later years were largely works of exhortation, aimed at the converted, at convinced Lutherans, designed to deepen beliefs already held, and were most often politically inspired and of direct political significance.

This change accompanied and supported the process of institutionalization. The time for large-scale proselytizing had passed. Now the Reformation needed to be consolidated and defended in the face of threats from Catholics, Turks, Jews and Jewish exegesis, and "fanatics." The task demanded exhortation rather than explanation. Emphasis was placed on the righteousness of the Protestant cause and on the wickedness and eventual futility of the opponents' cause. While there was still need for education in the tenets of the Protestant faith, stress now was placed on the deepening of beliefs already held. It was time to rally the troops, to whip up passions for the battles ahead. This stage in the movement's history was well-served by Luther's apocalyptic vision of the climactic struggle between the true and false church, between the followers of Christ and the minions of Satan. His highly charged rhetoric and liberal abuse of opponents proved useful to the movement's leaders and reassuring to its followers. Such were the treatises circumstances called for. Such were the treatises that Luther delivered.

Intentions and Results

Most scholarly work on Luther focuses on his theology. But the biographer's task is not done when he or she determines Luther's theology on a particular point, say, on the distinction between the church and secular authority or on the propriety of armed resistance against superior secular authority in matters of religion. There are further questions that must be answered, such as: what his contemporaries understood him to be saying, and what practical effect his actions and statements had for German history and the development of Lutheranism.

Consider, for example, Luther's relationship to the formation of Lutheran orthodoxy and the state-controlled territorial church, the *landesherrliche Kirchenregiment*. To create a lasting institution the Lutherans had to establish doctrinal norms and the means of inculcating and maintaining them among the pastors and the greater population. It should not be surprising, then, how concerned the theologians and secular authorities were in these later years with establishing summaries of true doctrine and with devising means of educating pastors and congregations in these fundamentals.

In this cooperative task Luther demonstrated a willingness to accommodate his concern for "evangelical freedom" to the practical requirements of order and institutional authority. His experiences with Karlstadt, the Zwickau prophets, Müntzer, the rebellious peasants, and the Sacramentarians had convinced him that there needed to be clear lines of authority within the institutional church including authoritative statements of the faith beyond the Bible. The Peasants' War and the results of the visitations of 1527 and 1528 had further convinced him that much of the population of the nominally Protestant territories had taken advantage of evangelical freedom to throw off the papal yoke with its fiscal and legal impositions without, however, replacing it with the yoke of Christ. Especially deplorable, he felt, was the manifest unwillingness of large segments of the population adequately to support their pastors or to provide for their Christian nurture and that of their children.

These, of course, are problems of institutionalization. No longer was the Reformation movement comprised largely of dedicated individuals. Now Luther and his colleagues had to deal with the problems of a mixed community composed of believers and non-believers. This challenge forced him to rethink his positions on such matters as congregational autonomy and even Bible reading as the best written source for encountering and determining the "word of God." He may never have abandoned his earlier convictions on these matters, but in practice he substituted university and pastoral authority for individual and congregational autonomy, and he supplemented, and perhaps for many common people even replaced, Bible reading with catechetical instruction and a prescribed order of worship.

Urged on by secular authorities and by his own concern for the institutional church, Luther helped shape several institutions that aimed at inculcating and maintaining the evangelical faith within the larger population. Consider, for example, one of the earliest needs of the nascent institutional church: a reformed service of worship in the vernacular. As Luther explained in his sermon of 29 October 1525, inaugurating his *German Mass,* he had long hesitated to issue such an *Order of Service* so as not to play into the hands of "fanatics"—he undoubtedly had Karlstadt in mind—who made a particular form of worship a matter of conscience. "But now that so many have entreated me in letters and treatises from all over," he explained, "and secular authority has urged me to it, we can no longer excuse ourselves but must recognize that it is God's will."[31] In his preface to the published version of *The German Mass and Order of Service* of 1526, he insisted on the importance of maintaining Christian liberty while also recognizing the need for order. He had written the *German Mass*, he said, for the sake of unlearned laity and for mixed congregations of Christians and non-Christians. It was, he continued, a form of catechization.[32] An exclusive community of true Christians would not need such an *Order*, he explained almost wistfully. But most of the population were not true Christians. Such compromises, we might add, are necessary whenever an attempt is made to institutionalize an ideology. Ideals must occasionally give way to practicality.

What gave Luther the authority to establish a new form of divine worship? Having repeatedly disavowed such authority in the past, it was ultimately the request of the Elector of Saxony that induced him to offer his *German Mass* as a model for others.[33] Luther had a cogent rationale for this position.[34] To Spalatin Luther explained that the electoral princes were not coercing faith in Gospel matters but rather were combatting external abominations. They had a responsibility to prevent public blasphemy such as the unreformed Roman mass. If they neglected their responsibility, God would punish them and their territory. This argument, although perhaps minimizing the actual coercive effects of imposing a uniform German service, did provide a convenient rationale for proceeding with the institutionalization of the Reformation.

The significance of the institution of the visitation for the development of the Lutheran territorial church needs hardly to be remarked upon. Some historians have made much of Luther's qualifications concerning the role of secular authorities in his preface to the Visitation Articles of 1528. The Elector, Luther wrote, had undertaken the visitation out of Christian love rather than out of any obligation flowing from his temporal office. He was, as Luther put it elsewhere, an "emergency bishop."[35] This restriction of the jurisdiction of the secular authority over the institutional church is significant theologically, but did not mean much in practice. This is not to criticize Luther for assisting in the establishment of the state-controlled church. He really had no other power to which he could turn to remedy the wretched conditions of the church at the local level. But it will not do to ignore his contribution to this development. In letters of 1525 and 1526 he urged the secular authorities to undertake a visitation, arguing that they had the right and the responsibility as "the highest guardian of the youth and all those who need it," to use force if necessary to see that the communities (*Gemeinden*) established adequate compensation for pastors and proper religious training for the population.[36] Throughout his later years he consistently supported and advocated the state-organized visitation.

Gerald Strauss has recently demonstrated the importance of catechization for the development of the institutional church.[37] Luther's *Small* and *Large Catechism* exercised a dominant influence on this development. His concern with true doctrine, exactly summarized, is apparent from the outset. The catechism should be taught to the young in such a way that not a single syllable would be altered. Variation and discussion should be reserved for the well-educated. And if any refused to accept the catechetical instruction, they were to be disciplined by pastor, family, employers, and the secular ruler. Luther saw this coercion as properly belonging not to the realm of faith but to the sphere of civil life. He wrote,

> Although we cannot and should not compel anyone to believe, we should compel the masses to know what is right and wrong among those with whom they reside, earn their living, and pass their lives. For he who wishes to live in a city, should know and observe the city law whose [protection] he enjoys, whether he is a believer or at bottom a rogue or scoundrel.[38]

Yet by equating the articles of the catechism with the secular laws of the city, he added his approval to a state-enforced religion.

Similarly, in 1535, Luther cooperated with the Elector in another major step toward the formation of the state-controlled, territorial church. In that year the Elector decreed that henceforth a prospective pastor must first present himself in Wittenberg to be examined by the university on his abilities and doctrinal orthodoxy and then to be ordained. On 20 October Luther carried out the first ordination under these new regulations.[39] And throughout the 1530's and 1540's he participated fully in the restructuring of the university, and especially the theological faculty, so that it might produce doctrinally sound pastors.[40]

Another step: in 1536-37, and at the request of the Elector, Luther penned the so-called Schmalkaldic Articles, which were to be presented as a confession of faith before the Catholic General Council. From their inception, however, the Elector also saw them as a confession of faith that could be used after Luther's death to hold the other Protestant pastors and preachers in Electoral Saxony (and probably in all Protestant territories) to the faith confessed by Martin Luther.[41] In 1538 Luther added articles against "fanatics" and "enthusiasts" to complement the articles against the papists. In his preface he explained that he had published these articles so that "if I should die before there was a council ... those who lived after me would have my testimony and confession to produce, in addition to the

Confession" [on the Lord's Supper of 1528, the third part of which was a general confession of faith]. This was necessary because there were "such poisonous people, not only among the opponents but also false brethren who wish to be of our party, who unhesitatingly presume to use my writings and teaching against me.... although they know well that I teach otherwise, and [they] wish to deck out their poison with my work and mislead the poor people under my name."[42]

These actions, and others like them, contributed to the formation of Lutheran orthodoxy. Whatever Luther's original intentions, the need to create a new clergy, and the decision to give the university responsibility for doing so and for passing on their fitness, combined with the framing of confessions of faith that were intended not only to challenge papists but also to unmask "false brethren," could not but further the tendency to identify true religion with true doctrine.

Let us consider a somewhat different example that illustrates the need to consider both intentions and results: the matter of armed resistance to the Emperor for the sake of the Gospel.[43] In 1530, under pressure from Landgrave Philipp, from the Elector, and especially from the jurists and political advisors, Luther grudgingly "allowed" the Protestant estates to adopt a positive law justification for such resistance. This stance left him profoundly uncomfortable. Yet despite his own theological reservations, as a practical matter his *Warning to His Dear Germans,* published in 1531, *encouraged* Protestants to resist a Catholic attack, even if led by the Emperor.

This conclusion is based on a distinction that the historian must make between Luther's intentions and how he was actually understood by others. In this regard, what Luther actually said may be less important than how he went about saying it. The intricacies of Luther's argument in his *Warning to His Dear Germans* may suggest to the twentieth-century scholar and perhaps even to some careful readers in the sixteenth century that Luther still harbored doubts about the propriety of Christians offering armed resistance to persecution by the Emperor, and that he still had an unwillingness, first announced in Torgau, to urge Christians to offer such resistance. But resistance was actually encouraged by the rhetorical force of this treatise, which found expression in a violent verbal attack on the papists, a lurid description of their misdeeds and intentions, and an almost gleeful prediction that the papists would be resisted, whether or not such resistance was proper. This was realized by Catholic opponents, who made some telling points about the provocative effects of Luther's violent and abusive language.[44] Even more to the point, perhaps, the rhetorical effect of the treatise was recognized by the League of Schmalkalden's leaders, who saw to it that the publication was reprinted numerous times both in 1531 and in 1546, when war actually broke out.[45]

The point of these examples, and they could be easily multiplied, is straightforward. The biographical significance of Luther's actions is not exhausted by a determination of Luther's stated motives, or of his theological rationale. The biographer must also determine how his actions were understood by others and what their practical effect was, irrespective of Luther's own intentions. Whatever Luther's personal or theological reservations concerning such matters as the formation of a state controlled church, the development of a rigid doctrinal orthodoxy, or the resistance to superior secular authority in matters of religion, as a practical matter his actions contributed to and supported each of these developments.

Conclusions

There is a good explanation why Luther scholars often ignore or minimize external constraints and concentrate on intentions rather than results. Commonly, they are seeking insights in Luther to be employed in contemporary theology. It is therefore natural for them to concentrate on Luther's theology, in its purity, irrespective of how it may have been understood, or more likely, misunderstood by his contemporaries. Such an approach, while perhaps legitimate in theological studies, can lead occasionally to the curious conclusion that Luther's co-workers, such as Melanchthon, never properly understood him. To such a conclusion the historian is prompted to ask what Luther's contemporaries in fact understood him to be doing. And the historian must further investigate what Luther's message actually accomplished, perhaps unintentionally. The answers to these questions will not only enrich our historical understanding of Martin Luther and his times; they will also add historical depth, and perhaps, in the process, provoke new insights, for contemporary theology.

Notes

1. See Helmar Junghans, "Interpreting the Old Luther (1526-1546)," *Currents in Theology and Mission,* 9 (1982), 271-281, statistic on p. 271.

2. Julius Köstlin and Gustav Kawerau, *Martin Luther: Sein Leben und seine Schriften,* 2 vols. (Berlin, 1903).

3. Heinrich Boehmer, *Der junge Luther,* 4th and subsequent eds., edited by Heinrich Bornkamm (Stuttgart, 1971); Martin Brecht, *Martin Luther: Sein Weg zur Reformation 1483-1521* (Stuttgart, 1981); Heinrich Bornkamm, *Martin Luther in der Mitte seines Lebens* (Göttingen, 1979).

4. Helmar Junghans, ed., *Martin Luthers Leben und Werk 1526-1546,* 2 vols. (Göttingen, 1983).

5. H.G. Haile, *Luther: An Experiment in Biography* (New York, 1980).

6. Hermann Kunst, *Evangelischer Glaube und politische Verantwortung: Martin Luther als politischer Berater seiner Landesherrn und seine Teilnahme an den Fragen des öffentlichen Lebens* (Stuttgart, 1977).

7. Eike Wolgast, *Die Wittenberger Theologie und die Politik der evangelischen Stände: Studien zu Luthers Gutachten in politischen Fragen* (Gütersloh, 1977).

8. Heiko A. Oberman, *Wurzeln des Antisemitismus: Christenangst und Judenplage im Zeitalter von Humanismus und Reformation* (Berlin, 1981).

9. Mark U. Edwards Jr., *Luther's Last Battles: Politics and Polemics, 1531-46* (Ithaca NY, 1983).

10. The list of theological works is too lengthy to cite, even for the older Luther. See the annual issues of the *Lutherjahrbuch* for titles.

11. Helmar Junghans, "Interpreting the Old Luther."

12. Wolgast, p. 298.

13. Karl Trudinger, *Luthers Briefe und Gutachten an weltliche Obrigkeiten zur Durchführung der Reformation* (Münster, 1975), pp. 8-10.

14. Edwards, *Luther's Last Battles.*

15. See *Luther's Last Battles,* pp. 20-23, 209-211.

16. Heinrich Bornkamm, "Probleme der Lutherbiographie," in: *Lutherforschung Heute,* ed. Vilmos Vajta (Berlin, 1958), p. 19.

17. Edwards, *Luther's Last Battles,* chapter 3.

18. Ibid., pp. 64-65; *WABr* 6, 154.

19. Ibid., pp. 166-171.

20. Wolgast, pp. 253-262.

21. See Wilhelm Maurer, "Luther und die Doppelehe Landgraf Philippus von Hessen," *Luther* (1953), pp. 49-120; William Walker Rockwell, *Die Doppelehe des Landgrafen Philipp von Hessen* (Marburg, 1904); and Walther Köhler, *Luther und die Lüge* (Leipzig, 1912), pp. 109-153.

22. Wolgast, p. 298.

23. For a detailed consideration of this point, see *Luther's Last Battles,* chapter 4.

24. Ibid., chapter 2.

25. Ibid., pp. 172-182.

26. Ibid., chapter 7.

27. Ibid., pp. 168-172.

28. Ibid., chapters 5, 7, and 8.

29. Ibid., pp. 163-164, 182-200.

30. Ibid., chapter 6; Mark U. Edwards, Jr., *Luther and the False Brethren* (Stanford, 1975), chapter 8.

31. *WA* 17, 1.459.

32. *WA* 19, 72-78, esp. p. 76.

33. *WA* 19, 44-53; Bornkamm, *Martin Luther in der Mitte seines Lebens,* pp. 415-419.

34. Ibid., pp. 425-426.

35. See Lewis W. Spitz, "Luther's Ecclesiology and His Concept of the Prince as Notbischof," *Church History,* 22 (1953), 3-31.

36. *WA Br* 4, 133-134.

37. Gerald Strauss, *Luther's House of Learning: Indoctrination of the Young in the German Reformation* (Baltimore, 1978), esp. chapter 8.

38. *WA* 30.1, 268-73.

39. *WA Br* 7, 302-303; *WA* 41, 454-459.

40. James Kittelson recently explored the implications of this development in his paper "The Impact of the Reformation upon Education in Germany," ASCH Meetings, Hope College, MI, April 1983.

41. Hans Volz, ed., *Urkunden und Aktenstücke zur Geschichte von Martin Luthers Schmalkaldischen Artikeln (1536-1574)* (Berlin, 1957), pp. 87-91.

42. *WA* 50, 192-194.

43. The following is drawn from my *Luther's Last Battles,* chapter 2.

44. For Duke Georg's evaluation, see WA 30/3:419-20. For Johann Cochlaeus, see *Hertzog Georgs zu Sachssen Ehrlich vnd grundtliche entschuldigung* (Dresden, 1533), pp. Cij-Ciij, Fi-[Fiv]ᵛ. Hij-Hijᵛ.

45. Joseph Benzing, *Lutherbibliographie. Verzeichnis der gedruckten Schriften Martin Luthers bis zu dessen Tod* (Baden-Baden, 1966), nos. 2908-2924.

THE HISTORICAL CONTEXT:
LUTHER AND HIS CONTEMPORARIES

ULRICH VON HUTTEN AND LUTHER'S OPEN LETTER TO LEO X

Thomas W. Best, *University of Virginia*

On 1 September 1520, at the behest of Karl von Miltitz, a former papal nuncio who dreamed of reconciling Luther with the Apostolic See, Johann von Staupitz and his new successor as Augustinian vicar general, Wenceslaus Link, called on their headstrong brother at Wittenberg. They asked him to assure the pope that he had never criticized Leo's character. In a report to Georg Spalatin, Elector Friedrich's chaplain, Luther declared on 11 September that he was willing to comply, since he would only be confirming what was true. He would have to guard, however, against reviling the papacy per se, he added.[1] Despite his acquiescence, he procrastinated, having renounced Catholicism the previous summer. On 3 October he informed Spalatin that he was changing his mind completely because of the bull *Exsurge domine,* which threatened him with excommunication unless he recanted.[2]

Miltitz was not content with indirect negotiations anyway, so Friedrich arranged for Luther to meet the ex-nuncio himself,[3] even though two such conferences the year before (at Altenburg in early January and at Liebenwerda on 9 October) had proved ineffectual. Luther cooperated, not only to please his patron but also to forestall reproach for scorning concord with Rome, as he wrote to Spalatin immediately after the talk with Miltitz on 12 October at Lichtenberg.[4] Again he consented to certify in a letter to the pope that he had found no fault with Leo as a person. He would also sketch his career, blame his polemics on the Leipzig theologian Johann Eck (an enemy he shared with Miltitz), and offer a truce as humbly as possible. He would attach a little treatise of unspecified nature, furthermore, and backdate the epistle to 6 September, in order that his concession might not seem to have been coerced by *Exsurge domine.* The letter together with its companion piece would be ready by 24 October.[5] According to Philipp Melanchthon, however, the epistle was not penned until a few days prior to 4 November.[6] During the first half of that month both it and the treatise, *On the Freedom of a Christian,* were printed in German, with a Latin edition of them following soon.[7] Because the initial publisher, Wittenberg's Johann Grünenberg, released the letter separately in German, *On the Freedom of a Christian,* in its German form, is offered to Hermann Mülpfort of Zwickau, whom Luther mistakenly addresses as Hieronymus. The tractate may possibly have been set down before 12 October, independent of Miltitz, but we have no proof that it was. Likelier is that it had been vaguely planned in advance of the Lichtenberg meeting,[8] without taking shape until afterwards and then specifically as the gift which Miltitz wanted for Leo. Thus it was probably drafted first in Latin, though the Latin text we have could be a subsequent revision.[9] By telling Mülpfort in the German introduction that the essay in Latin has been dedicated to Leo, moreover, Luther indicates that it was conceived in the language of the learned.[10] Surely the open letter, which postdated it, was originally composed in Latin, too, being likewise designed for the pope.

That epistle falls into four parts, of which the first is the longest, embracing paragraphs one through seven in the Latin version (one through twelve in German).[11] The gist of section one is that Luther has always thought well of Leo, no matter how sharply he has censured the Roman Curia, which he further berates. Not consistently distinguishing between pope and private individual, he pities Leo as a Daniel in Babylon and among the lions; also as a sheep among wolves, an Ezekiel among scorpions, and a driver whose horse no longer obeys. He asserts that he has better cause to commiserate with Leo, who should abdicate, than St. Bernard had to sympathize with Eugenius III. He has hoped to earn the pontiff's gratitude with his assaults on Christ's enemies at Rome, he alleges, mildly reprimanding Leo for failing to fight them also.

In the second section of the letter, which is the second longest part, comprising paragraphs eight through thirteen in Latin and thirteen through nineteen in German, Luther reviews his career since his audience with the legate Cajetan at Augsburg in October 1518. He blames both Cajetan and Eck for the disturbances of ecclesiastical peace in which he has participated, exposing Catholic corruption. Cajetan should have silenced his antagonists, he maintains, of whom conceited Eck is the most obstreperous. Miltitz' efforts to restore tranquillity are favorably described, and Leo is requested to consummate them by finally gagging the troublemakers. Luther volunteers to help by accepting any conditions other than retraction—a demand for which would make matters worse, he warns—and restrictions on Scriptural exegesis.

Part three of the letter, and the third longest section, consists of paragraphs fourteen and fifteen in Latin (twenty through twenty-two in German). In it Luther overtly mimics St. Bernard, who earnestly instructed his disciple, Eugenius III, on proper papal conduct in *De consideratione*. Pretending to be likewise moved by brotherly love, Luther cautions Leo against flatterers who exalt him, as if he were master of all instead of everyone's servant. A pope is not superior to councils and is not uniquely endowed with authority to interpret the Bible. If Leo fancies himself Christ's replacement on Earth, Luther admonishes, he has actually become an antichrist.

The last and shortest part of the open letter is limited to its final paragraph in both the Latin and the German versions, dedicating *On the Freedom of a Christian* to Leo. That tractate exemplifies the sort of endeavor to which he would devote himself, Luther avers, if Leo's minions left him alone. He describes it as a condensation of everything which constitutes a Christian life. What he meant, presumably, is that it expresses the essence of Christianity, and it does indeed contain the kernel of his theology. Poor as he is, he can proffer nothing else, he apologizes, excusing himself with a double-entendre: Spiritual gifts are the only ones which Leo needs.

The epistle departs in several conspicuous ways from Miltitz' expectations. In part one Luther dutifully exempts Leo from his crusade against Catholicism, but otherwise he continues to vent his spleen, damning the Curia in terms applicable to mystery plays, for instance, when he calls the court "a gaping maw of hell" in paragraph six of the Latin version, though it once was "a portal of heaven." In the letter's second section he makes not only Eck his scapegoat but also Cajetan, branding the cardinal in paragraph nine of the Latin text as imprudent and even disloyal. That egotist's despotism, he complains, is totally responsible for what has happened since the autumn of 1518. Undiplomatic as the strictures on Eck are, Luther had to plead self-defense in order to win a pardon. Carping at Cajetan in addition to Eck, however, was as gratuitously impolitic as precluding recantation and prescribing exegetical freedom. Then Luther unilaterally inserted part three of the letter, impugning papal absolutism by playing Bernard to Leo's Eugenius. Even if the Medici had been devout, he would not have welcomed such patronizing effrontery.

On the Freedom of a Christian, with its thesis of salvation by faith alone, can hardly be the treatise which Miltitz anticipated. "Beim Papst war kein Verständnis dafür zu hoffen," Julius Köstlin correctly remarked.[12] Believers, who are their own priests, need no good deeds, no obedience to laws, no sacraments, and no Church to enter heaven, the tractate teaches, partly by implication. In Latin it dares to deny explicitly that "any Christian has been put in charge of everything," dismissing such a notion as insane.[13] It reduces to the status of ministers, servants, and stewards the people "who are now extolled as Popes, Bishops, and lords."[14] It inveighs against Catholicism as a perverse tyranny in which "the paltriest men on Earth," exploiting misery for vice and scandal, have ousted true religion.[15] It stigmatizes papal traditions and the opinions of ultramontane theologians ("Theologistarum") as "pestilential, impious, and soul-destroying." By those "snares," which inculcate work righteousness, countless souls have been dragged to hell, it laments, "so that you can recognize Antichrist."[16] In its final sentence, squarely aimed at Leo, Luther concedes that his message offends human nature, as he himself is repugnant to "godless and blind pontiffs with their toadies."[17] Even more than his letter, his treatise turned into defiance the appeasement which Miltitz desired. *On the Freedom of a Christian,* particularly in its franker Latin form, is anything but the "augury of peace and hope" which Luther professes it to be in section four of the dedicatory epistle. As August Baur has observed, it is "der schroffste selbstredende Widerspruch und Gegensatz gegen die ganze Auffassung des Christenthums, auf welchem das päpstliche System, die römische Hierarchie beruhte."[18] Together with the letter it proclaims, in effect, that harmony with Rome is possible only on its author's terms.

Over two months before he drew up the *Sendbrief,* back on 18 August 1520, Luther vowed to Johann Lang in Erfurt that he owed no more allegiance to the pope ("Papae") than to "the very Antichrist," and he asked Lang not to judge him rashly, explaining that he had special grounds for such a conviction.[19] His reason was probably *Exsurge domine.* In finishing *De captivitate Babylonica ecclesiae praeludium,* around the same date, he jeered at the bull, quipping that the anti-Catholic *Prelude* constituted part of the revocation which the bull reportedly demanded.[20] We have already seen that, in early October, *Exsurge domine* caused him to abandon temporarily Miltitz' plan for a propitiatory letter to Leo. Just minutes before departing for Lichtenberg, on 11 October, Luther notified Spalatin that the bull had arrived in Wittenberg. Because of it, he exclaimed, "I am much freer now, being certain at last that the pope is Antichrist and that the seat of Satan has definitely been found."[21] By "the pope" ("papam") here he meant Leo especially, since Leo was the pope responsible for *Exsurge domine.* In his *Appellatio... ad concilium... innovata,* from 17 November, Luther accused Leo by name of being Antichrist.[22] The polarization of pontiff and Curia in the open letter's initial section and the attitude throughout the epistle—that, far from being Antichrist, Leo is an innocent victim—have to be rhetorical distortions. In other publications from the same period Luther spoke well of Leo as a person, or morally,[23] but after he had inspected an authorized copy of *Exsurge domine* it was almost impossible for him to believe that Leo as head of the traditional Church, or doctrinally, deserved to be contrasted with the papal court. Understanding that Leo had approved the bull, Luther privately classified both him and his counselors as predatory birds of a feather.

The feigning of sympathy and concern for him in his capacity as pope is not the only way facts are manipulated in the open letter. There is the misrepresentation of *On the Freedom of a Christian* as a peace offering in part four; and, in part two, the exaggerated argument that Cajetan and Eck are to blame for the shaming of Rome is belied by section one, where Luther fairly revels in more reprehension. He adopted an artificial stance, though he still could not become as conciliatory as Miltitz wished. In writing to Spalatin on the eve of the Lichtenberg conference, he explicitly proved his willingness to dissemble, for he divulged that he would continue to act as if *Exsurge domine* were spurious, despite knowing it to be authentic ("quamquam credo veram & propriam esse eorum"), and he recommended duplicity as the wisest policy for Elector Friedrich to pursue in regard to the bull.[24] Another case of his willingness to dissemble is his falsification of the open letter's date, for appearance's sake.

Forced by political pressure to cajole his greatest, most dangerous enemy, who was trying to extort the repudiation of what he held to be sacred truths, a no longer Catholic Luther became more aggressive than he had been in devising his two previous epistles to Leo (late May 1518 and either 5 or 6 January 1519).[25] Now convinced that Antichrist wore the tiara, he followed the lead of Ulrich von Hutten, who shared his animosity toward "Satan's synagogue." In an unctuous letter Hutten had dedicated to the pope a denial of papal jurisdiction—Lorenzo Valla's invective against the so-called Donation of Constantine, which the Vatican had cited for centuries as the legal basis for its pretensions to secular dominion. By imitating his fellow rebel, Luther could perceive, he might best preserve his integrity while also obliging his prince (much as he chided Leo by copying St. Bernard). He can scarcely have failed to discern, besides, that *On the Freedom of a Christian* complements Valla's tract, the two essays together stripping the papacy of both temporal and spiritual rule. As they parallel each other in content, so it is appropriate that they were published in similar fashion—ostensibly honoring one of their principal victims.

In 1440 Valla had argued on psychological, historical, and philological grounds that the document in which Constantine I purports to transfer the Western Roman Empire from his own control to that of Pope Silvester (314-36) and the latter's successors, whom he elevates above himself and all other officials, is fictitious. No emperor, even had he been cured of leprosy, as Constantine supposedly was, would have humbled himself to such an extent, humiliating his family, however strong his gratitude for physical and spiritual rescue, Valla reasons. Not only would Constantine's sons have objected; so would the citizens of Rome and Pope Silvester with them, since the people would not have wanted their empire weakened and pious Silvester would not have traded Peter's role for Judas'. Had the Donation actually taken place, notes Valla, it would be much better attested than it is, and records after Constantine reveal that popes were still not supreme. A close examination of the document, as contained among the supplements to Gratian's *Decretum,* shows its Latin to be anachronistic and its subject matter inaccurate. Valla's critique of the Donation leads him ultimately to a critique of the papacy for adhering to the Donation.

Circulating widely in manuscript, his exposé was printed first in 1506, evidently by Johannes Grüninger at Strasbourg. Collating the *editio princeps* with a more correct manuscript version copied in Bologna by his friend Friedrich Fischer, Hutten prepared a second edition which appeared toward the end of 1518, prefaced by his letter to Leo and accompanied by some ancillary material—a Greek account of the Donation in Bartholomaeus Picernus' Latin translation and several opinions (among them, Nicolaus Cusanus') tending to support Valla's rejection of the alleged transferral of power. The publisher was Andreas Cratander in Basel. One year later Cratander reissued that edition in different type, with a new title page, partial rearrangement of contents, and revised texts. When Hutten became acquainted with the *editio princeps,* which seems to have introduced him to the tractate himself, cannot be precisely determined, but he probably discovered it in Italy, where he studied law desultorily from 1515 to 1517. We know for sure that he visited Johannes Cochlaeus in Bologna as he was leaving Italy in late June 1517 and while Cochlaeus happened to have on loan the manuscript which Fischer duplicated for him. In a letter to Wilibald Pirkheimer dated 5 July 1517 Cochlaeus relates that Hutten asked for a transcription of the manuscript since he saw that it was superior to the 1506 edition. Hutten must have owned a copy of the *editio princeps* which he could at once compare with the manuscript and which he had already decided to have republished. By the end of November he had finished his redaction of Valla's essay and assembled the companion texts, except for his epistle to Leo. He penned that preface on 1 December, at the Steckelberg (his family's castle near Fulda), shortly before undertaking an ambassadorial mission to France for Archbishop Albrecht of Mainz.[26]

The letter can be condensed as follows: Friends who warned against the publication of Valla's polemic have been contradicted by Leo's love of peace, which sets the pope apart from his predecessors. Lacking peace, they were despots rather than genuine pontiffs, who imitate Christ. By restoring peace, Leo has also revived justice, faith, veracity, mercy, and freedom, which tyranny suppresses. Thanks to him, candid works like Valla's refutation, intolerable to previous, oppressive popes, can now be printed with impunity. Leo should welcome a composition by Valla especially, since Valla was dear to his ancestors, whose good taste Leo perpetuates. No Medici can sanction a lie like the Donation of Constantine, which is beneath the family's dignity. How much more Christian was Valla than "that ass" Picernus, who, in order to ingratiate himself with Julius II, professed to have translated a Greek form of Constantine's bogus grant which ostensibly verified the grant's legitimacy.[27] People apprehensive that Valla's philippic would displease Leo insult him by classing him with his thievish forerunners, who exploited German naiveté to clutch at imperial rule. Having nothing in common with them, he will bless their curser, even cursing them himself. Instead of being shepherds insuring the peace of their flock, they were wolves destroying peace. For the sake of wealth, they disposed of souls. In their lust for earthly gain they defended a fraud which any pontiff worthy of serving as Jesus' vicar would reject. Hutten is confident of earning Leo's gratitude by publicizing Valla's correction of history, and he is dedicating his edition of it to the Holy Father as proof that Leo honors truth. In closing, Hutten promises to look for further revelations like Valla's, if encouraged to do so.[28]

Though his letter tends to ramble, having an extemporaneous stamp, it is unified by its contrasting of Leo with precursors. Underlying its structural looseness is the idea that Leo will accept Valla's essay because he is unlike the popes who abhorred it. Whereas they were unchristianly rapacious, he is virtuous enough to merit his office. He is considered as antithetical to them as he is to his counselors in Luther's open letter to him, for which reason the first part of that epistle resembles Hutten's missive. Each is based on a daring juxtaposition, required for eliciting Leo's good will toward someone at whom the Church looked askance. Since earlier popes had repudiated Valla's treatise, Hutten needed to distinguish Leo from them. Since Luther had excoriated the Church's management (most notoriously in the afterword to his reprint of Silvester Prierias' *Epitoma*),[29] he needed to distinguish Leo from the Curia. On 30 May 1519 Erasmus had advised him to protest against abusers of papal authority rather than against popes themselves,[30] but section one of Luther's open letter transcends Erasmus' precept, conforming more to Hutten's example. Both Luther and Hutten lauded Leo besides rebuking a group of men closely associated with him. Though Hutten probably respected the pope in December 1517,[31] Luther surely assumed in October 1520 that the patriot had indulged in irony.

Was he definitely mindful of Hutten's letter when he devised a counterpart to it? On 24 February 1520 he had written to Spalatin that the Breslau canon Dominicus Schleupner, who was studying in Wittenberg at the time, had supplied him with a copy of Valla's diatribe as edited by Hutten. It was not necessarily from the 1519 edition but is likelier to have been. "Good Lord!" Luther cries to Spalatin. "What stupidity, or villainy, of the Romans . . . ! Such impure, such crass, such shameless lies, and for them to be reckoned among the articles of faith (capping the monstrousness)! I am so enraged, I almost believe the pope to be that Antichrist whom the world awaits. Everything he does, utters, and decrees is fitting."[32] From Luther's anger we may deduce that he had not been acquainted with Valla's essay before and had accepted the false Donation as authentic. Hutten contributed to his estrangement from Catholicism. Although he does not cite Hutten's prefatory letter, we can trust with full conviction that he read it along with the work by Valla. The indignation expressed to Spalatin lets us also safely infer that he did not forget either Valla's disproof or Hutten's dedication of it to Leo.[33]

His mention of the German humanist as Valla's editor is his first reference to Hutten in any extant writing, but the history of their relationship commences well before February 1520. Almost two years sooner, probably in March 1518, Hutten learned of Luther, though perhaps not by name. In a letter dated 3 April 1518 he said that at Wittenberg a faction had arisen against the pope, with another group supporting indulgences. He hoped that all participants would annihilate one another, for he lumped them contemptuously among the obscurantists whom the Reuchlin controversy had taught him to despise.[34] By October 1518 he seems to have heard a little more about Luther, but his opinion was still no higher.[35] It was the Leipzig debate, in the summer of 1519, which led him to appreciate the theologian who honored Scripture, not the pope, as Christianity's ultimate guide. Just two weeks after the disputation he wrote to Melanchthon, probably endorsing Luther.[36] By late autumn 1519 it is certain that he no longer disdained the monk, for he confesses in a note from 26 October that he dare not solicit Luther's aid in his revolt against papal tyranny, on account of his patron Archbishop Albrecht. Undeniably implied is a wish that the courageous evangelist were his ally, even though he rates Luther's Latin style inelegant enough to profit from Melanchthon's embellishment.[37]

At about the same time he presumed to publish a letter, dated 19 October

1519, in which Erasmus warily approved of Luther and which Hutten was charged with transmitting to its addressee, Archbishop Albrecht.[38] Early in 1520 he persuaded (or at least helped persuade) the condottiere Franz von Sickingen, who was already championing Johann Reuchlin at his behest, to harbor Luther in case Elector Friedrich withdrew protection. He relayed Sickingen's offer to Melanchthon on 20 January, from Mainz, and asked the professor of Greek to have Luther acknowledge it.[39] Because that letter was not delivered, he sent it again on 28 February, from the Steckelberg, reinforced by an accompanying note.[40] On 17 March Wolfgang Capito, in Basel,. advised Luther to reply to Hutten,[41] and on 28 April Crotus Rubeanus, in Bamberg, urged Luther not to spurn Sickingen's hospitality. Crotus also reported that Hutten, who wished the reformer well, would seek a position at the court of Archduke Ferdinand in Brussels, benefiting Luther and "proper studies" both if successful.[42] An optimistic Melanchthon, cheered by the enterprising mission, assured Johannes Hess on 8 June that Hutten was going to cut a path for liberty, aided by the greatest princes. "What might we not hope for?" he exulted.[43] On 30 April, to Capito, and on 5 May, to Spalatin, Luther disclosed that he had responded to Hutten's overtures. To Capito he stated that, at Melanchthon's instigation, he would have answered Hutten sooner had a messenger been available.[44] The April letter and one which he sent to Hutten on 31 May have both disappeared, along with a message to Sickingen from the same day.[45] In either of the two epistles to Hutten he perhaps confided, as Cochlaeus asserts, that he trusted Sickingen more than any ruler,[46] and in the later one he is likely to have congratulated Hutten on the satirist's recent dialogue collection, containing *Fortuna, Febris prima, Febris secunda, Vadiscus,* and *Inspicientes.* He should have acquired a copy during the first half of May. Whether *Vadiscus* affected him has been frequently disputed, since *An den christlichen Adel deutscher Nation,* dating from June and July, bears many resemblances to it but incontrovertible evidence is lacking.[47]

On 4 June, probably in response to the late April letter, Hutten wrote to Luther directly for the first time, unless some prior missive has vanished without a trace. His rather short and hastily worded note reveals that Luther had imparted certain plans to him, for it opens with the pledge that he will be deeply sorry if they are thwarted. He vigorously encourages Luther, who is already rumored to have been excommunicated, and he urges Luther to be careful, since the loss of such a hero would be grievous. He portrays himself as Luther's equally imperiled but less skillful coworker, helping to clear the gospel of pontifical obstructions. "You more felicitously; I according to my gifts," he concedes with winsome modesty.

He guarantees support regardless of what happens, for which reason Luther can safely apprise him of future projects. Together they should free the fatherland, assisted by Christ. Again in Mainz, he announces that he is departing that very day for Brussels, where he will petition the emperor's brother to intercede for their cause, and he reminds Luther of Sickingen's open door.[48] Unfortunately, we can only imagine how the letter's recipient reacted to it, but we know that it was printed in Wittenberg and that Melanchthon liked it. He dispatched a copy to Spalatin, along with one of Erasmus' epistles (probably the one to Archbishop Albrecht, published by Hutten), as proof that his colleague was esteemed by luminaries ("alterum orbis universi, alterum Nobilitatis decus").[49]

Luther may have communicated with Sickingen again on 30 June, for he promised Spalatin on 29 June that he would do so the next day.[50] Another knight, Silvester von Schaumberg, was offering him refuge, too. On 10 July, while he may still have been engaged with *An den christlichen Adel deutscher Nation,* Luther informed Spalatin that his enemies at the Curia should be cognizant of his alternatives to Bohemia. Were their machinations to effect his expulsion from Saxony, he could count on shelter in the middle of Germany, where he would rage against them all the more ferociously, no longer fearing to harm Elector Friedrich and Wittenberg University. Ominously for Miltitz, he precluded reconciliation and even further communication with the Romanists, whose favor he scorned no less than their furor. For him, as for Caesar at the Rubicon, the die was cast. If his books were burned, he would burn the canon law (and he did so exactly five months later).[51] Not only is the announcement of his rupture with the papal Church of interest to us; so is his expression "iacta mihi alea," because with the dialogue *Phalarismus* in 1517 Hutten had adopted it as a motto. Luther had written "aleam ieci" in March 1519 and "iacta erat alea" one year later,[52] perhaps independently of Hutten. By July 1520, however, he was aware that "iacta est alea" terminates both *Vadiscus* and *Inspicientes.*[53] Though he had also encountered the phrase in at least one recent work by a different author,[54] it is possible that he identified with Hutten as well as with Caesar when he abandoned hope for Catholicism.

On 31 August he had another note delivered to Sickingen, the contents of which are again unknown.[55] In early September—soon after Staupitz and Link had brought word of Miltitz' desire for a letter to Leo—Luther received a second note from Hutten, probably in reply to his late May epistle. It is also lost, but he summarized it copiously in his letter to Spalatin on 11 September. Incensed at the pope for plotting his assassination and commanding that Archbishop Albrecht convey him to Rome in fetters, Hutten is combating "sacerdotal tyranny" with sword as well as pen, Luther relates. Albrecht has prohibited antipapal publications by his former employee and by anyone else. "If he specifies my books," huffs Luther, "I will join forces with Hutten [iungam Hutteno et meum spiritum], defending myself in a fashion not calculated to gladden His Excellency." Spalatin should guard Elector Friedrich, Luther warns, for Hutten, whose trepidation he shares, has anxiously alerted him to the danger of being poisoned.[56] His attention to Hutten's message, which he wanted Spalatin to read in its entirety, signifies that it mattered to him. He appreciated Hutten's opposition to their common foe. On 3 October he repeated "the die is cast"—now in regard to Andreas Karlstadt's repudiation of the Roman Church. Because his letter of 11 September had temporarily gone astray, he notified Spalatin again of Albrecht's ban and Hutten's both literary and military campaign against Leo.[57] On 13 November he rejoiced that the hotspur had tilted at the papal legates Caracciolo and Aleander, whose capture he would have welcomed.[58]

When, despite the alienation cemented by *Exsurge domine* and under pressure from Elector Friedrich, Luther set about satisfying Miltitz in the autumn of 1520, he had been familiar with Hutten's name for half a year. In particular, Hutten had offered him a substitute protector; he had perused various works by Hutten, with whom he had also corresponded; and only one month earlier he had envisioned possible collaboration with the talented propagandist. Most importantly, Hutten had addressed a complementary epistle to Leo such as Luther himself was constrained to draft, dedicating a treatise to the pope which, like Luther's choice, diminished papal power. It is strange that no historian has ever wondered whether, in presenting his dubious gift to his persecutor, Luther imitated the editor of Valla's tract on the Donation of Constantine.[59] Are similarities not indeed apparent? Was Luther not indeed appropriately motivated? Had he not indeed been sufficiently impressed by Hutten's precedent? Was his relationship with Hutten not indeed conducive? His five-hundredth anniversary is high time for these questions to be raised. Latter-day Knaakes and Kalkoffs will reject them out of hand, but openminded scholars, who concede that Hutten may have influenced Luther in 1520, should take them to heart.

Notes

1. *WA Br* 2, 184.
2. *WA Br* 2, 191, 9-12.
3. *WA Br* 2, 195, 27-29.
4. *WA Br* 2, 197, 11-12.
5. *WA Br* 2, 197, 5-15, and Wilhelm Ernst Tentzel, *Historischer Bericht vom Anfang und ersten Fortgang der Reformation Lutheri,* ed. Ernst Salomon Cyprian (Leipzig: Gleditsch & Weidmann, 1717), pp. 449-452. In soliciting the letter and presumably also the treatise, Miltitz revived and modified proposals submitted by Luther at Altenburg in 1519. See *WA Br* 1, 290, 20-33.
6. Carolus Gottlieb Bretschneider, *Corpus Reformatorum,* vol. 1 (Halle: Schwetschke, 1834), p. 268: "Scripsit et ante paucos dies epistolam ad Rom. Pontificem *Leonem.* . . . " Since Melanchthon describes the letter as "modestam satis et piam," we must suspect that he did not read it closely, if he read it at all.
7. On 16 November, from Erfurt, Miltitz wrote to Wilibald Pirkheimer, "Ich schick och E. achbarkeyt alhie Eyne Epistel die Doctor martinus hat an bebstliche heylikeit geschriben *cum tractatulo de libertate christiana,* welcher noch nicht gantz gefertigt Im *latino* ist, sunder dewtz ist Er außgangen, welchen Ich Euch och mit Schigke. . . . " See Johann Bartholomäus Riederer, *Nachrichten zur Kirchen- Gelehrten- und Bücher-Geschichte,* vol. 1 (Altdorf: Schüpfel, 1764), p. 170.
8. See *WA* 6, 3-5, and 567, 25-31.
9. At any rate, nine new paragraphs were appended. See note 7 to this study. Wilhelm Maurer, *Von der Freiheit eines Christenmenschen, Zwei Untersuchungen zu Luthers Reformationsschriften 1520/21* (Göttingen: Vandenhoeck & Ruprecht, 1949), pp. 65-72, contends that the German version is the original. Cf. Birgit Stolt, *Studien zu Luthers Freiheitstraktat* (Stockholm: Almquist & Wiksell, 1969), pp. 8, 10-11, 90, 109, and 114-117.
10. *WA* 7, 20, 18-20.
11. Stolt, *Studien zu Luthers Freiheitstraktat,* p. 12, makes a separate division out of paragraph one in both versions, which she designates as the exordium.
12. *Martin Luther, sein Leben und seine Schriften,* vol. 1 (Berlin: Duncker, 1903), p. 365.
13. *WA* 7, 57, 8-10.
14. *WA* 7, 58, 16-18.
15. *WA* 7, 58, 23-30.
16. *WA* 7, 71, 36-39.
17. *WA* 7, 73, 11-12.
18. *Luthers Schrift Von der Freiheit eines Christenmenschen (de libertate christiana) nach Entstehung, Inhalt und Bedeutung dargestellt und entwickelt* (Zürich: Schultheß, 1876), p. 14. For the negative opinion of *De libertate christiana* held by Leo's legate Girolamo Aleander see *Deutsche Reichstagsakten, jüngere Reihe,* 2 (Gotha: Perthes, 1896), p. 500, lines 18-24. In the preface to his *Epitome de fide et operibus* (Cologne: Quentel, 1525) the Dominican inquisitor Jacob van Hoogstraten called *De libertate christiana* Luther's "most pestilential" book.
19. *WA Br* 2, 167, 15-17.
20. *WA* 1.6, 573, 12-15.
21. *WA Br* 2, 195, 22-23.
22. *WA* 1.7, 80-81. Notice that the equating of Leo with Antichrist is dropped from the German translation, pp. 88-89.

23. See for example *WA* 6, 584, 9, and 7, 296, 19.

24. *WA Br* 2, 195, 11-13 and 15-16. See also *WA Br* 2, 31, n. 3, plus *WA* 1.6, 577 and 595.

25. *WA* 1.1, 527-529, and *WA Br* 4, 292-293. The second letter was never sent. For a fragmentary and discarded draft of the first letter see *WA* 1.9, 173-175.

26. Regarding the 1506, 1518, and 1519 editions, see Wolfram Setz, *Lorenzo Vallas Schrift gegen die Konstantinische Schenkung* (Tübingen: Niemeyer, 1975), pp. 93-96 and 151-166. On the date of Hutten's preface to Leo see pp. 159-66 and Thomas W. Best, *The Humanist Ulrich von Hutten: A Reappraisal of His Humor* (Chapel Hill: U.N.C. Press, 1969), pp. 76-82. On pp. 162-163 of his book Setz mistakenly declares that the trip to France must have occurred·too early for Hutten to have been at the Steckelberg on 1 December 1517, as Hutten states at the end of the letter to Leo. On p. 166 Setz also errs in affirming that the 1518 edition was released before September of that year. Frank Hieronymus, "Huttenica, B. Huttens Ausgabe von Lorenzo Vallas 'De falso credita et ementita Constantini donatione declamatio,'" *Zeitschrift für die Geschichte des Oberrheins,* 127 (1979), 213-226, argues defectively that Hutten's first edition of Valla's treatise appeared in December 1519 and his second edition, in November 1520. Hieronymus omits Hutten's testimony in *Liberis omnibus ac vere Germanis* (Best, *The Humanist Ulrich von Hutten,* pp. 81-82, and Setz, *Lorenzo Vallas Schrift,* p. 162), while slighting the evidence furnished by Bernard Adelmann von Adelmannsfelden. Compare Setz' p. 164 with Hieronymus' final sentence in "Huttenica, B."

27. Even in the title of the preface to Picernus' translation, included in the 1518 and 1519 editions, Hutten questions Picernus' sincerity ("... quam è graeco in latinum se asseuerat conuertisse").

28. Eduard Böcking, *Ulrichs von Hutten Schriften,* vol. I (Aalen: Zeller, 1963), pp. 155-61.

29. *WA* 6, 347, 17-28.

30. *WA Br* 1, 413, 38-39. Also P.S. Allen and H.M. Allen, *Opus epistolarum Des. Erasmi Roterodami,* 3 (Oxford: Clarendon, 1913), p. 606, lines 41-42.

31. See Best, *The Humanist Ulrich von Hutten,* pp. 76-82.

32. *WA Br* 2, 48-49, 20-29.

33. In *An den christlichen Adel deutscher Nation* Luther refers to the Donation as "die ungehorete lugen." See *WA* 6, 434, 25-26. See also *WA* 50, 66.

34. *Ulrichs von Hutten Schriften,* vol. 1, p. 167, lines 11-22.

35. *Ibid.,* p. 216, lines 10-12.

36. *Ibid.,* p. 302, lines 34-35.

37. *Ibid.,* p. 313, lines 7-9 and 13-14.

38. *Opus epistolarum Des. Erasmi,* 4 (Oxford, 1922), 96-107.

39. *Ulrichs von Hutten Schriften,* vol. 1, pp. 320-321.

40. *Ibid.,* pp. 324-325.

41. *WA Br* 2, 71, 11-12.

42. *WA Br* 2, 91, 150-176.

43. *Corpus Reformatorum* 1, 201.

44. *WA Br* 2, 94, 30-31, and 98, 5-6.

45. *WA Br* 2, 111, 4-5.

46. *Commentaria Ioannis Cochlaei, de actis et scriptis Martini Lutheri Saxonis* (Mainz: Behem, 1549), p. 93. Notice the "suum" in "scripserat occulte ad Vlricum Huttenum suum Lutherus...."

47. See Walther E. Köhler, *Die Quellen zu Luthers Schrift "An den christlichen Adel deutscher Nation"* (Halle: Buchdruckerei des Waisenhauses, 1895), pp. 305-317, and Ernst Kohlmeyer, *Die Entstehung der Schrift Luthers An den christlichen Adel deutscher Nation* (Gütersloh: Bertelsmann, 1922), pp. 47-63.

48. *Ulrichs von Hutten Schriften,* vol. 1, pp. 355-356, and *WA Br* 2, 116-117. Clemen could well be wrong in note 1, p. 117.

49. *Corpus Reformatorum* 1, 263. See also p. 264: "Mitto... *Hutteni* epistolam...." Regarding the date, see *WA Br* 2, 115.

50. *WA Br* 2, 131, 15-16. See note 4, p. 132, and p. 208, 3-4. By 3 November Sickingen ought to have received three letters from Luther, not two. Did Luther change his mind on 30 June?

51. *WA Br* 2, 137, 13-31. Cf. 145, 40-42; 146, 8-12; 162, 10-15; and 169, 12-13. Also, *WA* 1.6, 405, 3-6.

52. *WA* 1.5, 20, 33, and 6, 157, 20.

53. He should even have read *De schismate extinguendo,* the preface to which reproves reactionary theologians and ends with "iacta est alea." See *Ulrichs von Hutten Schriften,* vol. 1, p. 352, line 4; also 356, lines 14-15 ("mittet eam Capito").

54. Hieronymus Emser's *A venatione luteriana aegocerotis assertio.* See the edition by F.X. Thurnhofer (Münster: Aschendorff, 1921), p. 97, line 2.

55. *WA Br* 2, 179, 8-9.

56. *WA Br* 2, 185, 16-28 and 48-51.

57. *WA Br* 2, 191, 29-30, and 192, 38-41.

58. *WA Br* 2, 213, 8-9.

59. Wilhelm Maurenbrecher nearly did so. On p. 254 of his *Studien und Skizzen zur Geschichte der Reformationszeit* (Leipzig: Grunow, 1874), he maintained: "Der radikale Ton in den großen grundlegenden und ewig jungen Schriften Luthers von 1520—wir meinen die Schriften 'vom Papstthum zu Rom', die 'an den Adel deutscher Nation', die 'von der babylonischen Gefangenschaft der Kirche' und die 'von der Freiheit des Christenmenschen'— erklärt sich aus der Einwirkung der Hutten'schen Schriftstellerei auf Luthers Geist, aus dem Vorbilde, das Hutten gegeben."

MARTIN LUTHER AND THE SELF-HATING JEWS

Sander L. Gilman, *Cornell University*

Too much ink has been spent already on the topic of "Luther and the Jews."[1] The topic which I shall be addressing is quite another one. How did certain Jews of the sixteenth century understand the Jew, and how did this perception, present in the public sphere, support (or perhaps contradict) Luther's formulation of his own understanding of the Jews? For just as historians of religion have found it necessary to divide Luther's perception of the Jews into stages, so too is it necessary to understand the concept "Jew" in the sixteenth century in a much more differentiated manner than has been. If we can accept the premise that there were at least three different Luthers (in terms of his attitudes toward the "Jews")—the young, Catholic Luther, who more or less ignored them; the rebellious Luther, who saw them as potential allies; and the old Luther, embittered by their refusal to convert to the new dogma—then we should be able to grasp the two, antithetical concepts of the "Jew" present within Christian (and Jewish) consciousness during Luther's lifetime.

The two models of the Jew are those of the "blind" Jew and the "seeing" Jew. Or, to choose two even simpler categories, the "bad" Jew and the "good" Jew. This split in the Christian perception of the Jew reflects both Church policy and community practice. The "blind" Jew is that Jew who refuses to acknowledge Christ. He is "blind" because he is inherently unable to see the truth of Christ as prefigured in the Old Testament, and acts as if that prophecy were not fulfilled. His blindness lies within the limitations of his reading and comprehension of the divine text. It is tied to his materialistic nature, for in being unable to see the allegorical truth of the Old Testament, the Jew remains mired in this world. One must stress that this blindness is viewed by the Church as the present state of the Jews. Jews can overcome this state of blindness through inspiration. Knowledge, learning, insight, doubt are not sufficient for the illumination of the Jew. Only the flash of divine inspiration, the sudden acknowledgement of Christ's divinity (and the instantaneous perception of the Old Testament as prefiguring his coming) frees the Jew from his blindness. In this moment, the Jew "sees" for the first time, and becomes the "good" Jew.

This model of conversion is a most complicated one, especially given sixteenth-century practice.[2] The general attitude toward the nature and the conversion of the Jew is fixed in canon law. However, there is a substantial shift in the public image of the convert in Germany from the high middle ages to the sixteenth century. There is one twelfth-century account of the voluntary conversion of a Jew, which is illuminating, both in its uniqueness and in its account of the process of conversion and the self-image of the convert. The "Letter on my conversion," written by the German monk Hermann, known before his conversion as Judah ben David ha-Levi, appears to be the first autobiographical account of a conversion to Christianity preserved following Augustine's fourth-century *Confessions*.[3] Hermann, in this letter, explains the reasons for his conversion to his new Christian co-religionists in terms which they would have found easy to comprehend. Upon finding himself in Mainz, he attended a series of sermons held by one of his creditors, Ekbert, the bishop of Mainz. He initially attended the sermons in order to keep an eye on Ekbert, whom he had lent money without sufficient collateral. Hermann became fascinated by Ekbert's mode of biblical exegesis, his ability to see in the Old Testament the eventual coming of Christ. Hermann's road to conversion, according to his own account, was extremely difficult. First, he had to overcome the anger and threats of his co-religionists; and second, he had to overcome the hesitancy of the Christian world. A monk, for example, to whom Hermann confessed his inability to see his way clear to conversion, damned him as innately unable to see the truth of Christ because he was a Jew! Hermann recounts his inner doubts at this moment, for, if indeed Jews are unable to see the truth, as they once had refused to see it at the time of Moses, then all of his inner turmoil was without purpose, as he would never be able truly to acknowledge the truth of Christ.

These two strands, the monk's charge that Jews were unable to "see" the truth, and Hermann's fear of his co-religionists reveal a set of Christian preconceptions about the nature of the Jew. Hermann's "Letter on my conversion" is a text aimed at an audience of Christians by one who now perceives himself to be part of this privileged group. It reflects a reification of the Christian attitudes toward the Jew by one who has passed through the stage of being Jewish to the higher stage of being a Christian. Hermann successfully disassociates himself from the image of the Jew through exorcizing the hidden Jew within through the act of writing. Hermann was a most successful Christian, who in later life became the founding abbot of the monastery at Scheda. In his epistle he presents the image of the Jew from which he feels himself freed. The Jew is closed-minded. He is a captive of the letter rather than the spirit of the Bible. He is materialistic. This essence of the Jew is supported by the Church's demand for a visionary experience, a mystical union with God, before the path to conversion is opened. Such moments are held to be impossible for Jews, at least for the idea of the "Jew" as held by the medieval Church, since Jews are bound to this world by their nature which is documented by their limited perception of revealed text. The Jew is vindictive and dangerous. He will turn on and attempt to destroy anyone who he feels threatens him. If he is struck, he will not turn the other cheek, but attempt to wreak vengeance. Hermann argues in his letter that these two qualities are both inherent in the "blind" Jew but can be overcome. The "blind" Jew can become a "good" Jew through the revelation of Christ. And this "good" Jew would be a better Christian than those merely born into the faith. This transformation necessitates a complete metamorphosis.

Hermann's autobiography presents a model of the split perceived by the convert between his present state and his image of himself as a Jew. Hermann uses the standard Christian criteria to classify his former self, and thus to exorcize it within the terms understood by his audience. His text, on the surface, wishes to teach that inner doubts and weakness can be overcome through faith. His sub-text is much more complex. For Hermann, embedded in the protective structure of the monastic orders, wishes to prove his membership within this privileged and powerful group. This group provides him with status and with power, qualities lacking in his incarnation as Judah ben David ha-Levi. To prove this power is not ephemeral, to show his status is not transitory, Hermann must provide, in his text, the antithetical model demanded by the Church. He must bear testimony, not only to his own initial weakness, but to the perfidy of his co-religionists. He must show the difficulty of conversion because of the innate, doubting nature of the Jew. He must reify the abyss demanded by the Church between the Christian and the Jew. Such a demand places Hermann, or any other convert, in an untenable position. For the dichotomy between Christian and Jew does not provide for a true identification with the persona of the former. There remains always the stigma of being the convert. (Indeed, this seems to be one of the demons Hermann is exorcizing in his letter.) What the convert must do is to turn this stigma into a sign of higher status, for the "seeing" Jew to be an even better Christian than his co-religionists. Hermann shows this by using his own autobiography as a paradigm for the ultimate insight which can be had into the nature of the self and thus into the truths of Christianity. He becomes his own text, and his allegorical reading of his conversion becomes the proof for his abandonment of the blindness of his former self, his perception of the world and its signs as transparent, revealing the glory of Christ, and his ability to see in his present state the pattern for the future.

Hermann's autobiography thus provides a pattern for the self-image of the convert as reflected in the written text. For the transformation of life perceived into text read is an important step. As Heiko Oberman has pointed out in his reading of parallel texts written by the best known of the sixteenth-century converts, Johannes Pfefferkorn, one of the central questions which must be asked of Pfefferkorn's pamphlets is their function as texts, texts to be read, texts which are both the stuff for interpretation as well as its model.[4] In reading these complex and often opaque texts, certain questions as to their function in society must be raised, but even more so the question of their function for the writer. For Hermann, the complexity of his text is limited, on one level, by the form of its transmission. While it was widely read, one can safely say that it was read primarily within the institutional structure of the monastery and reflected the monastic preoccupation with the inner workings of their own lives. When one turns to the pamphlet literature of the sixteenth century, one has moved from a limited public arena to the broadest, most accessible arena, that of the printed and marketed word. It is in this arena that the struggle of the convert for his identity takes place, and it is in this arena that Martin Luther finds a useful model for the Jew.

Luther is first exposed to the model of the "seeing" Jew during the debates concerning Johannes Reuchlin and his suggestions concerning the writings of the Jews. The debate between the Humanists and the Cologne Dominicans is too well known for recapitulation here.[5] Yet little attention has been paid until recently to one of the main actors, Josef Pfefferkorn, baptised in 1504, together with his wife, Anna, his son and his mother-in-law, and christened Johannes. Like Hermann's conversion it was voluntary, voluntary in the sense of the sixteenth century. Unlike other cases recorded in both Northern Europe and Spain of forced conversion (a contradiction in terms according to Canon Law, but acceptable practice within certain circles of the Church), Pfefferkorn evidently chose Christianity without any overt physical threats having been made against him.[6] The first pamphlets, written within three years of his conversion, were written to prove his new status as a "seeing" Jew. They also make the claim to a greater insight than that possessed by the Christian, since as a convert Pfefferkorn claims the special knowledge of a "blind" Jew made to see. Thus the central thrust of Pfefferkorn's pamphlets seems to be directed against the Jews and their books. Pfefferkorn based his claim to higher status on his knowledge of Hebrew and the Talmud, and his claim to status within the Christian community was accepted by his new co-religionists, since it provided them (they believed) with special, first-hand insight into the inner workings of the Jewish mind. Pfefferkorn was quite limited in his ability to claim special status. He drew on his identity as a Jew, and its implications within the Christian community, to provide for his needed self-definition as a better Christian than those who now surrounded him. Pfefferkorn's hidden agenda is thus twofold. He claims special knowledge of the Jews from the standpoint of the convert with the intent of encouraging the Christian reform of the Jews. More importantly for his own self-image, he also claims that this conversion will improve contemporary Christianity, an improvement perceived from the special perspective of the convert:

> My dearest Christians, you should understand and appreciate the great value and bounty which the Jews will bring to the Christian Church. And the following is true: Since the Jews are so attached to the five books of Moses, their experience of the sweetness of holy scripture through the gift of the holy spirit will make them even fierier in their adherence to the five books of Moses. Much as a hungry bear who has broken open a beehive will be not driven away because of the attraction of the sweets, so, too, it will occur with the Jews. When they taste the honey, they will say, this is a feast above all feasts, and I believe, as true as it is within me, that all of the worldly feasts are not to be compared with one who has understood the Old Testament in the light of the New....[7]

Pfefferkorn uses here the text to illustrate the nature and manner of the process of conversion, a conversion which is embodied (not symbolized) in the Jews learning to read correctly. For the image of the sweetness of letters is taken from Jewish tradition. When the Hebrew alphabet is first taught, the letters on the page of the primer are daubed with honey, so that the child will experience the sweetness of learning. Here Pfefferkorn takes the Christian metaphor of the sweetness of truth and superimposes it upon the Jewish image. Yet his Christian audience would not have been aware of this double level of meaning. A Christian reader would have only read the literal meaning of the text, the proverb about the bear, and would have been blind to the second level of meaning, a level of interpretation which only the Jewish convert could possess. Here the act of writing and its interpretation replicates the special role of the clarity of the convert's mode of exegesis. It stresses the hidden, special knowledge of the convert, illuminated by his new insight. His reading is thus better than that of the ordinary Christian, his insight deeper. An off-shoot of this claim to superior knowledge is Pfefferkorn's millennial claims, seeing in his conversion the first moment in the eventual conversion of all the Jews, and thus the second coming.[8] Such claims of special status raise the "seeing" Jew to a different level than either his "blind" former co-religionist or the Christian community.

Standing between the Jews and their future status as the vanguard of the second coming are the Jews' books. When Pfefferkorn lashes out against these books, against the Talmud and the Kabbala, he is attacking the real presence of Jewish misreading in the world. Thus when Reuchlin, almost alone, challenges him, Pfefferkorn is required by his model of the world to perceive Reuchlin as a tool of the Jews, perhaps even as a Judaizer. Reuchlin's attack appears to come from the highest level of the privileged group, and it attacks him specifically as a "baptised Jew."[9] Pfefferkorn sees his new status attacked. Reuchlin sets out to prove that Pfefferkorn does not have any special knowledge, and that he does not possess any greater insight into Jewish texts than the most ignorant Jew. Pfefferkorn feels himself attacked at his most vulnerable point. For missing from Pfefferkorn's early pamphlets, written before the publication of Reuchlin's *Augenspiegel* in 1511, is any mention of the insecurity felt by the convert. Pfefferkorn was able to repress this sense of status anxiety because of his special position within the Dominican community in Cologne (an analogous position to Hermann's). If we turn to one of his contemporary converts, a friend and fellow "seeing" Jew, Victor von Karben, the centrality of this status anxiety can be judged, as well as the importance of Pfefferkorn's repression of this feeling. Victor von Karben, "formerly a Rabbi among the Jews and now a poor, miserable priest," published a pamphlet stating his own case in 1508.[10] Better educated than Pfefferkorn, he too entered the lists of the popular pamphleteer as the prophet of the self. Karben had been one of the prize converts to Christianity, chosen to defend Christianity in a public debate held before the Elector of Cologne. In his pamphlet he bitterly states his sense of outrage at still being perceived as a "blind" Jew:

> And thus says the psalmist one spends the entire day like a poor dog, which has spent its day running and returns at night hungry. For there are many uncharitable and ignorant Christians who will not give to you but will rather show you from their doors with mockery, saying, "Look, there goes a baptized Jew." And then others answer: "Yes, anything that is done for you is a waste. You will never become good Christians." And thus they are mocked

and insulted by the Christians from whom they expect help and solace. And they are also hated by the Jews from whom they have come. Whatever joy or pleasure that one or the other might have had is turned to unhappiness and displeasure.... [11]

Victor von Karben, isolated in a tiny village on the Rhine, gives vent to the insecurity felt by the convert, suspended between two identities. For the Jews in their vindictiveness will always hate those who betray them, as they betrayed Christ; for the Christians, being a Jew is an immutable fact:

> And some come to me and ask craftily, "were you a Jew?" When I answer in the affirmative, they mock me and say, "Go to St. Andrew's Church in Cologne. A cat and a mouse. A dog and a rabbit." This means that as little as a cat and a mouse, as little as a dog and a rabbit can be friends, so little could I become a good Christian. And they said with satisfaction, "Though you act like a Christian, you are still a Jew at heart." [12]

Carved on the doors of St. Andrew's is the figure of a convert, by legend one of the former Deans of the Church, holding a cat in one hand and a dog in the other. This proverbial manner of depicting the "seeing" Jew as merely the "blind" Jew in new guise reflects the daily reality of the convert. No matter what the official attitude toward the convert, voluntary or forced, there remains within the popular image of the Jew the sense that the Jew remains a Jew. Thus the convert must be a different type of Jew, not merely a "good" Christian, but a "seeing" Jew. The populace perceives this demand for special status merely as further proof of the disingenuous nature of the "blind" Jew, who is willing to accept any mask in order to further his own ends.

While Pfefferkorn would have been spared much of the direct confrontation with such attitudes, he knew, if from his friend Victor von Karben, that such attitudes were prevalent in Christian society. When Reuchlin attacks him, all of the anxiety present, anxiety transformed into a claim for greater status, is released. He becomes vicious in his attacks on the Jews, demanding in his answer to Reuchlin, the *Brantspiegel* of 1512, the forcible baptism of young Jews and the exile of the rest. [13] This must be done because of the actions of "a few Christians who look through their fingers rather than see. These take presents and bribes from the Jews." [14] Reuchlin's action is not the act of a Christian, but rather the act of an agent of the Jews. And yet Reuchlin's rhetoric, as Pfefferkorn knows all too well, is the rhetoric of the Christian community concerning the converts. Thus

Pfefferkorn begins to address his audience as "we Christians" as the apotheosis of Reuchlin's addressing him as the "baptized Jew Pfefferkorn" throughout the *Augenspiegel*. When then the Humanists publish their various defences of Reuchlin, especially the *Epistolae obscurorum virorum* of 1517, the idea of Pfefferkorn as a spoiled Jew stands centerstage. Pfefferkorn becomes the quintessential renegade, proving his Jewish identity by acting like Judas. The supporters of the Dominicans, presented in the satire, are themselves unsure of Pfefferkorn:

> You ask me, in the third place, whether I think that Johannes Pfefferkorn will persevere in the Christian faith. I answer that, by the Lord, I know not what to say. It is a mighty ticklish point. You will recall to mind that precedent at St. Andrew's in Cologne—how a Dean of that Church, who was a baptized Jew abided long in the Christian faith, and lived an upright life. But upon his death he ordered a hare and a hound brought to him and enlarged, whereupon the hound in a trice seized the hare. Then he ordered a cat and a mouse to be brought—and the cat pounced on the mouse. Then he said to many who were standing around, "You see how that these animals cannot cast off their natures; and a Jew can never cast off his faith. Wherefore today I die a true Israelite," and so speaking he died. Thereupon the citizens of Cologne in memory of this event set up the brazen images which still stand in the wall before the cemeterey.[15]

Jews remain Jews no matter what they publicly profess. Thus the "bad" Jew Pfefferkorn must be punished, like Judas, he must be made to expiate his Jewishness through a public act. Yet such an act cannot in reality be carried out against Pfefferkorn, so the authors of the *Epistolae obscurorum virorum* create a double for Pfefferkorn, whom they destroy. This double exists throughout the text, always mentioned to qualify the true nature of a fictionalized Pfefferkorn. In one longer passage, from a letter written by a ficticious priest in Halle, he appears in some detail:

> Gentlemen, that you may understand the true nature of this suit against Johannes Reuchlin, let me tell you that the root of it all is Johannes Pfefferkorn, who resembleth in name, and in all else, that Johannes Pfefferkorn who was in this very place torn with red-hot pincers, and who in like manner had become a pervert from his faith, by reason of the wickedness that he had committed. If Pfefferkorn were safe here in jail, and the

executioners were to put the question to him as to what he had committed, he would make confession of not a whit less than his namesake.[16]

Pfefferkorn is supplied with a double, a double called Johannes Pfefferkorn, described as a convert, burnt by the Margrave at Halle.

Pfefferkorn's double is not merely a fantasy. Ulrich von Hutten had been the official representative of he Archbishop of Mainz in September 1514, at the torture and burning of a Jew called Pastor Rapp at Halle. Rapp was roasted over a slow fire while his skin was ripped from his body, as punishment for having falsely claimed to have been a priest. Under torture he admitted to the entire catalogue of charges usually lodged against the Jews from murder to defilement of the host. Hutten, in a Latin panegyric of 119 hexameters, glories in the death of Rapp, congratulating his readers that such a monster could have only been born to Jewish parents, and could not have been a Christian German.[17] Hutten also seems to be the writer who converted *Pfaff* (Pastor) Rapp into Johannes Pfefferkorn, creating a sacrificial victim in the world of reality parallel to the fictive Pfefferkorn whom he had maimed and tortured and used as a bloody broom in his 1517 revision of the *Triumphus Doctoris Reuchlini.*[18]

Rapp's punishment, as David Friedrich Strauss pointed out, is well within the terms of contemporary justice.[19] It provided a lesson to converts of exactly what could be done to those who claimed to be Christians, but were then unmasked as "blind" Jews. The literary fantasies of the privileged group had a frightening way of being turned into reality, at least as far as the Jews were concerned. Thus Pfefferkorn spends considerable time in refuting as a lie the charge that he was *Pfaff* Rapp. Indeed, in 1516 he published a pamphlet with the title *A Defence of Johannes Pfefferkorn, whom they did not burn!*[20] For Pfefferkorn knew what the outcome of the struggle with Reuchlin could mean for him. Reuchlin could be (and was) fined if he lost his suit; Pfefferkorn could be tortured and roasted over a slow fire. It is no wonder that the pamphlet war between Pfefferkorn and the Humanists increased in virulence, for, at least on one side the author had everything to lose, and on the other was the demand for the ultimate punishment.

To fit Martin Luther into this struggle means to recreate the model of the Jew he accepted during the 1510's. It is clear that Luther identified strongly with the political position of the Humanists. In a letter written to Spalatin in 1514 he mocks Ortwin Gratius, Pfefferkorn's Dominican patron and the translator of his works into Latin, and, as late as 1520, he asks Martin Bucer to keep him informed of the case pending against Reuchlin.[21] But

Luther's interest in Reuchlin is more than a passing concern about a fellow intellectual who has gone against the Church Establishment. Luther identifies himself with Reuchlin. In another letter to Spalatin, written in 1518, he literally sees himself as Reuchlin.[22] In projecting himself into Reuchlin's persona, Luther also accepts without question Reuchlin's denunciation of the convert as the "bad" Jew rather than as the "seeing" Jew. In 1514 Luther restates the Church's position that without divine intercession the Jews will continue to defame Christ and continue to be blind to his teaching. By 1523, Luther has shifted his focus ever so slightly. For Luther perceives the blindness and obduracy of the Jews as, at least in part, an artifact of the Church's treatment of the Jews. Luther's earlier perception of the convert as enemy, of the "seeing" Jew as the "bad" Jew, swings ever so slightly in his pamphlet of 1523, *That Jesus was born a Jew,* to perceive of a new world in which true conversion may take place.[23] The separation of the Jew as villain from the Archvillain, the Church, even moves Luther to a re-evaluation of Hutten's double for Pfefferkorn. In a pamphlet of 1533 directed against the abuses of ordination within the Church, Luther comments on those who fraudulently use the mass to reap riches for themselves, frauds "like that poor Jew who was burned at Halle on the Moritzburg."[24] Luther implies that the burning of Rapp was a sign of the corruption of the Church, since that which he had done was no different from the normal practices of the Church. Having freed Rapp from his function within the *Epistolae obscurorum virorum,* Luther is able to use the figure of Rapp as proof of the evil of the Church and of the treatment of the Jews within the Church. What is striking is that Luther retains this example of the treatment of the Jews in 1533, nineteen years after the burning of Rapp at Halle. Even though Luther has re-evaluated the function of Rapp within his shift of attitude toward the Jews in relationship to the Church, the image of the Jew as delineated within the Reuchlin-Pfefferkorn debate remains with him.

When the reader turns to the later pamphlets concerning the Jews, the return to the image of the "blind" Jew, the lying Jew, is evident. Without wanting to attribute this seeming reversal of the image of the Jew to a biological cause, such as organic brain disease, as has been done, one is pressed not to see in Luther's late attacks on the Jews some type of abberation.[25] And yet Luther's image of the Jew and the function which his reading of a text by a Jew may have had on his perception of the Jew points toward a continuity of Luther's image of the Jew, with its rejection of the convert. The rhetoric of Luther's late tractates is as harsh as that of Reuchlin's pamphlet and their program is summarized in the first and most extensive of these texts, *Against the Jews and Their Lies* (1543). Jews lie.

"From their youth they have been so nurtured with venom and rancor against our Lord that there is no hope until they reach the point where their misery makes them pliable" [. . .] "Jews lie shamefully."[26] And in their lying is the root of the deception. They lie within the legalism of their books, a legalism which is identical to that of the Church. And they do all of this under the guise of the religion of the Old Testament. They are incorrigible. Here one can compare Erasmus' comment to Pirkheimer in 1517 that Pfefferkorn " . . . could render no better service to his co-religionists than by betraying Christendom, hypocritically claiming to have become a Christian. . . . This half-Jew has done more harm to Christendom than all the Jews together."[27] For Luther all Jews are like Pfefferkorn. And Luther underscores this fact by adapting Pfefferkorn's program for the future treatment of the Jews. Burn their synagogues, destroy their homes, confiscate the Talmud and all other Hebrew books, including the Hebrew Bible, forbid the rabbis from teaching, ban them from carrying out trade, stop them from moving from place to place, demand that their children learn trades, and, if all else fails, drive them from the country.[28] This radical program is but Pfefferkorn's suggestions raised to a higher power, suggestions which Pfefferkorn himself could not have made since they would have endangered his own status as a convert.

It is the innate "blindness" of the Jews as readers of texts which is for Luther the key to the Jews' nature. Since it is precisely as a reader of the Jews' books that Pfefferkorn had come into conflict with Reuchlin and as a reader that he based his claim for status, it is about this point that Luther centers his perception of the Jew. In his second pamphlet, *On Shem Hamphoras* [the Ineffable Name] *and the Descent of Christ* (1543) Luther presents a detailed polemic against the nature and origin of the Jews' misreading of Holy Scripture:

> I, a damned *goy,* cannot understand where they have their great skill in interpreting, except, perhaps, that when Judas Iscariot hung himself, his bladder burst and his gut split. Perhaps the Jews had their servants there with golden pots and silver bowls to catch Judas' piss and other reliques (as they are called). Then they ate and drank the shit mixed with piss in order to become so sharp-eyed in interpreting the scripture. They see things in scripture that neither Isaiah nor Matthew, nor all the angels saw, and which we damned *goys* can never hope to see.[29]

Luther uses the "insiders" language to mock the special knowledge claimed by the Jew. Luther's rhetoric centers about the claims which the Jews made concerning their ability to read scripture, it is a claim which he perceives as one with their identity. In the *Tabletalk* of this period, Luther denied the special insight of the Jews into scripture. This refusal to give the claims of the "blind" Jews credence mirrored and reified his reception of the convert, of the "seeing" Jews. For to deny any special knowledge to the Jews, to deny them any insight at all into the mysteries of Scripture, undermines their ability to understand themselves, to read their own texts, as proof of their own conversion. Luther's reaction to converts, in the flesh rather than in their textual incarnation, illustrates this refusal.

In 1540 the Jew Michael of Posen came to Luther to discuss his conversion to the Lutheran dogma. Luther's reaction is swift. He identifies Michael with the assassins who had been rumoured to be threatening his life. His association of Michael (who bore no resemblance to the assassins) with the poisoners comes about because of a long-standing fear of the Jews as poisoners, a fear which can be traced as far back as 1525.[30] Michael's treatment is as a "blind" Jew, rather than as a "seeing" Jew seeking acceptance by his new co-religionists. Luther sees in Michael another Pfefferkorn, an individual whose claim to special exegetical abilities led to an attack on a Christian with whom Luther strongly identified. The idea of the irredeemability of the Jew appears in the *Tabletalk* again and again, with Luther recalling and recounting the tale of the Dean of St. Andrew's, a tale which, as we have seen, plays a central role in categorizing the nature of the Jew for the sixteenth-century Christian.[31]

Luther's ambiguous relationship to the very idea of the conversion of the Jews (and his virtual elimination of it from his teleology) is filtered through yet another layer of interpretation provided by yet another Jewish convert to Christianity, who shows the same model of self-hatred seen in Pfefferkorn and Victor von Karben. Antonius Margaritha's *The Entire Jewish Faith* was the subject of Luther's discussion during the winter of 1542-43, while he was formulating his final series of broadsides against the Jews. Margaritha, unlike Pfefferkorn, could claim a good Jewish education. Indeed what strikes one in a casual comparison of Margaritha's text with any of the Pfefferkorn pamphlets is the different tone. Not that the program is different, but in the wake of Pfefferkorn's authority as a "seeing" Jew having been undermined by Reuchlin and the Humanists, it was necessary to create a new level of scholarship upon which to base the status of the "seeing" Jew. Thus Margaritha's claim for serious scholarship about the Jews, as has been understood for almost a century of scholarship, simply masks much the same prejudices and presuppositions as found in Pfefferkorn's program, except cast in less polemical language and possessing more details, some accurate and some spurious.[32]

Antonius Margaritha was the grandson of the famed Nuremberg Talmudist Jacob Margolis and was the son of a rabbi. Unlike Pfefferkorn, whose proletarian background was the subject of much comment among the educated Humanists, Margaritha could make the claim of having a good Hebrew education. His conversion to Christianity in 1522, like that of his fellow voluntary converts, is ascribed to a sudden awareness of the blindness of his co-religionists and the truth of Christianity. In 1530 Margaritha published his work on the nature of Judaism. Not merely seen as a tool for the enlightenment of the Christian reading public and the reification of his new status as a "seeing" Jew, *The Entire Jewish Faith* was perceived by Margaritha as a challenge to the blindness of the Jews. Its author demanded, and got, a public disputation with the leader, or parnas, of the German Jewish community, Josel von Rosheim. At Augsburg in 1530, a *Reichstag* called to solidify the Emperor's power, a public disputation was held between Margaritha and Josel von Rosheim on the nature of the Jews' prayers, on their desire to make converts, and on their attacks on the Emperor and the state. Present was the Emperor Charles the Fifth, princes of the Holy Roman Empire, and representatives of both the Church and the Reformation (including Melanchthon). Josel von Rosheim was able to refute Margaritha point by point, showing how Jewish law and ritual expressly forbids the actions and beliefs attributed to the Jews by the convert.

Charles the Fifth had been accustomed to disputations between Jews and Christians as they were held in Spain.[33] There these debates were held to show the inherent truth of the Christian faith and there could be only one victor, the Church. In the debate between the "blind" Jew Josel von Rosheim and the "seeing" Jew Antonius Margaritha, the victor was not clear until the debate was over, and then the victory fell to the "blind" Jew. Margaritha was arrested by Imperial order as a danger to the social structure. Banished from Augsburg, he reappears in Leipzig in 1531, where he taught Hebrew at the university. In 1531, the third edition of his work appeared. He had concluded the first edition (and the second) with the formulaic statement that he knew that the Jews, once his book appeared, would curse him. The third edition, published after the debacle at Augsburg, turned that formulaic statement into an outcry at the perfidious Jews: "What has happened to me because of this book shall not be long suppressed. Still I pray to God, my creator, and Jesus Christ, that he save me from the stubborn and deceitful Jews. Amen."[34] Sometime after the publication of this third edition of *The Entire Jewish Faith* Margaritha converted for a second time, subscribing to the Augsburg Confession rejected by the Emperor on that occasion of Margaritha's public humiliation. Margaritha became a follower of Luther.

Margaritha's text presents an image of the "seeing" Jew, in its mode of interpretation, which is in contrast to the blindness of the Jews described. Central to Margaritha's argument is the lack of originality of the Jews. The Talmud, that focus of Pfefferkorn's fury, is to be divided into two parts. The original parts are the more modern ones and are the result of the revelations of Christ; the older segments, antedating the coming of Christ, are unoriginal.[35] This view, which appeared in the debate between Nahmanides and Hieronymus de Santa Fe, also a convert from Judaism, during 1413 at Tortosa, is vital since it stresses the centrality of the coming of Christ to any truthful revelation outside of Holy Scripture.[36] The seeming insight of the Jews, as documented by the Talmud, is merely a reflection of the truth of Christianity. The Jews can not make any claim to an independent revelation or tradition of interpretation. This view suspends the special status of the Jews after the destruction of the Temple, and draws the distinction which Luther needs and uses between the Jews of the Bible (with their prefiguration of the events of the New Testament) and the present-day Jews with whom he must deal. Indeed, the lesson which Luther cites as having learned from *The Entire Jewish Faith* is that Jews are just like Catholics: both believe that they can achieve salvation by actions in this world, rather than by faith alone. Both Catholic and Jew live in this world, rather than having a sense of the relationship between the material and the spiritual. And the blindness of both is made concrete by their mode of reading. The limited nature of the non-Protestant's understanding of the totality of the world is illustrated by Margaritha's presentation of Jewish ritual, a ritual which Luther immediately parallels to the Mass. For the Jews, like the Catholics, are corrupters of the True Word, untouched by insight. The lack of originality of the Jews in their mode of interpretation is further shown by their blindness to the true interpretation of Scripture. For, just as the Jews stole from the Christians after the revelation of Christ made their blindness overt, so too does the new revelation make the blindness of both Jew and Catholic evident.

Yet Luther based his reading of the nature of the Jew and his lack of originality on the revelation of a "seeing" Jew, one whose status as an expert had been severely undermined by the disputation at Augsburg, a disputation of which he must have had detailed, if indirect, knowledge. Margaritha's new status as the Protestant's "seeing" Jew would have countered some of Luther's doubt. For here was the ultimate proof of what revelation could accomplish. First, the "blind" Jew is made to see through divine intercession, and he converts to a faulty model of Christianity. And then, when the institution of the Church abandons him, he receives true insight and becomes a "truly seeing" Jew, a follower of the Reformation. And yet this shifting could be understood in the light of the Pfefferkorn model as evolved by the Humanists. For, if the Jew can never be truly converted, if he remains eternally the Jew, as the dog remains the dog, and the hare the hare, then Margaritha's shift from Judaism to Catholicism to Protestantism is living proof of this blindness. Seen from the standpoint of the Protestant, especially Luther, Margaritha's own biography gives substance to the charge that Jews are base and untrustworthy. Margaritha's striving for what Peter Gay perceives in twentieth-century German Jewry as "wholeness hunger," is silently understood as proof of the inherent, immutable nature of the Jew.[37] Margaritha becomes the living reification of both models of the Jew. The ambiguity felt by Luther in regard to his person is countered by his text, and yet text and person are perceived as one. The Jew is his own text, and it is a contradictory text.

In his pamphlet on *The Jews and Their Lies* Luther presents this dichotomy in all its confused fullness. Drawing heavily on Margaritha for the substance of his charges against the Jews, Luther nevertheless doubts the ability of the Jew to convert:

> No doubt it is necessary for the Jews to lie and to misinterpret in order to maintain their error ever against such a clear and powerful text. Their previous lies broke down under their own weight. But even if they were to lie for a hundred thousand years and call the devils in to aid them, they would still come to nought. For it is impossible to name a Messiah at the time of the seventy weeks, as Gabriel's revelation would necessitate, other than our Lord Jesus Christ. We are certain, sure and cheerful about this, as we snap our fingers at all the gates of hell and defy them, together with all the gates of the world and everything that wants to be or might be exalted, smart, or wise against us. I, a plain insignificant saint in Christ, venture to oppose all of them single-handedly and to defend this viewpoint easily, comfortably, and gladly. However, it is impossible to convert the devil and his own, nor are we commanded to attempt this. It suffices to uncover their lies and to reveal the truth. Whoever is not actuated to believe the truth for the sake of his own soul will surely not believe it for my sake.[38]

The inability of the Jews to be converted is not a tenet found in Luther's Christian sources on the Jews, at least not those cited in the opening of this pamphlet. Both Nicolas of Lyra and Paul of Burgos saw their expositions of Jewish law and ritual as means through which to achieve the eventual conversion of the Jews. Neither Margaritha nor Victor of Karben, whom Luther also read, provided this model. Indeed, they sought to undermine any notion of the inability of the Jews to be converted, as this view placed their own conversion in question. Luther sees in the model of the intractable Jew the figure of Pfefferkorn, and perhaps also of one aspect of Margaritha. But Luther does not ignore the potential presented by the other aspect of Margaritha's presence in his world. He concludes the pamphlet on *The Jews and Their Lies* with the formulaic statement: "May Christ, our dear Lord, convert them mercifully and preserve us steadfastly and immovably in the knowledge of him, which is eternal life. Amen."[39] This formula, with its promise of eventual conversion, is weakened somewhat in *On Shem Hamphoras,* where Luther prays for the potential conversion of "at least some" of the Jews, but still retains part of the ritual rhetoric with which the Jews are addressed.[40]

Luther's views on the nature of the Jews are reified by the presence of converts to Christianity in his world. The complex self-definition of these converts, their need to establish themselves as better Christians than the Christians themselves, their public attitudes toward their former co-religionists, as well as their use of their biographies and texts as exempla, all play a role in shaping the attitude of the Christian world toward the Jew. Since the initial model chosen by the convert is a model of the Jew viewed through the eyes of the Christian world, it is of little wonder that the Christian community found their attitude toward the Jew substantiated by the converts' testimony. Yet, within the converts' texts, a sense of the ambiguous position of the "seeing" Jew, neither "blind" Jew nor true Christian, can be found. When Luther initially confronts this contradiction, it is to give the image of the convert a negative quality. In desiring the conversion of the Jews to his own brand of Christianity, he swings to the other pole present within the model, and sees the potential for conversion as possible. When, following his letter *Against the Sabbatarians,* he again is confronted with the claims of the Jews in the form of a Jewish apologetic pamphlet, the entire model reverts to its original negative quality, as the public function of the pamphlet calls forth the negative associations held with Pfefferkorn. It is once again the stubborn Jew who is drawing Christianity (or at least Christians) into question. It is clear that Luther has sufficient personal reasons for his attitudes toward the Jews, reasons buttressed by theologians like Martin Bucer and Johannes Eck in their attacks on the Jews' books, but it is through the model of the Jew as perceived and presented by Jewish converts that

Luther found the reification of his own perception of the Jew, a reification replete with contradictions and ambiguities present in these Jews' understanding of their status and definition within the Christian world.

Notes

1. The literature on this topic cannot be measured. A quick overview of the literature, with the basic contours of the criticism, is to be found in C. Bernd Sucher, *Luthers Stellung zu den Juden* (Nieuwkoop: B. De Graaf, 1977).

2. See Guido Kisch, *Judentaufe* (Berlin: Coloquium, 1973), pp. 3-5 and Jeremy Cohen, *The Friars and the Jews: The Evolution of Medieval Anti-Judaism* (Ithaca: Cornell University Press, 1982).

3. For the text and its background see Gerlinde Niemeyer, ed., *Hermannus Quondam Judaeus: Opusculum de Conversione sua* (Weimar: Böhlau, 1963). See also J. Aronius, "Hermann der Prämonstratenser," *Zeitschrift für die Geschichte der Juden in Deutschland,* 2 (1888), 217-231.

4. Heiko A. Oberman, *Wurzeln des Antisemitismus: Christenangst und Judenplage im Zeitalter von Humanismus und Reformation* (Berlin: Severin und Seidler, 1981).

5. The basic study of the debate remains Ludwig Geiger, *Johann Reuchlin: Sein Leben und seine Werke* (Leipzig: Duncker und Humblot, 1871). See also his essays: "Johannes Pfefferkorn: Ein Beitrag zur Geschichte der Juden und zur Charakteristik des Reuchlin'schen Streites," *Jüdische Zeitschrift für Wissenschaft und Leben,* 7 (1869), 293-309 and "Die Juden und die deutsche Literatur," *Zeitschrift für die Geschichte der Juden in Deutschland,* 2 (1888), 321-327. On the question of the original language and rhetoric of Pfefferkorn's texts see Meier Spanier, "Zur Charakteristik Johannes Pfefferkorns," *Zeitschrift für die Geschichte der Juden in Deutschland,* 6 (1935), 209-228; Leonard Forster, "From the 'Schwabenspiegel' to Pfefferkorn," in *Medieval German Studies Presented to Frederick Norman* (London: University of London, Germanic Institute, 1965), pp. 292-295; and K.H. Gerschmann, "Zu Johannes Pfefferkorns 'Übersetzung der Evangelien,'" *Zeitschrift für Religion und Geistesgeschichte,* 21 (1969), 166-171.

6. I am making the distinction between "voluntary" and "involuntary" conversion based solely on the rhetoric of the converts. There is no such thing as truly voluntary conversion at a time which placed the Jew in the precarious position of tolerated pariah. For a case of clearly involuntary conversion within acceptable Church practice see Solomon Grayzel, "The Confession of a Medieval Jewish Convert," *Historia Judaica,* 17 (1955), 89-120. For a more general discussion of the pressures to which the Jews were subjected see Leon Poliakov, *The History of Anti-Semitism,* trans. Richard Howard (New York: Vanguard Press, 1965), vol. I, pp. 83-90, a chapter which Poliakov calls the "birth of a Jewish mentality."

7. *Der Juden Spiegel* (Cologne: n.p., 1508), fol. E4^v-Fl^r. All translations are mine unless otherwise noted.

8. See the discussion in Oberman, *op. cit.,* pp. 40-47 and Stephen Sharot, *Messianism, Mysticism, and Magic: A Sociological Analysis of Jewish Religious Movements* (Chapel Hill: University of North Carolina Press, 1982).

9. *Augenspiegel* (Tübingen: Thomas Anshelm, 1511), fol. 22^v, *et passim*.

10. *Hier inne wirt gelesen wie Her Victor von Carben . . .*(Cologne: Heinrich Quentell Erben, [1508]). Luther knew the Victor von Karben pamphlet in a Latin translation. Like Pfefferkorn's pamphlets, the original was written in German, since the need to establish the status of the author was its primary aim. Writing in German implied entering into the public lists as a "seeing" Jew rather than remaining within the complete shelter of the Church.

11. Karben, fol. a 4^r.

12. *Ibid.*

13. The *Brantspiegel* was evidently written without the express knowledge of Pfefferkorn's Dominican sponsors and marks his most personal and direct expression in the pamphlet war with Reuchlin. *Brantspiegel* (Cologne: n.p., 1512), fol. A2^v.

14. *Brantspiegel,* fol. D3^r.

15. Eduard Böcking, ed., *Epistolae obscurorum virorum* (Leipzig: B.G. Teubner, 1858), p. 45. The translation is from Francis Griffin Stokes, trans., *Letters of Obscure Men* (New York: Harper, 1964), p. 200.

16. *Epistolae,* p. 43; Stokes, p. 118.

17. Eduard Böcking, ed., *Ulrichs von Hutten Schriften* (Leipzig: B.G. Teubner, 1859ff.), pp. 5, 345ff.

18. See the discussion by Hajo Holborn, *Ulrich von Hutten* (Göttingen: Vandenhoek und Ruprecht, 1968), p. 50 and Thomas W. Best, *The Humanist Ulrich von Hutten* (Chapel Hill: University of North Carolina Press, 1969), p. 51.

19. David Friedrich Strauss, *Ulrich von Hutten* (Bonn: Emil Strauss, 1877), p. 74. This remains the best study of Hutten.

20. *Beschyrmung Johannes Pfefferkorn (den man nyt verbrant hat),* Cologne: n.p., 1514.

21. *WA Br* 1, 28f.; *WA Br* 1, 614f. (Bucer).

22. *WA Br* 1, 141f. in a letter to Spalatin, 15 February 1518.

23. See Luther's comments on his pamphlet *Dass Jesus ein geborener Jude sei, WA Br* 3, 102.

24. *WA* 38, 213 in *Von der Winckelmesse und Pfaffenweihe.*

25. This argument was put forth by Paul Reiter in what is perhaps the strangest apology for the late Luther's attitude toward the Jews, an apology which ignores all dynamic possibilities. Paul Reiter, *Martin Luthers Umwelt, Charakter und Psychose sowie die Bedeutung dieser Faktoren für seine Entwicklung und Lehre* 2 vols. (Copenhagen: Levin and Munksgaard, 1937-41).

26. *WA* 53, 419, 434. Here cited from the translation by Martin H. Bertram in *Luther's Works* (Philadelphia: Fortress, 1971) 47, 139, 151.

27. Cited by Geiger, *Reuchlin,* p. 342.

28. *WA* 53, 523-526.

29. *WA* 53, 636-637.

30. *WA Br* 3, 821.

31. *WA TR* 7038.

32. The most detailed study of Margaritha remains Josef Mieses, *Die älteste gedruckte deutsche Übersetzung des jüdischen Gebetbuchs aus dem Jahre 1530 und ihr Autor Antonius Margaritha* (Wien: W. Löwit, 1916). For the general background of the debate and its outcome see Selma Stern-Taeubler, *Josel of Rosheim, Commander of Jewry in the Holy Roman Empire,* trans. Gertrude Hirschler (Philadelphia: Jewish Publication Society, 1965).

33. See Haim Hillel Ben-Sasson, "Jewish-Christian Disputation in the Setting of Humanism and Reformation in the German Empire," *Harvard Theological Review,* 59 (1966), 385ff.

34. *Das gantz Jüdisch glaub* (Leipzig: Melchior Lother, 1531), fol. Dd 5^r.

35. *Ibid.,* fol. F 2^v.

36. See the detailed discussion in Hyam Maccoby, ed. and trans., *Judaism on Trial: Jewish-Christian Disputations in the Middle Ages* (Rutherford, N.J.: Fairleigh Dickinson University Press, 1982), pp. 89ff.

37. Peter Gay, *Freud, Jews, and Other Germans* (New York: Oxford University Press, 1978), pp. 3ff.

38. *WA* 53, 417; Bertram 47, 252-253.

39. *WA* 53, 552; Bertram 47, 306.

40. *WA* 53, 648.

LUTHER AND CALVIN ON CHURCH AND TRADITION

David C. Steinmetz, *Duke University*

Luther and Calvin never met, though they had friends in common, particularly Philip Melanchthon, whose affection for Calvin was regarded with suspicion by Luther's stricter disciples (though not by Luther himself), and Martin Bucer, whom Luther had won for his cause at the Heidelberg Disputation of 1518. In the ordinary course of events there would have been no reason to expect Luther and Calvin to meet, separated as they were by age, culture, and education. Calvin was born in the year that Luther first lectured on the Sentences of Peter Lombard. By the time Calvin was converted to the Protestant faith, Zwingli, Oecolampadius and Hubmaier were already dead and Luther had just turned fifty. Unlike Luther, who had received a scholastic theological education at Erfurt and Wittenberg, Calvin studied the classics at Paris and read law at Orléans and Bourges. Since Calvin understood no German (a fact which the Zurich theologians hinted darkly contributed to Calvin's inordinate respect for Luther), he was restricted to the Latin writings of Luther and Zwingli or to the works which had appeared in Latin or French translation. Only Calvin's swift rise to prominence in the Evangelical movement brought him to Luther's attention, and then not before 1539, when Luther was fifty-five and Calvin thirty.

We have far more evidence about Calvin's attitude toward Luther than about Luther's attitude toward Calvin. Not everything Calvin had to say about Luther was complimentary. Calvin deprecated Luther's tendency to find an edifying point in biblical texts without first subjecting those texts to hard and critical analysis.[1] While Calvin agreed with Luther that the defense of the truth required theologians to engage in polemical discussions (it was Calvin, after all, who called the relatively inoffensive and reform-minded Albert Pighius "that dead dog"), he could not agree with the ferocity of Luther's attacks on other Protestant reformers—even reformers with whom Calvin disagreed—or the self-indulgent character of his piques and rages.[2] Furthermore, while Calvin disagreed with Zwingli, whom he regarded as a theological second-rater, on questions relating to the eucharist, he was nevertheless forced to side with Zwingli against Luther on such sensitive issues as the importance of the session of Christ at the right hand of the Father or the impossibility of an unbeliever receiving in the eucharistic service more than the mere signs of bread and wine.[3] Indeed, as Brian Gerrish has persuasively argued, Calvin saw Luther in historical perspective, as an important, even decisive, theological teacher, but a teacher who had historical antecedents and who initiated but did not culminate a theological development.[4] The Lutherans were not wrong to venerate Luther; they were only mistaken in their inordinate veneration, a veneration which excluded historical change and development, which took the living Word of a prophet and codified it into inflexible law. The Reformation is about *sola fides, sola gratia, solus Christus.* It is untrue to itself when it rejects the succession of authentic teachers in the Church and appeals (against Luther's own self-understanding) to *solus Lutherus.* The *ecclesia semper reformanda* learns from Luther as it learns from any truly evangelical theologian, but it remains independent of him. *Sola scriptura* not *solus Lutherus,* the Bible and not Luther's teaching, is the only standard to which the evangelical theologian is bound.

Calvin is notorious, however, not for his negative but for his positive judgments of Luther. Karl Holl called Calvin Luther's best disciple and there are historical reasons for that judgment. Calvin signed the Augsburg Confession,[5] and in the controversy with Zwingli and the Zurich theologians sided instinctively with Luther on the question of the real presence of Christ in the sacrament. He was impatient with Protestant theologians like Bullinger and the Zurich pastors who were unwilling to acknowledge the deep and unrepayable debt which all evangelical theologians owed to the pioneering work of Luther. He was tolerant of Luther's polemical outbursts, though he disapproved of them and urged Melanchthon to exercise his best offices to encourage Luther to offer his arguments in a more moderate and conciliatory tone of voice. In a letter of November 25, 1544, Calvin wrote to Bullinger:

> I often say that even if he should call me a devil, I should still pay him the honor of acknowledging him as an illustrious servant of God, who yet, as he is rich in virtues, so also labors under serious faults. . . . It is our task so to reprehend whatever is bad in him that we make some allowance for those splendid gifts.[6]

For Luther's opinion of Calvin we have two principal sources, one written and one oral. The written source is a letter from Luther to Bucer dated October 14, 1539. In it Luther writes: "Farewell and please greet reverently Mr. John Sturm and John Calvin. I have read their books with special pleasure."[7] The oral source is an anecdote which Melanchthon reported by messenger to Calvin and which Calvin repeats in a letter to Farel:

> Certain persons, to irritate Martin, pointed out to him the aversion with which he and his followers were alluded to by me. So he examined the passage in question and felt that he was there, beyond doubt, under attack. After a while, he said: "I certainly hope that he will one day think better of us. Still, it is right for us to be a little tolerant toward such a gifted man." We are surely made of stone if we are not overcome by such moderation! I, certainly, am overcome, and I have written an apology for insertion into my preface to the Epistle to the Romans.[8]

If we ask what writing inclined Luther to be so favorably disposed toward Calvin, the only clue we have is the allusion to Cardinal Sadoleto in the 1539 letter to Bucer. Apparently the work which impressed Luther and which restrained him from attacking what he regarded as inadequacies in Calvin's position was Calvin's *Reply to Sadoleto,* an open letter addressed to the bishop of Carpentras and published in Strassburg by Wendelin Rihel in September, 1539.[9]

The *Reply to Sadoleto* deals with the doctrine of the Church and with the question of the relation of the authority of Scripture to the authority of the Fathers and Councils. Luther himself had just written a few months earlier a German treatise on the same subject entitled *On the Councils and the Church.*[10] Luther finished his treatise in March and was therefore unaware of Calvin's opinions. Calvin, though deeply indebted to Luther, did not read German and so was unable to consult Luther's essay. There is, therefore, in these essays no direct dependence of one author on the other. Nevertheless Luther saw in Calvin a spokesman for the whole Protestant movement and regarded his *Reply to Sadoleto* as the articulation of a position with which Luther wanted to identify himself. Indeed, he was so impressed with Calvin's treatment of the very questions with which he had struggled himself that he was unwilling to criticize Calvin or listen to the criticism of others. For a brief period of time in 1539 Luther and Calvin, the ageing reformer and the young French theologian, represented a common front against Rome on the central disputed issue of religious authority.

I want in what follows to compare Luther's *On the Councils and the Church* with Calvin's *Reply to Sadoleto,* noting the similarities and differences in their historical setting, their arguments and their style. The two treatises give a glimpse of what we might call an ecumenically Protestant position on the authority of Church, magisterium, Scripture and tradition. They sum up the best Protestant thinking prior to the convocation of the Council of Trent. They are important, not only as a clue to the deep affinity between Luther and Calvin, but also to the self-understanding of Protestantism at the end of its second decade.

I.

Luther's treatise was prompted by the decision of Pope Paul III to convoke a general council at Mantua in May, 1537. After a series of delays and postponements and the naming of Vicenza as a new site for the council, the outbreak of war between Francis I and Charles V forced the pope on May 21, 1539, to postpone the council indefinitely. Though many early Protestants, Luther among them, had called for a free council on German soil to settle the religious questions which divided Western Christendom, the Protestant League of Schmalkalden rejected the proposed council when it was finally offered to them. In the end the Protestant princes decided that the "council convoked by Paul III was not the free Christian council in German lands demanded by the Estates and promised by the Emperor" but a papally dominated assembly that was prepared to condemn Lutheran teachings without a hearing. "How could we feel safe at a council held in Italy," the princes demanded, "where the Pope wields so much power and where our enemies are so many?"[11]

During this period of increased interest in a council, Luther began to read extensively in the history of the early and medieval Church, particularly the *Historia Tripartita* by Cassiodorus Senator, the *Lives of the Popes* by Bartolomeo Platina, the newly published (1538) *Complete Councils* of Peter Crabbe, and the *Ecclesiastical History* of Eusebius of Caesarea together with the supplement to Eusebius which Rufinus composed.[12] Luther wanted to approach the question of Church councils from the perspective of history as well as from the standpoint of theology and exegesis. He wanted to examine concretely how councils in the past had functioned, what authority had been ascribed to them and whether they offered a viable instrument for the further reform and reconstitution of the Church. Because he became skeptical of the reliability of medieval historical sources during the course of his studies, he restricted his analysis to the Council of Jerusalem and the first four ecumenical councils, Nicaea, Constantinople, Ephesus, and Chalcedon.

On the Councils and the Church is divided into three main sections. The first section is largely negative.[13] By the application of a somewhat rough-hewn historical method Luther set out to demonstrate that on many issues the fathers and councils so contradicted themselves that it was impossible to find a doctrinal consensus. Of course, scholastic theologians and canon lawyers had always known that there were tensions and antinomies within the tradition. Late medieval theologians and lawyers attempted programmatically to reconcile and harmonize tensions and contradictions within the theological and legal traditions, confident that in the one Church led by the Holy Spirit into a unified vision of truth all such disagreements must be more apparent than real. Luther argues that this theological confidence is historically unfounded and cites numerous examples of conciliar decrees which are no longer followed in the Roman Church or which were contradicted by later councils. No one would dream of forbidding German Catholics the eating of *Blutwurst* or animals trapped in snares, though the Council of Jerusalem (attended, as Luther gleefully points out, by apostles and not merely by bishops in apostolic succession) forebade the eating of blood and required a limited Kosher observance by Gentile Christians. No Catholic prince (including the late Pope Julius II) would welcome the enforcement of the ancient conciliar restrictions on the participation of Christians in war and no Catholic bishop would think of invoking the opinions of Cyprian on the baptism of heretics or the readmission of apostates to communion. There is no way to harmonize these ancient decrees and opinions with modern theology and practice, to which they stand in absolute contradiction, and all attempts to do so since Gratian and Lombard have only made matters worse.

In the second section Luther attempted to define more narrowly the nature and task of a council.[14] After a lengthy discussion in which he scrutinized the records of the councils of Jerusalem, Nicaea, Constantinople, Ephesus, and Chalcedon, he concluded that a council could not, and had never been expected to, establish new articles of belief beyond the articles contained in Holy Scripture. Councils defend and explain teaching which the prophets and apostles had already articulated. Therefore there is nothing valid in the teaching of a council which is not first and more powerfully stated in Scripture itself. A council, then, "is nothing but a consistory, a royal court, a supreme court or the like, in which the judges, after hearing the parties, pronounce sentence, but with this humility, 'for the sake of the law.'"[15] The law which Luther has in mind is the Bible. The bishops in a council pass judgment on heresy, but only as that heresy can be proven to be heresy out of Holy Scripture. A judgment is not valid merely because it has been made by properly constituted and legally competent persons. However much Luther emphasizes the importance of offices in the Church, he does not simply invest those offices with the charism of truth. The decision of a council is valid not because it has been made by the proper persons under the proper conditions in a duly constituted assembly but because that decision is in harmony with the teaching of Holy Scripture. In that sense the authority of a council does not differ at all from the authority of any capable pastor or teacher. All three are servants of the Word.

The last section of the treatise shifts from the problem of councils and their authority to the larger question of the doctrine of the Church.[16] Because of his doctrine of justification by faith alone and his stress on the invisibility of the Church, Luther had been accused of holding a kind of "Platonic" ecclesiology, an idealized and utopian doctrine of the Church, which has no fixed place in space and time and which lacks the rootedness in this world which marks the corporation of the medieval Catholic Church. This essay focuses on the historical character of the Christian Church as Luther understands it and the visible signs by which it can be recognized. The discussion, therefore, is very practical and down to earth. The Church is an assembly of holy Christian people, holy because their sins have been forgiven and are now being mortified through Christ. Unlike other assemblies gathered for other purposes the Church preaches and hears the Word of God, baptizes, celebrates the eucharist, administers discipline, calls and ordains ministers, prays and bears the cross. While faith is invisible and election is a mystery, the characteristic activities which identify this society are public ceremonies which anyone can attend. The most important mark, however, is possession of the Word of God: "...even if there were no other sign than this alone, it would still suffice to prove that a Christian, holy people must exist there, for God's Word cannot be without God's people, and conversely, God's people cannot be without God's Word."[17]

II.

Unlike Luther, who took up a question that was troubling all of Germany, Calvin was prompted to write by what started out to be a purely local matter. In March, 1539, Jacopo Cardinal Sadoleto, bishop of Carpentras in southern France, sent a letter to Geneva, asking it to return to the Catholic faith. Sadoleto was one of the most illustrious members of the Sacred College of Cardinals, who had served every pope since 1513 in one important office or another, except Pope Hadrian VI. Sadoleto returned to Carpentras from Rome in 1538 at almost the same time that Calvin and Farel had lost a political struggle in Geneva and been expelled from the city by the triumphant party. It seemed an opportune time for the

Catholic Church to attempt to recall Geneva to the ancient faith of its ancestors and Sadoleto was quick to seize it. Whether Sadoleto acted on his own initiative or was commissioned to write by a conference of Catholic bishops in Lyons is unclear. What is clear is that he wrote an eloquent and persuasive appeal for reunion.

Geneva sent a copy of Sadoleto's letter to Bern. After mutual consultations which stretched over several months the city councils of Bern and Geneva finally decided in late July to ask Calvin to draft a response on their behalf. Calvin, however, was living happily in Strassburg, where he was minister to the French refugee congregation. Bern, therefore, sent Simon Sulzer, hat in hand, to Strassburg to ask Calvin to swallow past resentments against Geneva and Bern and to compose the kind of reasoned response which Sadoleto's reasoned and moderate letter deserved. After some hesitation and at the urging of his friends, Calvin agreed.

Calvin begins his *Response to Sadoleto* by making an assertion which is absolutely essential for understanding not only Calvin and the Reformed tradition but Luther as well. Calvin claims to have held both the office of Doctor and of Pastor in the church at Geneva and to have a legitimate Christian calling within the larger Christian community.[18] He did not merely go to Geneva; he was divinely sent. Like Luther who appeals again and again to the office which he holds in the Church as legitimation for his reform activity, Calvin rejects the notion that he is merely exercising his own right of private judgment or pursuing a vocation which has no public authorization. He is an office-bearer in the Church, standing in that valid succession which derives its legitimacy from faithful transmission of the ancient apostolic message. It is the Word which is transmitted which gives validity to the office of Pastor and Teacher, and not the office which gives authority and form to the Word.

Calvin does not accept Sadoleto's point that the Catholic Church was united on the eve of the Reformation, and the Reformation is a disruption of the harmony and peace of the Church.[19] Actually, the Catholic Church was broken when Luther's Reformation began, riven by dissension between pope and council, Franciscans and Dominicans, Scotists and Albertists, scholastics and humanists. Indeed, it was the brokenness of the Church, its loss of that unity in doctrine which the Church of Christ must have, which prompted the Protestant Reformation. Sadoleto is correct to believe that truth is one and that error disrupts unity. His only fault is failing to recognize that the Protestant Reformation, by recovering the true teaching of Scripture, is restoring unity to the badly fragmented Church of the later middle ages.

The charge of theological innovation is also beside the point. A doctrine is an innovation (and therefore a departure from the teaching of the apostles) when it is genuinely new; it is not an innovation simply because it is new to Cardinal Sadoleto. A more accurate reading of Church history must acknowledge that the later medieval Church has introduced doctrines and practices not known to the ancient Church. Hence the attempt of the Protestant reformers to recapture ancient doctrine and discipline is labelled innovation by a Church which has lost contact with its own past and which identifies modern belief and practice with the faith and discipline of the early Church.[20] One searches in vain in the early fathers and councils for the doctrine of transsubstantiation, for the practice of private confession and absolution, for purgatory and the intercession of the saints. In other words, while Sadoleto has appealed to antiquity, that was a formal appeal without theological content. If theologians study the ancient fathers, they will discover that the fathers support the Protestant reformers far oftener than they support Sadoleto. In point of fact the Protestant reformers are attempting to keep faith with the ancient teaching of the apostles as understood by the fathers against the later unwarranted innovations and novelties introduced by the Roman Catholic Church. The papists teach doctrines "sprung from the human brain."[21] They have leaders who neither understand the Word nor care greatly for it. The laity in the old Church venerate the Word but do not read or obey it. This deemphasis on the Word has led to the "supine state of the pastors" and the "stupidity of the people."[22] While Calvin is keen to find support for Protestant teaching in the fathers and early councils, he does not regard them as more than venerable interpreters of Holy Scripture. The Bible is superior to both fathers and councils, though fathers and councils are indispensable aids for the proper understanding of Scripture.

> For although we hold that the Word of God alone lies beyond the sphere of our judgement, and that fathers and councils are of authority only in so far as they accord with the rule of the Word, we still give to councils and fathers such rank and honor as it is meet for them to hold under Christ.[23]

Calvin contrasts the passive implicit faith recommended by Sadoleto with the active spirit of *docilitas* or learning readiness which characterizes true Christian faith. Real humility is submission to the Word of God and not passive submission to every opinion uttered by the Catholic Church or its hierarchy. "Sadoleto," Calvin complains, "you have too indolent a theology . . . all that you leave to the faithful is to shut their own eyes and submit implicitly to their teachers."[24] Implicit faith undercuts the theological responsibility of the people of God, while the active docility which follows conversion prompts men and women to study Holy Scripture in the sphere of the Church and in association with the fathers and councils. The Church has an instrumental authority since "we cannot fly without wings." It leads believers to the sources of truth and life. But the Church is not merely Mother; it is also school. Even simple believers have a theological responsibility which they must assume. Like Clement of Alexandria, Calvin believes that every stage of the Christian life is justified only in so far as one is pressing on, however hesitatingly and ineptly, to the next stage. The faith which justifies is never static.

Vincent of Lérins had argued that Catholic truth is the doctrine taught everywhere [*ubique*], always [*semper*] and by all [*ab omnibus*]. Sadoleto institutionalizes this ancient test of truth and makes it a test of the true Church. While Calvin admires and accepts Sadoleto's use of the Vincentian canon in his definition of the Church, he cannot accept the definition itself. Sadoleto's definition refers to the Church and the Holy Spirit, but omits all reference to the Word by which the Spirit of Christ forms and governs the Church. Yet a Church which is governed by the Spirit without the formative and restraining function of the Word is nothing more than a sect, a charismatic assembly which has lost touch with the historically grounded Word uttered in space and time.[25] The Word preserves the government of the Church from vagueness and instability. Therefore Calvin offers his own corrected definition of the Church modeled on the Vincentian canon:

> Now, if you can bear to receive a truer definition of the Church than your own, say, in future, that it is a society of all the saints, a society which, spread over the whole world, and existing in all ages, and bound together by the one doctrine and the one Spirit of Christ, cultivates and observes unity of faith and brotherly concord. With this Church we deny that we have any disagreement. Nay, rather, as we revere her as our mother, so we desire to remain in her bosom.[26]

Calvin also answers what he regards as Sadoleto's caricature of the evangelical understanding of justification by faith alone.[27] Faith is not mere credulity, not a mere assent of the mind to true doctrine, but a committal of the whole self to God. To be justified by faith means to be united to Christ in a bond of mystical union (Luther had spoken of being baked into one cake with Christ). Naturally anyone so possessing Christ and so possessed by him will perform good works. What is at stake is not the existence of good works but their status. Protestants deny only that these works contribute to justification or form even the partial basis for God's acceptance of the sinner. Good works are not merits in the Catholic sense, but only the fruits of faith.

Calvin ends his treatise with what appears to be an autobiographical confession of faith. He indicates that he was prevented from embracing Protestantism by his reverence for the Church in which he had been raised and only after a long internal struggle did he suddenly embrace the faith which then struck him (as it now strikes Sadoleto) as an innovation.[28] Sadoleto, of course, has recommended against such conversion and assured the Genevans that God would not condemn a man or woman who remained with the Church in which they had been baptized, even though they were convinced that that Church had erred and sinned against its own true nature. The difficulty with Sadoleto's position on conversion is that it could be embraced by Jews, Turks, and Saracens as a justification for their rejection of Christianity.[29] It is the perfect anti-missionary argument. Still in all, Calvin prefers to end on a positive note and concludes his *Reply to Sadoleto* with a prayer for Christian unity.

III.

I observed at the beginning of this paper that Luther and Calvin make a common ecumenical front in 1539 against Rome on the question of the Church and its teaching authority. That is not to say that there are no differences between them. There are certainly differences in style. While Calvin is painfully direct in his criticisms of the old Church and is not above occasional *ad hominem* thrusts at his opponent (particularly if he can disguise them in what appear at first glance to be compliments), he nevertheless maintains a fairly restrained and moderate tone, at least as moderate as the tone of Sadoleto himself. Luther, on the other hand, can never resist for very long the temptation to be a kind of theological Peck's Bad Boy, merrily ripping out the shirttails of his enemies and setting fire to them. Furthermore, while Calvin is content to outline a general theology of history and to avoid the discussion of specific historical cases, Luther builds his argument on the examination of specific historical texts and demonstrates the validity of his position on the basis of concrete examples. But these differences, and others like them, only serve to underscore the similarities in their fundamental argument.

1. *Fathers and councils.* Both Luther and Calvin agree that the authority of fathers and councils is subordinate to the authority of Holy Scripture. Luther takes the negative side of the argument and stresses the contradictions and tensions within the Church's theological traditions,

while Calvin stresses the positive agreement of the best of the fathers with Protestant teaching. The Catholic Church, in other words, appeals to a tradition which is in part contradictory and uncertain (e.g., the Council of Jerusalem on dietary laws or Cyprian on the baptism of heretics) and which in part undercuts the very positions which the Catholic Church seeks to establish (such as the doctrine of transsubstantiation or the discipline of auricular confession). So far from dreading an encounter with the Church's tradition, Luther and Calvin seem to relish the prospect, confident that a fair-minded reading of history will demonstrate the utter necessity of the Protestant appeal to Scripture alone as the authoritative source and norm of Christian doctrine.

2. *Vision of history.* Both Luther and Calvin reject the notion that Protestant reformers are theological innovators who have disrupted a 1500-year-old consensus in Christian doctrine. Innovations have been introduced by the Catholic Church during the Middle Ages which were not found in the earliest Church. The patristic age was more successful than later Christian eras in avoiding the introduction of theological novelties, though even the fathers were not altogether successful in suppressing theological innovation. Nevertheless, those fathers and councils are authoritative which have succeeded best in explaining and defending biblical truth. While Luther seems more skeptical of the value of patristic authors than does Calvin (though they share some of the same likes and dislikes), both agree on the importance of the fathers as exegetical guides to the interpretation of Scripture. What the Protestants are attempting to do is to persuade the Church to abandon its fascination with the theological and disciplinary innovations of the later Middle Ages and to return to Scripture and the fathers, Scripture as the authoritative text and the fathers as helpful interpreters (not infallible but better by far than the scholastics). In short, the Catholic charge of theological innovation has been met by a counter-charge of "tu quoque!" The defenders of the old Church have in the opinion of Luther and Calvin too restricted a vision of Christian history and invest the customs and doctrines of the relatively recent past with the dignity and authority which belongs to the ancient apostolic tradition alone. All with the result that what is truly ancient, such as the Pauline doctrine of justification by faith, seems to them to be a theological novelty.

3. *Office and magisterium.* While both Luther and Calvin agree in stressing the importance of offices in the Church, they also agree in subordinating the authority of the office to its proper functioning in a new and untraditional way. Traditional Catholic teaching had tied the authority of the office bearer to the office itself. A bishop has certain powers granted by God which are inherent in his office. Whether he uses

those powers wisely or abuses them shamelessly, the powers inhere in the office. The same is true of priest or pope or council. Luther and Calvin place authority in the Word of which the pastors, teachers, and councils are servants. That does not mean Luther and Calvin have embraced Donatism. The efficacy of Word and sacrament is not dependent on the personal faith of the minister. But the authority and legitimacy of the pastoral and teaching offices are derived from the Word which is proclaimed and not from the society or corporation which proclaims it.

The Protestants, in other words, are not conciliarists. They do not believe that a council, properly assembled and constituted, will necessarily be led by the Holy Spirit to an infallible definition of the truth. Councils have come to decisions which were nothing more than human, historically conditioned acts. If that is not so, then the Church is obligated to adopt the dietary laws of the Council of Jerusalem. The council is a court required to render judgment on the basis of an authority which is external to its own will and of which it is not the author. It is a useful court but it is not the source of the law by which it judges. Its decisions are authoritative and binding on the Christian community to the extent that they are in agreement with Holy Scripture. To the extent that they are not, they are invalid and bear no authority whatever. The same is true of the decisions of priests, bishops, theologians, and popes.

4. *Exegetical optimism.* Both Luther and Calvin reflect the exegetical optimism which marked early Protestantism. For a brief period of time Protestants thought it would be possible to write a theology which was wholly biblical and which excluded all philosophical and speculative questions. It became clear within a decade that such hope was not well founded. Nevertheless, Protestants remained optimistic about the clarity of Scripture and about the simplicity and persuasive power of the truth which it contained. Protestants were not well prepared for the internal disagreements within Protestantism when the careful exegesis of one group of godly and learned men clashed with the exegesis of another group equally learned and godly. On the whole, Luther and Calvin seem to believe that good exegesis will drive out bad and do not provide a great deal of help in suggesting a practical mechanism for reconciliation of conflicts. All we have in these two documents is the suggestion of Luther that a council can serve as a useful, though not infallible, court of judgment on disputed questions. The later history of Protestantism confirms that Protestants have tended to rely on synods, presbyteries, conferences, councils, and assemblies for the resolution of differences. But Luther and Calvin in these two treatises appear to leave the question hanging. It is the superiority of Scripture to tradition which is on their minds as they face Rome. Luther

and Calvin are confident that in every generation the lively and living Word of God will create communities of obedient hearers and doers of that Word. The unity which the Church seeks beyond all theological and doctrinal strife is the unity which the Word itself creates through the action of the Holy Spirit: "... for God's Word cannot be without God's people, and conversely, God's people cannot be without God's Word." On that point Luther and Calvin make common cause.

Notes

1. Calvin to Viret, 19 May 1540, *C.O.* 11,36 (no. 217).

2. *C.O.* 11, 698 (no. 544); 12, 99 (no. 657).

3. Cf. my article "Scripture and the Lord's Supper in Luther's Theology," *Interpretation,* 37 (July, 1983), 253-265.

4. Brian A. Gerrish, "The Pathfinder: Calvin's Image of Martin Luther," in *The Old Protestantism and the New: Essays on the Reformation Heritage* (Chicago: University of Chicago Press, 1982), pp. 27-48.

5. *C.O.* 9, 19, 91; 15, 336; 16, 263, 430; 17, 139; 18, 583-584, 733.

6. *C.O.* 11, 774-775 (no. 586).

7. *WABr* 8, 569, 29 (no. 3349).

8. *C.O.* 10.2, 432 (no. 197).

9. The Latin text is found in *O.S.* I, 437-489. References in this lecture are to the easily accessible English translation by John C. Olin in *John Calvin and Jacopo Sadoleto: A Reformation Debate* (New York: Harper Torchbooks, 1966), pp. 49-94.

10. *WA* 50, 501ff. References in this paper are to the English translation in Theodore G. Tappert, ed., *Selected Writings of Martin Luther,* vol. IV (Philadelphia: Fortress Press, 1967), pp. 197-370.

11. *C.T.,* vol. IV, pp. 73-78.

12. For a discussion of this writing in the broader context of the polemics of the older Luther see Mark U. Edwards, Jr., *Luther's Last Battles: Politics and Polemics 1531-46* (Ithaca and London: Cornell University Press, 1983), pp. 93-96.

13. "Councils," pp. 201-245.

14. "Councils," pp. 245-334.

15. "Councils," p. 325.

16. "Councils," pp. 335-370.

17. "Councils," p. 342.

18. "Reply," p. 50.

19. "Reply," p. 93.

20. "Reply," p. 62.

21. "Reply," p. 82.

22. "Reply," p. 82.

23. "Reply," p. 92.

24. "Reply," pp. 77-78.
25. "Reply," p. 61.
26. "Reply," pp. 61-62.
27. "Reply," pp. 66-69.
28. "Reply," pp. 88-90.
29. "Reply," p. 90.

MARTIN LUTHER AND THE ENGLISH BIBLE: TYNDALE AND COVERDALE

Heinz Bluhm, *Boston College*

Martin Luther was a man of many faces and many accomplishments. His versatility was boundless and his energy inexhaustible. While he surely did not create the modern German language, he enriched and endowed it more impressively and shaped it more significantly than any other author, whether of his time, before his time, or perhaps even after his time.

Among Luther's numerous achievements in the field of action and in the realm of thought, his work as a translator occupies a place of honor. His magnificent German Bible is one of the great translations of the Western world. Considered solely as a literary production, Luther's Bible can be compared in power and influence only to the Vulgate and the Authorized Version. So far as their effect on their national literatures is concerned, the German and English Bibles are in a class by themselves. Indeed both these great Bibles helped to fashion their respective languages and literatures. Both have taught style as well as substance to generations of writers. Both are integral parts of their national literatures. The Authorized Version along with Shakespeare, Luther's Bible along with Goethe are still towering peaks in these two important languages of the West.

Let us look at both national Bibles more closely. Both somehow transcend what is ordinarily meant by the term translation. They have the stature of primary works of literature. They lead lives of their own. They enjoy an existence apart from the originals of which they are ultimately but versions in another, a modern, tongue. Both the German and the English Bible are products of the Reformation, and both have deep roots in the Renaissance and Humanism. Of the two, the German Bible is the senior version, since it was begun earlier and completed earlier than the English Bible. If one influenced the other, it was surely a one-way affair.

Roughly speaking, the German Bible came into being in the course of a quarter of a century. It was undertaken late in 1521 and worked on till early in 1546. I do not say it was finished because Luther, tireless reviser that he was, would have continued revising if he had lived longer. Only death terminated the evolution of Luther's Bible. Besides the initial year of 1521 and the final year of 1546, six other dates are of primary importance: 1522, 1530, 1531, 1534, 1541, 1545. In 1522, the first and second editions of the New Testament appeared, the so-called *Septembertestament* and *Dezembertestament,* the former being the first Greek-based New Testament in any European language. In 1530 the most important revision of the New Testament was published. In 1531 came the great revision of the German Psalter, a rendering virtually unique among European vernacular Bibles. The year 1534 saw the first complete edition of the whole Bible, to be followed in 1541 and 1545 by further major revisions. Thus it took thirteen years to produce the German Bible in its entirety, and another eleven or twelve years of ceaseless improvement to bring it to its final literary perfection.

The Authorized Version has a longer history, more than three times as long as that of the Luther Bible. This history began in 1526 and ended in 1611. (I ignore the Wiclif Bible because it is based on the Vulgate, and hence is a translation of a translation rather than a translation from the original Hebrew and Greek. For the same reason I have ignored the eighteen pre-Lutheran High and Low German Bibles.)

Differently from the German Bible, the English Bible is the work not of one man but of a number of men. The German Bible is still truly "die Lutherbibel," Luther's Bible, even after a number of uneasy attempts at revision in the 19th and 20th centuries. The English Bible, on the other hand, has several fathers. Its chief creator, at least for the New Testament, was William Tyndale. Of the other men who helped shape it, Miles Coverdale is one of the most important: His Psalter, though not included in the Authorized Version, still survives in the Book of Common Prayer. Tyndale gave us the first printed New Testament in English in 1526, Coverdale the first printed complete Bible in English in 1535. Among the men who formed the intermediate English Bibles—those between Coverdale and the Authorized Version—as well as among the men who produced the final document of 1611, there were writers of superior linguistic ability.

It is quite clear that Luther came first and literally stole the show with the publication of his German New Testament in 1522. This was an event of European significance. On the Continent the *Septembertestament* quickly established itself as the source of all Protestant versions in the Germanic languages. In some cases it was Luther's New Testament rather than the Greek original that formed the primary basis of later Germanic renderings. Recently it has been claimed that even some Bibles in the Romance languages were influenced by Luther. For Tyndale no claim of far-reaching influence can be made: His authority did not extend beyond the English shores. Tyndale was clearly indebted to Luther, but he was not in bondage to him. Tyndale knew Greek himself and in all likelihood translated from the original. It is only natural that he should have consulted Luther's version. By 1524, when it is believed that Tyndale went to Wittenberg to meet Luther and Melanchthon, Luther was an international figure both as a religious leader and as a translator. It would have been just as unthinkable for Tyndale to proceed without consulting Luther's Bible as for Luther, several years earlier, to have proceeded without looking at Erasmus' new Latin translation, published as part of his edition of the Greek New Testament. Erasmus and Luther were international figures. A scholarly translator in the early decades of the sixteenth century could not and did not ignore Erasmus and Luther.

It has been convincingly shown that Tyndale used Luther's introductory material, his marginal notes, and his arrangement of the individual books of the New Testament. Thus Tyndale was under the general influence of the Wittenberg master.

There are also in Tyndale specific borrowings from Luther, some literary and others doctrinal. These, however, reveal themselves only on close study of the text. This is slow, painstaking, often exasperating work, to be done phrase by phrase, even word by word. Tyndale was a very able writer in his own right. It was not necessary for him to copy out Luther. He could render the Greek on his own.

To summarize: Tyndale apparently approved of the general tenor and spirit of Luther's version. He followed Luther's method, which was to translate clearly and idiomatically. In addition to this basic procedure, there are a number of instances of specific Lutheran influence. I have selected a few of these for presentation here.

Ephesians 4, 18

One of Luther's favorite literary devices was the resolution of a nominal genitive into a relative clause. A literal translation of the Greek would be "alienated from the life of God." In Erasmus' editions of the Greek text these words read as follows:

ἀπηλλοτριωμένοι τῆς ζωῆς τοῦ θεοῦ

Erasmus translated this literally into Latin, retaining the nominal genitive: "abalienati a vita dei."

We find a similarly literal translation in the Vulgate: "alienati a vita Dei."

Luther introduced a basic change. He converted the nominal genitive τοῦ θεοῦ into a relative clause, "das aus got ist." The whole phrase now reads: "entfrembdet von dem leben das aus got ist."

Tyndale follows Luther in converting the genitive τοῦ θεοῦ into a relative clause: "straungers from the lyfe which is in god."

Ephesians 4, 24

A similar literary device was the resolution of a nominal genitive into an adjective. A literal translation of the Greek would be: "The new man [is] created in righteousness and holiness of truth."

It is the last three words that are of interest here: "holiness of truth," reading in Erasmus' editions of the Greek text as follows:

ἐν ... ὁσιότητι τῆς ἀληθείας

Erasmus rendered it literally in Latin, keeping the nominal genitive construction: "per sanctitatem veritatis."

The Vulgate also translated the phrase literally: "in sanctitate veritatis."

Luther was the first to make a basic change. He converted the nominal genitive ἀληθείας into an adjective, "rechtschaffener," the whole phrase reading "ynn rechtschaffener heylickeyt."

Tyndale followed Luther precisely: "in true holynes."

Ephesians 5, 2

The same device as in Ephesians 4, 24 is employed in this verse. A literal translation of the Greek would be: "[Christ] gave himself up for us ... a sacrifice to God for an odor of sweet smell."

Again it is the final words that are of interest to us: "an odor of sweet smell," reading in Erasmus' edition of the Greek text:

εἰς ὀσμὴν εὐωδίας

Erasmus translated this exactly into Latin as "in odorem bonae fragrantiae." The Vulgate translated it less exactly as "in odorem suavitatis."

Luther again changed the nominal genitive εὐωδίας to an adjective "sussen," translating as follows: "zu eynem sussen geruch."

Tyndale once again followed Luther precisely: "of a swete saver."

If Tyndale was considerably influenced by Luther, Miles Coverdale, the creator of the first printed full Bible in English, was even more under his sway. In Tyndale it is mainly the general tenor rather than specific individual phrases that show the debt to Luther; Coverdale, in addition to subscribing to the principles underlying the German Bible, has a very large number of definitely Lutheran formulations. He himself indicated as much when he said on the original title-page of the first edition of 1535 that his version was "faithfully and truly translated out of Douche and Latyn." Though it has long been believed that the Zürich Bible was the German source referred to by Coverdale, I have been able to show that the primary source is Luther, since the Zürich Bible of 1524-29 is in many parts just a reprint of the Luther Bible.

In the three passages we have just discussed, Coverdale follows Tyndale. This is tantamount to saying that Coverdale agrees with Luther. I should like now to present to you a few passages in which Coverdale follows Luther even more closely than he follows Tyndale. In view of the decisive role that Paul's Epistle to the Romans played in Reformation thinking. I have selected passages from this famous epistle. Again, a very few examples must suffice.

Romans 1, 17

"The righteousness of God."

Erasmus' Greek

δικαιοσύνη ... θεοῦ

Erasmus' Latin

Iusticia ... dei ...

Vulgate

Iustitia ... dei ...

Luther

... die gerechtickeyt die fur got gillt

Tyndale

...the rightewesnes which commeth of God...

Coverdale

...ẙ righteousness that is of value before God...

Both. Tyndale and Coverdale have adopted Luther's idea of "iustitia passiva," 'passive justice.' Tyndale expresses it in his own words; Coverdale adheres more closely to Luther's extraordinary rendering of this crucial passage. It would seem that the full meaning of Luther comes across better in Coverdale than in Tyndale, who, while accepting Luther in principle, worded the idea somewhat less sharply than Coverdale.

Romans 3, 20

"For by the law is the knowledge of sin."

Erasmus' Greek

διὰ γὰρ νόμου ἐπίγνωσις ἁμαρτίας

Erasmus' Latin

Per legem enim agnitio peccati

Vulgate

per legem enim cognitio peccati.

Luther

Denn durch das gesetz, kompt nur erkentnis der sund.

Tyndale

For by the lawe commeth the knowledge off synne.

Coverdale

For by the lawe commeth but the knowlege of synne.

This is really an exciting verse in the two earliest renderings of the English Bible. Both Tyndale and Coverdale used the verb "commeth" as inserted by Luther in his German text. However, Tyndale did not add Luther's controversial "nur." Coverdale, a more thoroughgoing Lutheran, took over Luther's "nur" as "but" (in the sense of "only").

Romans 3, 28

"Therefore we conclude that a man is justified by faith without the deeds of the law."

Erasmus' Greek[1]

λογιζόμεθα οὖν πίστει δικαιοῦσθαι ἄνθρωπον
χωρὶς ἔργων νόμου

Erasmus' Latin

Arbitramur igitur fide iustificari hominem absque operibus legis.

Vulgate

arbitramur enim iustificari hominem per fidem sine operibus legis.

Luther 1522[1]-27[2]

So halten wyrs nu, das der mensch gerechtfertiget werde, on zuthun der werck des gesetzs, alleyn durch den glawben.

Luther 1530[1]-46

...gerecht..., on des gesetzs werck...

Tyndale

We suppose therfore [1534 For we suppose] that a man is iustified by fayth without the dedes of the lawe.

In the edition of 1534 there is a significant marginal note: "Fayth iustifieth."

Coverdale

We holde therfore that a man is justified by faith, without the workes of the lawe.

He has an even more important marginal note to this verse: "Some reade: 'By faith onely.'"

This is doubtless the most famous passage in Luther's translation of Romans, even of the entire New Testament. Neither Tyndale nor Coverdale chose, or dared, to go all the way with Luther's bold addition of "alleyn."[2] Yet each came to terms with it in a marginal note. Tyndale felt induced to state: "Fayth iustifieth." Coverdale was courageous enough to use the full Lutheran "By faith onely." However, he did not see fit to mention Luther's name. Instead he merely wrote "Some reade." The use of the plural could perhaps be explained by the fact that the edition of the Zürich Bible published from 1524 to 1529 had followed Luther in printing "allein durch den glouben." But neither Luther nor Zürich was named by Coverdale; it was probably too dangerous to do so at the time. One is reminded that the title-page of Coverdale's Bible similarly refrains from giving personal credit to Luther or to the Zürich translation but settles for the impersonal "done out of the Douche."

Romans, 4, 6

". . . the blessedness of the man, unto whom God imputeth righteousness without works"

Erasmus' Greek

τὸν μακαρισμὸν τοῦ ἀνθρώπου ᾧ ὁ
θεὸς λογίζεται δικαιοσύνην χωρὶς ἔργων.

Erasmus' Latin

beatificationem hominis, cui Deus imputat iusticiam absque operibus

Vulgate

beatitudinem hominis cui Deus accepto fert iustitiam sine operibus

Luther

... die selickeyt sey alleyn des menschen, wilchem gott zurechnet die gerechtickeyt, on zuthun der werck ...

Tyndale

the blessedfulness of the man vnto whom god ascrybeth rightewesnes without dedes.

Coverdale

... blessedness is onely that mans, vnto whom God counteth righteousnes without addinge to of workes....

Tyndale's version can be explained on the basis of Erasmus' Greek and Latin. Coverdale's, on the other hand, is in total agreement with Luther's free translation of the Greek. Coverdale's "onely" and his "without addinge to of workes" are fully explicable only on the basis of Luther's "alleyn" and "on zuthun der werck."

It will be noted that in this passage there is no influence of Luther on Tyndale, but only of Luther on Coverdale.

Romans 5, 13

"... But sin is not imputed when there is no law."

Erasmus' Greek

ἁμαρτία δὲ οὐκ ελλογεῖται, μὴ ὄντος νόμου

Erasmus' Latin

porro peccatum non imputatur, cum non est lex.

Vulgate

peccatum autem non imputatur cum lex non est.

Luther

aber wo keyn gesetz ist, do acht man der sund nicht.

Tyndale

but synne was not regarded, as longe as ther was no lawe:

Coverdale

but where no lawe is, there is no synne regarded.

Erasmus' Latin version is literal, the Vulgate nearly so. Tyndale's is freer, especially in that he replaces the present tense by the past in both clauses. Luther's version is freer still, actually reversing the order of the two clauses. It is manifest that Coverdale followed Luther completely.

Romans 7, 5

"... the motions of sins, which were by the lawe, did work ...

Erasmus' Greek

τὰ παθήματα τῶν ἁμαρτιῶν τὰ διὰ τοῦ νόμου ἐνηργεῖτο

Erasmus' Latin

affectus peccatorum, qui sunt per legem, vigebant

Vulgate

passiones peccatorum quae per legem erant operabuntur

Luther 1522[1]-1527[2]

da waren die sundlichen luste (wilche durchs gesetz sich erregeten) gewaltig

Luther 1530[1]-46

gewaltig was replaced by *krefftig*

Tyndale

the lustes of synne which were stered vppe by the lawe, raygned

Coverdale

the synfull lustes (which were stered vp by the lawe) were mightie

Tyndale's version is indebted to Luther for the verb "stered vppe," which does not occur in the Greek text at all; the Latin versions supply merely the copula "sunt." Coverdale retained Tyndale's verb and took over Luther's adjective—for—nominal—genitive construction "die sundlichen luste" as "the synfull lustes." He also adopted Luther's *gewaltig* (or *krefftig*): *mightie.*

There are several other striking examples in Romans of Tyndale's and especially of Coverdale's indebtedness to Luther, with similar interesting divergences between Tyndale and Coverdale. A full discussion of these is to be found in my forthcoming book, *Luther, Translator of Paul.*

One can see how much more heavily Coverdale depended on Luther than Tyndale did when one examines a particular book of the New Testament, such as Galatians. There are twenty-nine passages in Tyndale's translation for Galatians that are clearly traceable to Luther. All of these twenty-nine Lutheran formulations were, without exception, retained by Coverdale in 1535. In addition to these passages that Tyndale and Coverdale have in common, there are as many as 113 passages in which Coverdale, on his own initiative, followed Luther directly, independently of Tyndale.

Next I should like to consider a passage in Coverdale's translation for which he could not have relied upon Tyndale, for the simple reason that Tyndale did not translate that part of the Bible in which it occurs, namely, the Psalms. This passage is the second verse of the famous Twenty-Third Psalm. It reads as follows in English: "He maketh me to lie down in green pastures; he leadeth me beside the still waters."

Vulgate

In loco pascuae ibi me conlocavit super aquam refectionis educavit me

Luther 1524

Er lesst mich weyden da viel grass stett / vnd furt mich zum wasser das mich erkulet.

This, Luther's first rendering, in the Psalter of 1524, was retained in the important revision of 1528.

Luther 1531

Er weydet mich auff einer grunen awen / vnd füret mich zum frisschen wasser.

This remarkable new rendering, from the great revision of the Psalms of 1531, was taken over by Coverdale almost verbatim:

Coverdale

He fedeth me in a grene pasture, and ledeth me to a fresh water.

There can be no other source than Luther for this creative translation. The Zürich Bible of 1531 reads quite differently:

[Zürich 1531]

Er macht mich in schöner weyd lüyen. vnd fürt mich zu stillen wassern.

When one examines the whole psalm closely, one realizes that Coverdale's chief source was Luther's Psalter of 1531. Inasmuch as Coverdale's Bible did not appear till 1535, it is alternatively possible that he used Luther's first complete Bible of 1534, which contained the 1531 revised version of the Psalter. Whichever edition he did use, it was the work of Luther that provided the basis of Coverdale's rendering.

Conclusion

We have traversed a difficult route, the road from Luther's German Bible to the first two English Bibles—Tyndale's New Testament and Coverdale's whole Bible. The relationship among them is complex.

Tyndale was a Greek scholar in his own right and translated primarily on the basis of Erasmus' Greek New Testament, probably in its third edition of 1522. But he also had Luther's German New Testament in front of him, the first translation of the New Testament into any European vernacular, done out of the original language and enjoying a high reputation immediately upon its publication in September 1522. Tyndale was so impressed with Luther's theology and the quality of the prefaces and marginal notes in his translation that he printed them practically verbatim in his own New Testament in English. Beyond this *prima facie* evidence of dependence on Luther, he followed the latter in striving for a clear and idiomatic rendering, and in using some of Luther's favorite literary and stylistic devices. Impressed by Luther's religious thought, he actually rendered fundamental Lutheran concepts in Lutheran terms: He wrote "the rightewesnes that commeth of God" instead of the literal *iustitia dei,* and "congregacion" instead of *ecclesia.*

As for Coverdale, he knew no Greek and was therefore limited to English, German, and Latin for the sources of his own translation. His chief source for the New Testament was Tyndale. Whenever—and this was often enough—he parted company with Tyndale he followed Luther in spirit and in word. It has been asserted that he used the Zürich Bible rather than Luther. However, since the Zürich Bible as published from 1524 to 1529 is identical with Luther so far as the New Testament is concerned, it is ultimately Luther that he too followed. In those verses in which Coverdale used a Lutheran rendering originating in or after the great revision of 1530 and thus not found in the Zürich Bible of 1524 to 1529, it is obviously and incontrovertibly 1531 or post-1531 Lutheran versions that he followed. Coverdale, a more thoroughgoing Lutheran than Tyndale, is also a more faithful if less imaginative user of Luther's translation.

Tyndale and Coverdale, two of the principal shapers of the Authorized Version, have emerged as skillful translators in the wake of Luther's epoch-making and pace-setting German Bible. There own considerable mastery of the English language helped them immeasurably in their achievement of translations of the Bible into unforgettable English.

Luther, Tyndale, Coverdale: creator and imitators. Perhaps it is fairer to say emulators than imitators, though in different degrees, Tyndale being primarily an emulator and Coverdale rather more an imitator. There can, however, be no doubt about Luther's place in this triumvirate: He is the creative genius, the creator of the German Bible—the translation justly known and still designated as "die Lutherbibel," despite repeated attempts to modernize it. Whatever the general reading public may do, however many copies of "Die gute Nachricht" it may buy and even read, for liturgical use and, above all, for literary and scholarly study the Luther Bible is and remains, in Thucydidean terms, a κτῆμα ἐρ ἀεί, a possession for ever, an inexhaustible treasure. If it should ever be forgotten, an important part of the civilization of the West will have disappeared. Though this seems unthinkable for some of us, it may happen. The signs of the times point in that direction. It is the duty and high privilege of scholars to stem the tide of regressive ignorance and advancing ahistoricism that is inundating our intellectual and spiritual universe.

Notes

1. Erasmus has οὖν for γὰρ and Πίστει δικαιοῦσθαι for δικαιοῦσθαι Πίστει.
2. For a fuller discussion of Luther's *alleyn* see my *Martin Luther, Creative Translator*, pp. 125-137.

THE LITERARY IMPACT
LUTHER IN GERMAN LITERATURE

MARTIN LUTHER AND HANS SACHS

Eli Sobel, *University of California at Los Angeles*

Hans Sachs was born in Nürnberg on 5 November 1494, the son of a master tailor. In 1501 he began attendance at a Latin school and stayed until 1508. Those seven years equal his total formal education. In 1509 he was apprenticed as a shoemaker and at about the same time he was introduced to the versifying art of Meistergesang by Lienhard Nunnenbeck, a Meister of the Nürnberg Singschule. At age 17, Sachs began his journeyman years during which he travelled to Austria, Bavaria, the Rhineland, the Netherlands and most of central Germany. Having passed his Meisterschuhmacher examinations, in 1519, he settled back in Nürnberg with his own shop, married and fathered seven children by his first wife, who died in 1560. At age 68 he married a 27-year-old widow who was his only survivor at his death at age 82, in 1576.[1] If these facts were all, his life would read like that of a typical bourgeois, independent craftsman who happened to live his adult life in the age of the Reformation, in the era of the upheavals that nominally have their beginnings with the posting of the ninety-five theses by Martin Luther.[2]

Sachs, however, was also a prolific poet, polemicist and dramatist. His writings and literary interests began early—long before he had ever heard of Martin Luther—and reveal him as a deeply religious and observant Christian. In 1517-18, he completed his first great manuscript, a huge anthology of Meisterlieder: 398 poems on 459 leaves. Included were forty of his own Meisterlieder.[3] He had already, prior to 1518, published several Fastnachtspiele [Shrovetide plays] and numerous Spruchgedichte [gnomic or didactic poems]. In sum, and accepting the figures of his own *Summa* poem of 1566, by that year he had produced over 6250 pieces: 4275 Meisterlieder; over 1700 works in rhymed couplets; 208 Spiele (various drama- or play-form renderings); 73 spiritual songs; and only six surviving prose dialogues, the first four of which were all published in 1524, and were of major importance to the Lutheran movement. Even if all aesthetic considerations are disregarded, the literary legacy of Sachs is nevertheless of considerable importance for an understanding of the age of the

Reformation: the several items Sachs published in the period 1523-27 (and some later ones) are of special significance to the course of the Reformation in his native Nürnberg and in Germany. This is so even though one may not ordinarily think to class Sachs with the leading scholars, with such as Philip Melanchthon, Johannes Cochlaeus, Erasmus or Willibald Pirckheimer. Sachs was talented, an avid reader and, for a shoemaker, a rather notable collector of books and ideas—including the Greek and Roman classics and Italian renaissance writers, even though in translation.[4]

Sachs knew the Bible and studied it closely. His very first poems (1514-15) are Bible-text based. In 1520 Sachs had begun to collect Luther's and Lutheran works. By 1522 Sachs owned, and surely had studied, forty such publications. Then, in a Spruchdichtung, dated 8 July 1523, in the Sachs manuscript, there appeared in print Sachs's *Die Wittenbergisch Nachtigall/ die man yetzt höret vberall.*[5] The first edition includes a prose preface which was the first printed evidence of Sachs's prose style and language. The brief prose superscription to the work clearly indicates his purpose in the long poem (700 lines) to follow: it is addressed to all lovers of evangelical truth... wishing God's grace and joy in Christ Jesus. The 90-line prose preface is complete with marginal glosses, New Testament references. In the preface Sachs relates the way in which the community of Christ had for long stood under the yoke of the papacy and the love of neighbor had been lost. But then Dr. Luther began to write, and Luther was not to be refuted!

The *Wittenbergisch Nachtigall* poem was an immediate success. The opening lines were much cited, particularly those that derive from one of medieval Germany's much-favored genres, the dawn-song—the Tagelied or Wächterlied, with the cry of the watchman:

> Wach auf, es nahent gen den Tag
> Ich hör singen im grünen hag [meadow]
> Ein wunnigliche [blissful] nachtigall.

In brief, the first 100 lines introduce the allegory: the sheep are lured from their shepherd by the false light of the moon and leave their meadow, following the voice of a lion. This leads them into an arid place where they have only weeds and thistles to graze on. In addition, the sheep were trapped and became the prey of the lion, along with snakes and wolves who aided the lion. The lion, however, begins to loathe the nightingale's dawn-song for it announces the end of the lion's authority. But he cannot silence the bird, nor can the creatures in his service do so—the swine, goat, cat, snake, others. None can silence the nightingale, and many sheep return to their meadow and shepherd even though the wolves continue to try to force them to dismiss from their minds the previous events of the moonlight hours.

Sachs, having told his animal fable, then begins his explanation: the nightingale is Dr. Luther who led the sheep away from the seducing moonlight that stands for the teaching of the sophists. The lion is Pope Leo X, the desert in which the sheep are trapped is the clerical horde, the Roman church. The thorns and thistles are the Church liturgy, and the nets and traps that hold the sheep are the decretals, the canon regulations through which fasts, confession, celibacy and other rules were introduced. The wolves are the army of priests who do all for money; the snakes are the monks and nuns who sell their supposed good works to the laity. In sum, all the practices of the Church that deal with good works are denigrated, held to have no basis in the Gospels. This is Sachs's main point of attack and his chief support of the new doctrine—justification and salvation by faith alone; blessedness comes through faith in Christ.

Then follows a narration of the historical course of the Reformation up to the date of Sachs's composition, and his explanation of the animals named in the opening portion; it is no longer fable or allegory as Sachs writes: "das wilde schweyn deut Doctor Ecken" "Der Bock deuttet den Emser" "So bedeuttet die Katz den Murner" "Der Waldesel den Barfusser [Franciscan] zu Leipzig" "So deut der Schneck den Cocleum." These five Sachs singles out, with appropriate scornful descriptions of their activities, because they had written against Luther. But Sachs, master poet and now polemicist, has not finished with the animal figures he had introduced: the frogs are the higher schools whose scholastic erudition is now threatened; the wild geese are the conservative laity who wish to hold on to their inherited faith because it was good for so long and they therefore delay their judgment on whether it will still longer suffice.

This gives Sachs the theme for the closing portion of the poem: now that the truth has come to light, nothing of the old forms and customs will help. The bishops and certain worldly persons will try to exterminate the new teaching, but they are the servants of the Antichrist. Christ had prophesied their attacks, and the end of the Antichrist had long been announced in the Revelation of John. Babylon is now ripe for destruction because of the sins of its people; Babylon is Rome! Christians, return to Christ the Shepherd; let Christ be your comfort and consolation. Sachs's marginal glosses to the poem include, this time, not only biblical references but also quite specific historical data, references to diets, edicts, events pertinent to the Lutheran controversy and the publications of importance to his position—a remarkable display of erudition and wide reading by a shoemaker.

The published poem, with its woodcut title illustration of a nightingale safe in a tree surrounded by the animals, achieved seven editions within the year it appeared: four in Nürnberg, two in Zwickau and one in Eilenburg. The publication of the *Wittenbergisch Nachtigall* marked an end to the only sizable hiatus in Sachs's writing career—from 1520 to 1523. That he had three seemingly fallow years may be explained in several ways: he was newly-wed, in 1519, and as a good Bürger and husband he was busy with household and domestic concerns. Also, he had acquired forty of Luther's own and other Lutheran publications. According to Sachs's own inventory of his books, he also owned a pre-Luther New Testament, as well as the "Bibel, der erste Teil und der zweite Teil. Wittenberger Druck." He certainly had enough to read and study over two years. With the poem of 1523, Sachs, by his poetic support of the Reformation, became a notable figure—and not only in his native Nürnberg. Henceforth Sachs's coinage for Luther as the nightingale of Wittenberg was an adman's dream, a press agent's victory.

But, also in 1523, Sachs had composed a Meisterlied, practically unknown and available only in manuscript until 1941, titled "Die Nachtigal."[6] It is set metrically in Sachs's own *Meisterton*, the "Morgenweis," and consists of three *Gesätze* (tri-partite stanzas) of 27 lines each: a total of 81 lines, and greatly contrasting in size with the 700 lines of the published Spruchdichtung. Obviously, just as Sachs's enthusiasm for the new evangelical teachings had been growing, he wished to share this growth with others. But the publication of Meisterlieder was forbidden by the *Schule* rules and the "Nachtigal" Meisterlied was, therefore, available only to members of the Singschule and in manuscript form. The 700-line printed version of course allowed for expansions of many kinds: the addition of biblical citations, the political and historical glosses, eloquent and colorful interpretations.

Incidentally, the Meisterlied should not be titled "Das Walt Gott," an error in recent editions that, alas, may be perpetuated. It is true that those words appear *above* the Meisterlied, but they are only the pious ejaculation of Sachs as he begins work on a new, blank volume to be initiated into his personal collection [Mg 2]. In every one of Sachs's Meisterlied manuscripts, the *first* line in each poem heading invariably announces the *Ton* or *Weise;* this one being:

In der Morgenweis Hans Sachsen

then, without exception, follows the poem title, this one being:

Die nachtigal.

The word Wittenberg occurs only in lines 6-9 of the second *Gesätz,* when Sachs writes that the nightingale is he who sings out the coming of a new day, Dr. Martin Luther of Wittenberg.

The idea of the "singer of the night" has a long literary history from the classical world. The nightingale, in Greek legend, is the metamorphosed Procne bewailing the son she killed, and its song was so greatly admired that it became a symbol for singers and poets, along with the idea that the nightingale would rather die than stop singing.

Sachs, encouraged by the enthusiasm that greeted his *Wittenbergisch Nachtigal* and having developed a following of readers, now turned to a new, for him, literary form, the prose dialogue. In his lifetime he was to produce only seven such works.[7] The first four (all published in 1524) are the ones that concern Luther, the evangelical movement and the course of the Reformation in Germany. Their literary value is of no great consequence. They are valuable as demonstration of what Sachs considered the essentials of Luther's teachings. That they are in the vernacular immediately sets them apart from the Latin humanistic dialogues of the religious battles. In brief, the first two of the Sachs dialogues are polemics against the practices of the Roman church and Sachs's defense of the new faith. In the third dialogue, the *Schuster* becomes truly a "bible thumper." He criticizes certain Lutherans and their Christian attitudes. The fourth dialogue is Sachs's attack against Lutheran zealots. He wants all Lutheran followers to teach their opponents, the Roman church adherents, by their own Christian behavior; evangelicals must not harden others by their fanaticism and thus foster anti-Lutheranism and attacks on the evangelicals.

The first dialogue, in short title, is a "Disputation zwischen einem Chorherrn und Schumacher," that consists of 12 leaves, quarto, with title-page woodcut beneath which are quoted the lines of Luke 19, 40: "I tell you that, if these should hold their peace, the stones would immediately cry out." This first dialogue even achieved Dutch and English translations in the sixteenth century. The English version of 1547 is by Anthony Scoloker of Ipswich, *A goodly dysputacion betwene a Cristen Shoemaker and a Popysshe Parson, with two other parsons more, done within the famous citie of Norembourgh.* There is evidence, in addition, that an earlier English edition existed, for in the Index of Prohibited Books prepared by the Bishop of London under Henry VIII, dated July 7, 1546, there appears the entry: *A Godly disputation betwene a Chrysten Shoemaker and a popish persone.*[8]

Sachs's first dialogue was an obvious best-seller in Germany: eleven editions appeared in 1524, one of them in Low German. The bourgeois *Schuster,* the lay-person who is told by the *Chorherr* to stick to his trade, ably—even brilliantly—defends his position. His telling argument, in sum, is that the clerics who place the writings of the scholastics, canon law and papal decretals above all, and who do not know the Bible, the evangelical message, are not qualified to teach the gospel to the laity. The Roman clerics, in their blindness, do the opposite to what the Bible teaches and thus it becomes the duty of the laity to teach themselves from the holy scriptures, uncontaminated by the Roman clerics.

The thrust of the dialogue is perhaps best illustrated by an exchange early in the piece when the canon relates that he has just returned from his country house where he fed his nightingale who in this season was not singing. The *Schuster* says: "Ich weiß ein schumacher der hat ein Nachtigal, die hat erst angefangen zu singen." The canon replies: "Ey, der Teufel holl den schuster mitsampt seiner Nachtigall! Wie hat er den aller heyligsten Vater, den Bapst, die heiligen väter vnnd *vns* wirdige herren ausgeholhipt [maligned] wie ein holhyp bub [baker's apprentice]." When the canon is asked if he has a copy of the Bible, the canon tells his cook to fetch the "große alte Buch" and she brings him the decretals, then, after correction, the Bible—after she has first wiped the dust from it! When the Schuster refers the canon to a particular text, the canon retorts that the Schuster should look it up himself for he, the canon, knows much more useful things to read. The satiric treatment, the telling thusts, undoubtedly had great popular appeal.

The second dialogue, in short titled, "Ein Gesprech von den Scheinwercken der Geistlichen," consists of 8 to 10 leaves (in variant editions), quarto, with title-page woodcut and beneath it lines from II Timothy, 3, 9: "for their folly shall be manifest unto all men." This dialogue was also greatly popular, and achieved eight editions in 1524, and one, with greatly expanded title, over a century later, in 1629. The woodcut of the 1524 editions shows two men, Peter and Hans, sitting at a table. Entering through a door and approaching the seated men are two mendicant monks.

The dialogue is basically concerned with the monastic vows of poverty, chastity and obedience. When the monk says he hopes to obtain salvation through leading the monastic life, Hans confronts him with the emphasis on faith and advises the monk to leave the monastery. Hans keeps describing the uselessness of the monk's calling and reminds the monk of the consoling promises made by Christ. At the conclusion, Peter gives the monk a gift of two candles with the reservation that they not be used to read Scotus and Bonaventura but rather to read the Bible—and the monk agrees. Sachs's main thrust is that the monastic vows are not biblically derived. While the first dialogue attacked unworthy priests and their dogma, the second is directed against the *ecclesia militans,* the monastic orders, the main supporting agencies of the spiritual power of Rome. The old monk, although not prepared to give up his monastic life, even though he is prepared to acknowledge the errors of monastic individuals, agrees to think seriously about leaving his order. This, of course, involves the social aspects for him and illustrates how seriously Sachs, a good shoemaker, considered the sociological effects of the Reformation and the new teachings as a new way of life for those many in the Church.

The dialogue imparts a certain fairness to both sides, and also perhaps prefigures the thrusts of dialogues 3 and 4 that were to appear later, but within the same year, 1524. In the opening lines of the second dialogue the monk says: "Ich hör wol ir seyt Lutherisch." Peter, who is sitting with Hans, replies: "Nain, sonder Euangelisch."

The third dialogue, in short title, "Vom Geytz und anderen offentlich Lastern," consists, in various editions, of 8, 10 or 14 leaves, quarto, with title-page woodcut and beneath it the lines from Ephesians V, 3: "... fornication and all uncleanness, or covetousness, let it not be once named among you, as becometh saints." Seemingly this was the least popular of the Sachs dialogues of 1524, and achieved only four editions. The woodcut is of two men at a table with coins and a purse, to the right sits the Junker Reichenburger and to the left stands the priest, Romanus, who is pointing at the coins. This dialogue, unlike the three others of 1524, begins with a 30-line dedicatory preface, addressed to Hans Odrer zu Preßla [Breslau].

It is necessary to be aware that the word *Geytz,* in the title and the preface, meant to Sachs more than avarice. It had an amalgamated meaning of selfishness and self-interest, covetousness and all forms of base manipulations.

The content of this dialogue is mainly an exchange of volleys concerning money. Romanus is upbraided with the charge that his church and its dealings are all a fraud, all for the sake of money. But Romanus soon has Reichenburger cornered with his arguments that describe the manipulations of trade and commerce that make the evangelicals guilty in many ways: cornering of foodstuffs for extra profit, monopoly and cartel

practices, short weight, damaged goods foisted on innocent customers—
are such things in accord with the Gospels? But Romanus has more,
especially about taking unchristian advantage of employees and lending
money at interest. Reichenburger has no suitable reply; none, even when
Romanus says how little charity for the poor is given even though the Bible
commands it; in other words, the evangelicals have only the evangelical
word and not the works or deeds.

Reichenburger speaks hopefully of the time when the preaching of the
gospels will change people but Romanus counters that ages have gone by
without bearing fruit. In sum, Sachs is aware, and much concerned, that
the evangelicals have not yet learned to live good Christian lives nor cast off
their sinful ways. Sachs makes quite clear how aware he is of the
weaknesses of the new evangelicals—he expects and calls for a renovation,
a reformation of their inner and outer lives.

The fourth dialogue, in short title, "Vom ergerlich Wandel etlicher die
sich Lutherisch nennen," consists of 8 or 12 leaves, quarto, with a title-page
woodcut and beneath it the lines from II Corinthians 6, 3-4: "Giving no
offense in any thing, that the ministry be not blamed: but in all things
approving ourselves as the ministers of God." The woodcut is of two
friends, Hans and Peter sitting at a table as the Catholic Meister Ulrich
enters with rosary beads in his hands. Sachs again achieved a best-seller.
Eleven editions were printed, probably all in 1524, although some printings
are undated.

In this dialogue, Peter is the Lutheran Christian who inclines to
uncritical acceptance of all the Lutheran innovations while Hans, the
evangelical Christian, carefully analyzes the usefulness of each point, does
not wish to offend those holding to the old faith, and hopes to win them
over by teaching and even meeting them part way. The diverse positions of
Peter and Hans are immediately apparent in a discussion about eating meat
on Friday, as Peter describes how he did so in the presence of his father-in-
law, Meister Ulrich, a Catholic, who became angry. This gives Hans the
opening to defend his evangelical position—and enter Meister Ulrich. To
Ulrich, Peter is a heretic, not the Roman clerics Peter attacks. Hans pleads
that the words of Christ should prevail and that loving your neighbor is
what matters. Peter counters that he only follows Luther's examples, but he
is checked by Hans who says that people such as Peter use Luther only as a
cover for their misdeeds. The conclusion is that only through love will one
know the true faith—Hans' position—and Meister Ulrich is convinced and
prepared to attend Lutheran services. Hans is not a fanatic, not a rabble-
rouser. He does not approve of zealots who seek violent confrontation. For

him life must be a truly evangelical experience. And that is how Sachs formed and lived the rest of his life, as profusely attested by his writings.

In the four dialogues Sachs's "Christian" position is unique among all the other vernacular, pro-Lutheran publications. Sachs is a battler for reform, for the way an evangelical Christian must act, that the new teachings be upheld in life. The third and fourth dialogues give us Shoemaker Hans as a model for the Gospel message, a reminder and call for living a proper life—and not a call to theological battle. Sachs had a "this world" ethic. He truly felt himself secure in his humanism plus protestantism—a bourgeois sense of worthiness.

In 1523, Martin Luther, in his *Formula missae,* and in several letters pleaded for songs as part of his reform of the Catholic mass and other liturgical services. He appealed to the *poetae germanici* for *cantilenas,* to be put at his disposal, *quae dignae sint in ecclesia Dei frequentari.*[9] And Hans Sachs came through! His German hymns, songs and psalms to replace the Latin of the Roman church began to appear: in 1525, "Etliche geistliche, in der Schrift gegrünte Lieder für die layen zu singen." All eight Sachs songs that first appeared in printed pamphlet form were almost immediately included in the Nürnberg *Enchiridien* of 1525 and again in 1527. They were included in the Wittenberg *Gesangbuch* of 1533 and later editions, as well as in the later Nürnberg and other hymnals.

In 1525, Sachs published a collection of thirteen psalms, including the notation of four of his own musical settings—his musical skills having been developed in his musical inventions of Meistertöne for his original Meisterlieder. Each of Sachs's vernacular psalm renderings is in 7-line verses, with his treatments ranging from three to nine stanzas. His psalm versions were taken, *in toto,* into the Nürnberg *Enchiridion* of 1527.

In that same year, 1527, Sachs got involved in a publication that was to bring him an official rebuke from the Nürnberg city council and an official order that the work be suppressed.[10] All unsold copies were confiscated from the printer, as well as the 30 woodcut blocks used in the publication. Nevertheless, there were three further editions published in 1527; two without place of publication and one in Oppenheim. It is a modest volume: 18 leaves, quarto, including the 30 woodcuts. The conception of the work began with Andreas Osiander, one of Nürnberg's most fiery Lutheran preachers. The stimulus to Osiander to produce such a volume, according to Osiander's prose preface, was an old collection of woodcuts from the Carthusian cloister in Nürnberg. The woodcuts depicted, according to Osiander, the inner and outer degeneration of the papacy. Sachs's contribution to the volume, written on the persuasion and urging of

Osiander, Lutheran preacher at St. Sebald's Church, was 4-line verses under each of the 30 woodcuts as well as a 29-line concluding poem. Up to 1527 Sachs had played a comparatively passive role and was only indirectly involved in the learned disputes of the theologians. The verses by a shoemaker who dared, in print, to enter a purely theological dispute were unusual, a challenge at least, if not pure provocation. The Nürnberg city council, on 27 March, 1527, put it to Sachs officially; he was summoned to appear and told: "Nun sey solichs seynes ampts nit . . . darumb eins raths ernster bevelch, das er seins handtwerks und schuechmachens warte . . ." A shoemaker truly told to stick to his last!

The City Council edict had its effect, for in the next few years Sachs *published* little, although he continued to write as avidly as ever. His polemics in the cause of the Reformation then took a different turn. He now championed the new teachings, to spread the seeds of the Reformation, to protect and improve what had been won. He reworked biblical materials, especially the Gospels, to enhance the Protestant teachings. In a Spruchgedicht of 1535, his adherence to the basic Lutheran position is clear, in lines such as:

> der Glaub ist das ganz firmament
> ein ursprung andrer gaben allen

in a poem that concludes:

> der warhaft glaub, der ist die wurz
> der gibt uns Gott genzlich zu eigen. [12]

The poems of this period in no way enter the theological controversies; nothing of the transsubstantiation dispute, nothing of the Lutheran-Zwinglian dispute. Sachs writes on the moral consequences of faith, on the moral virtues rather than on dogma.

The close of a Spruchgedicht of 1539 perhaps most aptly illustrates what Sachs saw had occurred to God's word:

> erstlich von der Maulchristen
> darnach von romanisten
> und den religiosen
> sind eines tuchs drei hosen. [13] ["Die gemartert Theologia"]

He sought the pure teaching of the gospels, especially in the schools, as the prognostic of Judgment Day.

When Sachs learned of the death of Luther, he composed, on 22 March 1546, "Ein Epitaphium oder klagred ob der Leich Dr. Martin Luthers," a Spruchgedicht of 100 lines in the form of a dream sequence in which Sachs narrates how he suddenly felt saddened on the seventeenth of February and fell into a deep sleep and dreamt: he was in a temple and saw a covered casket; on the cover a shield with a rose and cross. As he looked and feared Luther's body might be in the casket, the white-clad figure of Dame Theology approached the bier and lamented the death of the man who had saved her from her enemies, had rescued her from her "Babylonian Captivity." When her troubled question arose about who would now be her champion, the poet—Sachs—consoled her with the words that God himself had taken her into His protection, and that many good men were yet alive to defend her, though Luther had gone to his eternal rest.[14]

With the death of Luther this particular account of the Sachs works must end. Sachs wrote thousands of pieces: tragedies, comedies, Fastnachtspiele and didactic poetry. His Bible was his greatest source, themes from the Old and New Testaments, the Psalter, the books of the Apocrypha. What before Luther had been saints' legends, greetings to Mary, rosary songs and the like were adapted—and the old works revised—to the new Lutheran teachings. Sachs's dramas, in later life, almost invariably dealt with Bible subjects such as Tobias, the Fall, John the Baptist, Job, the judgment of Solomon, the passion of Christ.

Sachs obviously strove to convince the lay reading or theatre-going German public that the message of the gospels was not a call to theological battle but rather a call and constant reminder to live a proper life. The *Wittenbergisch Nachtigal* and, especially, the fourth dialogue must not be read as the works of a visionary or a fanatic but rather as polemical literature written under the influence of the Lutheran ethic, as Sachs understood it. Sachs lived and wrote of the new evangelical way of life with a bourgeois faith in the state. He held firmly to the idea that "man is born to work as the bird is to fly," with freedom of conscience and the surety of faith.[15]

Notes

1. On Nürnberg in the 16th century, see Gerald Strauss, *Nuremberg in the Sixteenth Century* (New York: John Wiley, 1966). See also Steven E. Ozment, *The Reformation in the Cities: The Appeal of Protestantism to Sixteenth-Century Germany and Switzerland* (New Haven: Yale Univ. Press, 1975), and Gottfried Seebass, "The Reformation in Nürnberg," in

The Social History of the Reformation, eds. Lawrence P. Buck and Jonathan W. Zophy (Columbus: Ohio State Univ. Press, 1972), pp. 17-40.

2. The earliest biography of Hans Sachs is by M.S. Ranisch, *Historisch-kritische Lebensbeschreibung Hanns Sachsens* (Altenburg: B. Richter, 1765). For more recent biographical works, among many others, see Rudolph Genée, *Hans Sachs und seine Zeit: Ein Lebens- und Kulturbild aus der Zeit der Reformation* (Leipzig: J.J. Weber, ²1902), and Barbara Könneker, *Hans Sachs* (Stuttgart: Metzler, 1971), especially the bibliography, pp. ix-xviii.

3.Eli Sobel, "A Hans Sachs Anthology: The Meistertöne of MS Berlin *germ. quart.* 414," Diss. Univ. of Calif., Berkeley, 1947. See also Frances H. Ellis, *The Early Meisterlieder of Hans Sachs* (Bloomington: Indiana Univ. Studies, 1974).

4. On January 28, 1562, Sachs compiled, in manuscript, a catalogue of his personal library. For a printed reproduction of his holdings, see Erich Carlsohn, "Die Bibliothek von Hans Sachs," in an appendix [unnumbered pages] to Emil Weller, *Der Volksdichter Hans Sachs und seine Dichtungen* (1868; rpt. Wiesbaden 1966).

5. Text availabe in A. von Keller and E. Goetze, eds., *Hans Sachs Werke,* vol. VI, pp. 373 ff. This edition of Sachs's works (hereafter cited as *K-G*) consists of 26 volumes published in the Bibliothek des Litterarischen Vereins in Stuttgart (Tübingen, 1870-1908). See also *Hans Sachs: Die Wittenbergisch Nachtigall,* ed. Gerald H. Seufert (Stuttgart: Reclam, 1974) for a reprint with woodcut of the 1st edition and commentary. See *K-G,* vol. 25, p. 9, for Sachs's entry in one of his privately-bound volumes: "Diese puechlin [40 Luther tracts and sermons] habe ich Hans Sachs gesamelt, got vnd seinem wort zw eren vnd dem nechsten zw guet ainpünden lassen, als man zelt nach christi gepurt 1522 jar." In 1522, Sachs also owned and recorded as two items in his personal library: "Bibel, der erste Teil. Wittenberger Druck." "Bibel, der andere Teil. Wittenberger Druck."

6. Frances H. Ellis, *Hans Sachs Studies I: Das Walt got, A Meisterlied with Introduction, Commentary, and Bibliography,* Indiana Univ. Publications, Humanities Series No. 4 (Bloomington: Indiana Univ. Press, 1941).

7. For the dialogues and excellent critical text apparatus, see the edition by Ingeborg Spriewald, *Die Prosadialoge von Hans Sachs* (Leipzig: VEB Bibliographisches Institut, 1970). For analytical treatment of the Sachs dialogues and other works, see Bernd Balzer, *Bügerliche Reformationspropaganda: Die Flugschriften des Hans Sachs in den Jahren 1523-1525,* Germanistische Abhandlungen 42 (Stuttgart: Metzler, 1973), with comprehensive bibliography on pp. 219-231.

8. See Spriewald, *Die Prosadialoge,* p. 14, and Mary Beare, "The Later Dialogues of Hans Sachs," *Modern Language Review,* 53 (1958), 197-198. For an account of the Reformation epoch, see Barbara Könneker, *Die deutsche Literatur der Reformationszeit: Kommentar zu einer Epoche* (München: Winkler, 1975), with outstanding bibliography, pp. 184-269.

9. *WA* 12, 218. Luther's desire for songs in German is also expressed in a letter to Nicolaus Hausmann in Zwickau (1523): "...so irgend teutsche Poeten wären... uns geistliche Lieder zu machen...." German translation, from the Latin, in J.B. Riederer, *Abhandlungen von der Einführung des deutschen Gesanges in die evangelische Kirche* (Nürnberg, 1759), p. 34, and see p. 96 for a Luther letter to Georg Spalatin: "...daß das Wort Gottes auch durch den Gesang unter den Leuten bleibe."

10. *Eyn wunderliche Weyssagung von dem Babstumb/ wie es yhm biß an das endt der welt gehen sol/ jnn oder gemäl begriffen/ gefunden zu Nurmberg ym Cartheuser kloster vnd ist seer alt. Eyn vorred Andreas Osianders... Welche/ Hans Sachs yn teutsche reymen gefast/ vnd darzu gesetzt hat* (Nürnberg: Hans Guldenmundt, 1527).

11. For the text of the Council edict, see Gerhard Hirschmann, "Archivalische Quellen zu Hans Sachs," in *Hans Sachs und Nürnberg: Bedingungen und Probleme reichsstädtischer Literatur,* eds. Horst Brunner, Gerhard Hirschmann, and Fritz Schnelbögl (Nürnberg: Verlag des Vereins für Geschichte der Stadt Nürnberg, 1976), pp. 43-44.

12. *K-G,* vol. I, p. 353.

13. *K-G,* vol. I, p. 338.

14. For the text of the Luther epitaph, see *K-G,* vol. I, pp. 401-403. For a version in modern German, see Rudolf J. Weickmann, *Hans Sachs* (Schwabach: Peter Gersbeck, 1976), pp. 40-42.

15. See the Sachs citation and rendering of Job V, [7], in his *Dialog von den Scheinwerken der Geistlichen,* p. 119, ll. 554-559, in Spriewald, *Die Prosadialoge.* Sachs surely used the Luther Bible translation: ". . . wie die *Vögel* [italics added] schweben empor zufliegen." The King James version of Job V, 7, reads: ". . . as the *sparks* [italics added] fly upward." The Masoretic text, in English translation, also reads *sparks* and not *birds*—further evidence of Sachs's knowledge of Luther's Bible translations, his familiarity with Luther's works.

THE LUTHER-ERASMUS CONSTELLATION
IN THOMAS MANN'S *DOKTOR FAUSTUS*

Herbert Lehnert, *University of California at Irvine*

Only a nuclear holocaust could surpass the utter senselessness of the First World War. Seen from a detached vantage point, it was a suicidal self-negation of European or Western culture. The ability of industrialized society to produce wealth showed its extreme negative pole for the first time: utter destruction. During much of this war Thomas Mann was trying to make sense of the destruction. Sitting in his study in Munich he wanted to come to grips with his conception of German culture, which he wanted to present as a worthy cause to be defended. The resulting essay, *Betrachtungen eines Unpolitischen* [Reflections of an Unpolitical Man], subjected Thomas Mann to the hostility of many left-oriented critics, especially of the Expressionist generation. Mann defended German conservatism which he identified with Schopenhauerian pessimism. Yet Mann's book is complex to the extreme of being confused and confusing. It is not really defending a conservative, nationalistic, feudalistic ideology, but rather a culture where the free spirit in literature can prevail, where literature is not in the service of progress, has no obligation to contribute to the general will, is not forced to subscribe to an optimistic or any other fixed world view. In fact the *Reflections* are decidedly anti-totalitarian.

Thomas Mann opposed social meliorism as it was advocated by his brother Heinrich Mann and by the German Expressionist writers. Passionately he argued against the tradition of Rousseau which he considered to be the core of Western democracy. Germany, he insisted, was fighting for the preservation of its own culture, the tradition of the German *Bürger* who was neither *citoyen* nor *bourgeois,* neither an ideologue, a practical politician, nor a hard capitalist. The German *Bürger,* as Mann saw him, cultivated the flower of *Bildung* from skepticism and doubt, leaving politics to the specialists. The highest type of art, Mann writes, is characterized by "bildende Gerechtigkeit" (XII, 501).[1] This untranslatable phrase means something like "fairness which educates," "justice achieved by artistic form," or "artistic tolerance." Artistic justice was to be open-minded, independent of ideology and social goals. Rousseauistic democracy appeared as a fixed, optimistic ideology to him. Humanistic optimism holds that man, given the proper freedom, can and will improve himself, his lot, and the society around him. This world view clashed with the basic skepticism which Thomas Mann held all his life. Yet, as a producing artist, Mann could not divorce himself completely from humanism either. The conflict of nihilistic skepticism and a humanistic sympathy for man and his struggle permeates Mann's work. As we will see Luther and Erasmus become images for this conflict.

Radical doubt of the established bourgeois orientation can be traced to Mann's early years. Like his brother Heinrich he had refused to continue the family firm and, as a consequence, the status of the Manns as a leading family in the city republic of Lübeck lapsed. Thomas Mann had fled to art, away from the necessity of integrating himself into bourgeois society. This flight was accompanied by a profound doubt whether there was any sense to the social order at all, and whether any orientation like above and below, good or evil, had any autonomous validity. This doubt he found confirmed when he read Nietzsche and Schopenhauer. The world appeared illusionary to him.[2] Art that gives form to the imagination makes the illusionary character of the world conscious. Art presents alternatives to reality, illuminates and interprets social conventions, always dissolving their claims to represent absolute, factual truth. At the same time, a loving sense of humor and sympathy with the creatures of life, expressed in art makes life bearable. His refusal to take the world for granted also afforded Mann access to religion, even though he was not religious in any traditional manner. The very informality, even vagueness of his contact with religion, its refusal to be associated with an established church, he associated with his Protestant religious heritage.

The *Reflections* invoke many aspects of German culture, among them Luther's Reformation. The first chapter of the book calls German protest against the Roman Empire, against Western Catholicism, against the French Revolution a national characteristic. Mann quotes Dostoevski in agreement with this view. Luther's Reformation, Mann insists later in the book, was not simply an historical act of emancipation, as progressive, liberal ideology tends to see it, but rather an event of the soul, revolutionary and reactionary at the same time. Luther was an unpolitical man (XII, 513 f.). Luther and the Reformation were exemplary German, great in a sense that transcended the scope of any progressive ideology. Mann is heir to the 19th-century image of 'Luther the German' as derived from Madame de Staël and Heine.

Mann identified with Luther in the sense that he considered hiw own

Protestant roots peculiarly German. Yet analysis shows that he knew very little about the historical Luther. Only towards the end of his life, when he made studies for a play on Luther's marriage, did he begin to fathom the complexity of Luther's theology.[3] His Luther was a national figure, an unpolitical example of inwardness, resisting Rome and the Western Catholic world. Along with Nietzsche, Thomas Mann saw the Reformation as a renewal of Christianity with a precarious and multi-faceted relationship to Renaissance and Humanism.

When World War I was lost for Germany, Thomas Mann's world view was thrown into a crisis. He had seen the German national character, represented by a line of great men, Luther, Frederick II of Prussia, Goethe, and Bismarck, at stake. The allied strategy, he insisted, had aimed at purging the German soul of these great men so that Western civilization finally could take root in Germany.[4] In a letter of 1919 he contemplated the idea that this great Germanness (his words are "das große Deutschtum") from Luther to Bismarck and Nietzsche, was refuted and dishonored.[5]

Besides this extreme despair we also find more relaxed opinions: It might be possible to live with Western civilization.[6] Mann slowly began to notice that the danger of fanatical totalitarianism was rampant on the new right in post-war Germany. Democracy, he now realized, could, after all, incorporate the German tradition, could be based on Goethe's *Humanität,* could include Romanticism and the artist-dreamer. Yet Thomas Mann's eventual defense of democracy in Germany, since 1922, was no fundamental change in his world view. Rather, he stressed the humanistic, philanthropic, humanitarian aspect of his artistic praxis a little more. The skepticism against any optimistic ideology remained not only intact, it also retained its primary position. *Der Zauberberg* [The Magic Mountain] ends with a question mark—not by accident. The first great novel entirely conceived after the First World War is *Joseph und seine Brüder* [Joseph and his Brothers]. This novel plays with the tension between despair and humanitarian civilization, between religion and humanistic self-creation, between myth and progress. At its end Joseph has become a successful economist and administrator, the savior of his tribe and of its culture. But it is not he in his worldly glory who receives the principal blessing, but his brother Juda who is worthy of it because he is preoccupied by feelings of guilt and despair. While the surface action of the novel shows Joseph's vivid imagination yielding to civilized reality, the deep structure shows that culture, the cementing of reality, contained in Jacob's tales, is itself a product of the imaginative mind. Imagination subjects itself to a higher power, Jacob's God. In *Reflections,* Mann had confessed that he did not believe in a universal happiness to be provided by social democracy, but rather in despair, because despair opens the road to deliverance. The German word is "Erlösung" which also means redemption, and has a definite religious meaning (XII, 532). *Joseph und seine Brüder,* completed in 1943 in Pacific Palisades, California, still confirms Mann's belief expressed during the First World War.

When *Joseph* was conceived, in 1925, another plan competed with it. Thomas Mann wanted to write three stories: the first was to treat the Joseph story in more compact form, the second was to be about Philipp II of Spain and his vain struggle against modern Europe and the rise of the British Empire, the third was to be on Luther and Erasmus.[7] In an interview published in 1926 he spoke of being attracted to religion and religious interest permeated these three plans.[8] Around 1950 he again toyed with the Erasmus-Luther theme. What stimulated him must have been the contrast between Luther's inwardness and Erasmus' adaptation to the world, between religious conviction and detached doubt, between assertion of truth and ironic resignation from the follies of the world. Luther and Erasmus must have appeared to him like embodiments of a dichotomy that was very close to home. While his external existence as *Bürger* and established author defending the Republic made him identify with Erasmus' peaceful humanism, Luther, the destroyer of conventions, remained alive within his consciousness as well.

When Hitler subjugated Germany and much of Europe, and Thomas Mann had been driven to his American exile, a deeper despair about German culture than that of 1918/19 gripped him. He could take comfort in the thought that he took Germany with him wherever he went and that his Germanness was of a more sophisticated kind than Hitler's. Yet the despair was deep as his diaries of 1933 show. His hate must have become worse by the insight that behind all his contempt for the Nazis there was a kinship between him and them. Not only did they, in their crude way, strive for effective use of language, authoritarianism, nationalism, the religion of "Life," even racism, were tendencies in German cultural developments which Thomas Mann's own works showed. An Erasmus-like detachment appeared as an existential refuge. Germanness as it was invoked by the National Socialists became a precarious notion. Cocky nationalism, contempt for other nations, a fixed primitive ideology, extreme injustice to Germans of Jewish background and even their physical destruction, a desire to repeat the World War, no longer represented the Germanness that Thomas Mann wanted to carry with him. His Germany was sophisticated as well as skeptical, humane and open to the world.

Unfortunately, among the half-truths about Luther that Thomas Mann had picked up from Nietzsche was that of Luther, the coarse boor. Luther's coarseness in reality did not surpass the general standard of the 16th century, but in Catholic polemics, which Nietzsche had read, Luther was presented as a semi-educated peasant. Contempt of coarseness was a defense against the National Socialists which we can find in all of German Exile-Literature. In Mann's mind Luther, the rude, protesting folk-hero became dominant and this image slipped into disgrace. Luther, the representative of folksy Germanness came to resemble the primitivism and coarse savagery of the Nazis. Once Thomas Mann remarks that Luther shows "strong Nazi elements" (XII, 907). The low point of Mann's estrangement of Luther is in the essay *Die drei Gewaltigen* [The Three Mighty Men] first published in 1949 under the title *Goethe, das deutsche Wunder* [Goethe, the German Miracle] (X, 374-383). Goethe is praised here at the expense of two other great Germans, Luther and Bismarck.

This negative image of Luther, semi-informed as it was, had an impact on Thomas Mann's exile-novel *Doktor Faustus*. Yet in this fictional work the Luther theme is more complex than in the essay of 1949. While in the essay Goethe is a synthesis of Luther and Erasmus, so that Luther's deficiencies can be stressed, in *Doktor Faustus* Luther forms part of the German myth which is incorporated in the central character of the novel, Adrian Leverkühn. Luther, Nietzsche, and an artist of the Expressionist generation are superimposed on the character Leverkühn who is to represent the myth of German artistic productivity, a type of artist longing for the breakthrough, destroying conventions, and insisting on a new order. It was this free, unfettered artistic spirit that Mann had felt called upon to defend in *Betrachtungen eines Unpolitischen.*

When Leverkühn writes letters to his friend Zeitblom, the narrator of the fictive biography, he sometimes uses older forms of German adapted from his theology professor Kumpf. This language, early New High German, is meant to suggest Luther's, even though we know that Mann took much of it from the 17th-century novel *Simplicius Simplicissimus* by Grimmelshausen. Adrian himself calls the year which he devoted to Lutheran theology an act of self-discipline, comparable to entering a monastery of strict observance (VI, 175), obviously an allusion to Luther's biography. Another such allusion is that Leverkühn attends a school that used to be called "School of the Brethren of the Common Life" (VI, 16). Both Erasmus and Luther had attended such schools.

Not just Leverkühn, but also his friend Zeitblom attends the school. When I said that Adrian Leverkühn was to incorporate the myth of German artistic productivity this is fully valid only if Leverkühn is seen as half of the constellation he forms with Zeitblom, his devoted friend and biographer. Zeitblom is a teacher of classical languages and subscribes to the tradition of 16th-century Humanism (VI, 10). He is a Catholic but not a devout believer; he does not feel that his Catholicism conflicts with his humanistic world view and his love of the "best arts and letters" (VI, 15). This is an allusion to Erasmus, or at least to Erasmian humanism. The Leverkühn-Zeitblom constellation, to some degree, feeds on Mann's old plan to constrast Luther and Erasmus, Luther the stubborn demolisher of civilized convention, and Erasmus the the cautious and pliant humanist, servant of letters and style. In his 20th-century role, Zeitblom represents the educated German burgher, what in German may be called the *Bildungsbürger,* the type of faithful civil servant with university training and a vivid sense of culture. *Bildungsbürger* go beyond the ranks of civil servants, of course, but the modest, yet upper-class public official, somewhat detached from commercial competition, displaying an impartial interest in life and art as long as public order is not threatened, a judge, an administrator, a teacher, is the role model for the readers of German literature, for the public in the theaters and concert halls, much more so than the rich owner of industries. Professionals such as physicians, lawyers, even small town bankers and some employees strive to follow the civil service role model, that was and is so strong in Germany, by stressing the service character of their duties, their objectivity [*Sachlichkeit*]. Thus a bank employee will call himself *Bankbeamter,* a successful merchant before 1918 cherished the title *Kommerzienrat* which sounds like high civil service. Many want to add to their social prestige by participating in cultural activities.

German artists and *Bildungsbürger* live in symbiotic relationship. The latter want their usually modest life enriched and extended by the artists whose originality and boldness is appreciated, the former, much as they might claim to produce art only for its own sake, for their own satisfaction, or posterity (thereby adopting the standard of civil service: objectivity, *Sachlichkeit,* really depend on the admiration and receptivity of the *Bildungsbürger*).

Besides being Doktor Faustus, Leverkühn is Luther, Nietzsche and a 20th-century artist, Zeitblom is an Erasmian humanist, as Leverkühn's friend he has a little of Melanchthon in him. He is also a scholarly friend of Nietzsche's like Deussen or Overbeck, and a 20th-century *Bildungsbürger.* The constellation is treated like a myth. Myth, for Thomas Mann, meant types, forms of existence from the past which a successor enters and realizes for himself. Mann developed this idea during his work on the *Joseph* novel and presented it, in playful fashion, in the chapter of Eliezer, son and first servant of Abraham (IV, 419-424), in a more abstract form in the 1929 speech on Lessing, where he touches on the mythical nature of the

German national character (IX, 229-245). As in *Joseph* he adds a critical, rational balance to conservative myth. Lessing is shown as a believing skeptic, more a Luther of his time than the orthodox Lutherans. Mann invokes Lessing's mythical type of a writer dedicated to the truth specifically against rising fascism.

Yet, myth as type, in the way of a model eliciting emulation is also akin to the practice of fascism in hatching traditions for its followers to emulate, such as the Teutonic war hero. On their own low and coarse level, the Nazis appealed to the imagination with their myths, which was the secret of their success and the reason for some of their most stupid mistakes. On his own artistic level, Mann's construction of myths fed on his belief in the power of genius.

Nietzsche and the Symbolist tradition together support belief in the arbitrary power of the artist over myth. The Symbolist protest against the artist's dependence on reality led to the proclamation of the arbitrary freedom of the artist to create his own world. If, according to them, a real thing became a motif in a work of art, it assumed a new character. Its meaning was to be determined by the structure of the work. This means that art can change meaning at will, that the elements of the real world are at the disposal of the artist. Nietzsche's argument against the use of history in the 19th century, and especially against historical education, "historische Bildung," in *Vom Nutzen und Nachteil der Historie für das Leben* [Of the Advantage and Disadvantage of History for Life] is motivated by the fear that the burden of historical facts might impede the growth of genius and prevent greatness. Nietzsche's standard is creativeness as defined in the organic metaphor. His favorite type of history, monumental history, is in fact in danger of falsifying reality. Nietzsche goes so far as to say that at times there may be no difference between monumental past and mythical fiction.[9] Nevertheless, the only history he considers capable of service to life is monumental history, whose character is obviously artistic. Value derives from the image of the bold creator who liberates himself from the power of suffocating conventions.

In this same early essay on history, Nietzsche briefly developed what he calls the critical mode of dealing with the past. In this mode, man from time to time judges his past and condemns it.[10] From this section Thomas Mann could have taken another motto to *Doktor Faustus*. It was recognized soon after publication of the novel that Thomas Mann reversed the values expressed in *Betrachtungen eines Unpolitischen,* especially in regard to Luther, the Reformation, and its German character.[11] Art as breakthrough, art as the creation of a lonely genius rising above conventionality, the epoch of individualistic, bourgeois culture is condemned to death, playing out is own apocalypsis in Adrian Leverkühn's music which is inspired by his peculiar German devil. Zeitblom the intellectual burgher, the official educator, is helpless, can neither preserve culture nor control its demonized decline. Only the artist is the creator, only he can be the agent of destruction.

Like his fellow emigrés Max Horkheimer and Theodor Adorno with whom he had close contact during their years in California, Thomas Mann condemns the very culture in which his work had grown. Horkheimer and Adorno wrote *Dialektik der Aufklärung (Dialectic of Enlightenment)* approximately at the same time *Doktor Faustus* was written. Both works were published in 1947 by publishers who still specialized in exile literature. Horkheimer and Adorno stressed the negative potential of Western philosophical culture. Rationalism not only enables Western man to know much about objects, it also tells him how to control them. This power is subject to misuse and thus enlightenment no longer liberates humans but controls and subjugates them. In a similar way Leverkühn's art no longer liberates the cultured burghers from oppressive reality, but creates a system of total order in which the end of individualistic freedom is expressed. Mourning over the failure of the promise of German culture leads to a vision of its total failure. Adrian Leverkühn is prevented from personal contact with the non-German world, he never visits the city of Paris, because of the war, because of his pride, because of rejection by a woman. This motif means, on the symbolic level of the novel, that Leverkühn's art remains peculiarly German, its early use of texts by Shakespeare, Blake, Verlaine was only romantic universalism, not communication with the non-German world. The German art which here reaches its end is the art of the extremely original, the antisocial, alienated, lonely artist, the art of breaking through conventions, the art that refuses to communicate, but rather imposes its own order. While this view of art indeed has an affinity to Fascism, its insistence on its own order and on the invalidation of any common system of values derived in its modern form from Symbolism, and thus is really not merely German. In the symbolic system of meaning in Mann's novel it is, however, portrayed as peculiarly German.

More peculiarly German than Leverkühn's artistic principles is the constellation Leverkühn-Zeitblom, artist-burgher. The passivity of the *Bildungsbürger,* the helplessness with which he watches the proclamation of the end of individualistic culture, in Leverkühn's work and in the irrationalistic ideology of his fellow burghers, is a reflection of Mann's despair of Germany. Since Zeitblom's withdrawal from public life is a model of what Mann wished at times for himself, the author has included himself in his work, he partakes in his own accusation, just as much as he shares in the symbolistic principles of Leverkühn's art.

The Leverkühn-Zeitblom constellation has three aspects which are superimposed on each other: (1) The autobiographical aspect. It describes two modes of existence which Thomas Mann found in himself. (2) The historical aspect. Artist and *Bildungsbürger* really believed that they influenced the fate of the nation, but were unable to prevent the distortion of their rules as leader and follower, *Führer* and *Gefolgschaft* in National Socialism. The third aspect is mythical. The artist-burgher dichotomy is seen by Thomas Mann as the mythical repetition of the Luther-Erasmus constellation which is alluded to in Leverkühn and Zeitblom. The German artist's anti-conventional boldness is a Lutheran heritage. The destroyer of convention follows in Luther's footsteps. But also his inwardness derives from Luther. Luther's refusal to become the leader of the peasants' movement, his support of authority is specifically cited in Mann's hostile sketch of Luther in the essay *Die drei Gewaltigen*. In *Doktor Faustus* this inwardness is reflected in Leverkühn's withdrawal from public life, indeed from urban life. The Erasmus model, on the other hand, is that of a passive, ironic acceptance of the follies of the world. The Erasmian humanist does not rebel. He serves the classical tradition with stoic equanimity. If the public order lacks value, he is not going to tear it down, because he is horrified by the consequences. Classical education is elitist and, therefore, depends on the stability of the class system. Both Erasmus and Luther, both Zeitblom and Leverkühn are apolitical, yet contrast in their attitudes to the established order of values. While Luther attacks those values, stubbornly following the conceptions which his genius instilled in him regardless of the rest of the world, Erasmus and Zeitblom, as Catholics and Humanists, adhere to the traditions which keep the Western world together.

Looking back on Thomas Mann's *Doktor Faustus* from our historical vantage point casts doubt on this work's claim to mythical significance.[12] Germany, like any other country, is a social phenomenon. A myth or an intellectual tradition may contribute to its image. Yet, myths remain products of the imagination. That does not mean they are unreal. Self-deception can influence political decisions more than self-interest. Yet the image of an anti-Western Germany broke down and rapidly disappeared after the end of World War II. Wherever the German people had a chance, they voted by the ballot or with their feet for the West and for the restoration of democratic institutions.

Protestantism *per se* cannot be seriously used as the basis for an antidemocratic myth, since Protestantism is such a strong factor in history and present public life of both Britain and the United States. Since both of these democracies are or have been imperialistic, Protestantism also can serve neither as an anti-imperial nor as an imperial myth. Peaceful and progressive countries like Norway, Sweden, and Denmark are predominantly Lutheran.

Thomas Mann himself is a questionable witness when the democratic and the authoritarian traditions of Germany are weighed against each other. In his essay "Schicksal und Aufgabe," which contains the material used for a lecture called "The War and the Future" presented in many places in America in 1943, Thomas Mann explains that democracy for him is not a claim to equality from below, i.e. including the common people, but rather calls for goodness, justice, and sympathy from above. When "Mr. Smith or little Mr. Johnson"—these are his words—slaps Beethoven on the shoulder and asks him "how are you, old man," that, according to Mann, is not democracy but tactlessness and lack of respect. (Thomas Mann's German is: "Mangel an Sinn für Distanz.") But when Beethoven sings in his choral symphony: "Seid umschlungen Millionen, diesen Kuß der ganzen Welt," that is democracy, because Beethoven could have invoked his aristocratic status as a genius instead of calling all men his brothers (XII, 933). It is very likely that Thomas Mann himself received slaps on the shoulder when he traveled in the country. Any reader of his diaries can imagine how he would flinch on such an occasion. While the passage from "Schicksal und Aufgabe" is more outspoken than others, Thomas Mann's whole attitude during his democratic years retained a claim of cultural leadership, of authority. His obituary on Franklin Roosevelt, whom he knew personally, starts off comparing the president with Caesar, while later on he calls him an artist (XII, 941-944).

The historical significance of *Doktor Faustus* lies less in what the novel states about Germany and the German character, and more in the searching self-revelation of a German artist whose work was under the spell of Symbolism and Nietzsche. *Doktor Faustus* is significant as the imaginative fictional representation of the crisis of emancipated modern art. The setting is German because Mann knew how Nietzsche had influenced him, and he knew how Nietzsche's influence had undermined social concerns, humanism and the humanitarian character of German letters. He knew that the National Socialists invoked Nietzsche for the disregard of human rights. The setting is German also because of the peculiar constellation of artist and *Bildungsbürger*.

The author of *Doktor Faustus* must also have known that the National Socialists had arrogated to themselves the right to re-interpret the world in their ideology, repeating on their dismal level what art had done already in the era of Symbolism. His essay "Bruder Hitler" (XII, 845-852) written in 1938 in California, first published in English under the title "That Man is my Brother,"[13] playfully assumes an artistic kinship with Adolf Hitler even across a chasm of contempt. Neither emancipated modern art nor the receptive *Bildungsbürger* offer any defense against an anti-humanitarian totalitarianism, if the latter follows in Nietzsche's footsteps and promises a new world with new laws.

Mann's Adrian Leverkühn had first intended to assume a position of cultural leadership by teaching Lutheran theology at a university. The prospect of becoming a great modern composer proved to be an even stronger temptation. In order not to fall victim to any convention he separated himself from social ties. The devil's condition for providing a superhuman artistic breakthrough is that Leverkühn may not love. Leverkühn's extreme emancipation is social alienation. Even when he is with people an air of superiority sets him apart. The violinist Schwerdtfeger who temporarily breaks through Leverkühn's shell is sent to his death by Adrian. Social emancipation and artistic superiority are inseparable in Leverkühn, the ultimate modern artist. It is here that Thomas Mann's concern is centered, it is here where the historical significance of the novel lies, it is also here that Thomas Mann's ignorance of the real historical Luther becomes relevant.

Doktor Faustus purports to show the apocalyptic end of German art, the end of the flower of a bourgeoisie which saw itself in the image of the educated elitist civil servant. German art, especially literature, German education, the image a German citizen had of himself, his inner sense of freedom combined with respect for authority, all this was tied to the memory of Reformation Germany, tied to the type of elitist bourgeois civil servant which the Reformation had produced, university-educated, running a small state, as Goethe had exemplified it for the nation. Through Goethe and his contemporaries, the Romantics, the inward cult of art had intensified, had become a substitute religion for the upper class. Romanticism and Symbolism, no longer Protestant but anti-conventional, anti-pragmatic, anti-social movements, had cultivated the elitism of art to the point of alienation. What had been religious and communal had become something quite different. Leverkühn expressively takes back the promise of German classicism (VI, 634).

The question *Doktor Faustus* poses is this: can a society long endure if its art shirks social responsibility? The concern of modern art in the Symbolist tradition is not to open up a livable world, but rather to condemn the existing one because it fails to live up to superhuman artistic constructs. The affinity of this artistic tradition to Nietzsche is obvious. If we disregard the low intellectual level, it is easy to see how fascism indeed both apes the condemnation of the unglamorous, unheroic bourgeois world and worships superhuman strength. German fascism used Jews to mark the difference between evil subhuman, subversive modernity and its own good, Aryan, superhuman new world. By destroying Jews, National Socialism invoked an apocalyptic pattern. Both by its destructive aggressiveness and by its stress on will power and irrational conceptions, fascism contains within itself an uncanny tendency toward self-destruction. The same can be found in Symbolism, most of all in its apocalyptic motif. German Expressionism shows this tendency clearly, for example in Georg Kaiser's two dramas called *Gas* and *Gas Second Part* (1918, 1920), but it is also recognizable in the Symbolists' fascination with death. Italian fascism was influenced by it, its back shirts were its death symbols as were the black uniforms of the German SS. The tendency toward self-destruction, unfortunately, is not restricted to fascism. Since World War I it is rampant in German culture and has flourished. Adrian Leverkühn, who actively seeks the infection that destroys his brain, removing inhibitions that stand in the way of his superhuman artistic breakthrough, is a symbol of the complex of Symbolist formalism and aggressiveness, social alienation and self-destructiveness.[14]

The problem of arrogant alienation of art in the Symbolist tradition is far removed from Luther's Reformation. Luther cared for the common people, even though he did not want to emancipate them from secular authority. He did not aspire to an artistic-aristocratic status; on the contrary, he did not even want his work, his movement to be called by his name. Most of all, Luther's faith in God was the center of his personality and his theology. His faith saved him from the problems of a modern artist. Thomas Mann's view of Luther as a German genius is in line with a cliché prevalent in Mann's time, but is in error. Luther was not nationalistic in any modern sense, and his theology was far removed from any individualistic idealism. Luther's man is deeply dependent on God's mercy, not a self-willed, self-creating modern Prometheus.

Is Leverkühn's desire to break through conventions in the Luther tradition? For Luther the conventions to be removed were those man-made impediments that stood in the way of God's grace; for Leverkühn, conventions are those artistic forms to which the public has become accustomed. Luther's Reformation indeed had its socially destructive aspects and consequences, even though Luther was much less iconoclastic than the British Puritans. Yet Thomas Mann used the socio-historical implications of Luther's work to illustrate a destructive tendency that he found in his own art. After all, Mann was part of the Symbolist movement that had set itself apart from conventional bourgeois reality. Mann had escaped to art from the solid life style of his forbears.

That is way the theme of breakthrough can be identified in all of Thomas Mann's work, and in each case it is associated with self-destruction. When erotic love breaks through the aesthetic peace of little Mr. Friedemann in one of Mann's early stories, he is rejected and kills himself. When Gustav von Aschenbach in *Death in Venice* breaks through the shell of his artistic-aritocratic, disciplined life style, he dreams of a bloody Dionysian rite and soon afterwards eats contaminated fruits. Leverkühn's breakthrough destroys his own brain.

Luther's Reformation was meant as a renewal of faith. The dynamism of his times was destructive with or without the Reformation. It is very difficult to say whether the sum total of wars and destruction would have been different in the 16th and 17th centuries in Europe if Luther had not resisted the authorities or if he had been physically prevented from starting a movement. Be that as it may, the breakthrough theme in Mann's work is inseparable from the theme of alienated loneliness, a Romantic and post-Romantic theme, and thus quite different from Luther's intentions.

But is modern individualism, the cult of the self, not a Protestant phenomenon? Admittedly it was not Luther's intention to emancipate the individual, but did not the idea of the immediacy of the individual to God and elaborate introspection flourish in Lutheran Pietism and did not Lutheran Pietism influence Romanticism? To say this is not more or less than to say that Luther and the Reformation are indeed part of European and German history. They took place at the beginning of the bourgeois age. Humanism and the Renaissance informed modern individualism perhaps more than the Reformation. Only in a very broad sense can we speak of an influence of Reformation praxis on Romanticism, aestheticism, and modernism in art.

More direct is the influence of the Reformation on the development of the *Bildungsbürger*. The literate commoner who became indispensable in the service of the smaller German states was the product of the schools that were opened everywhere in Germany at the instigation of Luther, Melanchthon, Bugenhagen, and other reformers. The literate, well-educated administrator, the *Geheimrat,* became the model for the *Bildungsbürger*. Zeitblom was given a Catholic faith by Thomas Mann as an allusion to Erasmus, but his type harks back to the educated literate burgher, the product of the Reformation schools and the secularized German universities. The Catholic parts of Germany adapted themselves to the trend. The influence of the *Bildungsbürger* did not suddenly end in 1945. Rather it was restored in the Adenauer era in the Federal Republic.

This process of restoration explains much of the negative reception *Doktor Faustus* received in West Germany after its publication in 1947.

In a more symbolic way Leverkühn and Zeitblom are a valid reminder of the Luther-Erasmus constellation. Luther and Erasmus reacted to and were the expression of an era of change. Thomas Mann as observer of both World Wars, shaken in his belief in German culture, was himself forced to contemplate change. In *Doktor Faustus* he exposed the Leverkühn-Zeitblom constellation, an image of German culture, to his experiences. This constellation was to be anchored in history by alluding to two ways of reacting to instability, to the devaluation of cultural values. The Luther model is staying within one's own inwardness and intellectually breaking through the barriers of invalid tradition, disregarding the consequences. The Erasmus model is ironic acceptance of the external order for fear of turmoil, disregarding its lack of value. Zeitblom's passivity in the face of the subversion of his philanthropic humanism in Erasmian.

Both ways are inadequate. Leverkühn's art, by satire and by solemn religious lament, conjures up the end of the bourgeois era. By doing this it furthers its surrender. Thomas Mann has Adrian's work end in 1930, the year when the National Socialists first made significant inroads among the German electorate. Zeitblom's narration of Leverkühn's apocalyptic oratorio is accompanied by the story of a bourgeois circle pondering irrationalist ideologies in the style of the *Konservative Revolution.* Leverkühn's work is, like that of most Expressionists, forbidden under the Nazi government, but it helped undermine bourgeois culture and its ability to resist its own destruction. Zeitblom's amiable receptivity for the personality and the work of his friend prevents him from noticing how much Leverkühn's art has prepared the destruction which materializes while Zeitblom is writing his biography during World War II. The reader is to draw this conclusion by himself.

The bourgeois era did not end with Germany's second defeat, nor did the German contribution to Western culture end. What did end was the belief in a particular German culture. Since Thomas Mann associated Luther with his view of Germanness he had to bring Luther into *Doktor Faustus,* as questionable as its German myth is. In contrast to Mann we see more clearly that Luther was not merely a German phenomenon. Yet Mann's introspection goes beyond German cultural particularity. He had questioned bourgeois, individualistic, alienated art in its state of radical emancipation as apocalyptic Symbolism or apocalyptic Expressionism. This is not a peculiar German problem even though Mann treated it thus.

We can go one step further. Adrian Leverkühn cannot accept the artistic conventions of his time because he is part of a tradition which demands originality. Originality is an attribute of individualism. An original work is not derivative, the artist has to stand behind it as a person. Art is no longer a craft. If the work of art is thus personalized it can no longer be filled with playful ornaments. The work becomes a direct expression. In Leverkühn's case it is expressive lament. This personalized work has become too difficult and Leverkühn needs the devil to accomplish it (VI, 320 f., 662). The devil stands for alienation, for the absence of love. Without convention, craftsmanship and deceptive play the artist no longer produces a piece of entertainment but a document of himself. By being driven into himself to find the original source of his art, he is more and more alienated from convention, communication, community. By implication, the difficulty of the modern work of art is increased by the demand for greatness. It competes with the past and with other contemporary productions, it must be better and greater. If the demand for originality and the competition for personal greatness reaches the limits of human potential, it becomes inhumane. In this way *Doktor Faustus* touches the nerve of the bourgeois age which has to recognize its limits, just like Horkheimer-Adorno's *Dialectic of Enlightenment*.

Adrian tries to complement the personalization by the new order of his music and by invoking traditions. His apocalyptic oratorio uses an apocalyptic tradition reaching from the Old Testament to Dürer, Luther's contemporary (VI, 474-476). The Faustus Cantata uses the *Faust* book and alludes both to the Gethsemane scene in the passion of Jesus and to the final chorus in Beethoven's Ninth Symphony, each time by inverting the original sense.

The new order of Leverkühn's music, the twelve-tone technique, is described as strictest form and freest expression at the same time. Zeitblom calls this ambivalence "miracle and deep demonic wit" ["O Wunder und tiefer Dämonenwitz," VI, 646]. Modern alienated art is condemned as devilish, but its very extremity evokes the religious tradition which has always been at its base. In the Faustus Cantata and in his last speech and confession, Leverkühn expresses a hope for God's mercy, and Zeitblom adds his prayer. The greatest sin may be the greatest challenge to the grace of God. We can be certain that Luther would have been revolted by this speculative theology. But we have to understand this dialectic of disbelief and faith as Thomas Mann's way of allowing superhuman Leverkühn to revert to religious humility.

The end of German bourgeois culture is marked by the contrast to its beginnings in the age of the Reformation, and, at the same time, religion is shown as its essential part. Luther's belief in God's grace, Dürer's pious and yet characteristic woodcuts of the Apocalypse, the tradition of Faust from the Lutheran chapbook of 1587 to Goethe, Beethoven's and Schiller's invocation of a good God and the love of men—has all this reverted to demonic wittiness or does its end in catastrophe and devilish alienation provide access to God's grace? This is the question the novel poses at its end.

Thomas Mann's religious seriousness is clearly evident from the text. In the *Entstehung des Doktor Faustus* [The Genesis of a Novel] Mann tells how he originally had made the religious solace too obvious in Zeitblom's description of the Faustus Cantata. Adorno's unhappiness forced him to rewrite the passage, making it more allusive than direct (XI, 294). The new version contains the formula of a "transcendence of despair" (VI, 651). In it, I think, is a trace of the true Luther of whom Thomas Mann knew so little at the time.

Notes

1. References in the text correspond to Thomas Mann, *Gesammelte Werke* (Frankfurt a.M.: S. Fischer, 1960/74).

2. See Hans Wysling, *Narzissimus und illusionäre Existenzform: Zu den Bekenntnissen des Hochstaplers Felix Krull* (Thomas Mann Studien, 5; Bern: Francke, 1982).

3. See Herbert Lehnert, *Thomas Mann—Fiction, Mythos, Religion* (Stuttgart: Kohlhammer, 1965), pp. 140-223. A more detailed account of the sources of Kurt Aland, *Martin Luther in der modernen Literatur* (Witten: Eckart, 1973), pp. 185-430.

4. Thomas Mann, *Tagebücher 1918-1921* (Frankfurt a.M.: S. Fischer, 1979), pp. 7, 112.

5. Thomas Mann, *Briefe 1889-1936* (Frankfurt a.M.: S. Fischer, 1961), p. 165. 5 July 1919.

6. *Tagebücher 1918-1921*, p. 31.

7. See Hans Wysling and Marianne Fischer, *Dichter über ihre Dichtungen: Thomas Mann* (Frankfurt a.M.: Heimeran and S. Fischer, 1979), vol. II, pp. 66-73. Cf. *Gesammelte Werke*, XI, 138; see also the considerations about Philipp and the rising power of Britain by the fictive Professor Cornelius in *Unordnung und frühes Leid (Disorder and Early Sorrow)*, vol. VIII, pp. 633, 650.

8. Wysling/Fischer, p. 68.

9. Friedrich Nietzsche, *Werke*, ed. by Karl Schlechta, vol. I (München: Hanser, 1954), p. 223.

10. Nietzsche, *Werke*, I, 229 f.

11. See Werner Kohlschmidt, "Musikalität, Reformation und Deutschtum: Eine kritische Studie zu Thomas Manns Doktor Faustus" in: W.K. *Die entzweite Welt* (Gladbeck: Freizeiten Verlag, 1953), pp. 98-112 (first publication 1950).

12. For a critical evaluation of the myth of Germany see Bengt Algot Sørensen, "Thomas Manns Doktor Faustus: Mythos und Lebensbeichte," *Orbis Litterarum*, 13 (1958), 81-91, and in a review of the Mann-Kerényi correspondence by the same author: *Orbis Litterarum*, 16 (1961), 124.

13. *Esquire,* 11 (1939), No. 3, 31, 132-133.

14. His role as symbol for this complex of self-destructive aestheticism is not weakened when Leverkühn himself speaks of another art of the future, which will be the servant of a community. It, Leverkühn claims, will not *have,* but *be* a culture. This vision of a post-bourgeois community culture does not describe Leverkühn's type of art, a fact which Zeitblom stresses in a commentary following his report of Adrian's utterance (VI, 429). Adrian's vision only stresses the deficiency of the artistic modernity that he represents. It is not open to the needs of the community, it is irresponsible, it insists on suffering and superiority over the common man.

LUTHER'S LANGUAGE IN THE MOUTH OF BRECHT: A PARABOLIC SURVEY WITH SOME EXAMPLES, DETOURS, AND SUGGESTIONS

Reinhold Grimm, *University of Wisconsin at Madison*

For Felix Pollak,
my best listener.

In view of our pious endeavors, and given so much biblical exegesis, I feel entitled, indeed called upon, to introduce my subject by way of a full-fledged parable or, at least, a simile of sorts.

There is an old joke—not devoid of grace, I should say—that comes to us from both France and Italy, comparing the various ages of a woman to the five classical continents. (I hasten to asseverate that there are also such jokes about the ages of a man; but they are not nearly so parabolic and, alas, far less pious.) A woman, then, before reaching the age of twenty, is said to be, as one might expect, somewhat like Africa: namely, for the most part, "unexplored" and what in French is called *vierge*. Between twenty and thirty, she begins to resemble the alluring continent of Asia—or, in the Italian version, the subcontinent of India—and to present herself, more and more, as "profound and mysterious." At the height of her growth, the very peak of her career and achievement, *i.e.,* during her thirties, she is, of course, comparable only to America. But I have to quote that in French again, for we are told, laconically enough: *L'Amérique—technique.* Little choice is left when she starts going downhill. However, it seems to be equally natural, for Frenchmen as well as Italians, to liken a woman between forty and fifty to good old Europe. The latter claim most unkindly that she is all shattered and ruins, *tutta una rovina,* while the former, though admitting that she is "ravaged," cannot but add they still find her exceedingly charming, *mais si pleine de charme.* (I confess to siding with them.) Finally, beyond the age of fifty, it is Australia which needs must be invoked—or, according to the shivery and inconsequential Italians, Siberia—a remote part of the Earth, at any rate, that people tend to chat about, but where they scarcely ever go. *Tout le monde en parle et personne n'y va,* as the French version has it.

So much for my parable (which is, as are other parables, slightly dated). Yet its applicability to the corpus of Brecht scholarship—and I know what I am talking about—reveals itself as the more topical. Long since, Brechtians of any persuasion have left behind their youthful stages of innocence and mysteriousness; little indeed has remained untouched in their field. Nor can I swear a solemn oath as to the permanent profundity of their contributions. Even their American age, with *technique* running amuck, and the "Brecht Industry"[1] sputtering forth, or grinding out, article after article and book after book, appears to be drawing to an end, however reluctantly. In fact, most observers, whether Brechtians or not, will nowadays concur that Poor B.B., the erstwhile idol, has been severely damaged; and very few among them are likely to add that, nevertheless, they continue to be intrigued and fascinated by him. (Let me plead guilty, in passing, on several of these counts, including continued allegiance.) But be that as it may—and here I return, at long last, to the Bible and its re-creator in German—one thing ought to be clear: Regarding the relationship of Bertolt Brecht to Martin Luther, almost everybody concerned with the former has been speaking of it for decades, while hardly anybody has ever cared to go into it in detail. In so many years—unless, along with a host of bibliographers,[2] I am grossly mistaken—no more than a single tentative tract has been published which deals expressly with both.[3] And nothing, to my knowledge, has as yet come out, either in this country or abroad, devoted to the specific Luthero-Brechtian idiom and its workings or, precisely and emphatically, to "Luther's Language in the Mouth of Brecht."

Granted, there exists a plethora of secondary literature that treats Brecht's rich and powerful diction in general or his attitude toward Christianity and/or the Scriptures in particular. The material in question, by scholars and pastors alike, ranges from brief and isolated references to entire monographs comprising hundreds of pages. Somewhere, most of these authors, whatever their starting-points may have been, arrive at our topic and, somehow or other, comment on it. In volumes such as *Brecht und die Religion* ("Brecht and Religion")[4] or *"Wach auf, du verrotteter Christ!"* ("'Awake, Thou Rotten Christian!'"),[5] in essays such as "Brecht's Quarrel with God"[6] or "Brecht's Judging Jesus,"[7] in pieces which extract from his plays "the Fall,"[8] "Messianism,"[9] "Liturgical Elements,"[10] or, simply, "Biblical Themes and Motifs"[11]—to cite just a few examples from the most recent output—we encounter not only passages assuring us of the Marxist's development "From Anti-Theodicy to Eschatology," or of his celebrating a "Red Mass,"[12] but also, as often as not, sentences emphasizing his deep and lifelong indebtedness to Luther's German, both as a playwright and a poet. Vice versa, the same duality is effective in the pertinent studies, mainly by critics and philologists, that proceed from the opposite angle; yet I need not, nor shall I, bother with listing any of those near innumerable investigations.[13] Suffice it to say that, time and again, we are informed by either group of commentators that Brecht knew the Scriptures "extraordinarily well,"[14] considered them literature "of high quality," loved their "imagery," and kept exploiting them as his favorite quarry and inexhaustible source.[15] Such statements have become legion over the years; I might even be tempted to chime in with one of the pronouncements I myself have set down and repeated ever since the late 1950's and early 1960's,[16] were it not for the impassioned utterance following. For, ironically, the most remarkable attestation concerning Brecht and the Bible has been issued, in all probability, by a literary historian from Russia, who decreed that the Marxist writer from Germany was not only extremely well-read in the Gospel but could actually compete in matters biblical with any learned theologian![17]

This Eastern ecstatic, not surprisingly, didn't fail to stress,[18] in addition to the "poetic power" of the Lutheran translation, its roots in the "flexible" and "expressive" speech of the people, the lower classes, the proletariat... whereas his Western colleagues seem to prefer to content themselves with collecting and counting their items, and arranging them neatly in columns.[19] The clergy, on the other hand, and the students of divinity have something very different in mind. From the outset, and almost exclusively, theirs has been an interest in Brecht as a so-called *Gesprächspartner*: an interlocutor and discussant, that is, who would lend himself to being converted, "to a certain degree" at least, into a harsh and provocative voice crying in the wilderness of present-day ministry.[20] Doubtless, the worst outgrowth of this kind of appropriation, a veritable hotchpotch of random quotes from all over the Brechtian texts, plus unctuous edifying corollaries and modernizing mini-sermons, is the aforementioned to me (the labor of love of a Protestant parson) so inappropriately titled *"Wach auf, du verrotteter Christ!"* after a cynical line from Brecht's *Threepenny Opera*.[21] Small wonder that it was torn to bits, together with its Catholic counterpart, *Brecht und die Religion,* by an irate adherent of irreligion.[22] Still, the latter contribution is a rather more sophisticated piece of writing, as is that "single tentative tract"—as I had to term it—devoted specifically to Brecht and Luther. But both operate on a similar recuperative level nevertheless. What constitutes the book on religion is a discussion of the notions of God (*Gottesbilder*) and their socio-political functioning, with Brecht as a mere catalyst;[23] hence it can, for our purpose, largely be dispensed with. Not so that lone tract; for it is a head-on attempt at a Lutheran interpretation of Brecht's famous parable play, *The Good Person of Szechwan*, and he who penned it was none other than Franz Lau, the then editor of the *Luther-Jahrbuch*, the most important forum of Luther scholarship. Though admitting, frankly and humbly, to be a total ignoramus in practically everything Brechtian, except for this one play,[24] Lau did embark on his exegetic adventure. He did not go so far, it is true, as to suggest that there had been a real influence; but he did give in to the pastoral urge to transpose (or "to retranslate," as he phrased it, adding an untranslatable *je und dann wieder einmal*) the "atheistic anthropology" of *The Good Person of Szechwan* into the theological framework of Lutheranism.[25] And what exactly did Lau find? He found, or toyed with having discovered, nothing short of an intimate correspondence between Brecht's drama, especially through its split lead character, and some of the gravest and most contradictory aspects of the reformer's teachings: namely, the drastic views Luther advanced in his treatise on the bondage of the will, *De servo arbitrio,* and the weighty doctrine he propounded of those "two realms" obedient Christians inhabit, his *Zwei-Reiche-Lehre*. In conclusion, Lau came to submit, sleekly and candidly, that the Lutheran God is just as good-natured a sucker as Brecht's tender prostitute, Shen Te, and just as cunning and mean a scoundrel as Brecht's brutal slave-driver, Shui Ta. "Auch der Gott...Luthers...ist," to quote him *verbatim*, "guter Gott und ausgekochter Hund..."[26]

Lau's theses as they pertain to Brecht have been dismissed by both literary critics[27] and theologians;[28] and rightly so. Yet I cannot help assuming, if only playfully, the role of the devil's advocate for a moment. (Or must I settle for *angelorum*, instead of *diabolus*?) To be sure, as regards the doctrine of the two realms taken in any positive sense, it is completely alien to Brechtian thought; in fact, it is incompatible with Brecht's life as well as his work. All the more is it in concordance, though, not only with the thinking but with the whole work and life of a fellow writer and representative contemporary of his, Gottfried Benn. The very title Benn chose for his most personal and confessionary report reads, programmatically, *Doppelleben*.[29] Truly, as had done millions of his compatriots before him, so he, too, led a "dual life."[30] Its maxims, or tenets, were the same as centuries ago when it had originated: 'Secular authority, such as the state, has to be obeyed for the sake of order; it must not be questioned. Man's liberty resides within him and does not extend into the public realm.' Thus, only a trifle condensed, the literal verdict of the prominent historians, Koenigsberger and Mosse;[31] and not even their illustrious German colleague, Gerhard Ritter, who was otherwise quite apologetic, dared disagree. Luther's doctrine and the widespread passivity and obeisance it engendered, indeed the "obsequious servility" (the wording is Ritter's)[32] fostered by it, have exerted a lasting and detrimental impact on the fate of Germany—and, above all, her intellectuals, as Brecht would immediately throw in. Having been baptized, brought up, and confirmed in the Lutheran faith,[33] and immersed in Luther's catechism,[34] the Marxist author, a political activist on the page and on the stage, can't possibly have been unaware of these repercussions and their origin, whether or not he was acquainted with all the particulars of the *Zwei-Reiche-Lehre.* Clearly, in a negative sense, *i.e.,* as cause of a reaction and rejection as strong and determined as can be conceived of, Luther's doctrine of the two realms had in effect had an influence on Brecht and, by extension, his Chinese parable play,[35] in spite of his commentator's restraint and caution in that respect.

Conversely, and now in real defense of Lau, we must also take into consideration that Brecht, despite appearances, may well have known Luther's treatise, *De servo arbitrio,* and at a very early age to boot. In a note dating from 1920, he denied, as sternly as the reformer, albeit on entirely different grounds, the existence of free will; and in discussions with German intellectuals upon his return from exile, he employed basically the same graphic image from horsemanship, and likewise in a religious context, as had been coined by Luther in order to refute Erasmus. In the eyes of the young Brecht, free will is merely a "fiction" contrived by the capitalists; curtly and unequivocally, he declared: "Der freie Wille—das ist eine kapitalistische Erfindung."[36] In the eyes of the old Brecht, however, religion—lo and behold—"offers support"; but, as he mused with a fair dose of irony, would the horse be kindly disposed to the saddle supporting the horseman? And sanctimoniously retracting his simile for being lame, he went on to point out that, as a rule, it isn't the horsemen that are religious, but rather the horses:

> Die Religion gibt einen Halt. Aber das Pferd ist nicht gut zu sprechen auf den Halt, den der Sattel dem Reiter gibt.
> Das Beispiel hinkt, wie ich fühle. Es sind nicht die Reiter, die gemeinhin religiös sind, sondern die Pferde.[37]

Really, doesn't this have a familiar ring?

But there is more yet; for it seems not altogether improbable that Benn and Brecht, so strikingly at odds as to the Lutheran heirloom of the *Zwei-*

Reiche-Lehre, blithely banded together, as it were, by picking up and adopting, each in his own way, another piece from the vast Lutheran legacy. In the former's case, it happened explicitly though by chance, in the latter's—provided my assumption is correct—implicitly. What I am referring to is Luther's strange dictum that, should the world end tomorrow, he would today plant an apple tree: "Wenn ich wüßte, daß morgen die Welt untergeht, würde ich noch heute einen Apfelbaum pflanzen." These words, quoted in a radio talk to which Benn had listened,[38] inspired the poet to write a few lines of amused admiration that are not untypical of him. Admittedly, they are marginal to our pursuit; still, since they appear to be little known, and have escaped the attention even of Kurt Aland, the compiler of a huge documentation of Luther's portrayal in modern literature,[39] I think they deserve being adduced all the same. But I'll have to content myself with reciting them only in German, as they have never been translated (their first line, incidentally, serves as their title):

> Was meinte Luther mit dem Apfelbaum?
> Mir ist es gleich—auch Untergang ist Traum—
> ich stehe hier in meinem Apfelgarten
> und kann den Untergang getrost erwarten—
> ich bin in Gott, der außerhalb der Welt
> noch manchen Trumpf in seinem Skatblatt hält—
> wenn morgen früh die Welt zu Bruche geht,
> ich bleibe ewig sein und sternestet—
>
> meinte er das, der alte Biedermann
> und blickt noch einmal seine Käte an?
> und trinkt noch einmal einen Humpen Bier
> und schläft, bis es beginnt—frühmorgens vier?
> Dann war er wirklich ein sehr großer Mann,
> den man auch heute nur bewundern kann.[40]

The Brechtian evidence in question, again a poem, is in a less light-hearted vein. And neither does it mention Luther nor enter into a kind of dialogue with him; instead, its author created a secularized and highly topical variation on the reformer's dictum. Composed on a Danish island, and forming part of a trilogy entitled "Frühling 1938" ("Spring 1938"), Brecht's poem reads as follows:

Heute, Ostersonntag früh
Ging ein plötzlicher Schneesturm über die Insel.
Zwischen den grünenden Hecken lag Schnee. Mein junger Sohn
Holte mich zu einem Aprikosenbäumchen an der Hausmauer
Von einem Vers weg, in dem ich auf diejenigen mit dem
     Finger deutete
Die einen Krieg vorbereiteten, der
Den Kontinent, diese Insel, mein Volk, meine Familie
     und mich
Vertilgen mag. Schweigend
Legten wir einen Sack
Über den frierenden Baum.[41]

In Derek Bowman's translation:

To-day, Easter Sunday morning
A sudden snowstorm swept over the island.
Between the greening hedges lay snow. My young son
Drew me to a little apricot tree by the house wall
Away from a verse in which I pointed the finger at those
Who were preparing a war which
Could well wipe out the continent, this island, my people,
     my family
And myself. In silence
We put a sack
Over the freezing tree.[42]

While the external qualities of Brecht's lines, their rhymelessness and pithy rhythms, are surely characteristic of their author, one might perhaps hesitate to label their content and message as typically Brechtian. Are they not rather, as touchingly as amazingly, reminiscent of Luther's words and paradoxical attitude?[42a] Yet I shall leave it to the experts to verify these, or identify more, such strange correspondences in Brecht's work, either to the Lutheran heritage proper or to theology at large. Said experts, in doing so, will have to be more attentive, however. As they could learn from an intimate informant indeed, that is, one of the mothers of Brecht's children born out of wedlock, the budding thinker and writer, his laxness in Protestant ethics notwithstanding, maintained a keen interest in religion[43] well beyond the phase when he excelled as an eager pupil being prepared for his confirmation.[44] After all, didn't he even enroll in a course in theology, indeed in "religious development and pedagogy," during his student years in Munich—another demonstrable fact[45] that has gone unnoticed by the majority of Brechtians, scholars as well as pastors?

To Lau, those testimonies and biographical details were not yet accessible. His tract was published as early as 1962. But it didn't address itself to the Holy Writ in Brecht's writings, either. Luckily, this does not apply to what, in my opinion, must be hailed as the best and most conscientious treatment to date of *Brecht and The Bible*: the like-named book, based on a Harvard dissertation, of the American Germanist and Jesuit, G. Ronald Murphy. Though his approach is a limited one and primarily thematic, as already indicated by his subtitle, *A Study of Religious Nihilism and Human Weakness in Brecht's Drama of Mortality and the City*, he does not neglect the crucial elements of scriptural speech as used and transformed by the Marxist playwright. Murphy comes, in short, closer than anybody else to dealing with my subject, both in his monograph and in a sensational article of his. I therefore feel duly flattered that he has ranked me—*opus supererogatum*, theologically speaking—among his "academic parents," but I feel slightly embarrassed as well, because I definitely belong, to borrow a Brechtian witticism, to his illegitimate fathers. Which is to say that Murphy was able to draw and build on a number of previous studies (by Hans Mayer, Thomas O. Brandt, and others)[46] all of which he, in turn, exceeded considerably, broadening them wherever necessary, and correcting them as he saw fit. Understandably, for lack of time, I can only hint at some of his results and insights, acclaim and recommend once more his achievements . . . and put forward, mildly yet firmly, my 'paternal' reservations and qualms.

The article appeared first, of course. But that which was so sensational about it was not so much the fact that, on Murphy's prodding, a copy of the Bible had been found in Brecht's estate, inscribed and dated on the flyleaf, in his unmistakable spelling and handwriting, "bertolt brecht / 1926."[47] No, the real sensation—or so Murphy believed—was the subsequent discovery that this Brechtian Bible, which had come out in Berlin in 1924 in a thin-paper pocket version, contained in either testament a whole series of markings, and again in Brecht's own hand. "Now we have Brecht's Bible," Murphy rejoiced, proudly announcing that his find should prove "quite a boon" to further Brecht research. "There are in all thirteen texts noted by Brecht," we were informed: namely, three from *Genesis* (1: 1-7, 32: 15-17, and 26: 12), two each from *Samuel* and *Kings* (*1 Sam.* 17: 24-28, 39, 43-44; *1 Sam.* 18:4; *1 Kings* 11: 11-13; *2 Kings,* chap.s 18-19), one each from *Job* and *Proverbs* (15: 21-34 and 16: 19, respectively), two from *Matthew* (15:

28-33 and chap.s 21-22), and one each from *Mark* (6: 45-50) and *John* (9: 1-34). In the commentaries Murphy appended, he discussed all of these texts extensively, speculating in every instance on what may have caused the Brechtian choice. I am, with one exception, not going to repeat or question his remarks, nor to belittle the overall importance of his discovery; also, I trust I need hardly state that the Bible we are talking about is the Lutheran Bible: *Die Bibel / oder / die ganze / Heilige Schrift / des / Alten und Neuen Testaments / nach der deutschen Übersetzung / D. Martin Luthers.* However, we must bear in mind that it would be decidedly wrong to conclude that this Bible was the only one that was ever read by Brecht or, indeed, to Brecht (for that is what his grandmother was apparently wont to do from his early childhood on, thus improving his style, as he himself acknowledged, and endowing him with his "wonderful" mastery of his native tongue, as others soon came to realize).[48] There can be no doubt that the handy edition brought to light through Murphy's efforts is one of several Brechtian Bibles; it is a special, perhaps sensational, one merely insofar as Brecht, in a rare display of ironic syncretism, had glued in opposite the title page, as a frontispiece of sorts, nothing less than the picture of a smiling buddha comfortably seated on some step or wall! And I for one am not so sure, to say the least, that this relaxed proponent of nirvana "seems well chosen and placed" for permanent confrontation with the Scriptures, as Murphy comments on its reproduction in his monograph; rather, such an outlandish embellishment of the Bible seems to betray, on the part of its owner, critical distance as well as skepticism toward its tidings.[49]

Obviously, like most theologians and clergymen attracted to Brecht, the member of the Company of Jesus was keen on salvaging him, if merely "to a certain degree," for Christianity. Hence, in addition to what he had proffered in his article, Murphy asserted in his book that the Marxist writer and thinker felt attached in particular, not only to *Ecclesiastes* and *Isaiah* where the problems of "death" and "social goodness" are at stake, but also to the "Passion" and "Crucifixion," especially in Matthew's account.[50] As regards Brecht's affinity to the Old Testament, I do in effect concur; as to his love for the Gospel, however, I hold that Murphy far overshot the mark, although I must concede, in spite of my qualms, that there seems to be something even to that bold assertion. Still, to infer that Brecht downright empathizes with Jesus to the point of "identification"[51] is as one-sided and exaggerated as is the adverse inference that he outright "denigrates the Founder of Christianity," and preferably "by travestying" scenes of the Passion.[52] In a way, Brecht did neither and both; and Murphy's yielding to the redemptory temptation is so much the more astonishing since, at the very same time, he was not at all unaware of the complexities of the Brechtian usage of the Scriptures, the wide range of possibilities it encompassed, and the tensions and contradictions involved. As a matter of fact, some of his most perspicacious and valid observations stemmed precisely from this awareness. For not only did Murphy show, enlarging the work of his forerunners, how Brecht would model a whole "sequence of events" after the Evangel, from the Last Supper to the Agony in the Garden, and from the Betrayal of Christ to Christ's Arrest—in his *Life of Edward the Second of England,* for example—but Murphy likewise arrived at the weighty conclusion that Brecht sets up "serious conflicts between different parts of the Bible," if only "occasionally," and thereby succeeds in forcing it into a contradictory relationship with itself.[53] Undoubtedly, insights such as these, however cautiously formulated, had seldom been gained heretofore; or else, they had scarcely been pronounced.[54] That they have a direct bearing on our topic ought to be evident. Less weighty, granted, though equally applicable and relevant is Murphy's distinction between, on the one hand, Brecht's "quotational" and, on the other, Brecht's "situational" allusions to the scriptural text, and the same is true of Murphy's explanatory supplement: "Just as Brecht freely imitates the sound and tone of the Bible in statements entirely his own, so he also freely uses biblical situations for his own ends."[55]

And yet, not even so circumspect an exegete as the Jesuit priest was fully proof against the pitfalls of the theological appropriation! He became entangled in them not only when he drew up the sum total of his results, but already when handling isolated and specific cases. For instance, as he leafed through the pocket book he had so meritoriously helped locate, Murphy detected—this is the exception I reserved—"a long red line in the margin" of the Gospel according to Mark.[56] He was profoundly "shocked," as he himself confessed, "at the identity of this passage": namely, the story of Christ's walking on the water (*Mark* 6: 45-50). But wasn't Murphy, I venture to surmise, profoundly delighted, too? Anyway, for Brecht's selection of what the theologian defines as "one of the more clearly transcendental descriptions of Jesus," an incident "not easily susceptible to socially useful (let alone socialist) interpretation," he offered no fewer than three explanations in a row. First, Murphy pondered the enticing idea that Brecht might have had "a semi-religious interest in the dramatically metaphysical nature of the scene"; second, Murphy turned round completely and thought he could "safely speculate on a possible connection" with Charles Lindbergh's flight across the waters of the Atlantic, that "daring feat" of 1927 which, as a triumph of human collectivism and technology over the elements as well as the primitivism of religion,[57] had so impressed the dramatist that he wrote a radio play, his *The Ocean Flight* (originally, *The Flight of the Lindberghs*), in praise of it; and third, again performing a complete turn-about, Murphy fell back on a very modest though quite endearing reason for the predilection, otherwise inexplicable to him, which he saw evinced by the marking of this scriptural passage. For since even Brecht, "the old master dialectician," seemed not "broad enough to find intellectual room" for both the "divine and serene tone" of the Gospel and the "thoroughgoing, joyfully atheistic attitude" of his Lindbergh, that which had aroused his empathy was perhaps, so his devotee hopefully argued, "Christ's concern for his disciples' existential welfare," the affection and care expressed in his soothing words, "Be of good cheer: it is I; be not afraid."[58]

However, none of these three explanations, as well-meant or ingenious as they may be, is in any way convincing; each remains either wishful and vague, or simply too far-fetched. And what is worse yet, the sole textual evidence Murphy contemplated, beside his theological and psychological ruminations, is unquestionably the least plausible of all. Nevertheless, it is exactly here, if anywhere, that we can cogently demonstrate why Brecht marked his copy of the Scriptures. Indeed he knew perfectly well what he was doing, for he did make use of Mark's account in another famous text of his, albeit some fifteen years after the acquisition of his handy pocket Bible. Both situationally and quotationally, to adopt Murphy's terminology, those five verses culminating with Christ's walking upon the water are alluded to in Brecht's boisterous folk comedy, *Herr Puntila und sein Knecht Matti* (*Puntila and Matti, His Hired Man,* as Ralph Manheim has rendered its title). And do I have to declare that what we find in this play is something totally different from any of Murphy's supposed reasons, his pious or impious explanations? The scene is set in a private bar or tavern, so to speak, *i.e.*, the back room of a hotel; the characters present are Puntila, the great Finnish dionysiac, still going strong after two days and two nights of uninterrupted carousing, and his boon companion, the Judge, who has slipped under the table and is sprawling there, dead drunk and sound asleep; and the former addresses the latter thus:

> Wach auf, Schwächling! Laß mich nicht so allein! Vor ein paar Flaschen Aquavit kapitulieren! Warum, du hast kaum hingerochen. Ins Boot hast du dich verkrochen, wenn ich dich übern Aquavit hingerudert hab, nicht hinaus hast du dich schaun trauen übern Bootsrand, schäm dich. Schau, ich steig hinaus auf die Flüssigkeit—*er spielt es vor*—und wandle auf dem Aquavit, und geh ich unter?[59]

Manheim's translation is fairly accurate:

> Wake up, weakling. Don't leave me alone like this! Capitulating to a couple of bottles of aquavit! It can't be. You've hardly had a smell of the stuff. While I was rowing you across the aquavit, you crawled off into the bottom of the boat, you were afraid to look over the edge, you ought to be ashamed of yourself. Look, I'm stepping out (*he acts it out*), I'm walking on the aquavit. Do I sink?[60]

This is neither the token of a semi-religious interest nor the sign of a sympathetic attachment to Christ's attitude, nor even the expression of a determined if joyful atheism; but it is, indisputably, the scene from *Mark*, the 'shocking' biblical passage on the margin of which Brecht had drawn his long line, and a red one to boot. His allusions are unequivocal: *wandeln*, of course, is the precise Lutheran term, and the equation of the timid Judge in Puntila's imaginary boat with the frightened disciples in theirs on the Sea of Galilee should be no less palpable. To top it all off, there are yet other such biblical references in Brecht's scene that reveal themselves as both quotational and situational. This time, they are not only to *Mark* but also to *Matthew* and the synoptic Gospels in their entirety. Puntila's very call to "wake up," as well as the whole situation of his being awake and alone, as opposed to the Judge's weakness and falling asleep, cannot fail to evoke the events in the Garden of Gethsemane, on the Mount of Olives; in fact, earlier in the same scene, Puntila has already told the sleeping Judge reproachfully, quoting from the Gospel(s): "... der Geist ist willig, aber das Fleisch ist schwach" ("... the spirit is willing but the flesh is weak"). While Manheim, ever so slightly, departs from the text of the Authorized Version, which would read, "The spirit truly *is* ready, but the flesh *is* weak," the Brechtian original, as is manifest, adheres once more ot the exact Lutheran wording from both *Mark* 14: 38 and *Matth.* 26: 41.[61]

I think these correspondences, which could still be augmented to some extent, will suffice. Evidently, what is going on in Brecht's opening scene is a far cry from any loving identification, whether with Christ's concern for his disciples or with Christ's own agony. Yet the Brechtian allusions, for all their irreverent overtones, do not just bespeak an unfeeling 'denigration' of Jesus and his deeds and sufferings. Actually, such jokes, seemingly outright blasphemous, are very old: their tradition is 'venerable' (if that's the term) although they are apocryphal. As we learn from Erich Auerbach, for example,[62] they date back at least to the monastic life of the Middle

Ages, that Christian epoch of unblemished piety and purity, as Romanticism would have it; furthermore, they can be encountered in mundane works like Boccaccio's *Decameron,* which provides, among other things, gems such as "the resurrection of the flesh" (*la resurrezion della carne*) taken in a plainly sexual sense, as the erection of the penis. In the Italian's narrative, to be sure, this ribaldry will come as no surprise— significantly enough, however, it was dutifully refurbished (or, who knows, congenially fashioned afresh) by the young Brecht in one of the various "Psalms" he composed. For he, too, proclaimed "die Auferstehung des Fleisches," and in the same biblical yet thoroughly un-Christian sense as Boccaccio![63] Here as elsewhere, then, in assessing Brecht's relationship to the Bible, we must be heedful lest we succumb ourselves to one-sidedness and unjustified exaggeration. Neither the ribald punning in Brecht's youthful poem nor the riotous mockeries in his mature play— both of which could be supplemented, and the latter almost at will, with parallels from the bulk of his output—can serve as proof of his uncompromising negation or rejection of the values at issue; and, conversely and concomitantly, not even his most serious and wholehearted allusive utilization of the Passion or the Crucifixion itself, as a kind of time-honored model for the sacrificial death of the righteous, can be tendered as evidence to the contrary, and interpreted as an unconditional affirmation or acceptance of those values. It is true, the death scene in his tragic as well as most overtly Bolshevist play, *Die Maßnahme (The Measures Taken)*, where the Young Comrade, for the benefit of mankind in terms of world revolution, is shot and thrown into a lime-pit, *i.e.*, literally 'liquidated,' bears the title, "Grablegung," which is the German word normally applied to the Burial of Christ.[64] It is also true that the death of Kattrin, the mute daughter of the canteen woman in *Mother Courage and Her Children,* constitutes a virtual re-enactment of Christ's dying on the Cross, in the milieu and costume of the Thirty Years' War, and that it is one of the very few scenes in the playwright's entire *œuvre* where Brecht, the advocate of distance and alienation or *Verfremdung,* expressly wanted his audience to "identify" and "empathize" (*sich einfühlen*) with one of his characters.[65] Most Christlike indeed, Kattrin sacrifices herself for the salvation of her neighbors; and the comment of one of the witnesses—a soldier, by the way—after she has accomplished it, and been hit by the fatal bullet, is an unmistakable echo of the last words of Jesus, "it is finished." The soldier's lapidary summary, "Sie hats geschafft" ("She's done it"),[66] has exactly the same rhythmical structure, and almost exactly the same sound pattern, as Luther's rendition of *John* 19: 30, "Es ist vollbracht."[67] Still, none of all this will make the Marxist author a stern apologist of Christian values, much less a devout Christian preacher. We are invited, yes, to an "identification" or "empathy,"[68] but not at all with Christ...and "Grablegung," it should be noted, was deleted by Brecht in the final version of his *The Measures Taken,* and replaced precisely by "Die Maßnahme."[69]

One thing ought to be clear, though: We must never lose sight of the specifically Lutheran elements in Brecht's biblical language. They may even derive—Luther is omnipresent—from writings other than the reformer's Bible. In a similar scene, for instance, also from Brecht's *Chronicle of the Thirty Years' War,* Mother Courage, frantically trying to redeem her arrested son, Swiss Cheese, without trading away her indispensable wagon in order to procure the necessary ransom, snubs the Chaplain (*Feldprediger*): "Und Sie, stehn Sie auch nicht herum wie Jesus am Ölberg..." ("And you, don't stand around like Jesus on the Mount of Olives...").[70] The commentary given by Murphy is as benign and interesting as it is to the point, except for the (missing) Lutheran link:

> Proverb 'Wie Ochs am Berg' altered to a mild blasphemy by inserting Jesus and the Mount of Olives manages to suggest the Agony in the Garden, and though distorted by Mutter Courage ('herumstehen!'), the allusion is psychologically justified since it unconsciously reflects his, her, and their, waiting to see what will become of Schweizerkas, and its use here reflects as well a dreadful cynicism as to the eventual outcome.[71]

That's all very fine, and I don't deny that the proverbial dumbfounded ox may likewise by at hand, perhaps quite intentionally so on the part of the playwright. But I should maintain all the same that the real proverb underlying Brecht's phrase, and which enabled him to perform his 'mildly blasphemous' operation, is a different one, and one having a traceable origin in the history of the Reformation: namely, "herumstehen wie die Ölgötzen" ("to stand around like the anointed idols"). And this expression, particularly its derogatory key term, *Ölgötze(n),* stems, it goes without saying, from the mouth and pen of Luther: it is a coinage of his which first emerged in June, 1520, then was reiterated by him shortly afterwards, and at once attained near proverbial currency as an invective for Catholic priests, the products of consecratory anointment.[72] (Let me add in parentheses that I do not believe, therefore, the evidence offered by the authoritative etymological dictionary of the German language, our dear *Kluge-Götze,* to be conclusive; for it is highly unlikely that Luther was thinking of those sculptured groups of the sleeping disciples on the Mount of Olives, arranged, ever so often, on the outside walls of medieval churches, and that, as a consequence, such depictions of the *Ölberg* as they were and are called triggered off a "Klammerform *Ö*[berg]götze" which ultimately led to *Ölgötze*.[73] After all, the disciples in that popular scene are asleep, hence sitting, crouching, lying, but surely not standing around! There can hardly be any doubt that it was the priestly anointment of the consecration which prompted Luther's neologism, especially if we consider what he wrote in his appeal to the German-Christian nobility, his famous *An den christlichen Adel deutscher Nation* published in August, 1520: "Daß aber der Papst oder Bischof salbet, Platten macht, ordiniert, weihet, anders dann Laien kleidet, mag einen Gleisner und Olgotzen machen, macht aber nimmermehr einen Christen oder geistlichen Menschen" ["The fact that the pope or bishop anoints, makes tonsures, ordains, consecrates, robes differently from laity, may produce a hypocrite and anointed idol, but won't ever produce a Christian or spiritual man"].[74]) To repeat: Murphy is right as to the function of Brecht's richly ambiguous sentence; but it was a Lutheran quip or, more technically speaking, satirical image that laid the associative groundwork for it. Thus, while my example might again seem peripheral to our argument, it does illustrate more than sufficiently, on the one hand, how much Brecht was imbued with the language of Luther even beyond Luther's Bible, and, on the other, how little even Brecht's best theological exegete has paid attention to such elements, in spite of so many and manifold finds.

When I had just finished jotting down these remarks, the postman came and didn't ring twice but, nonetheless, delivered a parcel from Germany. As it turned out, it contained a brand-new volume by various hands on Brecht and his work and influence, with what appears to be the most recent contribution to our topic. The author is a young professor of divinity at the newly-founded University of Augsburg, Brecht's hometown; the title of his sizable tract is a blatantly rhetorical question, "B. Brecht—ein Gegenstand der Theologie?"[75] What a monstrous understatement! Of course he is "a subject for theology"; he is even subject *to* theology, and in a whole variety of ways, as we have seen. His latest critic could easily have convinced himself of so obvious a truism, if only by consulting a modicum of secondary literature. Or has it all been 'sublated' under the heading of Brecht's allegedly questionable suitability? Granted, the piece is by no means the worst of its kind I have come across; it is, in effect, quite thoughtful and, indeed, soul-searching. Yet nowhere does this latter-day Augsburg Confession supersede anything of that which has been amassed and achieved in its numerous antecedents, whether brought out by clergymen or by laymen. It even falls behind some of their insights and results. In brief, what we have is but another attempt at a pious retrieval (which goes so far as to perceive "crypto-Christian" traits in Brecht)[76] and but another failure to tackle Brecht's Lutheran language. However, in recompense for all that, the author, a Swabian like his "Gegenstand," has supplied us with glorious lapses such as a Kierkegaardian *Furcht und Zittern* ("Fear and Trembling") as an abbreviation of the Brechtian title, based on Balzac, *Furcht und Elend des Dritten Reiches* ("Fear and Misery of the Third Reich," more commonly known as *The Private Life of the Master Race*).[77]—Recreated as well as disappointed, though heaving a sigh of relief, I resumed my parabolic orbit, which was nearing its center anyhow.

As to the rest of it, then, let me enumerate a few more suggestions, as well as investigate a few more examples! To round off my survey without too many detours is about all I can do.

First, there is the problem of what an eager retriever might wish to advertise, outstripping even Brecht's fellow Swabian, as the Marxist's 'crypto-Catholicism.' For didn't Brecht disclose, toward the end of his life, that he was "der letzte katholische Schriftsteller"?[78] In German, this still remains a casuistic ambiguity; in English, naturally, it all depends on whether or not we choose to capitalize the decisive term. Was Brecht really claiming to be "the last Catholic writer"? Or was he merely intimating— though that wouldn't amount to a mean accomplishment, either—that he was "the last catholic writer"? I for one have always opted for the lower-case solution, and explained Brecht's enigmatic dictum as a proud statement of his self-confidence: he, after all, knew what he was worth, and wanted to be recognized as the (or, at least, a) truly all-embracing author of his time, mastering every single genre and branch of his craft.[79] But there has been voices that actually favor the capital C, as, for example, the late Ernst Ginsberg, a renowned actor. Unambiguously, according to him, Brecht proclaimed himself "the last Roman Catholic brain," a scribe and clerk seasoned not only in matters religious but in theological debate as well:

> Geben Sie acht, wenn Sie mit mir über Glaubensfragen diskutieren, mein Lieber. Ich bin der letzte römischkatholische Kopf.[80]

That the son of a Protestant mother and Roman Catholic father (not the other way round, as some zealots aver)[81] did in fact sympathize with Catholicism, preferring it to the Lutheranism in which he was raised, has been attested to repeatedly, both by biographical researchers and by those who were closely connected with him, scholars and personal friends alike.[82] And that in his writings he also took up and exploited the Catholic heritage, and no less ruthlessly at that, along with his Lutheran and countless secular legacies, is already a commonplace. We need only remember his *Hauspostille* (translated by Eric Bentley as *Manual of Piety*)[83] and the sundry themes and forms of the traditional breviary it includes.[84] Not even the very title of this most famous collection of Brechtian poetry does hark back, as has been assumed unthinkingly by almost every critic,[85] to Luther and his collection of edifying texts; for what the reformer published in 1527 was a *Kirchen-Postille* consisting of sermons, whereas the genuine *Hauspostill oder Christ-Catholische Unterrichtungen von allen Sonn- und Feyr-Tagen des gantzen Jahrs,* which appeared in 1690, came from the desk of a Rhenish priest by name of Leonhard Goffiné.[86] Moreover, even a cursory perusal of the four-volume catalogue listing the holdings of the Brecht Archives, the so-called *Bestandsverzeichnis,* will unearth notes and other pertinent material, such as the fragment of a "Traktat über den Katholizismus" ("Treatise on Catholicism")[87] and the title of a projected novel, "Der Katholik" ("The Catholic"),[88] as well as so revealing a head as "Missionsbuch[:] Gleichnisse der allein wahren katholischen und der allein wahren atheistischen Religion" ("Missionary Book[:] Parables of the Only True Catholic and the Only True Atheistic Religion");[89] indeed, for the 'manuscript to be' of a play entitled "Bier" ("Beer"), Brecht had availed himself of the galleys of a missal as a convenient wrapper![90] All of these items, admittedly, seem to date from the 1920's; but in Brecht's library, as I was able to ascertain years ago, there exist at least two more, and they belong to the mid-1930's and early 1950's, respectively. One is a copy of Ludwig Marcuse's monograph on Ignatius of Loyola that Brecht had acquired,[91] the other, a German edition of Ignatius' *Spiritual Exercises* themselves (received as a gift, as the inscription indicates, from the controversial Marxist philosopher and long-term prisoner of the East-German authorities, Wolfgang Harich).[92]

But why did Brecht's so 'cherish'—if, again, that is the apposite word— Catholicism at the expense of his native Lutheranism? The ready explantion that the former's colorful splendor may have proved seductive to him, the latter being too "bleak" or "bare" *(kahl)* for an imaginative mind, strikes me as quite superficial although it was uttered by an expert whose judgments I normally value highly;[93] it is at best, I think, a shop-soiled cliché. That, contrarily, the young Brecht felt impressed by a certain strictness, discipline, and consequentiality exuding from Catholicism, as he himself appears to have reasoned,[94] sounds much more probable to me, though even this explanation, despite its authenticity, can scarcely be said to be wholly satisfactory.[95] Hence, must we perhaps reverse our approach, as it were? Could it be that it was Brecht's vehement repugnance against fundamental tenets of Lutheranism that made him probe into Catholicism?[96] Namely, that which we can substantiate for his entire intellectual life, from its earliest days to its very last, is a deep-seated dislike and disgust of Paul, indeed scorn and hatred of that "favorite apostle of Lutheranism," as he was called, significantly, by a friend of Brecht's to whom we owe a good deal of our information.[97] At the age of twenty or so, the rebellious poet branded Paul as a gigantic "falsifier" (*Fälscher*);[98] in the year of his death, the playwright directing his *Galileo*—a work replete with things Catholic, however critically presented—hurled at Paul and Pauline thought the insult, "imbecility" (*Schwachsinn*), and denounced the Epistle to the Ephesians as sheer trash.[99] But, of course, not only is Paul the favorite apostle of Lutheranism, he was likewise, and foremost, the *Lieblingsapostel* of Luther himself. It was precisely through Paul's letters that the reformer had penetrated to his liberating experience of divine grace, the very essence of his (un- or anti-Catholic) theology. Thus we arrive at the perplexing—or, maybe, not altogether perplexing—result that what Luther held dearest in the Bible was held cheapest in it by Brecht, whose "favorite reading" *(Lieblingslektüre)* was nevertheless Luther's Bible![100] Which doesn't make the Marxist a crypto-Catholic, to be sure, as little as a crypto-Christian; nor did it prevent him in the least from being rather conversant, as has already transpired in several instances, with things Lutheran even beyond the confines of the scriptural text.

Second, then, there is this specific Brechtian 'Lutheranism' in its contradictoriness, both outspoken and discreet, that might deserve the closer scrutiny of theological scholars as well as others. It is a task all the more challenging since Brecht mentions Luther comparatively rarely, and sometimes in a deceptively flippant or near disparaging way. A note of around 1930, for example, reflects upon the "temptations" (*Anfechtungen*) a writer is prone to, and concludes that he had better incorporate them in his book, instead of trying to scare them away. Wouldn't Luther, Brecht asks rhetorically, and without even putting a question mark, have been better advised if he had used the ink in that legendary ink-pot he flung at the devil, during his Wartburg sojourn, for a detailed report on how exactly the devil manages to vex a man engaged in translating the Bible?

> Ob es nicht besser gewesen wäre, was den Tintenfleck auf der Wartburg betrifft, wenn Luther die Tinte, statt sie nach dem Teufel zu werfen, dazu benutzt hätte, aufzuschreiben, wie der Teufel bei einer Bibelübersetzung stört.[101]

Or take the lovely entry in Brecht's diary, his so-called *Arbeitsjournal*, which discusses the subtleties of sex and their deplorable lack in Germany or, at least, German literature:

> auffällig, daß wir in deutschland keinerlei anzeichen einer verfeinerten sinnlichkeit haben! die liebe ist dort (siehe faust!) etwas himmlisches oder etwas teuflisches, aus welchem dilemma man sich zog, indem man eine gewohnheit daraus machte! nur goethe und mozart wären zu nennen, und der letztere verlegte seine liebesdramen weislich auf ausländische schauplätze ... im mittelalter scheint der einzige kulturträger auch auf diesem gebiet der klerus gewesen zu sein.

Ultimately, Brecht decreed in these notes of March 8, 1941:

> —es wäre für die deutschen gesund, ihr erstes liebeslustspiel (ihr mandragola) etwa in einem LUTHER-UND-KÄTTER-drama zu bekommen![102]

I shan't translate, for obvious reasons, the entire entry, rewarding though it would be to study Brecht's views concerning sensuality; I must be content with stressing that he posits here, as the first true comedy of love for the Germans, a play on none other than Luther. The model named for it is the well-known work of a man who happens to be a contemporary of the reformer, Niccolò Machiavelli, whose comedy of love, sex, and cuckoldry, *Mandragola* or *The Mandrake,* dates from about 1513. And do I have to point out expressly that "KÄTTER" should not be confounded, as did occur in a learned disputation, with "Kätner," *i.e.*, the term for a cottager or poor peasant, and hence with Luther's stand in the Peasants' War, but that this mysterious word is, simply and most naturally, a dialect form of "Katharina," the name of Luther's wife? Less known, granted, yet likewise not unimportant is the fact that the idea to write a comedy on Luther and Catherine ("LUTHER-UND-KÄTTER") was first conceived by Richard Wagner, then weighed by Friedrich Nietzsche, and finally picked up by Thomas Mann, who actually undertook to compose such a drama, but abandoned his plan after elaborate preparations.[103] The founder of Lutheranism, at any rate, doesn't seem to have been so colorless and uninspiring, either for Brecht himself or for some of his worthiest predecessors ...

It goes without saying that the Marxist, in spite of my bantering, was familiar with Luther's stand in the Peasants' War and Luther's writings pertaining to it, his "Schriften gegen die Bauern,"[104] as well as with the other great Lutheran pamphlets; in fact, Brecht accorded the reformer—apart from what is self-evident, Luther's status as a translator—classical greatness not only as a lyrical poet but also as a pamphleteer. Not at all did he hesitate to admit that this "Klassiker . . . in der Lyrik und im Pamphlet" had been one of those whom he had emulated throughout his life, and from whom he had learnt and profited a lot.[105] And similar pronouncements can be found at the beginning and, once again, toward the end of Brecht's creative career. In the early 1920's, for instance, he bluntly suggested to emphasize the relevance of Luther, rather than that of Bismarck;[106] as late as 1955, he praised a recent booklet on Luther he had been given, and assured its author, a Lutheran pastor, that he had indeed read it, both with pleasure and interest, and would like to have "more of this nourishment." Whether by virtue of ironic mimicking or by chance, there is a faint biblical, Lutheran, almost pastoral ring in the words of Brecht's letter to the somewhat unbelieving minister:

> . . . wie Sie schon vermutet haben, waren meine Äußerungen über Ihr Luther-Büchlein völlig ernsthaft. Die Schrift hat mich vergnügt und interessiert. Ich war also durchaus berechtigt, es [*sic*] zu loben und mehr von dieser Speise zu verlangen.[107]

However, by far the most important reference to Luther in the whole Brechtian work and career is his mention, widely known and often adduced, in Brecht's essay of 1939, "Über reimlose Lyrik mit unregelmäßigen Rhythmen" ("On Rhymeless Verse with Irregular Rhythms"). Not only Brechtians, I am afraid, will be getting impatient because of my having withheld it for such a long time; so here it is:

> Der Satz der Bibel 'Reiße das Auge aus, das dich ärgert' hat einen Gestus unterlegt, den des Befehls, aber er ist doch nicht rein gestisch ausgedrückt, da 'das dich ärgert' eigentlich noch einen anderen Gestus hat, der nicht zum Ausdruck kommt, nämlich den einer Begründung. Rein gestisch ausgedrückt, heißt der Satz (und Luther, der 'dem Volk aufs Maul sah,' formt ihn auch so): 'Wenn dich dein Auge ärgert, reiß es aus!' Man sieht wohl auf den ersten Blick, daß diese Formulierung gestisch viel reicher und reiner ist. Der erste Satz enthält eine Annahme, und das Eigentümliche, Besondere in ihr kann im Tonfall voll ausgedrückt werden. Dann kommt eine kleine Pause der Ratlosigkeit und erst dann der verblüffende Rat.[108]

John Willett—resorting to "gest," an obsolete English word meaning "bearing, carriage, mien," and its adjective, "gestic"—has translated Brecht's passage as follows:

> The Bible's sentence 'pluck out the eye that offends thee' is based on a gest—that of commanding—but it is not entirely gestically expressed, as 'that offends thee' has a further gest which remains unexpressed, namely that of explanation. Purely gestically expressed the sentence runs 'if thine eye offends thee, pluck it out' (and this is how it was put by Luther, who 'watched the people's mouth'). It can be seen at a glance that this way of putting it is far richer and cleaner from a gestic point of view. The first clause contains an assumption, and its peculiarity and specialness can be fully expressed by the tone of voice. Then there is a little pause of bewilderment, and only then the devastating proposal.[109]

For the most part, this pledge of allegiance to the Lutheran language is self-explanatory; versed or not in the intricacies of the Brechtian theory of *Gestus* and *gestisch,* one will comprehend what its author is trying to convey. Yet quoting alone, as is customary, won't do. Brecht's parenthetical tribute to Luther (which has a series of weighty though more or less clandestine parallels) must and can be shown to be indicative, not only of their comparable ability of mastering German individually, as poets and pamphleteers, or translator and playwright, respectively, but also of a problem and predicament they shared and mastered, indeed resolved brilliantly, in the overall history of the German language itself. Just as Luther, after the divergent attempts of men like Niklas von Wyle and Heinrich Steinhöwel, who had rendered either solely the letter or solely the spirit of their texts, was capable of overcoming such extremes, shedding the faults and retaining the merits of both,[110] so, too, was Brecht when faced with the extremities German literature had reached by the time he made his entrance: the dual impasse, that is, either of Naturalism, with its slavish and slovenly imitations of everyday speech, or of Expressionism, with its bookish, stilted, and utterly stylized idiom.[111] Admirably, as had done Luther, Brecht succeeded in creating a language that was natural as well as controlled, popular as well as poetic—or rather, Brecht re-created it with the help of the Lutheran Bible, by 'watching Luther's pen,' in addition to 'the people's mouth.' The perfect unity thus achieved of content or message, on the one hand, and of form or structure and gesture, both linguistic and bodily, on the other, constitutes what the theoretician in his essay defines as *gestisch* and *Gestus,* although it certainly does not exhaust his multifarious concepts and their implications. For Brecht did not merely emulate the Lutheran language, but did in fact surpass it in his field: namely, in poetry and, specifically, through those "rhymeless verse[s] with irregular rhythms," the most consummate of which are invested with a dialectical quality developed straight from the application of his "gestic" principle.—But to expound all this not even meticulously, only adequately, would require a nice little essay of its own, something I needs must forgo.

Instead, let me continue, third, with 'biblical form and content,' and seize another Brechtian quote that has long been overdue, rampant as it is like a slogan, and which therefore can't be left out in our context. In response to an inquiry eliciting what had been one's "strongest impression ever"—*der stärkste Eindruck*—conducted by a fashionable magazine in 1928, Brecht calmly observed, "Sie werden lachen: die Bibel" ("You'll laugh: the Bible").[112] It was a serious reply, for all its flippancy; and what it referred to was, no question about it, the Bible of Luther. In truth, 'Lutheran' and 'biblical,' within the realm of Brecht's native tongue, were practically synonymous for him, as witness the recollections of his daughter, according to whom her father used to regale her "with comparisons of the Luther Bible [*Luther-Bibel*] and the King James Version,"[113] as well as his own words, "schimpfend mit biblischer (bzw lutherischer) kraft und plastik" ("cussing with biblical [*i.e.* Lutheran] force and vividness").[114] Since Barbara [Schall-]Brecht was born in 1930, and the Brechtian formulation dates from 1941, these testimonies can also serve to demonstrate that Brecht's strongest impression was a lasting one indeed. It was, I daresay, the most lasting of all his experiences... If that sounds too extravagant, or is deemed inconclusive, notice should be taken, among other things, of Brecht's lifelong exercises in biblical, *i.e.* Lutheran, style, both in his correspondence and when drawing up plot summaries,[115] of his habit on stage of reading aloud from the Scriptures, and writing down what he liked best,[116] and of the recital of scriptural passages (*Bibelstellen*) listed as a means of training for his actors and actresses.[117] And if even that is not yet enough, I recommend to ponder the two quotations following. The first is from a fragmentary poem Brecht scribbled, it seems, around 1918; the second, from his comments on a "miserable" oratorio a performance of which he had attended in 1920. In either instance, the young writer testified—'shockingly' again, perhaps, though in a different vein—to his experiencing the language of the Lutheran liturgy and Bible as a kind of physical onslaught of an almost erotic intensity. Compare:

Einst war Sitzen schön in Kirchenbänken
Wo der Segen mich zum Himmel schmiß![118]

And:

Aber gewisse Bibelworte sind nicht totzukriegen. Sie gehen
durch und durch. Man sitzt unter Schauern, die einem, unter der
Haut, den Rücken lang herunterstreichen, wie bei der Liebe.[119]

Even while the benediction had ceased to transport Brecht, catapulting
him sky-high, certain words of the Bible persisted in immersing him in a
more earth-bound ecstasy of orgiastic, indeed orgastic, dimensions! At the
time of the latter confession, which surely is remarkable in itself, he was, by
the way, occupied with plans for a piece on Jesus. Brecht had "many ideas"
for it, as he noted,[120] and unorthodox they were, for they bordered (I am
overstating the case just a bit) on a near Baalish conception.[121] But he never
tried his hand at this play; his Jesus as an ennobled Baal of sorts was too
"lyrical," he realized, and thus "unfit for drama" to begin with.[122] All the
more, however, did the impact of *Bibelworte* as phrased by Luther keep
piercing Brecht "through and through," as it were.

One could cite *ad infinitum* (and that is hardly an exaggeration) words
as well as names, titles, sentences, paragraphs, scenes, chapters, acts, and
even entire works of Brecht's, permeated with biblical lore in its Lutheran
wording; there are, literally, hundreds and hundreds of them in his
enormous *œuvre*. Of course, I can give here only a few scattered examples
amassed rather at random, and shall, furthermore, skip the poetry almost
completely because I have elsewhere dealt with it at some length.[123] Yet
even such dainty morsels will amount to an overabundance. Brechtian
names lifted from the Scriptures—whether occurring in published material
or in the holdings of the Brecht Archives—include Habakkuk[124] and
Salome,[125] Miriam[126] and Job,[127] Ezekiel,[128] Uriah,[129] and the Prodigal
Son,[130] indeed Eleazar, the son of Aaron, from *Ex.* 6: 23/25,[131] and
Malchus, the servant of the high priest, from *John* 18: 10.[132] Brechtian
titles of biblical origin comprise those of three one-act plays ("Er treibt
einen Teufel aus" ["He Casts Out a Devil"], "Lux in tenebris" ["The Light
Shineth in Darkness"], "Der Fischzug" ["The Draught of Fishes"])[133] and,
naturally, that of the full-fledged drama, *Baal*; but already the very first
play the fifteen-year-old penned and 'published,' another piece in one act,
is entitled, most tellingly, "Die Bibel" ("The Bible").[134] (And no less
striking, incidentally, is the discovery that this mimeographed text of 1913

contains exemplary passages of what Brecht, decades later, was to describe as his "gestic" speech!)[135] Also, while it seems quite understandable that there should appear a figure by the fabulous name of "Trinity Moses" (*Dreieinigkeitsmoses*) in a play, or opera, such as *Rise and Fall of the City of Mahagonny,* fraught as it is with the Judaeo-Christian tradition as a whole, both the Old and the New Testaments,[136] the converse fact that a radio play about a general and gourmet of the 1st century B.C., set in ancient Rome and a proletarian Hades, should introduce a "Dreifaltige Stimme," of all things, cannot but strike us again as extraordinary and most telling. For this *dreifaltig* voice—not, mind you, *dreifältig*—isn't a "threefold" one, as it has been rendered,[137] but, as precisely as anachronistically, a "Trinitarian Voice."[138] And yet, it emanates, needless to underscore, from Brecht's *The Trial of Lucullus* (*Das Verhör* [or *Die Verurteilung*] *des Lukullus*)! No wonder, then, if the mythical Greeks in his adaptation of the Sophoclean *Antigone,* characters like Creon or the Elders of Thebes, draw on parables or similes from the Gospel, *e.g.* the cutting down of the fig tree and the cutting off of one's hand.[139]

With these and the preceding examples, we have been crossing over, gradually yet steadily, into the vast and variegated area of scriptural subject matter in a strict sense, though it goes without saying that form and content are in effect inseparable. Wherever we look, words, images, and motifs which are biblical as well as Lutheran can be seen to pervade smaller or larger parts of the Brechtian writings; even post-scriptural Christian lore of purely Catholic provenance, such as the struggle of St. Joan with the powers that be, which inspired Brecht to no fewer than three dramatic treatments,[140] presents itself clad, so to speak, in a Lutheran garb. Indeed, giving vent to a pun in the manner of George Bernard Shaw, whose work was far from alien to Brecht,[141] one might safely posit that something clerical and/or Lutherical figures prominently in every single one of the twenty-odd volumes of Brecht's collected works plus supplements. To stick to the Bible, we find both Absalom riding through the woods and the moment of eternal damnation ("Absalom reitet durch den Wald oder Der öffentliche Mann" and "Das Tanzfest oder Der Augenblick der ewigen Verdammung," as two early short stories are entitled);[142] further, we encounter the fragments of a drama on "David"[143] and of a libretto, "Sodom and Gomorrah,"[144] together with two "Songs of Solomon"(in the *Threepenny Opera* and *Mother Courage and Her Children,* respectively)[145] and with a combined and most powerful inversion of the Parable of the Talents and the Last Judgment, the culmination of Brecht's *Threepenny Novel* (or, as it was first translated, *A Penny for the Poor*).[146] Certain favorite motifs of his, such as the Flood (*Sintflut*) and, interestingly, the story of Judith, emerge not only twice but recur several times. There are, for instance, a couple of brief narrative pieces, "Von der Sintflut,"[147] and a fragmentary radio play, "Die Geschichte der Sintflut,"[148] along with numerous other citations;[149] and there are likewise two texts or plans for films, "Die Judith von Saint Denis"and "Die Judith von Shimoda,"[150] along with the aforesaid one-act play of 1913, which forms a (counter)reformation variant of this story, and with an early but, once more, quite precocious tale—missing in the Brechtian estate, unfortunately—which seemed to motivate Judith's beheading of Holofernes by her disgust for his "sweaty feet" (*Schweißfüße*),[151] and thus to prefigure that debunking of idealized heroism so dear to the mature author (just think of Brecht's famous novella about Socrates).[152] On the other hand, certain plays virtually abound with biblical motifs, encompassing either several at a time or whole clusters and sequences thereof: as, for instance, the story of Judas betraying Jesus, in *Life of Edward the Second of England*;[153] the derision of Christ and the Parable of the Good Samaritan, in *The Caucasian Chalk Circle*;[154] or, in *The Good Person of Szechwan*,[155] the story of Lot, the angels, and the rain of fire.[156] Yet even in plays that have no—secret or overt—scriptural foundation whatsoever, but instead are based on historical facts like colonialism, fascism, and the revolutionary events since 1871, or on sociological phenomena like brainwashing, human alienation, and bootlegging gangsters, we hit upon lavish biblical imagery and receive broad hints at the Bible. Examples can be gleaned from *A Man's a Man* and *In the Jungle of Cities* (Peter's denial),[157] from *Drums in the Night* (the Prodigal Son's filling his belly with husks)[158] and *Roundheads and Peakheads* (the soldiers' casting lots for Christ's coat),[159] as well as from that weird satire linking Hitler and Al Capone, *The Resistible Rise of Arturo Ui*, where a rule from *Deuteronomy* ("Thou shalt not muzzle the ox when he treadeth out *the* corn") grotesquely justifies the whims of a professional killer,[160] or, last but surely not least, from Brecht's drama on the Paris uprising, *The Days of the Commune*, where the Christian, or biblical, admonition of the moderates, "All they that take the sword shall perish with the sword," is countered, unflinchingly, by the equally biblical yet totally un-Christian rejoinder, "And all they that don't take the sword?"[161]

The Marxist playwright, as a matter of fact, went so far as to have the Book itself appear on stage, not only as an abstract object of ideological criticism, *i.e.*, a religious document the use or abuse of which is being debated, but also as a most concrete object for the business of the players, *i.e.*, as one of the props. The bible thus attains a dramaturgical or, indeed, genuinely theatrical function. For instance, in a scene titled "Die

Bergpredigt" ("The Sermon on the Mount") from Brecht's *Fear and Misery of the Third Reich*, the contradiction as perceived by him between *Matth.* 22:21 ("Render therefore to Caesar the things which are Caesar's; and unto God the things that are God's") and *Matth.* 5: 9 ("Blessed *are* the peacemakers") is unmasked verbally, though quite effectively, while in a scene from Brecht's huge didactic play, *The Mother*, an actual copy of the Bible is brought in from the wings, and eventually torn to pieces during a violent discussion, after accusations such as:

> Warum von Gott reden? Daß in 'seines Vaters Hause' viele Wohnungen sind, das sagt man euch, aber daß in Rostow zu wenige sind und warum, das sagt man euch nicht.[163]

(In Lee Baxandall's rendition:

> Why speak of God? Although they say there are many mansions in 'our Father's house,' there are certainly too few in Russia. But that they never tell you, and they don't tell you why.[164])

Still, it is—in good Lutheran fashion—the biblical text that counts in these scenes, for all their showmanship. And, clearly, Brecht launches his attacks on the Gospel not only by taking it to the letter, but also by pitting its teachings against one another; moreover, what looms up here, however implicitly, is once again the concept of the two realms. Ultimately, the Bible in the Brechtian writings reveals itself always, linguistically or otherwise, as Luther's Bible. In fact, its omnipresence in them is such as to have prompted their author in various cases to indulge in what the Russian Formalists called 'laying bare the device.'[165] Which is to say that the very method employed is laid open, or even expressly mentioned by name. To wit, a play composed as early as 1923/24, Brecht's adaptation of Marlowe's *Edward II*, makes its Judas figure, Baldock, meekly and unmistakably observe: "Die Bibel lehrt uns, wie's zu halten ist" ("The Bible tells us how it's done").[166] Later examples of Brechtian *obnazhenie priëma* can be found especially in the *Threepenny Opera*; but since this work is so well known, its similar if bluntly sarcastic observations by Mac the Knife and Jonathan Peachum—praise of the "tricks" and "saws" they owe to the Bible, or lament that, alas, it's getting worn out more and more—need hardly be cited.[167] Nor do I have to reiterate that, in reality, Brecht's Scriptures were anything but wearing off; quite to the contrary, they proved to be an inexhaustible treasury to be ransacked at will, both for his art and his daily life.[168] And that applies, it should be noted, to the

Apocrypha as well, [169] not just to the canon of the Holy Writ in its Lutheran version . . .

Verily, Luther's language in the mouth of Brecht; the Bible of the reformer in the hands of the Marxist! Hence I shall, fourth, briefly analyze two final biblical Brechtian texts (one from each of the testaments) marked as authentic by the author himself, and thereby try to produce some 'crowning evidence' at last. Both my examples—strings of scriptural quotes, rather than coherent passages—are from Brecht's *Galileo,* or *Life of Galileo* (*Leben des Galilei*), one of his greatest and, for our end, most typical and yielding works.

The first text derives from Scene 7, which bears the heading, "Aber die Inquisition setzt die kopernikanische Lehre auf den Index" ("But the Inquisition places the Copernican doctrine on the Index"); it is the so-called *Bibelduell,* the stichomythia with sayings from the Bible, between Galileo, on the one hand, and Cardinal Barberini, later Pope Urban VIII, on the other, occurring in a ballroom during the Roman carnival. To characterize it in a nutshell, it constitutes the sprightly yet portentous prelude to the clash of the obligations of the scientist with the exigencies of those in power, political and economical as well as spiritual. That which is at stake is, in a word, truth. Should it be spread? Should it be withheld? Barberini's companion and colleague, Cardinal Bellarmine, provides the cue:

BELLARMINE: Gehen wir mit der Zeit, Barberini. Wenn Sternkarten, die sich auf eine neue Hypothese stützen, unsern Seeleuten die Navigation erleichtern, mögen sie die Karten benutzen. Uns mißfallen nur Lehren, welche die Schrift falsch machen.
Er winkt grüßend nach dem Ballsaal zu.

GALILEI: Die Schrift.—'Wer aber das Korn zurückhält, dem wird das Volk fluchen.' Sprüche Salomonis.

BARBERINI: 'Der Weise verbirget sein Wissen.' Sprüche Salomonis.

GALILEI: 'Wo da Ochsen sind, da ist der Stall unrein. Aber viel Gewinn ist durch die Stärke des Ochsen.'

BARBERINI: 'Der seine Vernunft im Zaum hält, ist besser als der eine Stadt nimmt.'

GALILEI: 'Des Geist aber gebrochen ist, dem verdorren

die Gebeine.' *Pause.* 'Schreiet die Wahrheit
nicht laut?'
BARBERINI: 'Kann man den Fuß setzen auf glühende
Kohle, und der Fuß verbrennt nicht?'[170]

Ralph Manheim and Wolfgang Sauerländer, in a translation largely
identical with the one prepared by Charles Laughton in collaboration with
Brecht, have rendered this piece of dialogue as follows:

BELLARMINE: We must go with the times, Barberini. If star
charts based on a new hypothesis make
navigation easier for our seamen, let's use
them. We disapprove only of doctrines that
put scripture in the wrong. (*He waves a
greeting to the ballroom*)
GALILEO: Scripture.—'He that withholdeth corn, the
people shall curse him.' Proverbs of Solomon.
BARBERINI: 'A prudent man concealeth knowledge.'
Proverbs of Solomon.
GALILEO: 'Where no oxen are, the crib is clean: but much
increase is by the strength of the ox.'
BARBERINI: 'He that ruleth his spirit is better than he that
taketh a city.'
GALILEO: 'But a broken spirit drieth the bones.' (*Pause*)
'Doth not wisdom cry?'
BARBERINI: 'Can one go upon hot coals, and his feet not be
burned?'[171]

Don't such lines, really, sound authentic enough? The "Scripture" dutifully
invoked; "Proverbs of Solomon" named twice; not to mention quotation
marks, archaisms, appropriate images and motifs, and what have
you... Accordingly, all critics and scholars so far, whether laymen or
clergymen, have taken it for granted that Brecht in this text quotes the
biblical verses literally, copying them, as it were;[172] only one single
investigator, though without further consequences, dropped the casual
remark that Brecht's quotations are handled freely.[173]

On closer scrutiny, however, we detect things which are much more
complicated. Namely, while it is undoubtedly true that all six lines, or seven
quotes, can be traced to some verse or other from *Proverbs*, it is no less true
and demonstrable that the playwright has altered, consciously and
cunningly, each and every sentence and phrase (and, sometimes, even

word) in his seemingly faithful quotations.—Already in *Prov.* 11: 26, with which Galileo starts out, Luther's *Leute* ("people" in a general sense) has been replaced by *Volk* (with a clear implication of "the lower classes"): as a result, Brecht's biblical verse at once takes on a sharper, more socially critical edge.—The ensuing reply by Barberini, granted, is rooted primarily in *Prov.* 12: 23 ("Ein verständiger Mann trägt nicht Klugheit zur Schau"); yet the Brechtian wording, which also echoes *Prov.* 10: 14, 10: 19, and 14: 3,[174] is different, and so is, consequently, the message it imparts. For Luther's almost urbane maxim—fit for Gracián or the French moralists, or some Chinese sage, for that matter—is turned into a grave forewarning and foreboding! Doubtless, Barberini intimates Galileo should beware lest he endanger himself by distributing "knowledge" to the ignorant, *i.e.* the poor and oppressed, who must be shut off by all means from such *Wissen* (which is, it will be remembered, a key concept both in Brecht's play and in his entire work).—Admittedly, Galileo's verse about the "oxen" (equaling *Prov.* 14: 4, which is reproduced by Brecht's English translators *verbatim* from the Authorized Version, as most of his quotes or pseudo-quotes) does not contain ideologically motivated changes, since its model reads: "Wo nicht Ochsen sind, da ist die Krippe rein; aber wo der Ochse geschäftig ist, da ist viel Einkommen." Nevertheless, the playwright aimed at, and succeeded in, propounding the biblical thought more graphically and urgently, and in a more *gestisch* way to boot; he rendered, congenially indeed, Luther's language even more Lutheran.—With Barberini's next reply, half an outspoken menace, half a warning still, the "Bible duel" has departed farthest from its scriptural source. Just compare the Holy Writ and the cardinal's unholy twist of it: "Ein Geduldiger ist besser denn ein Starker, und der seines Mutes Herr ist, denn der Städte gewinnt"—"Der seine Vernunft im Zaum hält, ist besser als der eine Stadt nimmt." At most, then, the Brechtian phrasing amounts to a liberal variation on *Prov.* 16: 32, its ideological changes being quite trenchant; for not only do they discard the notion of patience, but they also substitute "reason" instead, another key concept of Brecht's, whose scientist-hero so believes in its "gentle force" (*die sanfte Gewalt der Vernunft*).[175]—Galileo is, of course, fully aware of the purport of the crucial rebuff he meets with, wherefore his redoubled answer assumes all the more weightiness. What he proclaims initially ("Des Geist aber gebrochen ist, dem verdorren die Gebeine") was modeled after *Prov.* 17: 22 ("...ein betrübter Mut vertrocknet das Gebein"); what he pronounces subsequently ("Schreiet die Wahrheit nicht laut?") was formed after *Prov.* 8: 1-3 ("Ruft nicht die Weisheit, und die Klugheit läß sich hören? / Öffentlich am Wege und an der Straß steht sie. / An den Toren der Stadt, da man zur Türe eingeht, schreit sie..."). Either portion of this rewording of the Bible can again be shown to be highly "gestic" as well as most trenchant. The latter, Galileo's impassioned outcry, condenses no fewer than three consecutive scriptural verses into one poignant and lapidary rhetorical question, with the momentous replacement of "wisdom" and "prudence" by "truth"; the former—note its structural similarity to Brecht's favorite, "if thine eye offends thee, pluck it out"[176]— deftly draws on additional books from the Old Testament, above all *Isaiah* (he who is wretched is "zerbrochenen Geistes") and *Ezekiel* ("Unsre Gebeine sind verdorrt, und unsre Hoffnung ist verloren, und es ist aus mit uns"),[177] all of which are combined with, and superimposed on, the original clause. Obviously, as anyone familiar with the Brechtian drama will agree, Luther's biblical speech is here employed in construing, by virtue of an ingenious montage, both a forceful and bold rebuttal on the part of the protagonist and, at the same time, a bitter and ironic reproach on the part of the playwright. If only figuratively, Galileo, unbeknownst to himself, predicts the outcome of his story and anticipates the ultimate judgment that will be passed on him.—The third reply by Barberini, which now is a veritable barb and a snide and undisguised threat, terminates the whole futile exchange. But it also (in masterly effigy, so to speak) seals Galileo's fate. For the words of the cardinal, an equally pungent rhetorical question, conjure up the shadow of Giordano Bruno—*der Verbrannte*, as he is called[178]—whose condemnation to the stake looms large in the play from its very beginning; likewise, they constitute yet another exemplar of Lutheran "gestic" language streamlined and even 'dialecticized' by Brecht. Once more, compare his model (this time, *Prov.* 6: 28) to what has become of it in his hands: "Wie sollte jemand auf Kohlen gehen, daß seine Füße nicht verbrannt würden?"—"Kann man den Fuß setzen auf glühende Kohle, und der Fuß verbrennt nicht?" The improvement achieved by Brecht's laconic repetition of *Fuß/Fuß*, over Luther's apparently richer alternation of *gehen/Füße*—to name but the simplest though most efficient device—ought to be self-evident; besides, it is strongly reminiscent of some of the most brilliant lines from the *Threepenny Opera.*[179]

Do I have to state expressly that such comparisons are not meant to belittle the reformer's accomplishments in the least? Yet, all the same, his disciple's creative manipulations certainly aren't loose quotational exercises; no critic can afford to neglect them, much less ignore them altogether. Nor can we content ourselves with Murphy's pithy definition, "semi-biblical *Nachdichtung*,"[180] as meet as the notion of emulative appropriation may be for a starting-point. Not even the more elaborate description of the Brechtian technique as one of "adapting the texts slightly so as to make them more sharply contradictory," and of "freely synthesizing a biblical teaching without bothering to quote exactly," while "always being careful to use biblical German,"[181] can be said to be more than preliminary, for all the insights it betrays; it scarcely proves to be sufficient, either linguistically or ideologically. As will have come to the fore in my fleeting analysis, if mainly indirectly, not just the Lutheran Bible but the King James Bible, too, must have played a significant role in the composition—or, to be more precise, the reworking[182] and first translation—of Brecht's biblical stichomythy. The playwright knew the Authorized Version quite well, as did his friend and erstwhile collaborator, Laughton; and we are therefore bound to suspect that it served as a kind of productive catalyst, or regulative agent, during their co-operation. But, though by no means unimportant, this was merely a brief episode in the long and complex process of the 'Brechtianization' of the Scriptures. Surely the Authorized Version did not supplant Brecht's *Luther-Bibel*, whether in his *Bibelduell* or elsewhere in his work and life (a fact which, I hope, has also transpired occasionally as we went along, and could further be substantiated by way of a more painstaking interpretation). And what pertains to the linguistic complexities applies to the ideological ones as well. Namely, that which provides the dramatic frame—if you wish, the archetypal constellation—for the scriptural duel between Galileo and Barberini is nothing less than the temptation of Jesus by the devil on the pinnacles of the temple, according to *Matth.* 4: 3-10! However, the sides of the soteriological encounter have been inverted by Brecht: The cardinal, *i.e.* the Church or institutionalized Christianity, occupies the position of Satan, whereas Reason and Humaneness, *i.e.* the scientist and his quest for truth and a knowledge accessible to the people, occupy that of Christ. I trust I can refrain from commenting on this shrewd and, as some might say, truly diabolic device of Brecht's; all I want to add is the exegetic piquancy that he that recognized where the playwright had virtually set his stage, and whom he had chosen as his characters' doubles, was neither a Catholic priest nor a Lutheran minister... but a Soviet scholar, the same staunch expert I cited at the outset in a similar theological instance.[183]

To bring up, finally, the second of my two texts, or pieces of 'crowning evidence.' It stems from Scene 14 of Brecht's *Life of Galileo*, the title of which as it affects our investigation runs: "Galileo Galilei lebt in einem Landhaus in der Nähe von Florenz, bis zu seinem Tod ein Gefangener der Inquisition" ("Galileo Galilei spends the rest of his life in a villa near Florence, as a prisoner of the Inquisition"). In this scene, the penultimate of the play, the great scientist is almost blind, having ruined his eyesight in countless hours of nightly research; moreover, not only is he in the claws of the papal henchmen, but he is also cared for—that is, nursed as well as henpecked—by his elderly daughter, Virginia. The short section I am going to adduce shows him, after she has denied him the benefit of being read to from his beloved Horace, as he grudgingly consents to finish his weekly letter to the archbishop, who keeps feeding him with edifying questions and quotations. Naturally, Galileo is mad at that pious spinster of a daughter of his, but cannot risk to disclose his feelings; thus, while Virginia is sitting down to take his dictation, he snaps:

GALILEI: Wie weit war ich?

VIRGINIA: Abschnitt vier: Anlangend die Stellungnahme der Heiligen Kirche zu den Unruhen im Arsenal von Venedig stimme ich überein mit der Haltung Kardinal Spolettis gegenüber den aufrührerischen Seilern...

GALILEI: Ja. *Diktiert:*...stimme ich überein mit der Haltung Kardinal Spolettis gegenüber den aufrührerischen Seilern, nämlich, daß es besser ist, an sie Suppen zu verteilen im Namen der christlichen Nächstenliebe, als ihnen mehr für ihre Schiffs- und Glockenseile zu zahlen. Sintemalen es weiser erscheint, an Stelle ihrer Habgier ihren Glauben zu stärken. Der Apostel Paulus sagt: Wohltätigkeit versaget niemals.—Wie ist das?

VIRGINIA: Es ist wunderbar, Vater.

GALILEI: Du meinst nicht, daß eine Ironie hineingelesen werden könnte?

VIRGINIA: Nein, der Erzbischof wird selig sein. Er ist so praktisch.

GALILEI: Ich verlasse mich auf dein Urteil. Was kommt als nächstes?

VIRGINIA: Ein wunderschöner Spruch: 'Wenn ich schwach bin, da bin ich stark.'

GALILEI: Keine Auslegung.

VIRGINIA: Aber warum nicht?

GALILEI: Was kommt als nächstes?

VIRGINIA: 'Auf daß ihr begreifen möget, daß Christum liebhaben viel besser ist denn alles Wissen.' Paulus an die Epheser III, 19.

GALILEI: Besonders danke ich Eurer Eminenz für das herrliche Zitat aus den Epheser-Briefen [*sic*]. Angeregt dadurch...[*etc.*][184]

I am resorting again to the more recent translation of Manheim and Sauerländer:

GALILEO: Where was I?

VIRGINIA: Section four: Concerning the reaction of the church to the unrest in the arsenal in Venice, I agree with Cardinal Spoletti's attitude concerning the rebellious rope makers...

GALILEO: Yes. (*Dictates*)...agree with Cardinal Spoletti's attitude concerning the rebellious rope makers, to wit, that it is better to dispense soup to them in the name of Christian charity than to pay them more for their ships' cables and bell ropes. All the more so, since it seems wiser to strengthen their faith than their greed. The Apostle Paul says: Charity never faileth.— How does that sound?

VIRGINIA: It's wonderful, father.

GALILEO: You don't think it could be mistaken for irony?

VIRGINIA: No, the archbishop will be very pleased. He's a practical man.

GALILEO: I rely on your judgment. What's the next point?

VIRGINIA: A very beautiful saying: 'When I am weak then I am strong.'

GALILEO: No comment.

VIRGINIA: Why not?

GALILEO: What's next?

VIRGINIA: 'And to know the love of Christ, which passeth knowledge.' Paul to the Ephesians three nineteen.

GALILEO: I must especially thank Your Eminence for the magnificent quotation from the epistle to the Ephesians. Inspired by it...[*etc.*][185]

Inspired indeed! Could any good Christian be more obliging than the Marxist playwright? Not only does Brecht quote profusely from the Gospel, and quite sovereignly at that; nor does he merely identify the sources of most of these quotations, either by author or by epistle; but he even adds the exact chapter and verse in the concluding instance. To be sure, the sarcastic mock devotion and, still more so, the unexpected plural Galileo dishes out *(Epheser-Briefe,* tacitly corrected in the English version) might give us pause, for there is, after all, only one such epistle. Or should Galileo's 'lapse' be intentional? Did Brecht perhaps commit this 'error' with his tongue in his cheek, as another sort of 'laying bare the device,' however subtly? His writings do contain at least a couple of comparable— if markedly cruder—cases in point. For example, in his adaptation of George Farqhar's *The Recruiting Officer* (*Pauken und Trompeten* [*Trumpets and Drums*]) of 1954/55, he invented an imaginary second book of *Deuteronomy*, with a ludicrously biblical verse in it: "Gott, heißt es im Deuteronomium, Buch 2, Kapitel 27, Vers 14: Gott sieht die schwarze Ameise auf dem schwarzen Stein in der schwarzen Nacht" ("It is written in Deuteronomy, Book 2, Chapter 27, Verse 14: The Lord sees the black ant on the black stone in the black night").[186] Similarly, already Brecht's Peachum in the *Threepenny Opera,* as early as 1928, was prone, in all likelihood, to such flights of scriptural fancy.[187] Hence, should the same hold true for his Galileo? Could there by anything fishy about those several Epistles to the Ephesians?

But the elusive playwright, while not meticulous to the point of being pedestrian—*fußgängerisch,* as he faithfully translated this expression[188]— appears to be fairly reliable here, in particular if we begin with his concluding quote. It is authentic beyond dispute, even though it actually turns out, in a Lutheran variant of the standard Luther rendition,[189] to be a combination of *Eph.* 3: 18 and 19 ... which does, however, decidedly not read, "daß *Christentum* liebhaben [instead of *Christum* liebhaben] viel besser ist denn alles Wissen," as one of my fellow critics happened to cite it,[190] naively or wishfully exposing—or so Brecht would argue—himself and his Pauline ilk. Also, if the "very beautiful saying" that is unworthy of a commentary in Galileo's opinion, "When I am weak then I am strong," remains without mention of sources used, it more than makes up these lacunae by its exactitude, since it is in fact a near literal quotation (not from Paul's Epistle to the Ephesians, granted, but from the second of his Epistles to the Corinthians).[191] Yet how about Brecht's third, or first, evangelic quote, so pompously introduced and warranted by the apostle's very name and mission? Well, as "wonderful" as it may sound, it can be spotted neither in Paul's epistles nor elsewhere in the Gospel; indeed it does not exist anywhere in the entire Bible, inasmuch as I have been able to ascertain. Or as Brecht himself, with a marvelous pinch of understatement, once put it: "Streng genommen, in der Bibel steht der Satz nicht" ("Strictly speaking, the maxim is not in the Bible").[192] True enough: His quote is a pure and untainted product of his imagination ... at least as far as the Lutheran Bible and the German text are concerned. For "Charity never faileth" does occur in the English Bible, albeit in an entirely different context; and its correspondence in Luther's text is also entirely different: namely, "Aber die Liebe höret nimmer auf..."[193] Need I emphasize that, as before, this salient fact—a lawful forgery foisted by Brecht on the one he loathed as the worst of all forgers—seems to have gone unnoticed by clergy and laity alike?[194]

We have to concentrate on the original, though, in order to grasp what is in effect going on in the playwright's manipulatory quotation. For his deceptively plain and simple sentence, three words only, constitutes a perfect grammatical and syntactic ambiguity. Clearly, "Wohltätigkeit versaget niemals" can—and hence must—be read in two ways: (a) as a nominative followed by an archaic verb form (namely, 3rd pers. sing. ind.) in the present tense, plus the adverb; and (b) as a preceding accusative dependent on another archaic verb form (namely, imp. plu.) and the accompanying adverb. Both these readings, equally justified and fully convincing, are based on the twofold meaning of the term, *versagen,* which, as an intransitive verb, denotes "to fail," but as a transitive one, "to deny or refuse." Accordingly, in the former case, we arrive precisely at Galileo's cynical advice dripping with bloody irony, "Charity never faileth (or fails)"; in the latter, however, what we obtain is a very laudable, most humanitarian, and genuinely Christian exhortation, "Never deny (or refuse) charity!" And this imaginary biblical saying does have, of course, a real equivalent in the Bible or, to be more specific, the Gospel: to wit, in the Epistle to the Hebrews, a book that was attributed, in traditional theology at least, to none other than Paul. Do not forget to be charitable: "Wohlzutun... vergesset nicht..." Thus we are admonished by Luther in *Heb.* 13: 16; or as the Authorized Version has it: "But to do good... forget not..." Brecht must have chuckled with malicious delight when 'forging' (in the most emphatic sense of the word) his ambiguous quote, although he abstained from ever divulging its hidden message. All he vouchsafed his cast—and, by implication, ourselves—was the curt and grim remark that Galileo's "use of clerical quotations" (*Verwendung klerikaler Zitate,* as Brecht chose to phrase it) is "downright blasphemous" (*rein blasphemisch*).[195] Yet who would take the old fox's studied devotion at face-value, anyway? Galileo is as shrewdly conscious of his double-talk, or veiled quip, as was the playwright. For how else could he ask Virginia his sardonic questions? And how else could he pay his sanctimonious homage to her? Remember:

Wie ist das.... Du meinst nicht, daß eine Ironie hineingelesen werden könnte?... Ich verlasse mich auf dein Urteil.

> How does that sound?... You don't think it could be mistaken
> for irony?... I rely on your judgment.

With or without supplementary hints, Brecht's free-wheeling mimicry of
Paul reveals itself as overwhelmingly 'authentical' in ever pertinent
respect—and yet, conversely, as absolutely 'antithetical' at one and the
same time. In sum, then, his masterfully forged scriptural quote is
thoroughly biblical, indeed Christian, as well as thoroughly Brechtian,
indeed Marxist; and the common denominator for this stunning
ideological equation is its thoroughgoing linguistic Lutheranism: Brecht's
total absorption of Luther's German into his own poetic speech. His two
English translators were, to all intents and purposes, ill-advised when
doing away with those 'erroneously' multiplied "epistles" and, thereby, the
tiny signal indicating that not only something but a whole lot is fishy about
Galileo's magisterial utterance. (To be fair, though: How in the world
could they—or any translator, however ingenious and conscientious—
have done justice to Brecht's manœuvre?)

Yet I shall proffer no further examples or suggestions, nor stroll off on
any more detours, parabolic or otherwise. Luther's language in the mouth
of Brecht has spoken for itself, as has the Brechtian thought by means of
the Lutheran tongue. That the heretic from Augsburg approved of, and
accepted, parts of the Bible even ideologically, notably from the Old
Testament, such as sections of *Proverbs,* and that he disapproved of, and
rejected, most of the New Testament, in particular the epistles of that
"falsifier" he so fiercely condemned, has by now become sufficiently
manifest. As a matter of fact, there are texts in his *œuvre* which bring
about—with the selfsame mastery as displayed in his drama, and dire
consequences beyond anything advanced even by Murphy—an outright
refutation of the Holy Writ by the Scriptures themselves, pitting the
testaments against each other (*Ecclesiastes,* for instance, against hateful
Paul) and thus exploding the Gospel.[196] Brecht, whose favorite book
(*Lieblingslektüre,* in agreement with Galileo) and both strongest and most
lasting *Bildungserlebnis,* or formative experience,[197] was the Bible, was
simultaneously, to harken back to Galileo once more, a most skilful and
determined "Bible-smasher" (*Bibelzertrümmerer*)[198] brutally bent on
destroying the Evangel. And must I repeat expressly that he accomplished
this formidable act likewise through Luther? Truly, Brecht's linguistic
allegiance and indebtedness to him, as well as the creativeness and
productivity they kindled, have not been surpassed anywhere in the entire
bulk of modern German literature; at best, they were paralleled in certain

works of Friedrich Nietzsche, who in turn influenced Brecht so profoundly.[199]

The reformer's disciple and friend, Erasmus Alberus, wasn't far of the mark, according to the experts,[200] when he declared that Luther was "the father of the German language, just as Tully had been the father of Latin": *Lutherus linguae Germanicae parens, sicut Cicero Latinae.*[201] I humbly submit that I am perhaps not too far of the mark, either, in declaring that the most eloquent and prolific scion of Martin Luther in our times was indeed Bertolt Brecht, the Marxist poet and playwright. May he and his ancestor whom we commemorate—and, by implication, yourselves—forgive me for my dog-Latin when I conclude:

Stirps autem Lutheri prolixissimus facundissimusque aetate nostra Brechtus.[202]

Notes

1. See my review article, "The 'Brecht Industry': A Polemical Assessment," *Monatshefte,* 69 (1977), 337-46.

2. Cf. Klaus-Dietrich Petersen, *Bertolt-Brecht-Bibliographie* (Gehlen: Bad Homburg [*etc.*], 1968); A.A. Volgina, *Bertolt Brecht: Bio-Bibliografičeskij Ukasatel'* (Moskva: Kniga, 1969); Jan Knopf, *Bertolt Brecht: Ein kritischer Forschungsbericht. Fragwürdiges in der Brecht-Forschung* (Athenäum Fischer: Frankfurt, 1974; itself a rather questionable report); Stephan Bock, *Brecht, Bertolt: Auswahl- und Ergänzungsbibliographie* (Brockmeyer: Bochum, 1979); as well as my *Bertolt Brecht* (Metzler: Stuttgart, [3]1971).

3. Franz Lau, "Bert Brecht und Luther: Ein Versuch der Interpretation des 'Guten Menschen von Sezuan'," *Luther-Jahrbuch 1962* (Wittig: Hamburg, 1962), pp. 92-109.—I have not been able to consult Egon Gramer, "Rad- und Richtungswechsel, vierfach. Variationen über ein Sprichwort: Luther, Brecht, Karsunke," *Diskussion Deutsch,* 9 (1978), 476-80; within our context, however, such "variations" would seem to be marginal at best.

4. Hans Pabst, *Brecht und die Religion* (Styria: Graz [*etc.*], 1977).

5. Gerhard Krupp, *"Wach auf, du verrotteter Christ!" Christliche Kommentare zu Bert Brecht* (Kommissionsverlag Rufer: Essen, 1972).

6. Edward M. Berckman, "Brecht's Quarrel with God: From Anti-Theodicy to Eschatology," *Comparative Drama,* 10 (1976), 130-46.

7. John Ditsky, "Brecht's Judging Jesus: Christian Analogies in *The Caucasian Chalk Circle,*" in *New Laurel Review,* 7.1 (1977), 40-48.

8. Hector MacLean, "Brecht's *Die heilige Johanna der Schlachthöfe* and the Fall," *Seminar,* 13 (1977), 29-41.

9. Sammy McLean, "Messianism in Bertolt Brecht's *Der gute Mensch von Sezuan* and *Der kaukasische Kreidekreis,*" *ibid.,* 14 (1978), 268-84.

10. Klaus Lazarowicz, "Die Rote Messe: Liturgische Elemente in Brechts 'Maßnahme'," *Literaturwissenschaftliches Jahrbuch,* N.F. 16 (1975), 205-20.

11. Siegfried Mews, "Biblical Themes and Motifs in Brecht's *Herr Puntila und sein Knecht Matti,*" in *University of Dayton Review,* 13.3 (1979), 53-63. Again, this is a contribution I have, unfortunately, been unable to consult.

12. See above, n.s 6 and 10, respectively.—It should be noted, by the way, that Lazarowicz's interpretation of *The Measures Taken* as a kind of political "mass" is no fewer than thirty years old. In essence, already pamphletists of the Cold War, but surely others as well, have advanced theses not dissimilar to those proffered by the Munich theater historian; cf. Herbert Lüthy, *Fahndung nach dem Dichter Bertolt Brecht* (Arche: Zürich, n.d. [1973]), esp. pp. 38ff. (the essay in question was first published in 1952) and compare my "Ideologische Tragödie und Tragödie der Ideologie: Versuch über ein Lehrstück von Brecht," in *Tragik und Tragödie.* Hrsg. von Volkmar Sander (Wissenschaftliche Buchgesellschaft: Darmstadt, 1971), pp. 237-278 (first published in 1959). Of course, the fact that Brecht's "paraliturgical ritual" became, very much *against* the intentions of its author, a tragedy remains indisputable, regardless of what Lazarowicz (cf. p. 215) may maintain; it was, after all, precisely this insight which prompted Brecht to ban all further productions.

13. Mention has to be made, however, of Albrecht Schöne's seminal essay, "Bertolt Brecht: Theatertheorie und dramatische Dichtung," *Euphorion,* 52 (1958), 272-290; for, symptomatically again, the one by Ditsky (see n. 7 above) is but an exaggerated variation on its "Christian Analogies." Compare esp. Schöne, pp. 291ff.

14. Cf. Krupp, p. 143.

15. Cf. Pabst, p. 263.

16. See my *Bertolt Brecht: Die Struktur seines Werkes* (Carl: Nürnberg, ⁶1972 [first published in 1959]), pp. 44ff., "Kreuzzug gegen Brecht?", in *Theatrum Mundi: Essays on German Drama and German Literature Dedicated to Harold Lenz on his Seventieth Birthday, September 11, 1978,* ed. by Edward R. Haymes (Fink: München, 1980), pp. 136-144 (first published in the privately distributed journal, *Radius* [June 1963], Nr. 2, pp. 35-41), and "Bertolt Brecht," in *Deutsche Dichter der Moderne: Ihr Leben und Werk.* Unter Mitarbeit zahlreicher Fachgelehrter hrsg. von Benno von Wiese (Schmidt: Berlin, ³1975), pp. 561-591 (first published in 1965; republished, under the title "Porträt mit biblischen Zügen," in my *Brecht und Nietzsche oder Geständnisse eines Dichters: Fünf Essays und ein Bruchstück* [Suhrkamp: Frankfurt, 1979], pp. 77-104).

17. Ilja Fradkin, *Bertolt Brecht: Weg und Methode,* Aus dem Russischen von Oskar Törne (Röderberg: Frankfurt, 1974), p. 370 (the original Russian version appeared in 1965).

18. Cf. *ibid.,* p. 371.

19. Though I am speaking figuratively, the article singled out by Berckman for special praise does in effect boil down to mere statistics; cf. Barbara Allen Woods, "A Man of Two Minds," *German Quarterly,* 42 (1969), 44-51, and Berckman, p. 130.

20. Cf. Pabst, p. 248.—Earlier attempts at such a conversion are, to name but two, the articles by Dietmar Schmidt, "Die Christen und das Unbequeme bei Bertolt Brecht," in *Almanach auf das Jahr des Herrn 1960* (Wittig: Hamburg, 1962), pp. 65-76, and Jochen Klicker, "Bert Brecht—Frage an die Christen: Verfremdung als Problem christlicher Existenz," *Kommunität,* 5 (1961), 75-63 (as to Brecht's concept of alienation or estrangement, see, for instance, my "Verfremdung: Beiträge zu Wesen und Ursprung eines Begriffs," *Revue de littérature comparée,* 35 [1961], 207-236).

21. As far as translations are available, and whenever it may seem feasible, Brecht's titles (though rarely his texts) will be quoted in English only; all German quotations, unless otherwise specified, will refer to Bertolt Brecht, *Gesammelte Werke in 20 Bänden* (Suhrkamp: Frankfurt, 1967), abbr. *GW* + volume(s) and page(s).

22. See Jost Hermand, "Unter Christenmenschen: Krupp, Pabst u. Co.," *Brecht-Jahrbuch 1979* (Suhrkamp: Frankfurt, 1979), pp. 121-130, who also points out the ludicrous inappropriateness of Krupp's title.

23. Cf. Pabst, p. 17 *et passim.*

24. Cf. Lau, p. 94.

25. Cf. *ibid.*, p. 107.

26. *Ibid.*

27. See, for instance, Helmut Jendreiek, *Bertolt Brecht: Drama der Veränderung* (Bagel: Düsseldorf, 1969), p. 240, where this is done implicitly.

28. See, for instance, Pabst, pp. 9f., where this is done explicitly.

29. Gottfried Benn, *Doppelleben* (Limes: Wiesbaden, 1950); cf. also his *Gesammelte Werke in vier Bänden,* hrsg. von Dieter Wellershoff (Limes: Wiesbaden, 1958ff.), vol. IV, pp. 69ff. and 448f.

30. For more details, see Dieter Wellershoff, "Fieberkurve des deutschen Geistes: Über Gottfried Benns Verhältnis zur Zeitgeschichte," in *Die Kunst im Schatten des Gottes: Für und wider Gottfried Benn,* hrsg. Reinhold Grimm u. Wolf-Dieter Marsch (Sachse u. Pohl: Göttingen, 1962), pp. 11-39, as well as my "Innere Emigration als Lebensform," in *Exil und innere Emigration. Third Wisconsin Workshop,* hrsg. von Reinhold Grimm u. Jost Hermand (Athenäum: Frankfurt, 1972), pp. 31-73.

31. Cf. H.G. Koenigsberger and George L. Mosse, *Europe in the Sixteenth Century* (Holt, Rinehart and Winston: New York, 1968), p. 130.

32. Compare Gerhard Ritter, *Die Weltwirkung der Reformation* (Oldenbourg: München, ²1959), p. 75: "Das Endergebnis war ein friedsam loyaler Untertanengehorsam ehrbarer Staatsbürger, nicht selten gesteigert zu kriechender Servilität, die uns heute abstößt."

33. See, above all, Werner Frisch and K.W. Obermeier, *Brecht in Augsburg: Erinnerungen, Dokumente, Texte, Fotos* (Aufbau-Verlag: Berlin u. Weimar, 1975), p. 53 *et passim.*

34. It has even been asserted, though without any proof: "Als wichtigste Schullektüre sind der *Kleine Katechismus* von Luther und die *Hauspostille* [!] zu nennen"; cf. Pabst, p. 220. For Brechtian treatments, see *GW* 8, 38; 6, 2353ff.

35. Brecht's version of J.M.R. Lenz's play, *Der Hofmeister* ("The Tutor") constitutes a direct German confrontation; cf. *GW* 6, 2331-94.

36. *GW* 20, 10.

37. *GW* 20, 315.

38. See Thilo Koch, *Gottfried Benn: Ein biographischer Essay* (Langen/Müller: München, 1961), p. 61 fn.

39. Kurt Aland, *Martin Luther in der modernen Literatur: Ein kritischer Dokumentarbericht* (Eckart: Witten u. Berlin, 1973). Not only is Benn totally ignored by Aland, but even Brecht is barely mentioned; cf. my review of this book in *German Studies: Section III,* 8 (1975), 147f.

40. Benn, *Gesammelte Werke,* vol. III, p. 448.

41. *GW* 9, 815.

42. Bertolt Brecht, *Poems 1913-1956,* ed. by John Willett and Ralph Manheim, with the co-operation of Erich Fried (Eyre Methuen: London, 1976), p. 303.

42a. Compare also Thornton Wilder, *The Eighth Day* (Popular Library: New York, 1967), p. 172: "The planting of trees is the least self-centered of all that we do. It is a purer act of faith than the procreation of children." Interestingly, the character in Wilder's novel who proclaims this view is a German.

43. Compare Paula ("Bie") Banholzer's report as quoted in Frisch / Obermeier, p. 125.

44. Compare the words of a class-mate of Brecht's, quoted ibid., p. 46: "Brecht nahm offensichtlich den Konfirmandenunterricht recht ernst."

45. A course on "Religionspsychologie (Religiöse Entwicklung und Erziehung, Grundprobleme der Weltanschauung)" is listed for Brecht's first semester, which lasted from October, 1917 to February, 1918; cf. *ibid.*, p. 117.—I do not want to conceal that, according to another erstwhile beloved of Brecht's, Marie Rose Aman, the same eager pupil was said to have burnt both the Bible and the catechism: "So sollte er die Bibel und den Katechismus verbrannt haben." However, if this remark proves anything, it is precisely the youthful Brecht's posession—or, at least, repeated and well-known perusal—of a Bible, the more so since the sentence immediately preceding the one quoted reads: "In Schülerkreisen wurden damals über Brecht unmögliche Dinge verbreitet." Cf. *ibid.*, p. 92.—I have been unable to consult Eberhard Rohse, *Der frühe Brecht und die Bibel: Studien zum Augsburger Religionsunterricht und zu den literarischen Versuchen des Gymnasiasten* (Vandenhoeck u. Ruprecht: Göttingen, 1983), a voluminous dissertation comprising "etwa 576 Seiten und 3 Faltkarten" which appeared after the completion of my manuscript. Rohse's "vorzügliche Arbeit" is said—see Walther Killy, "Luther-Ruhm and Luther-Kitsch: Die deutsche Literatur und der deutsche Reformator," *Die Zeit*, 45 (11 Nov. 1983), pp. 13f.—to contain sensational findings; however, judging from the "bislang unbekannte Stelle" quoted by Killy, some reservations might be in order. For this allegedly unknown entry in Brecht's diary has been available in print for approximately eight years, and is of course adduced in the present essay; cf. n. 119 below and the respective quotation.

46. See esp. Hans Mayer, *Bertolt Brecht und die Tradition* (Neske: Pfullingen, 1961), pp. 48ff., and Thomas O. Brandt, *Die Vieldeutigkeit Bertolt Brechts* (Stiehm: Heidelberg, 1968), pp. 13ff.; also, compare my "Bertolt Brecht" of 1965 as well as my *Bertolt Brecht* of 1959, pp. 44ff. (both cited in n. 16 above).

47. See G. Ronald Murphy, "Brecht's Pocket Bible," *German Quarterly*, 50 (1977), 474-484; all quotations are from p. 474.

48. Cf. Frisch / Obermeier, p. 159.

49. See the page facing the title in G. Ronald Murphy S.J., *Brecht and The Bible: A Study of Religious Nihilism and Human Weakness in Brecht's Drama of Mortality and the City* (Univ. of North Carolina Press: Chapel Hill, 1980); of course, this applies also, and to an even greater extent, to the glued-in photograph of a racing car (!) which can be found on the back-inside cover, and which the author wisely refrained from reproducing.—I am most grateful to Father Murphy for having made available to me, with a magnanimity I have seldom experienced in the profession, all his pertinent material, and this despite my forewarning that I might have to disagree with him in some instances.

50. Cf. *ibid.*, p. 89; also, compare Pabst, p. 285, who speaks, more cautiously, of Brecht's "kritische Hochschätzung Jesu wie der Bibel." One of the very few dissenters is Klaus Peter Hertzsch in his type-written dissertation, "Bertolt Brechts Ethik und Anthropologie in ihrer Bedeutung für die Hermeneutik der Rechtfertigungslehre" (Halle, 1968).

51. Cf. Murphy, *Brecht and The Bible*, p. 89.

52. Cf. Woods, p. 48.

53. Cf. Murphy, *Brecht and The Bible*, pp. 5 and 7.

54. But see my "Bertolt Brecht," p. 571.

55. Murphy, *Brecht and The Bible*, p. 63.

56. Cf. Murphy, "Brecht's Pocket Bible," p. 481; all subsequent quotations are from this page.

57. It is interesting to note that Murphy renders Brecht's term, *das Primitive*, simply as "the primal" or "the primeval"; also, referring to the play's atheistic message only fleetingly, he does not mention its militant irreligiousness at all.—For the Brechtian text, see *GW* 2, 565-585; esp. compare pp. 575ff. ("Ideologie") where we read lines such as the following:

Darum beteiligt euch
An der Bekämpfung des Primitiven
An der Liquidierung des Jenseits und
Der Verscheuchung jedweden Gottes, wo
Immer er auftaucht.

58. Cf. n. 56 above.—Strangely enough, Murphy in his article does not mention another red line marking *Matth.* 14: 28-33, i.e. the related incident of Peter's attempted and abortive walking upon the water. In am at a loss as to an explanation of this omission, unless it was due to sheer oversight.—See also n. 61 below.

59. *GW* 4, 1613.

60. Bertolt Brecht, *Collected Plays*, ed. Ralph Manheim and John Willett, vol. VI (Vintage Books: New York, 1976), p. 109.

61. It follows that Brecht may have drawn on either *Mark* or *Matthew*, whereas Puntila's walking upon the water reveals itself, on closer scrutiny, as a combination of both: Like Peter, he steps out of the boat; like Christ, he does not sink.—For the Brechtian quotation(s), see *GW* 4, 1612 and Brecht, *Collected Plays*, vol. VI, p. 108.

62. Compare Erich Auerbach, *Mimesis: Dargestellte Wirklichkeit in der abendländischen Literatur* (Francke: Bern, ²1959), p. 216.

63. See *GW* 8, 242; also, compare my *Bertolt Brecht*, pp. 33 and 85.

64. Compare Bertolt Brecht, *Die Maßnahme*. Kritische Ausgabe mit einer Spielanleitung von Reiner Steinweg (Suhrkamp: Frankfurt, 1972), pp. 31 *et passim*.

65. Compare his remarks in *Brechts 'Mutter Courage und ihre Kinder.'* Hrsg. von Klaus-Detlef Müller (Suhrkamp: Frankfurt, 1982), p. 181: "Zuschauer mögen sich mit der stummen Kattrin in dieser Szene identifizieren; sie mögen sich einfühlen in dieses Wesen und freudig spüren, daß in ihnen selbst solche Kräfte vorhanden sind..."

66. See *GW* 4, 1436 and Bertolt Brecht, *Collected Plays*, ed. by Ralph Manheim and John Willett, vol. V (Vintage Books: New York, 1972), p. 208.

67. As far as I know, Murphy was the first to recognize this; see his *Brecht and The Bible*, pp. 79 and 82.

68. Cf. *ibid.*, p. 89.

69. See *GW* 2, 660.

70. See *GW* 4, 1388 and Brecht, *Collected Plays*, vol. V, p. 167.

71. Murphy, *Brecht and The Bible*, p. 75.

72. See Friedrich Kluge and Alfred Götze, *Etymologisches Wörterbuch der deutschen Sprache* (de Gruyter: Berlin, ¹⁶1953), p. 537.—Brecht himself, by the way, owned the 15th edition of *Kluge-Götze*.

73. Ibid.

74 *Hutten - Müntzer - Luther, Werke in zwei Bänden.* Ausgewählt u. eingeleitet von Siegfried Streller (Aufbau-Verlag: Berlin u. Weimar, 1970), p. 19; also, compare p. 45.

75. Klaus Kienzler, "B. Brecht—Ein Gegenstand der Theologie?", in *Bertolt Brecht— Aspekte seines Werkes, Spuren seiner Wirkung*, hrsg. Helmut Koopmann u. Theo Stammen (Vögel: München, 1983), pp. 85-110.

76. Cf. *ibid.*, p. 89.

77. As might be expected, it is here that Kienzler discovers Brecht's "Grundbotschaft"; cf. *ibid.*, p. 109.—However, it must be admitted in all fairness that the volume as a whole constitutes quite a valuable contribution.

78. Quoted in Siegfried Melchinger, *Drama zwischen Shaw und Brecht: Ein Leitfaden durch das zeitgenössische Schauspiel* (Schünemann: Bremen, 1957), p. 174; but compare also n. 80 below.

79. See my "Der katholische Einstein: Brechts Dramen- und Theatertheorie," in *Brecht: Neue Interpretationen,* hrsg. Walter Hinderer (Reclam: Stuttgart, 1984); forthcoming.

80. Ernst Ginsberg, *Abschied: Erinnerungen, Theateraufsätze, Gedichte* (Arche: Zürich, 1965), p. 144.

81. Cf., for example, Berckman, p. 134.

82. In particular, compare the testimonies of an early friend of Brecht's and of the custodian of the Brecht Archives; cf. Hans Otto Münsterer, *Bert Brecht: Erinnerungen aus den Jahren 1917-22. Mit Photos, Briefen und Faksimiles* (Arche: Zürich, 1963), pp. 133f., and Herta Ramthun as quoted by Pabst, p. 288. Also see Frisch / Obermeier, p. 125, for Banholzer's report.

83. Bertolt Brecht, *Die Hauspostille / Manual of Piety.* A Bilingual Edition with English Text by Eric Bentley and Notes by Hugo Schmidt (Grove Press: New York, 1966).

84. See, for instance, Pabst, p. 83.

85. In fact, this even applies to the best and most thorough treatments we have, those of the East-German scholar, Klaus Schuhmann; *e.g.,* compare his *Der Lyriker Bertolt Brecht 1913—1933* (Rütten u. Loening: Berlin, 1964), pp. 68 ff. *et passim.*

86. Of course, there were also *Handpostillen, Herzpostillen,* and so on, right down to Brecht's own *Taschenpostille,* the precursor of his *Hauspostille;* see the 3rd edition of *Die Religion in Geschichte und Gegenwart (RGG)* and compare esp. ^3RGG V, 477f. and ^3RGG II, 1683.

87. See *Bertolt-Brecht-Archiv: Bestandsverzeichnis des literarischen Nachlasses,* bearb. von Herta Ramthun (Aufbau-Verlag: Berlin u. Weimar, 1969ff.), henceforth abbr. *BBA +* Nr.(s); here, *BBA* 462/86.

88. *BBA* 435/67 (1921).

89. *BBA* 813/15 (1920).

90. *BBA* 424/41-45; some pages are extant.

91. It had appeared in 1935, entitled *Ignatius von Loyola.*

92. The inscribed date is 1951.

93. Compare Ramthun's remarks (cf. n. 82 above): "Von klein auf hat Brecht mehr mit dem Katholizismus als mit dem Protestantismus, dem er selbst zugehörte, sympathisiert. Das mag daran liegen, daß ihm die evangelische Kirche zu farblos und zu kahl erschien, während sich die katholische Kirche doch sehr prunkvoll und farbenfroh zeigte...."

94. See again Frisch / Obermeier, p. 125.

95. For the most recent assessment along both these lines, see Albrecht Weber, "Brecht— Der Augsburger," in *Bertolt Brecht—Aspekte seines Werkes, Spuren seiner Wirkung,* pp. 239-275; here, p. 250.

96. Weber seems to be on the right track when he states: "Tief gezeichnet schien Brecht von der lutherischen Rechtfertigungslehre..." However, he doesn't pursue this comparison any further. Cf. ibid.

97. Münsterer, p. 133.

98. Cf. *ibid.*

99. Brecht as quoted by Käthe Rülicke, "*Leben des Galilei:* Bemerkungen zur Schlußszene," in *Sinn und Form: Zweites Sonderheft Bertolt Brecht* (Rütten u. Loening: Berlin, 1957), pp. 269-321; here, p. 294. Literally, Brecht speaks of a "Schundroman."

100. Compare *GW* 3, 1317: "Die Bibel und der Homer sind meine Lieblingslektüre." As far as the former is concerned, Galileo's confession is equally applicable to Brecht.

101. *GW* 18, 82.

102. Bertolt Brecht, *Arbeitsjournal.* Hrsg. von Werner Hecht (Suhrkamp: Frankfurt, 1973), vol. I, p. 248.

103. Cf. my *Brecht und Nietzsche*, p. 169 as well as Aland, pp. 369ff.

104. Cf. Bertolt Brecht, *Briefe*, hrsg. u. kommentiert von Günter Glaeser (Suhrkamp: Frankfurt, 1981), vol. I, p. 604 (spring 1949). For an express listing of other pamphlets, plus a critical remark, see ibid., p. 539 and vol. II, p. 1065.

105. See *GW* 19, 503.

106. See *GW* 20, 38.

107. Brecht, *Briefe*, vol. I, p. 743 (April 21, 1955). The work in question is Karl Kleinschmidt's *Martin Luther: Ein Beitrag zur Geschichte der deutschen Reformation* (Kongreß-Verlag: Berlin, 1953); cf. *ibid.*, vol. II, p. 1152.

108. *GW* 19, 398.

109. *Brecht on Theatre: The Development of an Aesthetic*, transl. and notes by John Willett (Methuen: London, 1964), p. 117.

110. See Heinz Otto Burger, *Renaissance* [/] *Humanismus* [/] *Reformation: Deutsche Literatur im europäischen Kontext* (Gehlen: Bad Homburg[etc.], 1969), pp. 157ff. and 458.

111. Among other things, compare *GW* 15, 32ff. (untitled notes on "Sprachverlotterung") and 12, 458f. ("Über die gestische Sprache in der Literatur," from *Me-ti* / *Buch der Wendungen*).

112. "Die losen Blätter," Beilage zu *Die Dame*, 56, Nr. 1 (Oct. 1928), p. 16; cf. also Mayer, pp. 48f.

113. Barbara Schall-Brecht in a radio interview broadcast by the Deutschlandfunk on June 12, 1983.

114. See Brecht, *Arbeitsjournal*, vol. I, p. 317 (Nov. 18, 1941).

115. Compare, for instance, Brecht's letter to Dora Mannheim written in 1920, on the one hand, and his unpublished plot summary for *A Man's a Man*, on the other; cf. Brecht. *Briefe*, vol. I, pp. 65f. and Patty Lee Parmalee, *Brecht's America*. With a Foreword by John Willett (Ohio State Univ. Press: Athens, Ohio, 1981), p. 100.

116. Compare the report by Lotte H. Eisner, "Sur le Procès de Quat' Sous," *Europe*, 35 (1957), nos. 113/4, pp. 111-123.

117. See *GW* 15, 423.

118. Bertolt Brecht, *Gesammelte Werke*. Supplementband III (Suhrkamp: Frankfurt, 1982), p. 36.

119. Bertolt Brecht, *Tagebücher 1920-1922. Autobiographische Aufzeichnungen 1920-1954*. Hrsg. von Herta Ramthun (Suhrkamp: Frankfurt, 1975), p. 49. Similarly, and as late as between 1928 and 1932, Brecht wrote in another fragmentary poem, albeit without biblical reference:

Immer noch, wie im Pawlowschen Versuch
Veranlassen Gocken in mir Prozesse
Sicherlich chemischer Art, Gedanken metaphysischer Richtung...

Cf. Brecht, *Gesammelte Werke*, suppl. vol. III, p. 244.

120. Cf. Brecht, *Tagebücher...*, p. 15.

121. Compare *ibid.*, pp. 49f.: "Im übrigen wäre die Jesusgestalt zu zeichnen durch Eindringlichkeit und Lässigkeit. Ein Mensch für die Menschen, für jetzt, für den Platz, wo er ist, schnauft, redet, leidet.... Es sind mystische Visionen, ein guter Mensch unter einem Feigenbaum, das Herz auf der Zunge, ein lebender Eindruck, ein ganz nabelloser Mensch, ein gelungenes Geschöpf, zwecklos, ohne Benötigung irgendeiner Rücksteifung (Pflichterfüllung oder so). Ein unverletzbarer Mensch, weil widerstandslos. Ganz lavierend, biegsam, wolkengleich, voll von Sternenhimmeln, milden Regen, Weisheiten, Fröhlichkeit,

Vertrauen, Möglichkeiten. Der gute Mensch in einem." If this Jesus isn't a distant relative of Baal's, then he certainly is a close one of Brecht's Chinese "Glücksgott," whose drama also remained unwritten; cf. *GW* 17, 947f.

122. Compare, *Tagebücher...,* pp. 49 and 50: "Das Ganze ist lyrisch, ungeeignet fürs Drama, weil unlogisch, ja alogisch, eine reine Zerstörung des Folgebegriffs"; Jesus "kann nicht gestaltet werden im Drama: Er bietet keinen Widerstand."

123. In a lecture on "Luther's Bible in Brecht's Poetry," delivered at Queens College, N.Y., on Nov. 10, 1983.

124. Cf. *BBA* 813/125: "Er heißt vielleicht Habukuk oder George Morg..."

125. Cf. *BBA* 437/94-5: "Das Wunder Salome, ein Opfer wilder Barberei!"

126. Cf. *BBA* 4/6 (also title of a fragmentary poem).

127. Cf. *BBA* 450/24: "Der Hiob, der aus einer Kneipe in eine Gesellschaft gerät..."

128. Cf. *BBA* 209/1; Brecht writes erroneously, "Echeziel."

129. See Bertolt Brecht, *Texte für Filme II: Exposés* [/] *Szenarien* (Suhrkamp: Frankfurt, 1969), p. 654, "Der Uriasbrief" (for a projected film) and compare BBA 235/53 and 503/47-8. Also, there is a character by name of Uria [*sic*] Shelley in Brecht's play, *A Man's a Man*; cf. *GW* 1, 298.

130. Cf. *BBA* 813/76-8.

131. Cf. *BBA* 152/44.

132. Brecht's use of this name is 'shocking' indeed: It appears in a poem titled "Historie vom verliebten Schwein Malchus"; cf. *GW* 8, 201ff.

133. Cf. *GW* 7, 2745-2813; the biblical references are *Luke* 13: 32 (among others), *John* 1: 5, and *Luke* 5: 9. Brecht's translators appear to be unaware of those to *Luke,* for they have rendered the two titles as "He Drives Out a Devil" and "The Catch," respectively; cf. Bertolt Brecht, *Collected Plays,* ed. by Ralph Manheim and John Willett, vol. I (Vintage Books: New York, 1971).

134. Cf. *GW* 3029-38.

135. Compare, for example, *GW* 7, 3035: "Großvater, wenn der Tag des Gerichtes kommt, wie wirst du dastehen?" The similarity to "Wenn dich dein Auge ärgert, reiß es aus!" ought to be obvious. (Incidentally, the edition has an exclamation mark at the end of this sentence; but the photocopies made available to me many years ago by Brecht's widow, the late Helene Weigel, clearly indicate that there has to be a question mark.)

136. See Gunther G. Sehm, "Moses, Christus und Paul Ackermann: Brechts *Aufstieg und Fall der Stadt Mahogonny,*" in *Brecht-Jahrbuch 1976,* pp. 83-100; also, compare Murphy, *Brecht and The Bible,* pp. 49ff.

137. Cf. Brecht, *Collected Plays,* vol. V, p. 100 *et passim;* the translator is Frank Jones.

138. Compare also Ignace Feuerlicht, "Brecht's *Lukullus,*" *Monatshefte,* 75 (1983), pp. 369-383.

139. Cf. *GW* 6, 2303 and 2327.

140. To wit: *St. Joan of the Stockyards, The Visions of Simone Machard,* and *The Trial of Joan of Arc at Rouen, 1431.*

141. See, for example, Karl-Heinz Schoeps, *Bertolt Brecht und Bernard Shaw* (Bouvier: Bonn, 1974).

142. Cf. *GW* 11, 16f. and 15, respectively.

143. See *Bertolt-Brecht-Archiv: Bestandsverzeichnis,* vol. I, pp. 280ff.; also, compare Münsterer, pp. 138f.

144. Cf. Parmalee, pp. 95ff. and Helfried W. Seliger, *Das Amerikabild Bertolt Brechts* (Bouvier: Bonn, 1974), pp. 62ff.

145. Cf. *GW* 2, 467ff. and 4, 1425ff.

146. Cf. *GW* 13, 1149ff.

147. Cf. *GW* 11, 101ff.

148. Cf. *Bertolt-Brecht-Archiv: Bestandsverzeichnis,* vol. I, pp. 300f. and Vol. IV, p. 185; also, see Parmalee, pp. 101ff. and Seliger, pp. 93ff.

149. Compare, for instance, *BBA* 1086/68 and *GW* 17, 952.

150. See Brecht, *Texte für Filme II,* pp. 366ff. and 647, respectively.

151. See Münsterer, p. 145.

152. Cf. *GW* 11, 286ff.

153. Cf. *GW* 1, 249ff.

154. See *GW* 5, 2078 and 2024f.; also, compare Schöne's and my remarks (cf. notes 13 and 16 above, respectively).

155. For the overall plot, compare *Gen.* 18: 20-19: 29; as to the rain of fire, cf. *GW* 4, 1536.

156. In addition, compare the parody of the Passion in the *Threepenny Opera,* among other things.

157. Cf. *GW* 1, 344 and 150.

158. Cf. *GW* 1, 118.

159. Cf. *GW* 3, 945.

160. Cf. *Deut.* 25: 4 and *GW* 4, 1772.

161. Cf. *GW* 5, 2129.

162. Cf. *GW* 3, 1170ff.

163. *GW* 2, 884; cf. *John* 14:2.

164. Bertolt Brecht, *The Mother.* With Notes by the Author. Transl. and with an Introduction by Lee Baxandall (Grove Press: New York, [2]1965), p. 117.

165. See Victor Erlich, *Russian Formalism: History—Doctrine* (Mouton: The Hague, 1955).

166. See *GW* 1, 254 and Brecht, *Collected Plays,* vol. I, p. 214.

167. Cf. *GW* 2, 446 and 398.

168. Compare, for instance, Brecht, *Briefe,* vol. I, p. 81 ("Solchen müssen alle Dinge zum besten [*sic!*] dienen") and *Romans* 8: 28; Brecht, *Briefe,* vol. I, p. 83 ("Mit Teufelszungen und Erzgurgel") and *1 Cor.* 13: 1; Brecht, *Briefe,* vol. I, p. 141 ("Feuerwolke") and *Ex.* 40: 38. These and so many other quotes, which could be supplemented even from the 1950's—*e.g.,* Brecht, *Briefe,* vol. I, pp. 638 and 662: "Karyatiden, die angesichts des revolutionären Sodoms zu Salzsäulen erstarren," and "wenn Du willst, stecke ich das kleine Lichtlein unter fünf Scheffel"—bespeak the absolute ease and intimacy with which Brecht handled the biblical language of Luther.

169. Compare *GW* 8, 260 ("Gegen Verführung") and the apocryphal *Wisdom of Solomon* (*Die Weisheit Salomos*) 2: 1-19.

170. *GW* 3, 1286.

171. Brecht, *Collected Plays,* vol. V., p. 49; for the Brecht-Laughton version, see *ibid.,* p. 429.

172. Compare, for instance, Pabst, pp. 176f. and Brandt, p. 23. Even Herbert Knust, to whom we owe the most recent—and, it should be emphasized, otherwise quite painstaking—monograph, does not question the 'authenticity' of the Brechtian quotations; cf. his *Bertolt Brecht: Leben des Galilei* (Diesterweg: Frankfurt [*etc.*], 1982), pp. 35f.

173. Cf. Krupp, p. 112.

174. All three of these verses suggest the same: "Die Weisen bewahren [*retain*] die Lehre"; "wer aber seine Lippen hält, ist klug"; "die Weisen bewahren ihren Mund."

175. Cf. *GW* 3, 1256.

176. See, for instance, *GW* 3, 1337; 6, 2381; 8, 401.

177. Cf. *Is.* 66: 2 and *Ezek.* 37: 11; also, compare *Ezek.* 37: 2.

178. Cf. *GW* 3, 1255.

179. Compare *GW* 2, 447f.: "Nur wer im Wohlstand lebt, lebt angenehm!" Brecht's source in this case, K.L. Ammer's [*i.e.* Karl Klammer's] rendition of Villon, juxtaposes *schwelgt/lebt*, which is, needless to say, incomparably weaker.—As regards Brecht's insertion of *glühend*, it was lifted, in all likelihood, from *Is*. 6: 6.

180. Cf. Murphy, *Brecht and The Bible*, p. 19.

181. Cf. ibid.

182. Compare, for example, Ernst Schumacher, *Drama und Geschichte: Bertolt Brechts 'Leben des Galilei' und andere Stücke* (Henschelverlag: Berlin, 1965) and *Brechts 'Leben des Galilei.'* Hrsg. von Werner Hecht (Suhrkamp: Frankfurt, 1981).

183. See Fradkin, pp. 372f.; also, compare Pabst, p. 176.

184. *GW* 3, 1332f.

185. Brecht, *Collected Plays,* vol. V, pp. 85f.; for the Brecht-Laughton version, see *ibid.*, pp. 458f.

186. See *GW* 6, 2672 and Bertolt Brecht, *Collected Plays.* Ed. by Ralph Manheim and John Willett (Vintage Books: New York, 1972), p. 294.

187, Compare *GW* 2, 403: "Meine Tochter soll für mich das sein, was das Brot für den Hungrigen—*er blättert nach*—; das steht sogar irgendwo in der Bibel." I have been unable to locate any such saying in the Scriptures, whereas the context strongly supports my suspicion of a playful case of *obnazhenie priëma*. A learned theologian, however, lists Brecht's sentence unabashed, as biblical... although without identifying it by book, chapter, and verse, as he usually does; cf. Pabst, p. 171.

188. Cf. *GW* 17, 1296.

189. See *Die Bibel oder die ganze Heilige Schrift des Alten und Neuen Testaments nach der deutschen Übersetzung D. Martin Luthers.* Nach dem 1912 vom Deutschen Evangelischen Kirchenausschuß genehmigten Text. Mit erklärenden Anmerkungen (Privil. Württemb. Bibelanstalt: Stuttgart, n.d.), Part II, pp. 312f.

190. Pabst, p. 177 (my emphases).

191. Cf. *2 Cor*. 12: 10.

192. See *GW* 4, 1364 and Brecht, *Collected Plays,* vol. V, p. 147.

193. See *1 Cor*. 13: 8.

194.The 'lawful' aspect, *i.e.* the fact that Brecht's 'creation' is grounded, no matter how contradictorily, in Paul's epistles all the same, had escaped even my own notice. I am, therefore, most grateful to my colleague at the University of Michigan, Mary C. Crichton, who kindly directed my attention to it.

195. See *GW* 17, 1132.

196. Compare, one last time, Brecht's poem, "Gegen Verführung."

197. On another level, this formative experience was, of course, Marxism; cf. my *Brecht and Nietzsche*, pp. 77ff.

198. See *GW* 3, 1316 and Brecht, *Collected Plays,* vol. V, p. 73.

199. See my *Brecht and Nietzsche*, esp. pp. 156ff.

200. Compare, for instance, Burger, p. 258: "Wenn man... auf die Sprachkunst [instead of mere *Sprachgeschichte*] abhebt, hat Erasmus Alberus nahezu recht..."

201. Quoted ibid.

202. Brecht was himself fond of such Latin dicta; see, for instance, his *Ego, poeta Germanus, supra grammaticos sto.* Quoted by Lion Feuchtwanger, "Bertolt Brecht," in *Sinn und Form: Zweites Sonderheft Bertolt Brecht,* pp. 103-108; here, p. 106.

DIETER FORTE'S PLAY *LUTHER, MUNZER, AND THE BOOKKEEPERS OF THE REFORMATION*—OR THE DIFFICULTIES OF WRITING HISTORICAL TRUTH

Guy Stern, *Wayne State University*

As few others in German history, Martin Luther has captured the literary imagination of his contemporaries and successors. Through the ages, beginning in his own lifetime, he has inspired poems, short stories, novels, and dramas—some of them laudatory, some of them condemnatory.[1] Several early dramatists devoted whole cycles to Luther: Martin Rinckart, for example, became a one-person popularizer of the Reformation. Simon Lemnius, a student dismissed from the University of Wittenberg, avenged himself by penning a scurillous pornographic play about the reformer.[2] In fact in the nineteenth century we encounter the curious phenomenon that a German playwright, Zacharias Werner, idealized Luther in one drama, converted to Catholicism, recanted, and then demonized him in a lengthy poem.[3]

Most of the dramas have concentrated on one particular aspect of Luther's life. John Osborne's *Martin Luther* and *Young Luther* by the notorious pre-Fascist Adolf Bartels come to mind as dramatizations of the early Luther; other phases were dramatized by Malmberg's *The Professor of Wittenberg,* Josef Buchhorn's *Turning Point in Worms* and Friedrich Lienhardt's *Luther at the Wartburg.* Leopold Ahlsen's drama-in-flashbacks, on the other hand, shows Luther on his deathbed, but recapitulates events from various stages of his life.[4] If we were to include dramas in this enumeration in which Luther has only a peripheral role or appears in a fictional guise, an additional and at least equally imposing bibliography could be compiled which would range again from the time of the Reformation, e.g. Friedrich Dedekind's *Papista conversus* to Goethe's *Götz von Berlichingen* to recent German plays such as Stefan Schütz' *Kohlhaas.*[5]

But despite this plethora of dramatic treatments it appears likely that no drama since the time of the Reformation when, of course, the very name of Luther could evoke emotional responses pro and con, has stirred such controversy as Dieter Forte's play *Luther, Münzer, and the Bookkeepers of the Reformation* (as the work has been titled in the English translation by Christopher Holme).[6] Its success or *succès de scandale* came all the more surprising, since it was the very first full-length drama by a thirty-five-year-old German playwright who, until that point, had written only advertising copy, short stories, and television scripts.

Dieter Forte was born in 1935, went to a commercial school where he specialized in advertising, associated himself with the so-called Group 61, a group of writers coming from and/or writing for the working class.[7] He received several grants designed for working-class writers, a travel stipend from the German Foreign Office and then a minor literary prize. Before becoming a celebrity he wrote a very brief autobiographical sketch, all but forgotten today, for the appendix of an anthology:

> After my years in school [I took up] various jobs: errand boy, apprentice in a business, advertising specialist, press photographer, artist-painter. Finally I wrote, with some success, short stories and travelogues for newspapers and magazines. Later on plays, television scripts, and radio plays. [Then followed] a year and a half in Hamburg as a free-lance contributor, occasionally as reader and assistant to the drama director of North German television. Just now [i.e., in 1966] I live as a free-lance writer in Düsseldorf.

Forte then lists his publications, all of them titles of radio plays (originals and one adaptation), publications in periodicals and newspapers, plus a few translations in progress.[8]

After the premiere and publication of his Luther and Münzer drama, which was to be translated into English, French, Italian, Dutch, Hungarian, and Rumanian, Forte continued his attack on capitalism in a play, *Jean Henry Dunant or the Introduction of Civilization* (1977). He also published his earlier and new television plays (1980), other social protest dramas, such as *The Death of Kaspar Hauser* (1979), an adaptation of Webster's *White Devils* (1972) and in the same year, one of *Cenodoxus* by Jakob Bidermann, a seventeenth-century German Jesuit. It is fair to add that none of his subsequent works reached either the quality (wherever we fix it) or success of his Luther drama.[9]

The reasons for its success are not hard to adduce. For one it was first performed in 1970, when the waves of the student protest movement—conjured up by pointed parallels in the very first scene of the play—were still running high, a working-class and proletarian perspective was valued, and an iconoclastic attitude towards all organized religion was being promulgated. Also the drama superbly uses popular television techniques and combines, in spots, tragedy, and melodrama, sermon with farce. Finally it wildly intermingles historical costumes and modern dress. In the performance I witnessed in Saarbrücken (in the summer of 1972), the directors, Martin Buchhorn and Werner Wachsmuth, exercised an option allowed by Forte's stage directions and had the Pope Leo X played by an actress. She wore a miniskirt. [10]

The plot can be quickly summarized. The action takes place on a multi-levelled stage with the many locales suggested by moving the focal points and actors from stage-right to stage-center and stage-left in a great many variations. [11] Forte utilizes the key events of the Reformation from 1514 to 1525 as the turning points of his plot—Luther's posting of his theses, the disputations at Augsburg with Cajetan, the social protests of Thomas Münzer, the death of Emperor Maximilian, the intrigues at the Vatican and at various German courts, the election and accession to the throne of Charles V, the Diet of Worms, the Peasant Uprising, Luther's condemnation of it, his marriage to Katharina von Bora, and the execution of Thomas Münzer. To accommodate such a vast panorama and a time span of more than a decade, Forte assembles more than eighty, quickly unfolding tableaux, one often dissolving into the next (especially when he wants to suggest simultaneity of action). Also the actors do not exit, but simply are "blocked out" of a scene or the spotlights are removed from them when their roles are not required.

But the historical events are merely the background for the focal action of the play, perhaps best described as a complex game between puppet masters and their marionettes, with one person often being manipulated while he or she manipulates others. The master puppeteer is Jacob Fugger. As the world's first multimillionaire he becomes the symbol of capitalism through the ages who holds a monopoly on everything from the sale of relics to the African slave trade, from mining products to consumer goods. He is the ultimate power broker: he determines who shall be emperor or king, pope or bishop, whether war or peace prevails.

The manipulated princes, especially Frederick the Wise of Saxony and Archbishop Albert of Brandenburg in turn manipulate the Emperor, their underlings, each other—and most importantly for this play, the theologians and intellectuals in their realm, especially Luther and Melanchthon. Luther, in his turn, becomes the puppet master of his followers, of the poor and downtrodden, the peasants and workers. Only one person does not seek power, wealth, or self-aggrandizement among the affluent, sophisticated, or educated classes: Thomas Münzer emerges as the hero of the drama who seeks betterment for mankind—égalité, fraternité, liberté—unselfishly and honestly. While all the other characters, especially Luther and the Pope, are doubters, cynics, non-believers, or hypocrites, Münzer sees religion as the opiate of the masses, a vehicle for exploitation and suppression, and openly preaches the denial of God. By so conceiving his main characters, Forte (as will be shown in detail) strips Luther of any redeeming qualities as a man, theologian, or writer, while Münzer, with the possible exception of being too much of an idealist, is cleansed of all blemishes.

The conclusion of the drama is consistent with such premises. At the end all the reactionary forces have advanced their goals: the princes have gained more land, power, and wealth; the Pope has refortified his position; the emperor has won a war. Luther, an unwitting or knowing tool of all of them, has become a wealthy, smug, married bourgeois and philistine. All of them, however, are now entirely in the hands of the plutocrats, represented here by Jakob Fugger's monopolistic trade empire. The masses, the workers and peasants, have been defeated and decimated in a series of bloodbaths, their parliament dissolved, and their spokesman, Thomas Münzer, betrayed and captured. The play closes with three simultaneous actions taking place on stage. The Fuggers, their books showing a record profit, pray a *Te Deum* to almighty capital; Luther, his wife, and the princes burst out into the singing of "A Mighty Fortess is Our God"; while Münzer, all but blocked out by them, is being beheaded.

As might be expected, Dieter Forte, during and after the opening of his drama and its subsequent publication, attempted to make a case for his revisionist approach to Reformation history. In telling of the genesis of the drama—research and writing took more than five years—Forte emphasizes that the subject suggested by the sub-title, "The Introduction of Bookkeeping," is central, since (to his mind) that invention was as revolutionary and epochal for medieval economics as electronic data processing became for ours. Having once recognized that fact, Forte found the contradictions and divergences in standard histories and biographies suddenly resolved. His exhaustive research proved to his complete satisfaction that the addition of only one piece to the political and economic jigsaw puzzle of the age produced a consistent and complete picture. The missing piece was the figure of Jakob Fugger, banker and businessman, whose money had controlled every important event of the era, including the bloody suppression of the Peasant Revolution. From that point onward Forte rejected all traditional accounts of the Reformation and the Peasant War. "I then felt challenged . . . I now wanted to prove that one can draw a historical portrait, factual down to non-essentials, and bring about entertaining theater as well [...] I stayed as neutral as a human being can be. After all, I did not need to change anything—[the story] is suspenseful enough as it stands."[12]

Also Forte maintains repeatedly that he has been historically accurate throughout his play. In a prefatory note to the drama, reproduced in many playbills, he states: "The texts retain for the most part the original words. Figures and facts are accurate. All currencies have been converted into modern Deutschmarks."[13] He also asserts that he has not tinkered with the chronology; in fact he goes to the extraordinary length of indicating the exact age of each character in the dramatis personae. And he has defended himself, repeatedly, against charges that he has bowdlerized history: "I can't help it if Münzer spoke in that way [i.e., anticipating Karl Marx and Ernst Bloch]. These are his texts...I have not written a propaganda drama."[14] Elsewhere he makes a similar claim for the accuracy of Luther's speeches. And his view of Fugger, he asserts, came from an extensive study of his account books: "The fact that Fugger emerges not as 'a helper of mankind,' but as someone who made money out of mankind should not be put down to me. It is after all *his* bookkeeping."[15]

Forte, in short, claims that he did not want to write an *Agitationsdrama* or anti-religious propaganda piece, or an exposé, for that matter. He asserts, correctly, that the more sensational aspects of his drama appear in many history books, even in the conservative times of Leopold von Ranke.[16] If these were not the goals of Forte, what then was the underlying purpose of his play? He wanted to compose, he claims, the first German drama about money, monopoly, and power.

> For the first time a drama on a German stage demonstrates how decisively money can intervene in the interrelationships of power and how extremely rewarding profits can be made through politics, if people engage in cold-blooded calculations and systematic manipulation... [then] if much money is amassed in one place and is administered by a very few, power is automatically generated. I will return to this theme in future plays. Perhaps people will then see my first drama in a different light, not only as pointed towards Luther and Münzer but even more so to the introduction of bookkeeping.[17]

(We will not examine here whether scenes in *Faust, Part II* or Brecht's *Threepenny Opera* and *Saint Joan of the Stockyards* undermine Forte's claim to originality.) Finally Forte suggests that he wanted to bestir the memory of his countrymen, so that they might recall one of the few triumphs, however short-lived, of German liberalism: the Peasant War, the early victory of the revolutionaries, their invocation of a parliament, their betrayal by Luther, Fugger's financial intervention, and the extirpation of more than one hundred thousand of them.

What argument, finally, does Forte advance in defense of his revisionist treatment of Luther's life and works? For one he denies that these revisions are of primary importance to his drama. In a letter to the French producers of his play he argues that German directors and audiences, rather than the work itself, have focused attention on Luther, thereby falsifying his intentions:

> ... Numerous elements which can be important for German audiences ... whose acquaintance with history is more precise— since, in fact, the play revolves around matters that they have learned in school—will become altogether secondary in France.... The German productions all too often have limited themselves to the single problem concerning Luther.[18]

Elsewhere, however, Forte admits that he did become an idol smasher of Luther's image, even though a reluctant one. During his research, he explains, he came to view Luther as a cog in the machinery of early capitalism, whose role it was to divert the suppressed from their desperate lot on earth by promises of a better life in the beyond. Forte admits that this view deposes Luther from his pedestal and "shatters his image." But Forte adds immediately: "That was not my primary goal." Nor had he intended, he adds, to draw black-and-white characters for the sake of "upgrading Münzer and downgrading Luther." Much effort, he argues, went into his depiction of Luther, including the showing of his positive sides. What he, Forte, had *not* wanted to do was to tell once again Luther's tormenting crises of faith and the political dilemmas in which he found itself. That story, severed from the context of its socio-political setting, had been told all too often by the Protestant church. In saying so he sounds almost apologetic. "That Luther comes out of this differently from the man we knew will no doubt be painful for many. But these are, after all, his own words."[19]

So much for Forte's apologia in his own behalf. He argues his case well; his play is entirely absorbing, and his occasional bitterness—for example at the fact that a television version of his drama was cancelled in favor of a scholarly discussion about it—appears not unfounded. (It is another matter whether he should have vented his resentment in a generally favorable article commenting on the TV series *Holocaust*.)[20] Before exposing the weaknesses of the play, not to say its hollowness, one can readily subscribe to the words of the well-known Protestant theologian Helmuth Thielicke, one of the severest critics of the drama, who nonetheless welcomed "in principle the fact that Luther is being shown from a different side."[21]

My own objections transcend criticism directed at a single play. Forte, without actually labelling his work, defines it as a documentary drama, a form employing new and technologically sophisticated stage devices, not possible or accepted before our times and, more importantly, achieving veracity by virtue of employing, totally or in good part, documents and other primary source materials. I am convinved that with the emergence of this new form an exploration of its ethics and aesthetics has become necessary. This need become obvious, at the latest, with the appearance of the documentary *The Investigation* by the German playwright Peter Weiß, which recreates the Auschwitz trial by piecing together various parts of the court transcript. But Weiß' selections reflect his own point of view: he illumines the suffering and endurance of the political prisoners and obscures those of the persecuted Jews. In a subsequent article Weiß justifies his selectivity by saying that the creator of documentary drama can impose a usable pattern on the fragments offered by reality. He concedes that his type of documentary is unabashedly partisan and that in "fighting rapacious conquest and genocide the technique of black-and-white depiction is justified."[22] Weiß offers, essentially, a description of agit-prop theater. One may not like it or approve of it, but Weiß has provided a suitable aesthetic for this type of propagandistic documentary drama.

But Forte claims that he tried to be objective, that he eschewed black-and-white situations and characters, and that he was content to let the facts tell their own story. Hence Weiß' straightforward partisan ethics and aesthetics do not apply to Forte.[23] The following, however, might. The list below may constitute an aggregate of criteria together with their rationale. Finally Forte's play will serve as a test case for these criteria.

1. In a documentary drama or in one that relies heavily on authentic texts (as here the sermons of Luther and Münzer), there must be some indication where the use of authentic documents leaves off and authorial imagination sets in; otherwise the audience is deluded into thinking *both* authentic.[24] Luther's sermons, if somewhat bowdlerized in their modern dress, are genuine. His conversations with his various contemporaries, on the other hand, cannot be authenticated by available source materials. Forte uses these conversations not so much to shift or distort historical events or Luther's part in them, but to reveal motivations behind them.

Invariably he attributes Luther's motives not to religious fervor or even zeal or, where Luther obviously errs, to shortsightedness, but to hypocrisy, self-seeking, cynicism, or opportunism. To cite one example: Luther, in all probability, married late in life (as even Marxist sources speculate)[25] to become integrated in an emerging new society. But Forte makes Luther appear as a hypocrite who uses his wife as the convenient "middleman" for accepting bribes and "douceurs" which he, ostensibly, won't deign to accept (p. 119). Another example: Earlier in the drama the victorious peasants establish, in Heidelberg, a parliament, the first in German history. While it is salutary that Forte invokes this all-but-forgotten event—about which no further details are known—he does damage to the credibility of his work by the way he dramatizes the incident. The proceedings sound, in their parliamentary language and content, like those that took place in 1848 in the Paulskirche. Obviously Forte wishes to make a point here about the tragic ineffectuality of German liberalism. But by compensating for lacking information about one age by drawing on sources from another, more than three hundred years later, Forte strains, perhaps breaks, the suspension of disbelief on the part of his audience. The very fact that the drama is, in many places, suffused in documentation, lends an all but fraudulent patina of factuality to the author's unsubstantiated inventions and substitutions.

2. In order to draw parallels or analogies to a later age, especially the author's own, the playwright of a documentary drama must not misrepresent either the past or the present. Dieter Forte is, in theory, in agreement with this criterion and knows of the difficulties in putting it into practice. In reviewing a historical novel, set in the same period as his drama, Forte theorizes that there are three ways to "utilize historical material as example for today's situation." In the first method the view and the intention of the author is apparent from the start. History thus becomes the tool for proving the preconceived views of the author. One might call such a work, Forte continues, "tendentious literature"—and such an approach courts many weaknesses. "After all, who likes to see the world through tinted glasses?", he asks rhetorically.

A second method, according to Forte, is to retain the historical material within its context, but to "work it up" in such a way that the reader, without much commentary by the author, realizes the—anything but fortuitous—analogies to the present. The danger of that method is its potential antiquarianism or quaintness of style and language. Finally, according to Forte, the author can escape the dilemmas posed by these two methods through an ironic approach. "[It] allows him to change his perspective constantly—to look from today back to yesterday, then again to take aim at today from [the perspective] of history."[26]

Essentially it is this last approach which Forte attempts to follow in his drama. But he adheres to it only intermittently. All too often he becomes a victim of the pitfalls of the first two methods which, in theory, he had rejected. Two examples of many: Forte is tendentious, when he argues that the modern world has turned completely mechanistic and that man has become a mere cog in a production line.[27] Given this conviction (and a commendable zeal to counteract such a world), he transforms the world of the Reformation into such a negative utopia. When Jakob Fugger, for example, advocates a modicum of restraint in slaughtering the insurgent peasants, he reasons that enough farm workers must be left alive to produce agricultural products (p. 176). On the other hand there are passages that creak under the load of medievalisms. The page-long sermons of Luther and Münzer, even though translated into approximations of modern German, are a heavy encumbrance on the drama—and have, consequently, been greatly curtailed in various productions.[28] At the conclusion of the play the two time frames all but coalesce: the present is being imposed on the past, and the past on the present. Fugger cites Dow-Jones averages and the *Wall Street Journal,* reporters conduct interviews as though daily newspapers have been invented already, and they conclude their conversation with Luther with the stereotyped formula of the *Spiegel*-magazine: "Dr. [Luther], we thank you for this interview" (pp. 203-207 and 152, resp.). In fact there is scarcely a page without such "aggressive anachronisms," as one analyst of the drama has labelled them.[29] But many are more subtle. The drama opens with the presentation of a student revolt (which Münzer supports and Luther condemns). But the scene and the dialogues are so structured that the reader is led to believe that student riots in the sixteenth century equal those of our times (p. 31).

Finally when Forte employs the method he had advocated as ideal—and tries to move across the centuries on the time machine of irony, he is curiously inconsistent. There is indeed broad irony afoot, when he has the princes decide on the new Kaiser through playing poker, a card game not as yet invented, or when he employs modern gutter language, or when Frederick, in talking of his relics-for-sale industry, sounds like a Madison Avenue huckster. In fact, much of the fun and the theatrical success of the play relies on such incongruities. But, unfortunately, all sense of irony abandons Forte when he brings Luther or Münzer on stage. Their stolid seriousness moors the time machine of irony.[30] And, with none of the methods of blending past and present consistently adhered to, the play stays a documentary drama in name only. Curiously, it is not the anachronisms that destroy its credibility. As Goethe already pointed out, no historical work can do without anachronisms.[31] His own drama, *Götz von Berlichingen,* also set in the sixteenth century, has his characters quote works not written as yet and feast on potatoes not as yet brought over from America. But Forte, by his mélange of approaches to history, does not use anachronisms; his entire play becomes one. A prominent German essayist and an early critic of Forte's play, recognizing some of these failings from the start, called it a "montage of facts" and adds: "[It is] a dishonest play. It pretends to be a documentary . . . hence does not lay claim to the authorial privilege of literary invention and yet it has almost nothing to do with the historical truth of the Age of Reformation."[32]

3. While the next aesthetic criterion is not new and has been iterated and reiterated by writers and critics since the eighteenth century—e.g. by Shaftesbury, it takes on a particular ethical dimension in documentary dramas: Historical characters must be treated fairly, neither demonized nor sanctified. Dieter Forte, despite his protestations to the contrary (cited above) does both. Luther emerges as a coward, constantly poised to recant, as a plagiarist, who steals a good part of his theses from his colleague Karlstadt, hypocritical, opportunistic, anti-Semitic, a male chauvinist, a philistine, dumb, provincial and vulgar, bloodthirsty, obsequious to the nobility, devious to colleagues, and condescending or domineering to social inferiors.[33] In answer to criticism Forte has maintained that he has also shown positive aspects of Luther's character (I found none) and that Luther, in fact, actually wrote what the play attributed to him.[34]

The last assertion deserves closer analysis as an example-in-reverse of the ethics and aesthetics of a documentary drama. Some of Luther's remarks are not authenticated by sources, e.g. a dialogue with Spalatin, the chancellor of Frederick the Wise, in preparation for Luther's appearance in Worms, which portrays Luther as a duplicitous politician (pp. 72-75). It is difficult to see how such a person could have aroused religious fervor in himself and others. But many other utterances of Luther, while authentic, constitute distortions either through omission or chronological rearrangement. When showing Luther as grasping and money-hungry, and a defender of plutocrats, does not the ethic of a documentary drama appear to demand the balancing observation that Luther refused payment for his writings (unlike Erasmus, among others) and that he preached, all his life, against usury, even when it was practiced by powerful and supportive princes?

Similarly Forte distorts by drawing Luther's character synchronically rather than diachronically. To be sure Forte argues, as previously quoted, that "the chronological order has been preserved."[35] That claim does, indeed, stand up when applied to the sequence of historical events. But as far as character portrayal goes, the older, more conservative and compliant Luther has been superimposed on the young, rebellious reformer. In one of the very first scenes, the young Luther delivers himself of a diatribe against students and universities which, at worst, might have been uttered by the old:

> LUTHER: No morals or decency any more. Instead of learning they run around with girls and ask you silly questions in the bargain. No proper order.... The universities ought to be reduced to rubble, the whole lot of them. They only corrupt the youth. Hotbeds of unbelief and criticism, all of them. There's nothing in the world reeks more of hell and the devil than a university (p. 12).

Given a Luther of such small-mindedness, it is no wonder, despite being one of the chief protagonists, that he emerges as a rather dull figure. Not only Forte's critics, but also some of his well-wishers and friends have seen in his Luther a man without character and one of the drama's weakest components. As one of Forte's French director-producers put it: "Forte decidedly denies the figure of Luther any psychological motivation, any ambition, and even any authentic religious concerns."[36] She might have added that even Luther's achievement as a translator of the Bible is dismissed as constituting just one of many Bible translations of the times.

Münzer, on the other hand, is raised to heroic, even saintly proportions. He appears as the sixteenth-century apostle of his chiliastic vision, an advocate of a communal, if not communistic life style, and as an angel of hope vis-à-vis the retrogressive forces—capitalistic and materialistic—sustained or strengthened by the teaching of Luther and the Pope. Forte apparently drew heavily on Ernst Bloch's pioneering works on Thomas Münzer.[37] But Forte would have done well to reread Bloch. Bloch knew, as Forte appears to forget, that both Luther and Münzer were driven primarily (though not exclusively) by differing interpretations of an envisioned religious utopia. And Bloch, the admiring rediscoverer of Münzer, also saw his weaknesses:

> Yet Münzer was undoubtedly vain, and worse, he [was] boastful, did not completely weigh his threatening words

correctly. His first and even his last letter to the Count of Mansfeld show signs of immaturity.... To be sure that happened only sporadically, only rarely does his assurance of power appear so hollow. The question remains, however, how far Münzer really was what he pretended to be, first of all politically, as a leader and man of importance, of immediate and far-reaching vision.[38]

Forte ignored these shortcomings in Münzer as he ignored the merits of Luther. With Forte's play we have returned to a dramatic world of unblemished saints and satanic villains or to revolutionary Marxist heroes and capitalistic exploiters.

4. Hence a documentary play, to become more than ephemerally effective theater, must proceed dialectically. Heiner Kipphardt, in the postscript to his play *In the Matter of J. Robert Oppenheimer,* quotes Hegel on the principles of writing history. He set himself the guidelines that he "ought change the historical facts as little as possible and as much as was dramatically necessary."[39] While Forte would probably subscribe to this method in principle—he quotes Büchner to the same effect[40]—he really made of his drama an antithesis to the Luther legend and substituted for a one-sided theological explanation of the Reformation and the Peasant Revolt a purely socio-political one, or to paraphrase one of his critics, he replaced religious polemics with the polemics of the pocketbook.[41] But to do so, especially in an ahistoric age, is yet another form of misleading an audience. One of Forte's critics deplored this as a type of irresponsibility: "Many young people, as the evening discussion in Hamburg demonstrated, accept [his image of Luther as a stupid...knave of the exploiters] without further reflection, for their knowledge of history has reached the zero-level long ago."[42]

In summary, Dieter Forte, when he wrote his play, had a unique chance to combine, in one play, subjects which two earlier German writers had left unfinished. Gerhart Hauptmann left behind a drama fragment about the Anabaptists, Thomas Mann (perhaps because drama was not his métier) left merely notes to a play about Luther's marriage.[43] Forte took up their cudgel when the way for his revisionist approach towards Luther had been paved by a decade of social protests and attacks on national shrines and cultural heroes. Forte's way had also been smoothed by the iconoclastic anti-Papal play *The Deputy* by Rolf Hochhuth; the emergence of a Protestant Hochhuth had even been anticipated.[44] Yet Forte missed this opportunity. Against Hochhuth's modern morality play he set an exposé and a diatribe. And thus, German literature, if not world literature, after having produced both satanic and hagiographic images of Luther for centuries, still owes us a plausible reincarnation of the reformer.

Notes

1. No complete bibliography on "Luther in Literature" exists as yet. Kurt Aland's *Martin Luther in der modernen Literatur. Ein kritischer Dokumentarbericht* (Witten: Eckart, 1973) confines itself to selected modern authors, including Forte, but concentrates on Thomas Mann. Friedrich Kraft's "Die bösen Bälge. Der arme Mann Luther und die Dramatiker von viereinhalb Jahrhunderten," *Zur Sache. Kirchliche Aspekte heute,* Heft 8 (Hamburg: Lutherisches Verlagshaus, 1971), pp. 75-98, yields excellent information, but treats the subject survey-fashion.—My own computer search at the Library of Congress produced several little-known treatments, e.g. Louise A. Vernon, *Thunderstorm in Church* (Scottsdale, Pa.: Herald Press, 1974) together with an additional bibliography *Martin Luther in English Poetry* (St. Louis: Concordia Publ. House, 1938). Also Prof. Walther Killy, University of Göttingen, mentioned his own bibliographical research-in-progress to me.

2. See Martin Rinckart, *Der Eißlebische christliche Ritter* (Eisleben: Jacob Gaubisch d. 'A', 1613), *Indulgentiarius confusis* (Eisleben: Jacob Gaubisches Erben, 1618), *Monetarious seditiosus* (Leipzig: Rehfeld and Grosse, [1625]) which brings, at that early date, a confrontation between Luther and Münzer. For further bibliographic information see Gerhard Dünnhaupt, *Bibliographisches Handbuch der Barockliteratur,* vol. III (Stuttgart: Hiersemann, 1981), p. 1540ff. Also see Lemnius, *Monachopornomachia,* ed. G. Vorberg (München: G. Müller, 1919).

3. See Zacharias Werner, *Martin Luther oder: Die Weihe der Kraft* in his *Theater* (Wien: L. Grund, 1818), vol. III, pp. 3-308; *Weihe der Unkraft, ibid.,* vol. VI, pp. 293-312.

4. See Osborne, *Luther. A Play* (London: Faber and Faber, [1961]; Bartels, *Martin Luther. Eine dramatische Trilogie. I. Der junge Luther. II. Der Reichstag zu Worms. III. Der Reformator* (München: Callwey, 1903); Constantine F. Malmberg, *The Professor of Wittenberg* (Burlingston, Iowa: The German Literary Board); Buchhorn, *Wende in Worms* (Cottbus: Heine, 1937); Lienhardt, *Luther auf der Wartburg* (Stuttgart: Greiner and Pfeiffer, 1909); Ahlsen, *Der arme Mann Luther* (Gütersloh: Mohn, 1965).

5. Friedrich Dedekind, *Papista conversus. Ein newe christlich Spiel von einem Papisten, der sich zu der rechten Warheit bekeret und darüber in Gefängniß und Gefahr des Lebens kompt. Darauß er durch Gottes Hülffe gnediglich erlöset wird....* (Hamburg: Heinrich Binder, 1596). Schütz' drama was performed in Kassel in 1973 (where I saw it). I have not yet found a printed version.

6. German original (Berlin: Klaus Wagenbach, 1971); English transl. (New York, St. Louis, etc.: McGraw Hill, 1972). Page numbers in my text refer to the transl. Where Holme's translation appears in need of revision, I have substituted my own.

7. Forte contributed to Fritz Hüser and Max von der Grün's anthology *Aus der Welt der Arbeit, Almanach der Gruppe 61 und ihrer Gäste* (Neuwied and Berlin: Luchterhand, 1961). Forte's name does not appear in a later anthology, Egon E. Dahinten, ed., *Stockholmer Katalog der Dortmunder Gruppe 61* (Stockholm: Standard Kartong, [1969]).

8. Hülser and von der Grün, eds., p. 342f. Further information from Wilhelm Kosch, *Detusches Literatur-Lexikon*, 3rd rev. ed. (Bern and München, Francke, 1978) and from *Kürschners Deutscher Literatur-Kalender*, 1978.

9. There has been an intimation that Forte's later plays were treated unfairly by the critics. See Michael Töteberg "Volksnah und doch nicht tümlich. Fernschspiele von Pevny/Turrini und Forte als Buch," *Die Tat*, Nr. 31 (1 Aug. 80), p. 10: "These [later] plays failed so completely with the theater critics, that it is truly suspicious. Has Dieter Forte become a victim of a turning point of trends [*Tendenzwende*] in the theater?"

10. This costuming occured at various German stages. Forte, in an interview, explained it as follows: "I had reflected thoroughly [about having the pope represented by an actress]. I did not mean any particular pope, but the Institution, a feminine, emancipated culture. The Pope, God's deputy, a demiurge, is neither man nor woman [but] neuter; it's immaterial who plays him. . . . [The miniskirt] symbolizes the contrast between Mediterranean and German culture, between the barbarians and the popes who read Plato. . . ." See [Arthur Joseph], "Es geht nicht um Theologie, sondern um Geld. Arthur Joseph spricht mit Dieter Forte," *Theater heute*, XIII, Nr. 1 (1 Jan. 72), 41-42.

11. Georg Hensel, a reviewer for *Theater heute*, called it a "windshield-wiper technique of staging." See his "Luther, der Knecht des Kapitals," *Theater heute*, XII, Nr. 1 (1 Jan. 71), 19.

12. Joseph, p. 41. Forte has repeatedly elaborated on his definition of "reality" in the theater. He believes that the stage can examine a world whose depiction is filtered, distorted, and oversimplified by the technical media as to its true substance and "it can show, with the simplest means, how results are brought about." See his "Reiz des Vergänglichen," [i.e., printed version of symposium lecture "Theater zwischen Tradition and Utopie," Klagenfurt, 1973], *National-Zeitung*, Basel, LXXXI (8 Sept. 73), "Am Wochenende," 3.

13. German version, p. [5], English, p. [1].

14. Joseph, p. 42.

15. Forte, "On my method," in his *Luther, Münzer . . .*, trl. Hume, p. 209.

16. Forte appendixed a bibliography to the (German version) of his play, "Literatur (Auswahl)," p. [142], in which he lists Ranke, *Die Geschichte der Päpste*, Wiesbaden, 1957 and *Deutsche Geschichte im Zeitalter der Reformation*, Köln, 1957.

17. Joseph, p. 41.

18. Forte's letter of June 1972 to Elisabeth Tréhard is cited in her "Questions à l'auteur," *Cahiers de la production théâtrale* [*Comédie de Caen*], No. 5 (1973), p. 9. (My transl. from French.)

19. The two passages occur, respectively, in Joseph, p. 42 and in Forte, "On my methods," p. 209.

20. Forte, "Geschichtstabu," in "Holocaust und die Folgen [Themen der Zeit]," *Die Zeit*, Nr. 11 (9 March 1979), p. 64.

21. As quoted from his remarks during a debate about Forte's play in the Thalia-Theater, Hamburg, May 1971. See W. Alexander Bauer, "Diskussion in Hamburg. Punktesammeln für Fortes *Luther*," *Marbacher Zeitung*, Nr. 106 (10 May 1971), p. 26. Agreement between Forte's supporters and detractors stopped at this point, however. The critic and author Walter Böhlich, who championed the play even before its successful premiere in Basel (conversation with me, Summer 1972, house of Prof. Klaus von See, Frankfurt), maintains that the core of the Luther portrayal, the discrepancy between the reformer's avowed ethics and his actions, are founded in fact. Thielicke has countered that Forte pilloried Luther for the socio-policial ills that grew out of (and perverted) his reforms.—For an additional account on the debate, see K.W. "Ein Autor verteidigt seinen Luther," *Frankfurter Allgemeine Zeitung*, Nr. 102 (4 May, 1972), p. 22.

22. Weiß' *Die Ermittlung* in his *Dramen* (Frankfurt a.M.: Surhkamp, 1968), II, 7-199. Also see his "Das Material und die Modelle. Notizen zum dokumentarischen Theater," *ibid.*, 464-472.

23. Forte, during a debate in the Haus der Kirche, Berlin, June 1971 (in which he participated by phone) is quoted as saying: "Against the reproach of 'anti-religious propaganda' he defended himself as against the charge that he had wanted to write a Marxist play." See G.G. "Ein engagierter Mensch. Theologen und Historiker diskutieren über Dieter Fortes Luther-Stück," *Der Tagesspiegel,* XXVII, Nr. 7826 (13 June 1971), 4. Also see Joseph, p. 42.

24. This objection occured already to some of the reviewers of the premiere in Basel. See Hermann Dannecker, "Typisch deutsch im Umwerten der Werte," *Schwäbische Zeitung,* Nr. 283 (8 Dec. 1970), p. 11: "The unprepared spectator cannot spearate between original texts, which furthermore had to be 'translated' into contemporary German, and [passages] which the author had added on.

25. For a concise summary of past attitudes to Luther in the GDR see Siegfried Streller, "Einleitung" in *Hutten-Müntzer-Luther. Werke in zwei Bänden,* "Bibliothek deutscher Klassiker" (Berlin and Weimar: Aufbau, 1970), vol. I, pp. iv-xxxiv; on Luther's marriage, p. xxxiii. As indicated by recent mailings from various cultural offices of the GDR, there has been a major shift towards a more positive view of Luther during the Luther anniversary year. For a detailed analysis see James M. Markham, "East Germany Finally Embraces Luther," *The New York Times,* Sunday, May 8, 1983, Section 1, pp. 1, 3.

26. Forte, "Der Student und die Bauern" [i.e. review of Horatius Haeberle, *Kopf und Arm* (München: Droemer, 1976)] in *Der Spiegel,* XXX, Nr. 44 (25 Oct. 76), 221-222.

27. See his interview with Hans-Peter Platz and Aurel Schmidt "Der Schriftsteller und das Theater," *Basler Magazin,* Nr. 47 (25 Nov. 1978), pp. 2-3.

28. As reported by Hensel, p. 20 (see note 11) such cuts were applied as early as the premiere in Basel. Because of the inordinate length of the play "each director breaks out of the [six-hour-long] total drama those parts that interest him." See Wolfgang Stauch von Quitzow, "Alles nur Marionetten. Dieter Fortes 'Luther'-Drama bei den Ruhrfestspielen," *Mannheimer Morgen,* Nr. 119 (29 May 1979), p. 40.

29. See B[ernard] Lortholary, "La Réforme selon les manuels scolaires et Dieter Forte," *Cahiers de la production théâtrale* [Comedie de Caen], Nr. 5 (1973), p. 28.

30. Early reviewers, without (understandably) connecting it to Forte's unresolved dilemma with a documentary drama, clearly saw the inconsistency in his ironic approach. See Karena Niehoff, "Demontage einer Legende," *Süddeutsche Zeitung,* Nr. 84/85 (8-9 Apr. 1981), p. 37: "More than apparent is Forte's stylistic indecisiveness between persiflage and historical drama in the case of Luther, Münzer and the minor characters attached to them. As soon as one or the other comes on stage Forte is no longer in the mood for jokes or leg-pulls, and is entirely overpowered by his embittered intent to dismantle radically one legend and to construct a massive, towering new one." Also see O[tto] Gillen, "Verzeichnetes Lutherbild," *Baden-Württemberg,* VIII, Heft 5 (1971), p. 21, who criticizes the lack of "ironic distanciation" in the performance at Karlsruhe.

31. Goethe, in defense of Alexander Manzoni's alleged anachronisms, wrote that "all literature [trades] in anachronisms." See "Theilnahme Goethes an Manzoni," W.A. I, 42^1, 172. Forte commits such mild anachronisms, despite his claim that "facts and figures are accurate." For example, he has two characters quote from Machiavelli's *The Prince,* a work not published in book form until 1532.

32. See Heinz Beckmann, "Schelte für die Hochschaukler," *Zeitwende, Kultur, Theologie, Politik,* 42 (1971), 279.

33. To document, selectively, passages revealing these negative characteristics: pp. 12 and 44 (plagiarism); p. 40 (hypocrite), 151 (male chauvinist), 149 philistine (i.e., anti-scientific), p. 36 (stupid); p. 151 (provincial); p. 151 (vulgar); pp. 95 and 163 (bloodthirsty), pp. 130ff and 165 (obsequious), pp. 44 and 67 (devious), p. 101 (condescending).

34. Joseph, p. 42 and Forte, "On my method," p. 205.

35. Forte, "On my method," p. 208.

36. Elisabeth Tréhard, "Analyse dramaturgique de la pièce," in *Cahiers* (see note 18), p. 16.

37. Forte, in his "Literatur (Auswahl)," lists Bloch's *Thomas Münzer* (Frankfurt a.M., 1969) and *Atheismus und Christentum* (Frankfurt a.m., 1969).

38. See Bloch, *Thomas Münzer als Theologe der Revolution, "Gesamtausgabe"* (Frankfurt a.M.: Surhkamp, 1969), vol. I, p. 98.

39. Kipphardt, "Nachbemerkung," in his *In der Sache J. Robert Oppenheimer,* rev. ed. (Frankfurt: Suhrkamp, 1981), pp. 149-151.

40. In his "Geschichtstabu" (see note 20) he quotes Büchner's request to dramatists: "His highest task is to come as close as possible to history as it really happened."

41-42. See Hensel, p. 20.

43. See Gerhart Hauptmann, *Die Wiedertäufer* [Fragment] in his *Sämtliche Werke,* ed. Hans-Egon Hass (Berlin: Propyläen Verlag, 1963), vol. VIII, pp. 697-848. Thomas Münzer is not mentioned in the drama. Also cf. Thomas Mann's plans for a drama *Luthers Hochzeit.* He left 47 octavo pages of notes. For a detailed description of their contents see Aland (note 1), ch. viii.

44. Comparisons between *The Deputy* and Forte's Luther drama have frequently been drawn, for example by Reinhard Baumgart, "Ein Bühnenluther als Bühnenfutter," *Süddeutsche Zeitung,* XXVII, Nr. 164 (10-11 July 1971), *Feuilleton,* p. 12.

REVOLUTION AND REFORM
LUTHER AND HIS TIME

LUTHER AND ROME: THEN AND NOW

Harry J. McSorley, *University of Toronto*

The topic I have chosen is broad indeed. It deals not only with two very different ages but is also more inclusive than the theme, Luther and the papacy, on which we have some illuminating recent studies, the agreed results of which I gratefully presuppose, without being able to rehearse here in the space alloted me.[1] I chose the broader theme "Luther and Rome" so as to allow me, especially in Part I of the essay, to deal with other actors than the Pope on the Roman Catholic side who played key roles in Luther's transition from a Catholic reformer of the Catholic Church to the excommunicated Augustinian friar whom history acknowledges as the Father of the Protestant Reformation.

Subscribing thoroughly to the view of Peter Manns in his admirable recent essay, based on his more than thirty years of Luther research, that "the reality [of Luther] is far more complicated than the historians and above all, the theologians until now have admitted",[2] I think it would be redundant for me to offer any disclaimers concerning completeness. I simply wish, on the basis of selected texts, to draw attention in Part I to some of the factors that contributed to the tragic rupture of the relationship between Luther and Rome then, and to contrast them in Part II with a different set of factors contributing to a more positive appreciation of Luther by Rome and, vice-versa, of Rome now by Lutherans.

I
Luther and Rome—Then: Truth, Misunderstanding and More

1. *Truth*

It would take more than one lecture to speak about the Christian and Catholic truth discovered or re-discovered by Luther that still commends itself to Protestant *and* Catholic Christians today.[3] I list here simply three such truths at the very heart of Luther's theology:

    i)   Against the late scholastic theology that he had been taught Luther, as early as 1515 or 1516, came to see with the Scriptures that, without the liberating grace of Christ everyone was held in bondage to sin and that the sinner's will was totally unable—unfree—by its own power to do anything to attain justification and the forgiveness of sins.[4] Putting Luther's basic tenet more positively and more familiarly, he early came to see that we are justified solely by faith in Christ and solely through his liberating grace.

ii) The truth concerning the article of justification discovered by Luther during his effort, as a Doctor of Sacred Scripture, to renew the theology of his day, was programmatically translated into the practical life of the church when Luther sent his 95 Theses on the reform—not the abolition—of the theology and practice of indulgences to his 27-year-old archbishop, on October 31, 1517.[5]

iii) Not just in 1517 or 1518, but as early as 1509, Luther knew, without in any way challenging the legitimate authority of the popes, councils or even church traditions that were truly universal, that the supreme authority and norm of all church doctrine and practice was Holy Scripture.[6]

It was this set of convictions, strengthened by new "insights into the Word and faith as the foundation of salvation", that gave Luther the courage to stand fast and accept the challenge to his status in the church and the threat to his very own life that was set before him in 1518 when his reformation program unexpectedly entered on a collision course with the pope and virtually the entire ecclesiastical establishment of his day.[7]

Why wasn't Luther's truth grasped by the rest of the Church? Why did his truth very shortly become a source of division in the Church? Here are some of the factors that have to be considered in answering these questions.

2. *Misunderstanding*

That there was a great deal of serious misunderstanding on all sides which contributed to Luther's excommunication is evident to anyone who reads the sources. A crucial instance of this is implied in Joseph Lortz's oft-quoted phrase: Luther was rejecting a Catholicism that was not fully Catholic when he attacked the new, Ockhamistic version of the once-condemned semi-pelagian error.[8] Surprisingly, this thesis has been verified by none less than Heiko Oberman who, while successfully refuting in part the thesis of Heinrich Denifle and Lortz that late medieval nominalism was radically uncatholic, nevertheless had to concede that on the doctrine of justification—the key concern of Luther—the Ockham-Biel wing of Nominalism was "at least Semi-pelagian".[9]

Reacting against this doctrine, Luther erroneously thought that all the scholastics except Gregory of Rimini held to the Ockham-Biel view. In actual fact, had he known the medieval tradition better, Luther could well have cited Catholicism's "common doctor", Thomas Aquinas, against his late scholastic foes.[10]

For another illustration of the serious misunderstanding that was involved at the very outset of Luther's public conflict with Rome, we have Luther's own words in the letter he sent to Pope Leo X May 30, 1518 accompanying his lengthy explanations of the 95 theses on indulgences:

The theses, he writes, were drawn up for discussion only in and around Wittenberg. "They were drawn up in such a way", says Luther, that he would find it "incredible that they be understood by everyone, for they are disputations, not doctrines or dogmas, expressed rather obscurely, and enigmatically, as is the custom. Otherwise, had I been able to foresee [that they would circulate everywhere] I certainly would have taken care to make them more readily understood".[11]

In light of this testimony, it seems to me difficult to deny that misunderstanding played a major role in the process by which Luther's Catholic reform became a reform movement outside of communion with the Roman Catholic Church. Yet there are some who seem nervous about using the very category of misunderstanding in interpreting the Reformation, apparently fearing that, by drawing attention to the important role played by misunderstanding, one is thereby *reducing* the divisive outcome of Luther's reformation to a set of "mere misunderstandings". To allay that fear and to help balance the picture I have entitled this first section of the essay, "Truth, Misunderstandings and *More*".

3. *Mistakes*

A mistake is really a form of misunderstanding, but I single it out here only to get away from its suspect brother. I have never found anyone denying that mistakes—or errors—were made by both Luther and Rome, but one doesn't see it affirmed too much either. And yet mistakes abound on both sides that contributed in a major way to the divisive outcome of Luther's reform. To draw from just one very fateful encounter between Luther and "Rome"—the Leipzig Disputation in 1519—we see serious mistakes on both sides that, by definition, tarnished the claim to truth upheld by each side.

Despite the native brilliance and acumen of both disputors—and the great sense and truth they each spoke—we find serious theological, historical, or exegetical errors being made that contributed to the widening of the gap between Luther and Rome.

We find Luther, for example, insisting on an exegetical point that has been abandoned by modern protestant biblical scholars: namely, that the "rock" foundation of the church according to Mt 16,18 cannot be Peter, but only Christ. For Luther, any Church Fathers who said Peter was the rock, must have been yielding to human weakness.[12] One would also have to agree with the historian Harold Grimm that "Luther was not historically accurate in maintaining [at Leipzig] that the jurisdiction of the church of Rome over the others was a product solely of the preceding four hundred years and of papal decretals".[13]

One has to agree also with Grimm that at least some of "the claims made by Catholic tradition and defended by Eck [concerning papal authority and Roman jurisdiction] were exaggerated".[14] For his part, Eck, with virtually all the Catholics of his day, made the grievous error of unchurching the Greeks, seeing them not only as schismatics but also as heretics, and of clearly implying that they were not to be regarded as belonging to the Church.[15] In this way Eck could invalidly invalidate their theological witness against the excessive claims of the medieval papacy.[16] Aside from exegetical[18] and historical mistakes which befell Eck as well as Luther, one can also point to Eck's view of church councils which left no room for critical judgment or thoughtful reception on the part of the believer. The believer's proper response to the decrees of lawfully assembled councils, according to Eck, was simply "the obedience of faith" which makes the intellect a captive.[18] The New Testament words of Gal. 1,8 and 1 Thess. 5,21 ("Test all things") that are so important for Luther's critical view of church authority and, in theory at least, for that of the Catholic tradition through Augustine and Aquinas, play virtually no role in the Counter-Reformation ecclesiology of John Eck.[19]

4. *Lack of Understanding, Lack of Evangelical Charity and Lack of Justice*

Along with misunderstandings and mistakes the divisive result of Luther's reformation is incomprehensible unless we look at Rome's lack of understanding in the face of Luther's sincere, well grounded and Catholic reform proposals.

According to the Catholic Luther scholar, Erwin Iserloh, Luther's honest request for reform of the scandalous indulgence preaching and practice was rejected out of a lack of "understanding and priestly conduct" on the part of the bishops and the pope. This failing by "Rome" in the confrontation of 1518, says Iserloh, combined with Luther's own fierceness [*Heftigkeit*] and impatience, drove Luther to say things about the church, the pope, councils,and the priestly ministry that placed him outside the Church of his day.[20]

In speaking of lack of understanding, then, we move beyond the realm of the purely intellectual and scholarly into that of the ethical—or unethical—behaviour of scholars, theologians, and prelates.

We note first of all that Luther's Archbishop was enmeshed in a massive conflict of interest when Luther wrote to him about reforming the very practice of indulgences that was keeping Albrecht fiscally solvent. Unaware of the deal that had been struck between Albrecht, the pope, and the Fuggers, Luther, who approached Albrecht with his October 31, 1517 letter calling for reform of what Peter Manns calls the "heretically misunderstandable" contemporary practice of indulgences,[21] can be compared to Little Red Riding Hood thinking she was talking to Granny instead of you-know-who! How, with such dirty hands—or paws—could Albrecht possibly have responded as he should as a Christian pastor to the plea of one of his fellow priests? Instead of being converted from his ways by Luther's genuinely prophetic letter, Albrecht followed the path that least threatened his income.

This story of a Catholic prelate with his finger in the till is matched by another tale of less than Christian behaviour toward Luther by his supposed friend, John Eck. Early in 1518 at the request of the Chancellor of Eck's University of Ingolstadt, Bishop Gabriel von Eyb, to give him an opinion on Luther's 95 indulgence theses, Eck wrote a series of highly critical comments alongside a number of Luther's theses.[22] These found their way to Luther who was greatly offended that a friend—without first contacting him to learn the *meaning* of the theses would, without understanding them, pass such judgments on them as "erroneous", "frivolous", "seditious", "rash", and "irreverent towards the pope". This unhappy affair testifies not only to the fact that, according to Luther, Eck *misunderstood* the theses, but worse, that he violated the rules of friendship and Christian charity by failing to contact him before condemning him and also by failing to presume a better interpretation of the theses as befits friends.[23]

Luther tried to set a good example of what Christian charity requires by replying to Eck at length but *privately* in his *Asterisks* so as not to return to Eck the evil he had done to Luther.[24] Unfortunately, however, in the reply, Luther resorts to the name-calling, the patronizing remarks, the insults and the explicit or implicit charges of heresy that we find privately in Eck and publicly in the responses of John Tetzel and Sylvester Prierias. Through these three Roman actors, as Peter Manns puts it, "Luther allowed himself to be provoked into developing his high polemical endowment".[25] Though lack of understanding can still be found in the ethically neutral sense of an inability to understand the position of the other—such as was the case in the non-dialogical meeting at Augsburg in October 1518 between Luther and Cardinal Cajetan[26] the relation between Luther and Rome was, from 1518 on, marred by increasing harshness, rudenss, ridicule—in short—lovelessness on both sides, often accompanied by calumnious misrepresentation of the position of the other side. One may call this a "moralizing" view of the Reformation if one wishes, as long as one does not ignore two things: (1) the fact that, without such moral failing—or what Vatican II called "culpa" or fault on both sides—an essential condition for Christian division would have been lacking and Luther's reformation could have followed a much more fruitful course within the church;[27] and (2) that Luther himself felt he was the victim of malicious and rash judgments by his opponents.

Is Luther thinking of the uncharitable accusations made against him when, in his German interpretation of the Our Father for the laity, published April 5, 1519, he includes this teaching in his comments on the 5th Petition—Forgive us our trespasses as we forgive those who trespass against us—

> Don't think that a slanderer, a false accuser or one who judges evilly will have his sins forgiven, neither the smallest nor the greatest, . . . unless he leaves aside and changes his wicked tongue.

Reminiscent of his words to Eck, Luther invokes here, "the noble, precious, golden rule of Christ" contained in Mt. 11,55ff. "If your brother sins against you . . . go to him and tell him his fault between you and him alone"—and says: "Notice that you're not to tell[the grievance] to anyone else, but only you and he" are to be involved.[28]

When the theological faculties of Louvain and Cologne published their censures of some of Luther's teachings in February 1520, Luther raises the question of Roman "subjectivism", that is, judgments made without biblical support. "We are Masters of Theology . . . whatever we say is Gospel and whatever we condemn is heresy",[29] is Luther's sarcastic rendering of their position.

Even if the judgments of the two faculties against him were correct and grounded on the Scriptures, says Luther, they should have dealt with him according to charity or according to the Christian law.[30] Very important here is that Luther does not try to defend every phrase he wrote. He asks instead why, out of charity, the learned theologians did not simply say to the people: "Don't be offended, brothers, by Luther's writings: he has disputed many things and has said some things perhaps more profoundly than everyone can grasp: if even the divine Scriptures have their dangerous places, how much more human writings".[31] The professors, Luther says, would expect me to follow that rule of charity—which is even a part of the natural law—and he would be prepared to do so if, contrary to the professors' procedure, he didn't have to denounce a person's name publicly as well as his doctrine. To date, he says, I have not named anyone even though I have often attacked their doctrines.[32] He then repeats the evangelical rule of dealing privately with a brother, that we had noted in his 1519 exposition of the Lord's Prayer, and asks why they didn't admonish him in a private letter, "so that I might either explain myself or change or show myself pertinacious".[33]

Lest I seem to be stacking the dice here in favour of St. Martin versus the uncharitable professors, it has to be mentioned that the professors are confronted with the *unprecedented* problem that the age of Gutenberg has brought about: how to deal privately with a professor with non-conformist ideas who is disseminating them by means of best-sellers.

Lack of evangelical charity often includes injustice. In the case of Luther and Rome this often takes the form of simply distorting or falsifying the actual teaching of the adversary. The very titles of Luther's replies to Eck as well as the content demonstrate at least the perceived presence of this literally vicious factor in the deteriorating relations between Luther and Rome. Consider for example: *A Defence of Luther Against the Malign Judgment of John Eck* (1519)[34] and *Concerning the New Bulls and Lies of Eck* (1520).[35] As late as August 1520, as he was just becoming aware of the existence of the papal bull, *Exsurge Domine,* that threatened him with excommunication unless he retracted 41 propositions taken from his writings, Luther could state formally in a document sent to the young Emperor:

> I ask all my friends and enemies . . . there where I have acted or spoken excessively, to put the best interpretation on my words and acts . . . For my part I offer to everyone that I will put the best interpretation on what they do. . . . [36]

Mention of *Exsurge Domine* in the context of a discussion about lack of understanding, love, and justice as key factors contributing to the division between Luther and Rome requires that at least something be said here about the *official* way Luther was dealt with at Rome.[37]

Following the lead of Ludwig von Pastor,[38] Erwin Iserloh thinks Luther was not done an injustice by the excommunication. Rather, having started with a well-grounded polemic, Luther allowed himself to take positions that the Church had to censure.[39] A substantive question, however, is: did Rome have to censure them as *"heretical"*? Recall that Luther himself had shortly before proposed to the universities of Louvain and Cologne that they warn people about the "dangerous" aspects of his teaching. Further, in what sense of the term was "heresy" being used? In the narrow sense of a denial of an article of faith held by the Universal Church East and West? Or was it one of the several broader senses that had currency in the middle ages? Another such question is: which propositions did *Exsurge Domine* censure as heretical—and which only as "offensive to pious ears"? The document doesn't tell us that rather important piece of information, a failing that Luther immediately pounced upon.[40] As such, it is a pitifully inept document that, given what was at stake, was a disaster for both Luther and Rome. For Luther, because it unnecessarily hardened his opposition to Rome, to put it mildly, with the result that against all his intentions he had to continue his reform out of communion with Rome. For Rome it was a disaster because it cut off the most gifted theologian of the age and with him millions who believed Rome had indeed done an injustice to Luther. Finally, is a condemnation just that didn't *appear* to be just—even to learned Catholics of the day, many of whom, John Eck had to admit to Leo X's successor in 1523, could not see what was wrong with some of the condemned propositions?[41]

The judgments of von Pastor and other Catholics about the justness of Luther's excommunication deal solely with the substantive aspects of the case. Still needed, it seems to me, is an analysis of the equity of the Roman procedures from the standpoint of this history of the canon law of procedures. Until that study has been made, I do not think it anachronistic to say Luther was not done justice from the procedural point of view. Luther and his supporters, especially Elector Frederick of Saxony, consistently called for impartial and learned bishops or other persons to try his case.[42] Only by redefining terms can Luther be said to have been provided with an impartial—or just—investigation by Rome. The sole fact that John Eck—a bitter enemy of Luther, whose pre-judgments against and personal animosity towards Luther were matters of public record— was even allowed near Rome when it was preparing its judgment on Luther is sufficient to rule out Luther's having received a just verdict. And yet we know he not only was in Rome, but played a key role in the shaping of that fatefully divisive document, *Exsurge Domine*.[43]

When Luther received the bull of Leo X, he seems to have called off his offer to put the best interpretation on people's words by putting the worst possible interpretation on the authors of the Bull—he was the Antichrist. Against the Antichrist, no holds were barred. Neither evangelical charity nor the radical requirements of the Sermon on the Mount were to be exercised toward those who were the enemies of God.[44] The worst interpretation was to be placed on even the most promising signs of reform in the Roman Catholic Church. A notable example of this is the painfully honest reform document prepared by a committee of cardinals at the request of Pope Paul III in 1537. The secret document was leaked and printed in Italy in 1538.[45] Luther published a German translation of it with a preface and marginal comments. Instead of welcoming and supporting the recommended reforms of monastic life, indulgences, the papal and ecclesiastical usury, simony and trading in benefices that had produced such non-pastoral prelates as Albrecht of Mainz—Luther contemptuously ridicules the document. His bitterness is so great that he is unable to see what the document says. Despite the document's several explicit criticisms of misconduct by popes and cardinals, and its urgent call for change,[46] Luther claims in his preface that, according to the document, "Neither [the pope] nor the cardinals have ever done anything wicked. They are all pious and should have what they have, and what is more, they are to remain as they are".[47] And, in response to the criticism of the cardinals of those theologians who taught that the mere will of the pope is the rule and guide for all his decisions and actions so "that he can do what he wants without fear"—a doctrine which the cardinals say is the source of "all the abuses in the church of God,"[48] Luther, instead of rejoicing that *his* critique of Roman and papal subjectivism is now being urged within the Roman curia, writes in the margin: "Bring the fire! These cardinals have become heretics since they condemn this old article of *faith* on which the papacy is based."[49]

Luther and Rome—then? A tragic, unecessary mélange of truth, misunderstanding, mistakes, meanness, misrepresentation, mutual condemnation and division.

II
Luther and Rome—Now: Understanding—and More

The kind of self-criticism within the Roman Church of which we have just had a sample did not become a majority view in Rome overnight, but neither were the cardinals condemned as heretics, contrary to Luther's suggestion.[50] It is not my purpose here to rehearse the long process of inner Roman Catholic reform starting with Adrian VI, Cardinal Cajetan—even John Eck—the Bishops of the Council of Trent and the new or renewed religious congregations. But there is one crucial element of the 16th-century Roman Catholic Reformation—or Counter-Reformation if you like—that should be singled out here as providing at least one of the roots of the newer relationship between Luther and Rome that is coming into being today.

1. *Love Urges Understanding*

I refer to a foundational teaching of the founder of the most important single institutional expression of the Catholic Reformation other than the Council of Trent. At the beginning of the *Spiritual Exercises,* the very first counsel St. Ignatius Loyola offers in this:

> To help those giving the Exercises as well as those receiving them, it ought to be presupposed that any good Christian should be more ready to save than to condemn a statement made by his neighbor. And if one is not able to save it, let him ask the neighbor how he understands it, and, if he understands it badly, let him correct him lovingly; and if that isn't sufficient, let him seek every suitable means by which the proposition, correctly understood, might be saved.[51]

This rule has touched the lives not only of the Jesuits but of millions of other Catholics, lay and religious, who have allowed themselves to be guided by the *Exercises.* No more than the Sermon on the Mount, or the eighth commandment, however, has it immunized Catholics against uncharitable interpretations of Protestant teachings. This is a spiritual teaching that coincides perfectly, as we have seen, with Luther's pleas for charitable and benign interpretations of his teaching and with his resolve— at least before *Exsurge Domine*—to do the same for others. It is a teaching that surely animated the great Jesuit Cardinal Bea, who as first President of the Vatican Secretariat for Promoting Christian Unity, steered through the Second Vatican Council's *Decree on Ecumenism* which called for "a change of heart", a renewal of the mind and "an unstinted love" along with public and private prayer for unity as the very "soul of the whole ecumenical movement".[52] Speaking directly of Luther in that spirit, the incomparable student of the Council of Trent, Hubert Jedin, could write: What we Catholics "can do and have to do is not only show complete justice to Luther, but also to embrace him with love, which is the sign by which one recognizes the disciples of the Lord".[53]

2. *Understanding*

The *Decree on Ecumenism* also called on Catholics "to acquire a more adequate understanding of the respective doctrines of" those whom it called "our separated brethren".[54] Theology and other subjects, especially those dealing with history "must be taught with due regard for the ecumenical point of view, so that they may correspond more exactly with the facts."[55] Speaking more bluntly, and with direct reference to Catholic textbook treatments of Luther, Cardinal Bea wrote shortly after Vatican II: "Even today many [Catholic theologians] confront Luther's theological thought with great lack of understanding and they have not succeeded in breaking through the clichés of controversial theology because of the insufficient attention they give to the various structures of Luther's thought and statements.... Entering into Luther's thought and working out the genuinely Christian values in his teaching can also serve to illuminate the Catholic truth ... and to show where a unity in the testimony of faith already exists."[56] This statement, bearing the dateline "Rome, in June 1967", symbolizes powerfully the dramatic change in the attitude of "Rome" toward Luther after 450 years!

The study of the change in attitude toward Luther by Catholic Luther scholars starting in the late 1930's has been told too many times to repeat here.[57] And there is simply not sufficient space for adequate discussion of the changing *Lutheran* attitude to Rome, above all as this has been expressed in various levels of Lutheran-Roman Catholic dialogue around the world. What I do wish to do in this final section is mention some further highly symbolic *official* expressions on the part of Rome that indicate not just a change of heart but also of mind by Rome in its assessment of Luther.

3. *Repentance and Reception of Luther's Truth by Rome*

The above-mentioned contemporary Roman Catholic Luther scholarship in tandem with biblical scholarship and research into the Council of Trent is virtually unanimous in recognizing the catholicity of Luther's central and original reformation protest on behalf of the doctrine that we are justified before God solely because of the grace of Christ working in us through faith.

Such scholarship provided the foundation for Cardinal Bea's successor in the presidency of the Secretariat for Christian Unity, Cardinal Willebrands, to say to the Lutheran World Federation's Assembly in 1970:

> Catholics have in the past not always assessed Luther's person, nor stated his theology correctly. This has served neither truth nor love, nor the unity we are striving to bring about between Lutherans and Catholics.... Which Catholic today can deny that Luther was a deeply religious person who searched honestly and devotedly for the message of the Gospel...?
>
> Luther recognized the deep meaning of the word "faith" and many Lutherans and others have to this day learned to live out of that faith that he taught.... Today joint investigations by Catholic and Lutheran scholars have shown that the word "faith"

in Luther's sense excludes neither the works of love nor hope. It can be said then with good reason that Luther's concept of faith—if one takes it in its entirety—actually means nothing other than what we in the Catholic Church mean by love....

Luther was a man for whom the doctrine of justification was the article on which the Church stands or falls. In this he may be our common teacher that God must always remain the Lord and that our most important human response has to remain absolute confidence in and the worship of God.[58]

Ten years after the historical address of Willebrands, which represented the first official positive Roman Catholic pronouncement on Luther's person and teaching, Pope John Paul II in a general audience on June 25, 1980, sent greetings to all the Christians who on that and on the following days were gathered in Augsburg, Germany, and around the world to commemorate the 450th anniversary of the *magna carta* of Lutheranism, the Augsburg Confession. The Bishop of Rome regretted the fact that "the last powerful effort" to reconcile Roman Catholics and Lutherans at the Diet of Augsburg in 1520 did not succeed in averting a visible division between them.

However, said the pope, with reference to recent scholarship on the unity negotiations at Augsburg:

With all the more gratitude we learn today with increasing clarity that at that time, although the building of a bridge did not succeed, important principal pillars of the bridge have nevertheless remained intact through the storm of the ages. The intensive dialog of many years with Lutherans ... has allowed us to discover anew how broadly and firmly based are the common foundations of our Christian faith."[59]

At this point the pope, strictly for reasons of protocol, we are assured by good sources,[60] abbreviated the German portion of his address, which was otherwise given in Italian, thereby omitting citations from the Augsburg Confession itself that were part of the original German text that had already been made available to the Lutherans at Augsburg. Whether this should be considered a misunderstanding, a mistake, a miscalculation or simply a massive failure in ecumenical public relations is up to you to decide. It is devoutly to be hoped that you put the better interpretation on it! In any event, the words of Pope John Paul II, written, but not yet uttered, are nonetheless historic. After confessing the Trinitarian faith shared by both Lutherans and Catholics, which was never really a matter of contention between them, John Paul II went on not just to cite but to *confess* the article of justification in the positive form in which it is expressed in the German version of article four of the Augsburg Confession:

> We receive forgiveness of sins and are justified before God by grace on account of Christ through faith, that is, when we believe that Christ has suffered for us and that on our acount of him our sins are forgiven and righteousness and eternal life are given to us.[61]

Here we have not just a reception but a positive confession by the Bishop of Rome of the very heart of the Christian faith that was Luther's central reformation concern.[62]

That this is not an over-interpretation of the pope's real intention can be gathered from the fact that, less than five months later, John Paul II was to confess this same faith before representatives of the Council of the Evangelical Church in Germany. With explicit reference to the fact that reflection on the Augsburg Confession has made Catholics and Lutherans newly conscious of their common faith, the Bishop of Rome confessed his faith in the saving work of Christ, neither in the language of *Augustana* nor in that of the Council of Trent—but in the words of Paul the Apostle whose Letter to the Romans, said the pope, was called by Luther—citing the reformer for the first time in papal history—"the true center of the New Testament and the purest Gospel".[63] With his quotation of Luther's Romans Commentary in the addresss to the Lutherans at Mainz, John Paul, according to George Hunston Williams "made an effort to imagine the reality of Christian faith as experienced by Luther in using the very words of Luther himself. . . . [64]

John Paul II's confession in this same address that all have sinned against the grace of unity and therefore all require even more than sin,[65] was made even more specific in another address the same day to representatives of the Working Group of German Christian Churches. There John Paul explicitly identified himself with the words of Pope Adrian VI, who, less than two years after Luther's excommunication, confessed the guilt of the Roman Catholic Church—especially its leaders—for the division.[66] With Adrian he said:

> The sickness is deeply rooted and has many forms: we must therefore proceed step by step and deal first with the worst and most dangerous evils by means of the proper medicine so as not to make everything even more confusing by a too hasty reform.[67]

This means, added the pope, that renewal of the Christian life is the first and most important step to unity.[68]

We see then in our time an astonishingly different attitude and manner of speaking on the part of Rome toward Luther and his cause than was expressed in the papal Bulls of 1520 and 1521. Out of a concern for justice and love, Rome has been able to begin listening to Luther as a Christian teacher and has been discovering in him and in the great *Confession* written by Melanchthon, but animated by Luther, as John Paul II put it, "not only a partial consensus on some truths, but an agreement on central foundational truths. That allows us to hope for unity even in those areas of faith and life where we are still divided."[69]

4. Reception of a Petrine Ministry by Lutherans?

Two things need to be said in closing.

There are still issues on which Lutherans and Catholics are divided. And, though we can discern a dramatic change on Rome's part toward Luther, Luther can of course no longer speak except through his writings—and to some extent through his spiritual descendants.

The central and original issue of the Reformation, as we have seen, is no longer regarded as an issue on which the churches need be divided. Differences remain, but proof has not been forthcoming that these are church-*dividing* differences.

As for the still divisive question of the papacy itself, does not the fact that more and more Lutherans and Catholics—including the pope—are discovering that they confess the same faith in Christ and his saving work in us *itself* put the entire papal question into a new light? The Lutheran/Catholic dialogue in the U.S.A. has pioneered the ecumenical effort by Lutherans to recognize the important role that a renewed and reinterpreted Petrine ministry can play in the church universal.[70]

Nowhere is the doctrine of justification and the question of the papacy linked more directly than in Luther's statement of 1531:

> "Once [it] has been established, namely that God alone justifies us solely by His grace through Christ, we are willing not only to bear the pope aloft on our hands but also to kiss his feet."[71]

But Luther added: "we are not able to obtain this from the pope."[72] And thus, the pope remained for him the Antichrist. Today, however, the very fact that the pope can and *does* confess that we are justified before God by grace for the sake of Christ through faith has to undermine Luther's charge that the pope is the Antichrist. Compare Luther's charge that: Everything the papists "say and do aims at leading us away from Christ and toward ourselves and our work"—and thus is "Against Christ"[73] with the words of Pope John Paul II as he was leaving Germany after his 1980 visit:

> The prayer of the Lord [that "all may be one", John 17,21] is for all of us a source of a new life and a new longing. As Bishop of Rome and successor of St. Peter I place myself completely and entirely in the stream of this longing! In it I recognize the language of the Holy Spirit and the Will of Christ, to which I would like to be obedient and true to the utmost. I want to serve unity, I want to travel every road which Christ is leading us . . . to unity in that one flock, *in which he alone is the sole and trustworthy Good Shepherd.*[74]

We don't know for certain how Luther would see "Rome" today, but we can find in his written work an opening to a papacy—at least by what he called "human right"—that would preach the Gospel and not impede its being preached. We can, moreover, hear the words of some contemporary Lutheran theologians who heard the pope preach and speak during his German visit:

> One thing must be clear at the outset: we are no longer dealing with the papacy and popes of the late middle ages, which Dr. Martin Luther justly[75] and heavily attacked. The popes of recent history are no longer concerned with power and wealth, but with a living Christ in the entire Church, and they themselves want to live according to this Christ with great seriousness. In assessing these facts the request of [Lutheran] Bishop Hanselmann has found widespread agreement, namely, that Luther's designation of the pope as "Antichrist" be officially stricken from our present-day Lutheran vocabulary and declared to be irrelevant.[76]

Luther and Rome—Now? Conversion of mind and heart, Christian love seeking justice and truth, the overcoming of mutual understandings and caricatures, growing agreement on the fundamentals of the faith that were

Luther's chief concern, mutual commitment to overcoming the division: Or, in the words of John Paul II on his departure from Germany: "I have the firm hope, that the unity of Christians in the power of the Spirit, of Truth and of Love, is already on the way".[77]

To share John Paul's hope, as so many millions of Christians do today, is not to yield to a naive optimism that fails to take seriously or to grapple with the remaining obstacles to the restoration of Christian unity. It is rather to open one's eyes to the incontrovertible fact that more progress has been made toward restoring communion among Lutherans, Roman Catholics and other Christians in the past twenty years than in the previous four hundred. This progress involves genuine theological convergences not only on what Luther regarded as secondary matters—such as the papacy— but also on that which he regarded as the very heart of his reformation concern, the doctrine that we are justified or made right with God solely by grace through faith in Christ.

Nor does this firm hope rise or fall with what the pope or the popes may have done or failed to do in the past or may still do in the future that really or apparently works against Christian unity. Christian hope—even for the pope—is not based on the pope, but on faith in the power of God to reconcile all things and persons in Christ (Ephesians 1 and 2; Colossians 1) and in the power of the prayer derived from Jesus that all his followers may be one so that the world might believe he has been sent by God (John 17). Such a well-grounded hope—and not some facile or hormonally conditioned optimism—enables Christians to have the confidence of Luther that the Lord Sabaoth "will win the battle" against all the forces that alienate people, whether they be Christians or not, from God and from one another.

Notes

1. Specialized studies: Remigius Bäumer, *Martin Luther und der Papst,* 3rd ed. with a new chapter on the scholarly discussion on Luther and the Pope since 1971 (Münster, Aschendorff, 1982); Scott H. Hendrix, *Luther and the Papacy.* (Philadelphia: Fortress, 1981); see also Harding Meyer, "Das Problem des Petrusamtes in evangelischer Sicht", in Karl Lehmann, ed., *Das Petrusamt* (München and Zürich: Schnell and Steiner, 1982), pp. 110-128. The biography of Luther up to the Edict of Worms in 1521 by Martin Brecht, *Martin Luther: Sein Weg zur Reformation* (Stuttgart: Calwer Verlag, 1981) also illuminates the relations in this early period, even though Bäumer, p. 188, judges that no essentially new viewpoints have emerged in the last decade on this theme. See also Marc Lienhard, *Martin Luther* (Paris: Centurion; Geneva: Labor et Fides, 1983), pp. 429-446.

2. Peter Manns and Helmuth Nils Loose, *Martin Luther* (Freiburg: Herder; Lahr: E. Kaufmann, 1982), p. 52.

3. I have partially addressed that task in, Part II of "Luther: Model for Church Reform or Doctor of the Church?", an essay to be published elsewhere in 1984.

4. For this see my study, *Luther: Right or Wrong?* (New York - Minneapolis: Paulist Press/Augsburg Publishing House, 1969), pp. 217-238.

5. "Disputatio pro declaratione virtutis indulgentarium": *WA* 1, 233, 1-238, 22; *LW* 31, 25-33. Letter to Albrecht the Archbishop of Mainz and Magdeburg, October 31, 1517; *WA Br* 1, 110-112; *LW* 48, 45-49. The foundational text of Luther's critical ecclesiology, Gal. 1,8—"If an angel form heaven should teach otherwise, let him be anathema"—is already cited here.

6. Marginal Notes to the *Sentences* of Peter Lombard; *WA* 9, 46, 16-20 (1509).

7. Otto Hermann Pesch, *Hinführung zu Luther* (Mainz: Grunewald, 1982), p. 97. According to Pesch, this is the essence of Luther's "reformation breakthrough", as distinguished from various earlier "reformation turning points".

8. J. Lortz, *Die Reformation in Deutschland* (Freiburg: Herder,[4] 1962) vol. I, p. 176.

9. H.A. Oberman, *The Harvest of Medieval Theology* (Cambridge, Mass.: Harvard, 1963), p. 426. For a response to Wilhelm Ernst's view, *Gott und Mensch am Vorabend der Reformation* (Leipzig, 1972) that it is incorrect to call Gabriel Biel a new kind of Semipelagian, see Denis Janz, "A Reinterpretation of Gabriel Biel on nature and grace", *Sixteenth Century Journal,* 8 (1977), 104-108, and H.A. Oberman, *Werden und Wertung der Reformation* (Tübingen: Mohr,[2] 1979), pp. 168-169. A.E. McGrath, "The Anti-Pelagian Structure of 'Nominalist' Doctrines of Justification", *Ephemerides Theologiae Lovanienses,* 57 (1981), 108-119, also seeks to clear Biel of the charge of 'semi-Pelagianism'. Beyond what I have written in my essay, "Was Gabriel Biel a Semipelagian?" in: L. Scheffczyk, W. Dettloff and R. Heinzmann, eds., *Wahrheit und Verkündigung: Michael Schmaus zum 70. Geburtstag* (München: Schöningh, 1967), vol. II, pp. 1109-1120, a piece McGrath seems to have overlooked, I would simply point out here: (1) Assessments of Biel's 'semi-Pelagianism' have to be made not only by looking at the texts of Biel, but also at those of the Second Council of Orange. (2) These texts and the surrounding documents reveal that the so-called Semipelagians were, as Owen Chadwick has put it, nowhere near fifty per cent Pelagian; *John Cassian,* 2nd ed. (London: Cambridge Univ. Press, 1968), pp. 127. They were, in fact, ninety per cent Augustinian, except for such views as that held by Biel, that sinners can take the first step toward salvation by their natural powers instead of by the inspiration of the Holy Spirit working within us to enable us to will even this first step, as Orange II taught. (3) The fact that one *believes* God has covenanted or made a pact with us out of his goodness and liberality does not prevent one from being a Semipelagian or even a Pelagian. Pelagius himself, it should be recalled, could praise God's *benignity* in revealing to us the commandments and in giving us the further gift of free will in order keep them.

In the position of McGrath, like that of other recent authors before him: "The very existence of this pact [namely, the alleged agreement by God "that the *viator* can take the initiative in his own salvation"] demonstrates that it is God who has taken the initiative in salvation by ordaining the covenant". McGrath, pp. 115-118. After studying the text and the context of Orange II, are we to believe that if the Semipelagians of old had been able to convince their critics that God has *covenanted* with us to allow us to initiate saving faith by our own natural will power without the inspiration of the Holy Spirit correcting our "wounded liberty"—are we to believe that Orange II would have said: "Now that we know you are covenant theologians, we have no disagreement with you?" Of course we would not expect that, because the implicit argument going on between Semipelagians and Orange II is precisely what kind of covenant, pact or plan of salvation is it that God has ordained. For

Orange II, it is in the Scriptures that we are to find this covenant or plan, and the Semipelagians simply were not integrating into their view of the revealed plan of salvation the teaching of such biblical texts as Proverbs 8,35 (Septuagint), Phil. 1,6 and 2.13, and I Cor. 12,3. (4) In order to indicate the existence of differences in the circumstances, mode of expression and rationale used by Biel and others to defend essentially the same thesis as the historical Semipelagians, I prefer to designate Biel's view as Neo-semipelagian.

10. See my study, "Thomas Aquinas, Pupper van Goch and Martin Luther: An Essay in Ecumenical Theology", in: *Our Common History as Christian: Essays in Honor of Albrecht Outler*, eds. J. Deschner, L.T. Howe, and K. Penzel (New York: Oxford U. Press, 1975), pp. 99-129.

11. *WA* 1, 528, 36(—529,2): ".... sic editae, ut mihi incredibile sit, eas ab omnibus intelligi... Alioqui... curassem ut essent intellectu faciliores."

12. *WA* 59, 464, 998-465, 1027. See my essay "Some Forgotten Truths About the Petrine Ministry", *Journal of Ecumenical Studies*, 11 (1974), 210-213, Pesch, pp. 40-41, points to other important biblical texts where Luther's interpretation is no longer defensible. See also p. 67 where Pesch speaks of Luther's "boundless optimism" concerning the ability of the Scriptural texts to interpret themselves, and of the fact that "Luther simply cannot imagine that anyone who knows Hebrew and Greek might interpret Scripture differently than he does".

13. Harold Grimm in: *LW* 31, 311. For a specific example of a "historical mistake" made by Luther in citing Gratian's *Decretum*, see Pierre Fraenkel, "John Eck's *Enchiridion* of 1525 and Luther's Earliest Arguments against Papal Primacy", *Studia Theologica*, 21 (1967), 110-163 (esp. pp. 154-156).

14. *Ibid.* The work of Wilhelm de Vries, for example, "Das Petrusamt im ersten Jahrtausend" in: K. Lehmann, ed. *Das Petrusamt* (see note 1 above), pp. 42-66 and Yves Congar, "Church Structures and Councils: East and West", *One in Christ*, 11 (1975), 224-265, shows us a historical relationship between the Eastern churches and Rome that was more real than Luther, and less authoritarian than Eck had realized.

15. And for centuries after, until the *Decree on Ecumenism* of Vatican II made it clear that the Orthodox churches belong to the one Church of Christ.

16. For example, *WA* 59, 453, 642-651 and 482, 1554-483, 1566. For a helpful alignment of the respective arguments of Luther and Eck (before, during and after Leipzig) based on the testimony of the Eastern Church see Pierre Fraenkel (note 14), pp.142-151.

17. Among his more glaring exegetical mistakes in his use of I Cor. 3,12-15 as a "very clear text" in support of the existence of purgatory: *WA* 59, 531, 3041ff. For a critique of this interpretation see Joachim Gnilka, "Fegfeuer", *Lexikon für Theologie und Kirche*, 2nd ed., vol IV (Freiburg: Herder, 1960), col. 47.

18. *WA* 2. 491, 1794-1798.

19. See my essay mentioned in note 12 and the very important monograph of Hermann Schüssler, *Der Primat der Heiligen Schrift als theologisches und kanonistisches Problem im Spätmittelalter* (Wiesbaden F. Steiner, 1977). Even in his later *Enchiridion*, Eck makes no effort to embrace the critical thrust embodied in Gal. 1,8 and 1 Thess. 5.21. Cf. the index of biblical texts in the magnificent critical edition of Pierre Fraenkel, *Johannes Eck: Enchiridion locorum communium adversus Lutherum et alios hostes ecclesiae*, 1525-1543 (Münster: Aschendorff, 1979), p. 429. Eck does concede, however, that following the example of Paul in Gal. 2, 11-15, "it often happens today that the pope and other superiors are reprehended by inferiors": Fraenkel, *Johannes Eck*, p. 68.

20. E. Iserloh, "Aufhebung des Lutherbannes?", in: R. Bäumer, ed., *Lutherprozess und Lutherbann* (Münster: Aschendorff, 1972), p. 74.

21. Manns (note 2), p. 93. This verdict is based upon a fascinating presentation by Manns of the historical development of indulgences among the German peoples on pp. 91-93.

22. For details see Erwin Iserloh, *Johannes Eck (1486-1543): Scholastiker, Humanist, Kontroverstheologe* (Münster: Aschendorff, 1981), pp. 22-28; E.G. Schwiebert, *Luther and His Times* (St. Louis, Concordia, 1950), pp. 333-336. For Eck's comments, which Luther called "Obelisks", and Luther's reply, the *Asterisks,* see *WA* 1, 281-314. For Luther's letters on the matter see *WA Br* I, 157-158 (to Egranus, March 24, 1518) and to Eck in *WA Br* I, 178 (May 19, 1518); partial translations of the letters in Schwiebert, pp. 334-335.

23. Cf. *WA* 1, 281, 9-16; esp. 11-12: "...quam *temerarium* sit aliena, praesertim *non intellecta* damnare...amaricari amici non praemoniti *omniaque meliora praesumentis* de amico placita, imo quaesita." *WA Br* 1, 178, 5-6; 12-13; 16-17 (Letter to Eck, May 19, 1518): "Et hoc est testimonium fidelis amicitiae tuae...imo *evangelicae charitatis, qua fratrem monere prius quam accusare ivbemur...* Id plane admiros, qua tandem fronte tu solus audeas meas sententias iudicare, *antequam cognoscas et intelligas...*[Q]uidquid *non intellectum* damnaveris, idio sit damnandum, quia Eccio non placet." (my emphasis). The latter phrase reflects Luther's critique he would level at Catholic theologians and popes for the rest of his life. Lortz's much-disputed thesis concerning Luther's alleged "subjectivism" failed to take into account Luther's similar complaints against "Rome".

24. *WA Br* 1, 158, 24-25 (letter to John Egranus, March 24, 1518); 178, 20-21 (to Eck, May 19, 1518).

25. Manns, p. 114. Luther told Eck he would have spoken more temperately had he *published* the *Asterisks: WA Br* 1, 178, 23-24. This dubious distinction will soon disappear in Luther's polemical work.

26. See Pesch (note 7), pp. 107-111, who sees Luther and Cajetan as at least understanding one another, though differing on the relation of Scripture to papal teaching, but not on the question of the kind of certitude required for reception of the sacrament of penance. On the first point, in the absence of an official manuscript and in view of Cajetan's clear earlier teaching that the *pope* and the entire church are subordinate to Scripture, there seems to be reason not to accept, as Pesch does, the accuracy of the view Luther attributed to Cajetan, namely that the pope is superior to both Scripture and to councils. Cf. the Luther texts cited by Pesch, pp. 108-109 and the Cajetan reference in my essay, "Some Forgotten Truths..." (note 12 above), p. 229, note 80. On the second point see my essay "Luther and Trent on the Faith Needed for the Sacrament of Penance", *Concilium,* 61 (1971), 89-98. On the "historical impossibility" of Eck understanding Luther's real concern see Manns, p. 120.

27. Manns, pp. 120-121, suggests that the divisive outcome of Luther's work was determined by a "historical necessity" involving all-too-human factors but one which never reached the level of "theological necessity", for not even Luther's three great reformation works of 1520 are "unequivocally, completely or definitively 'uncatholic'". Moreover, even the themes dealt with at Leipzig or later such as church ministry, sacrament, the Mass, or Monasticism can, according to Manns, be expressed in a thoroughly "catholic" way without doing violence to Luther's specific approach.

28. *WA* 2, 120, 25-27; 30-32.

29. *WA* 6, 181, 28-30; cf. 190, 32-34, where he uses his favorite adage to caricature what he regards as Roman subjectivism: "sic volumnus, sic iubemus, sit pro ratione voluntatis".

30. *WA* 6, 185, 21-26.

31. *WA* 6, 185, 27-30.

32. *WA* 6, 185, 30-34. This claim can be verified, even though Luther is not thinking here of works in which he defends himself against critics such as Eck or Prierias.

33. *WA* 6, 186, 24-27.

34. *WA* 2, 621-654.

35. *WA* 6, 576-594. In this work Luther provides further evidence for the judgment reached long ago by a Catholic scholar, Friedrich Zoepfel, after examining a later work by Eck against Luther, that Eck more than once misrepresents and distorts Luther's teachings: Karl Meisen and F. Zoepfel, eds., Johannes Eck: *Vier deutsche Schriften* (Münster: Aschendorff, 1929), p. XVII.

36. *Erbieten (Oblatio sive protestatio)*, 1520, *WA* 6, 477, 20-21 and 26-27.

37. Recent literature: Peter Manns, *Martin Luther*, pp. 121-123; Remigius Bäumer, ed., *Lutherprozess und Lutherbann* (Münster: Aschendorff, 1972); Daniel Olivier, *Le Procès Luther* (Paris: Fayard, 1971); reviewed by E. Iserloh, *Theologische Revue*, 68 (1972), 390-391; Marc Lienhard, *Martin Luther* (note 1), pp. 403-412.

38. *Geschichte der Päpste*, vol. II, part 1, 1-4. ed. (Freiburg: Herder, 1906), p. 270, sees the polemical writings of the summer of 1520 as "complete proof" that their author was not done an injustice by the church's condemnations.

39. "Aufhebung des Lutherbannes?" in: *Lutherprozess* (note 38), p. 78.

40. *WA* 6, 599, 20-602, 33: *Adversus execrabilem Antichristi bullam* (1520).

41. Georg Pfeilschifter, ed., *Acta Reformationis Catholicae*, vol. I (Regensburg: Pustet, 1954), p. 143, l. 29-33. Otto Pesch, p. 68 thinks that even in terms of the presuppositions operating in the church in Luther's day, the process against him was a scandal.

42. *WA* 1, 188, 5-10 (Letter to Spalatin, August 8, 1518); 294, 8-14; 307, 16-20 (to Frederick, January 1519); *LW* 48, 71; 104; see p. 150 for a reference to Erasmus's request to Albrecht of Mainz in October 1519, that Luther be treated fairly. See Pastor, 4, 1, p. 271 for a letter of Frederick to Leo X, July 1520, making a similar request.

43. R. Bäumer, in *Lutherprozess*, p. 36. If Luther's other public enemy Prierias was involved, as Roland Bainton says, *Here I Stand* (New York: Abingdon, 1950), p. 144, the above judgment would have to be made even more forcefully.

44. For the textual evidence see Part I of the essay mentioned in note 3.

45. *Consilium delectorum cardinalium... de emendenda ecclesia...* in: Carl Mirbt and Kurt Aland, eds., *Quellen zur Geschichte des Papsttums und des römischen Katholizismus* (Tübingen: Mohr,[6] 1967), vol. I, pp. 530-537; German translation *WA* 60, 291-308; English translation of the German: *LW* 34, 240-267.

46. Cf. Mirbt/Aland, p. 531 at notes 2 and 3; 532 at note 1; 533-534 (Praeterea); 535 (Diximus); *WA* 50, 292, 5-20; 294, 28-31; 300, 4-8; 302, 36-303, 6; *LW* 241, 253, 258.

47. *WA* 50, 290, 29-32; *LW* 34, 239.

48. Mirbt/Aland, 531; *WA* 50, 292, 5-25; *LW 241.*

49. *WA* 50, 292, 17-21 (marginal note); *LW* 34, 242. Despite the document's explicit rejection of papal arbitrariness, Luther continues to make this accusation in his preface; he also offers a caricature of papal infallibility that the document itself attacks: *WA* 50, 288, 16-28; 289, 6-16; *LW* 34, 236-237.

50. For the mixed reaction that the Cardinals memorandum aroused in the curia see Hubert Jedin, *Geschichte des Konzils von Trient*, vol. I (Freiburg: Herder, [2]1951), pp. 341-347; *A History of the Council of Trent*, tr. E. Graf (St. Louis: B. Herder, 1957), vol. I, pp. 426-434.

51. J. Calveras and D. de Dalmases, eds. *S. Ignatii de Loyola Exercitia Spiritualia*, Rome: Institutum Historicum Societatis Iesu, 1969, n. 22, pp. 164-165; cf. pp. 112, 115-116. My translation.

52. *Decree on Ecumenism*, nn. 7 and 8.

53. H. Jedin in: "Wandlugen des Lutherbildes in der katholischen Kirchengeschichts-schreibung", Karl Forster, ed., *Wandlungen des Lutherbildes* (Würzburg: Echter, 1966), p. 101.

54. *Decree on Ecumenism*, n. 9.

55. *Ibid.*, n. 10.

56. Augustin Kardinal Bea, "Geleitwort" to August Hasler, *Luther in der katholischen Dogmatik* (München: Hueber, 1968), p. 3.

57. Otto Pesch offers an up-to-date survey of literature documenting that change in "Katholiken lernen von Luther", in: Karl Lehmann, ed. *Luthers Sendung für Katholiken und Protestanten* (München and Zürich: Schnell and Steiner, 1982), p. 182, n. 7.

58. Jan Kardinal Willebrands "Gesandt in die Welt", in H.W. Hessler, ed., *Evian 1970: Offizieller Bericht der Fünften Vollversammlung des Lutherischen Weltbundes,* (Witten/Berlin: Eckart Verlag, 1970), pp. 97-99. My translation, English translation in LaVern Grocz, ed., *Sent into the world* (Minneapolis: Augsburg, 1971), pp. 62-64.

59. German text in: *Una Sancta,* 35 (1980), 197. My translation.

60. *Ibid.,* note 5, by the editor.

61. *Ibid.,* note 7.

62. For a rejoinder to an opinion that attempts to drive a wedge between Luther and the Augsburg Confession, see Vinzenz Pfnüre, "'Ökumene auf Kosten Martin Luthers?'" *Ökumenische Rundschau,* (1977), pp. 36-47.

63. *Acta Apostolicae Sedis,* 73 (1981), 71-75, esp. pp. 72-74. (Nov. 17, 1980 at Mainz).

64. G.H. Williams, "The Ecumenism of John Paul II," *Journal of Ecumenical Studies,* 19 (1982), 706.

65. *AAS,* 73 (1981), pp. 72-73; George Williams (note 64), pp. 686 and 701 sees in John Paul "an almost evangelical stress...on change or conversion of the heart and personal sanctification or holiness". Compare the conversion and renewal that, as we have said, Vatican II regards as the very world of ecumenism and also the first three of Luther's 95 theses on indulgences and their explanations dealing with lifelong conversion concerning which neither *Exsurge Domine* nor Trent had any complaint: *WA* 1, 530, 15-533, 34; *LW* 31, 83-88.

66. *AAS,* 73 (1981), 76.

67. *Ibid.,* p. 76.

68. *Ibid.*

69. *AAS,* 73 (1981), 73. The pope cites here the words of the German Catholic bishops of January 20, 1980.

70. *Papal Primacy and the Universal Church,* ed. P.C. Empie and T.A. Murphy (Minneapolis: Augsburg, 1974).

71. *WA* 30.1, 181, 1-3, 10-13; *LW* 26, 99 (*Galatians Commentary* 1531-1535 on Gal. 2:6). Cf. *WA* 18, 786, 26-31; *LW* 33, 294, where the papacy, along with indulgences, is considered a secondary question.

72. *WA* 30.1, 181, 13-14; cf. *LW* 26, 99.

73. *WA* 30.3, 314, 9-15.

74. Pope John Paul II, Parting words at the Munich-Riem airport, Nov. 19, 1980 in: *Verlautbarungen des Apostolischen Stuhls,* ed. Sekretariat der Deutschen Bischofskonferenz, Bonn, 25 (1980), p. 140: "...Christus [führt] uns...zur Einheit in jener Herde...in der er allein der einzige und sichere Gute Hirt ist." (my emphasis).

75. The Evian Assembly of the Lutheran World Federation in 1970 did not think Luther was *completely* just in that his attack "upon the Roman Catholic Church and its theology was not entirely free of polemical distortions, which in part have been perpetuated to the present day." L. Grocz, ed., *Sent into the World* (Minneapolis: Augsburg, 1970), pp. 156-157; German text in *Evian 1970,* p. 207.

76. J. Greifenstein, H. Jehle, G. Kretschmar, E. Ratz, im Auftrag der Kommission für Catholica-Fragen der Evangelisch-Lutherischen Kirche in Bayern, "Wir Evangelischen und der Papst", *Una Sancta,* 36 (1981), 195.

77. *Op. cit.* (note 75), p. 140: "die Einheit der Christen [ist] schon auf dem Wege".

MARTIN LUTHER'S NEED FOR REFORM—AND OURS

Harry J.Haile, *University of Illinois at Urbana*

Ironically, the humane studies, although they look back on the most venerable heritage of interpretive science, appear in our time to harbor the last holdouts for nineteenth-century positivism and materialism. The 500th birthyear of one of the great interpreters of all time, Martin Luther, has produced the most egregious examples of stubborn and superstitious adherence to the doctrine of objectivity. Martin Brecht's updating of that august line begun by Julius Köstlin and continued by Otto Scheel and Heinrich Böhmer is organized around the old topoi. Where any have been eroded, as the nailing of the theses, he avers it is not important *(daran liegt nicht viel)*, thus muffling the salient point: the essence of the Luther legend was precisely the presumed factuality of historical narrative. In his more popular rendition, Walther von Löwenich details precise circumstances of the thesis-posting. He adorns the facts only when it heightens the drama, calling, for example, the narwhal tusk rubbings administered to the dying subject only *köstliche Medikamente.*

For contrast, let us turn to a standard text in a confessedly materialistic 20th-century field, *Principles of the Law of Property.* Here the author argues at the start that he is not dealing with tangibles at all, but rather with a concept consisting in reciprocal understandings, sometimes very complex ones (p. 2). He then quickly admits (p. 5) that the courts in fact create property.

This is a view most typical of current intellectual climate. Thinkers have generally rejected the materialism which in the last century so fostered our magisterial propensity for definition, analysis, "objective" truth. It was a philosophy (naively abjuring philosophy) probably derived eventually from Newtonian mechanics. Likewise, the contemporary world view was profoundly affected by the revision that took place in physics during the early decades of our own century: 1) that recognition associated with Albert Einstein that "space" does not mean the Newtonian void, but the very shape of the world's contents, all firmly joined over the most remote reaches, and 2) the primacy of consciousness as it emerged from wave mechanics and was argued most articulately by physicists of the 1920's and 1930's. Especially Werner Heisenberg, Erwin Schrödinger, Eugen Wigner, and Niels Bohr, impressed by the epistemic implications of quantum physics, felt is was very important to let scientists in other fields understand that in physics, the quondam paragon of positivists, researchers were inquiring primarily into states of their own private consciousness.

As we look back on that epoch, we see little evidence that Bohr or Heisenberg or Schrödinger succeeded in communicating with other specialized branches. Especially the biologists, sociologists and humanists continued in antiquated reductionism. But change was in the air.

By 1922, for example, the 13th edition of Jakob Burckhardt's classical study of the Italian Renaissance, which had been regularly revised and expanded since 1860 in order to maintain all the "facts" correct and complete, was issued *not* in yet another revision, but in the original form. How shall we understand that? Philosophers of history like Wilhelm Dilthey, Benedetto Croce, and R.G. Collingwood had been disclaiming "scientific" objectivity for history—ironically, just at the same time when physicists were claiming that objectivity was not scientific. One of the most quoted books at mid century was by a physicist turned historian, the slim volume by Thomas Kuhn, *Structure of Scientific Revolutions,* which presented the history of science as a sequence of culturally determined points of view. Borrowing his key word from language teachers, Kuhn called these points of view paradigms. Scientific understanding had ceased to be incremental, as in those first twelve revisions of Burckhardt's masterpiece, but was felt to be interpretive.

Many historians today recognize their study as human, no less than physics telling us first of all about the state of some researcher's consciousness, then only secondarily about any presumed object under investigation. The past, according to Arthur Danto, can scarcely be more soundly predicated on available present data than can the future be projected from them. Other scholars, like Hayden White, have gone so far as to aver that any creation in the medium of language is fictional. Probably the best introduction to this view was the collection by Robert H. Canary and Henry Kozicki, *The Writing of History,* published at Wisconsin in 1975. It concludes with a most helpful bibliographical essay on current attitudes toward historiography. In sum, just as lawyers accept property as a concept the law itself has created, so historians are coming to recognize history as their own narrative.

If this is so, then we might say we have two options before us when we ask about Martin Luther: we can accept the narrative by historians of the last century, or we can permit our own Luther image to arise from the stresses and aspirations of the present epoch. As professor lecturing on Genesis and consciously exemplifying interpretation of the past for his own students, Luther himself most emphatically urged the latter course. He said we can easily see the problems confronting Noah if we will but consider the troubles besetting the church today. Why, Doctor Luther could recount many an event in Noah's life which Moses omitted to record—consider that great leader's struggles, for example, with the sectarians! But before following Luther's precept and relying on present experience to envisage the past, let us glance at how biographers have attained their understanding of this colorful character.

The central issue in the early novel was not subject matter at all, but point of view upon the narrated world. Think of Lawrence Sterne, Trollope, Goethe. The most remarkable configurations have been achieved in our own time by James Joyce, William Faulkner, Thomas Mann, Patrick White. Another rising Australian is Thomas Keneally, whose 1975 thriller, *The Passenger,* tells of a young woman whose husband cannot face up to her pregnancy. He insists on an abortion; she resists; he easily obtains a psychiatrist who commits the young wife and prescribes destruction of the fetus as requisite to the mother's therapy. The heroine is rescued, however, from the psychiatric ward by a gentle swindler who, having himself been ripped from the womb by Caesarian section, longs to experience authentic birth, if only vicariously. After numerous perils are overcome, the novel ends in happy prospect of a successful parturition. All this has been narrated in the present tense by the, as yet unborn, fetus.

Point of view, so well understood by the early novelists, can make all the difference. During the 19th century, however, the novel was most frequently told from an omniscient vantage point, as if from the moon, where all sides of the matter could be easily overviewed. The same was true of positivist historical writing of the day. Grasping any writer's point of view is crucial for the understanding of his narrative. Take, for example, Doctor Luther at table.

Saint Anne was patron saint of the miners, so Luther and his students, from mining families in a mining region, knew her powers well. They included the sorcery of rendering men and boys impotent. One time when Luther was looking back in doctrinaire regret upon his years in the monastery he drew the summation: "Anne was my saint, Thomas my apostle, and James was my epistle"—more literally, he was celibate, a doubter in Christ and a believer in good works. Another time he told how as a student on his way to Erfurt he had been so frightened by lightning he had sworn, "Help! Saint Ann, I'll become a monk! But *Ana* means grace in

Hebrew, so the Lord took it by grace and not by law." That ribald remark by the older man is, so far as I am able to make out, the entire documentation for Anne's role in Luther's Damascus-like revelation in Stotternheim, by which historians and psychologist's like to explain his entrance into the monastery—as if explanation were the purpose of history writing. The experience itself is, incidentally, attested from another point of view in a later letter from Crotus Rubeanus, but it is the above quoted remark at table which (sans the quip about Hebrew) comes soberly into the omniscient history book.

In the 1530s there was much note-taking at Luther's table, boarders who missed a session assiduously copying out records kept by colleagues. Old Conrad Cordatus, in making one such copy, could not resist adding his own detailed knowledge of the layout of the Black Cloister. When Luther marveled at having been granted appreciation of God's grace here in the filthy crapper, Cordatus added, "in the tower." Thus, in the omniscient narrative of 19th-century Luther biography, was born the 'Tower Experience', where the Evangelical doctrine was discovered, all of a sudden flash, in the unlikeliest of places.

After Doctor Luther's death Philip Melanchthon spoke about developments in Wittenberg before his own arrival there. His remark on this occasion that the 95 theses had been posted on the door of the Castle Church provided the omniscient positivists with the scene in which their Great Reformer, Thor-like, smote Christendom asunder (*Götterdämmerung* seemed somehow prefigured in the industrialization of Europe). From that moment in 1517 these writers dated the beginning of their "Protestant" Reformation—borrowing a word which had not come into use until 1529, matching it with a medieval expression, and thus attaching to Luther the very odium he resisted all his life long, that of a schismatic innovator.

How shall we characterize this point of view? First of all, we notice the solid Victorian, or Wilhelminian, values: Luther's austere, even deprived childhood, a stern father who produced in the son neuroses popularized by Doctor Freud (specialists in history, theology, etc. were often unacquainted with the superior psychological understanding in earlier writings by Kleist, Tieck, Schlegel, not to mention Goethe). Luther as Germanic hero now stood for aggressively nationalistic pride in Bismarck's *Gründerjahre,* he was macho-masculine, bellicose in his much-vaunted righteous anger, he crushed foes with his thundering. Actually, Doctor Martinus, a composer of polyphony, sang the alto line. Once when he complained his high voice lacked resonance, Philip assured him it carried well. A fine, cutting tone is of course best for debate and for that subtle irony which has escaped so many sobersides. At the famous Leipzig confrontation with the redoubtable, bull-necked Eck in 1519, Luther stepped to the rostrum sniffing a daisy. His voice was probably more like that of Truman Capote than Oral Roberts. The favorite literary form of the 19th century was drama, that genre which resolves tedious inner process into separate, palpable events: Stotternheim, the Tower Experience, the Nailing of the Theses, the Diet of Worms, dashing Ritter Jörg at the Wartburg. Note how the centuries-long, vegetable process of German Bible scholarship, flowering during the decades of exemplary team work in Wittenberg among Aurogallus, Luther, and Melanchthon and then serving as model for other collaborative blossoms, like that authorized by King James, comes into Luther biography as a sensational "one-man translation," accomplished in eleven weeks at the mountain fortress.

Current scholarship has brought some of the non-stageable material to the fore: the arduous further career of Luther the peace seeker trying to preserve the Church, of the learned historian setting conciliar authority over against autocratic one-man rule, of the astute negotiator jockeying for council location, representation, and agenda. How much is a man's mind set by his immersion in tradition, how much by surrounding social forces? Today the real importance of Martin Luther is probably no longer as Germanic warrior, angry rebel, or righteous prosecutor of the glorious cause, but rather as patient, persistent scholar, peace seeker, and negotiator.

Philip Melanchthon, self-conscious humanist, loved to attach classical sobriquets to notable contemporaries. Thus the puissant landgrave of Hesse became "Alexander"; Luther, whom Philip knew best, he called "Arcesilaus," after an ancient Greek skeptic, follower of Plato who lived during the 4th and 3rd centuries B.C. We do not know Arcesilaus' literary personality, because none of his writings survives, but his philosophical position is reported by Plutarch, by Luther's beloved Cicero, and others. Arcesilaus rejected the Stoic doctrine of syncatathesis, which assumed rational understanding. He denied the reliability of sense impressions from the outer world, and he denied the infallibility of inner, deductive powers as well. Arcesilaus is therefore remembered as the proponent of epoche: the suspension of judgment. While he conceded that a moral man must eventually take action, Arcesilaus reminds us that most of the truly important issues remain, for mortal judgments, imponderable. —This, Luther as Melanchthon knew him.

As for me in my time, I have found Luther to be best characterized by his own constant teaching of *epikeia,* a concept which he drew both from

Aristotle and from Paul, and which he translated as "gentleness," the willingness to make concessions in favor of agreement, even to give up one's sacred principles to accommodate other people.

How different is this tender friend of Melanchthon from the bellicose thunderer of church history! So where is the truth? —in the middle, perhaps? I think not. But there is, across the whole spectrum of possible points of view, always a common denominator: inseparable from this figure seems to be the idea of reform.

Reform was nothing new with him, of course. Modern historians are quick to remind us that Christianity has been a reform religion since earliest beginnings. G.B. Ladner, in his classic treatment, drew attention to *The Idea of Reform: Its Impact on Christian Thought and Action in the Age of the Fathers,* as, fundamentally, the individual effort to become more like the creator: *reformatio ad imaginem dei* in fulfillment of Genesis 1.26-27, "God created man in his own image." The idea of reform is beautifully preserved in an evangelical hymn from early in our own century: "Lord, send a revival, and let it begin in me." Martin Luther was acting on the idea of reform on that day in 1505 when he entered the Augustinian monastery in Erfurt. *Reformatio ad imaginem dei* was the central problem of his life, as it is of any man's: revival in the soul, ongoing effort to fulfill that ancient promise of Genesis.

Reformatio ad imaginem dei is also the central problem of any society, so let me try to discuss Luther the way he understood Noah, as facing the same problems we know today. Heiko Oberman has already been at pains to dissociate Luther from "reform" in the sense of tinkering about with the institutions of this world. This is a modern, journalistic usage of the term. Of course, everything would be just dandy if we could get rid of the bad guys—or, as the Marxist would say, the reactionaries—and replace them with the good guys who agree with us. That begs the question: The whole sense of society is to raise up good people. Reform in Luther's medieval sense remained the central concern of the German tradition right on through the great epoch of Friedrich Schiller and German idealism.

But society has become so complex, who can overview it all? It is dominated by very large, highly ramified organizations. Their lofty "operators" are far removed from the human operation. Why, the very qualifications for becoming president of, say, General Motors, have next to nothing to do with automobiles. Luther's cardinal of Mainz was appointed to the single most powerful post in entire Germany because he came of good family, was an affable lad (in his twenties), a patron of the arts, and had exquisite taste (he is said piously to have preserved the bones of his favorite mistress in his reliquary). As to theology, Albert knew about as much on that score as the president of some great state university knows about the liberal arts and sciences—or anything else being taught on his campus save the specialization in the administration of higher education.

If the grand lords are so remote, and themselves are animated by no compelling vision, if they lose no sleep about the little people touched by their machinery, what can we expect of their scribes in chancellery? One can read the instructions for the sale of indulgences as they went out over Cardinal Albert's signature and disturbed a remote professor, on 32 pages of double-column fine print in the Saint Louis edition of Luther's works. It is doubtful the cardinal ever read them or—as was the preference of great lords in that day—had them read aloud in his presence—but they certainly do lend classic form to the bureaucratic thoroughness of the clerics who compiled them: such lovingly fastidious attention to the fine details of the enterprise and its transaction was clearly to encourage whatever sins may be incidental to acquiring the wonderful advantages just ripe for seizing at this unique, once-in-a-lifetime opportunity.

The authors of these instructions were learned men, skillfully engaged in that sort of pursuit which modern organization theory calls "suboptimization": within one's own strict department, the achievement of excellence, without respect to any larger unit—in this case, the Church— and possibly even at cross purposes with it. I and my own colleagues produce huge quantities of scholarly writing with expertise quite comparable to that of the Cardinal's administration. Fortunately, no one is affected by our *akribeia*. In other fields today, like law and medicine, the result of suboptimization can be that outright predatory professional behavior of the sort Luther sharply rebuked.

He reserved his strongest language, however, for any who would presume to reform the church through outward improvements. He insisted reform could come only through the pure doctrine. Translated into our own point of view, his strenuous objection to the supremacy of law and good works has to be grasped as a structural issue. His humanist contemporaries, all good, rational men, sincerely believed a workable world had to be based upon systematic reward for merit. It is easy for us to discover the same honest attitude in the world at any time. Luther's retort that you cannot teach an apple tree to grow apples instead of thorns strikes the worldly as poetic, but unrealistic. Let these same worldlings, however, but take a look at the world produced by good works, and ask whether the doctrine really turns out to yield, in practice, all it promises in theory. The head of a large English department with which I am acquainted recently circulated the point system he uses to award salary increases and other advancements. It provides points for committee memberships, more for chairpersonships, and just recognition for longer and for shorter articles as well as books; it factors in the respective prestigiousness of the journals and/or university presses where they appear; it distinguishes between publications, lectures and the like which were invited, and those humbly submitted (fewer points for the latter). I am sure similar procedures are familiar from other branches.

In these we may discover as Luther discovered in Noah's world features of the Renaissance Church which no Renaissance source tells us about. Rewarding merit, for example, has the further advantage of routinization. The Head of the English Department no more needs to judge the importance of a particular contribution—indeed, might he not be blamed for attempting?—or assess its style than one ought inquire about peculiar features cut into rosary beads; you count them, that's all. The final consequence of good works can be an infallible decision-making mechanism which relieves functionaries of personal responsibility.

There are, to be sure, troublesome side effects observable in our society no less than in the Renaissance Church: great precision and detail in formulating rules, preoccupation with correct procedure for applying them, and ubiquitous litigiousness when it turns out that "not all the law is in the chancellor's books," as Luther in his endless heckling of the legal profession once put it. Furthermore, even our hard-wired computers turn out results which some insist on subjecting to interpretation.

Indeed, the need for reform, like the possibility for reform, resolves itself into the same problem with which I began: a question of interpretation. The sort of society I have described profoundly affects, through its doctrine of law and good works, man's concept of man. It lays a behaviorist, materialist interpretation both on the past and on the present human condition as essentially one of test animals in a Skinner box, human conduct being the, in principle, calculable product of material desires. Thus the works doctrine is recursive, being an interpretation calculated to induce certain actions which in turn foster that kind of interpretation.

Although it is today so widespread that examples pop up everywhere, surely the most succinct formulation of what one might call the Marxian-Skinnerian ideal of man was that famous line by the East German dramatist Bertolt Brecht:

Zuerst kommt das Fressen,
Dann kommt die Moral,

"First you got to get grub, then you can have your morality." Luther would just as glibly put it exactly the other way around, and quickly follow through with all kinds of other instructions: "Take no thought of what ye shall eat"; "He who would save his life shall lose it"; and so on. Well, which is right? Which does come first, teaching and being taught what is right— or by grace just knowing it? Luther gave his answer when he said you do not sit down with a book and instruct the apple tree, it knows what to do already. That was one of his frequent metaphors for the recurrent Pauline contention which Luther also so gladly cited, that the law is not written in tablets of stone, but in the tablets of the heart.

Just incidentally, it may be the Pauline-Lutheran view which is today supported by modern genetics and so-called socio-biology. But that observation is diversionary, because most scientists have a religious commitment to reward of merit.

Eventually, it seems to me, the idea of reform must be led back to that fundamental religious question over which Doctor Luther brooded his whole life long: is the creator, exalted far beyond our meager powers of comprehension, and is creation essentially and finally good, or not? Perhaps it is indifferent. Or perhaps, as the Manichaeans heretically averred, two forces strive eternally one against the other. How is man's frail understanding to grapple with such awesome ultimates? "I despaired," Luther said, "and cast myself upon Christ."

Faith, after all, is not acceptance of the reasonable and probable. "Believing Christ died for our sins is not faith," Luther scoffed. "That is historical fact. Even the pope and the devil believe that." Faith, in Luther's sense, is not conviction at all, much less what we have become convinced of. On the contrary, it is what we believe because we must. There is no other light to shine "across the void of mystery and dread."

So, in conclusion, I would say however you take Luther's life it stands for reform. Reform in Luther's sense begins in self-confidence, with that humble faith which led him firmly to set his notorious "alone" after Paul's "through faith"—and then to boast about it.

WAS LUTHER'S REFORMATION A REVOLUTION?

Max L. Baeumer, *University of Wisconsin at Madison*

READING THE ENLIGHTENMENT

An increasing number of historians today speak of the Reformation as a revolution, emphasizing the violent social and political changes of this movement rather than its spiritual and religious character and significance. Some neo-socialists give the impression as if the fathers of Marxism had been the first to consider the Reformation a revolution. This is not the case. In 1756 Voltaire in his *Essai sur les moeurs et l'esprit des nations* (Chap. 128) calls the Reformation the first great "revolution of the human spirit" within the political system of Europe. But Voltaire considers the Reformation still a "barbaric pollution" of that splendid 16th century of arts and enlightenment. At approximately the same time d'Alembert sees the Reformation as the second of three *révolutions d'esprit*. The are: First, the Renaissance of arts and sciences after the fall of Constantinople in the 15th century, second, the religious reformation of Martin Luther in the 16th century, and third, the advent of modern philosophy with René Descartes in the 17th century. These three "revolutions," according to d'Alembert, mark the great progress of humanity in a continously rising enlightenment.[1] A few decades later, with the background of the French Revolution of 1789, two conservative monarchist writers, Louis Gabriel de Bonald and Joseph de Maistre, explain Luther's Reformation totally negatively as a rebellious defection from the Holy Mother Church.

In Germany in 1774, and in direct opposition to French rationalism and enlightenment, Johann Gottfried Herder, Lutheran theologian, poet and one of the initiators of the German Storm and Stress movement, evaluates the Reformation as the result of a number of irrational revolutionary turnovers or *Umwälzungen* of the human spirit to the improvement of the world. "Reformations" he asserts, are "revolutions" in "passions and concurring movements." Seven years later, in 1782, the enlightened theologian Johann Salomo Semler asserts that actually the popes were to blame for the "great revolution of the Reformation, but that it is also true and rightful to describe this revolution as a great blessing of God."[2]

The comparison of the Reformation with the French Revolution, which became so important for the founders of Marxism can already be found in an anonymous article of the *Schleswig Journal* of 1792 in which the Reformation is praised for "the overthrow of the hierarchy and the loosening of the shackles of the intellect, while the American and French Revolutions brought the overthrow of despotism and liberation from the manacles of slavery."[3] Karl Marx, 60 years later, uses exactly the same words, *Befreiung von den Fesseln der Sklaverei,* for his own description of the Reformation.[4] But already one year before the French Revolution, in 1788, the historian of constitutional law, August Ludwig Schlözer in Göttingen, called the beginning of the revolution in France a *National-Reformation.*[5] Georg Forster, one of the most active German supporters of the French Revolution, who considers that revolution *ein Naturereignis,* "a phenomenon of nature" and "a product of nature's justice," talks about the Protestant revolution of the sixteenth century as one of the good revolutions because it led to freedom of the religious spirit in Germany.[6]

It is obvious that before and at the time of the French Revolution, the Reformation is not only seen as a revolution of the spirit, but also as a national revolution, liberating the religious spirit. After the Wars of Liberation from the yoke of Napoleon, the Reformation becomes the symbol of the national liberation of Germany. From now on and up to the present time, Luther and the Reformation are perceived, above all, in the light of German nationalism, and the Reformation itself is seen as a revolutionary liberation of Germany. None other than Goethe demanded in 1817—what subsequently became reality—namely that the Anniversary Festival of the Reformation should be merged with the National Festival of the People's Battle of Leipzig, celebrated thirteen days earlier and commemorating the victory over Napoleon in October 1813. This combined festival, Goethe states, will put "the German spirit in a lively motion."[...]"It will be celebrated by all fellow believers, and in this sense, it will be more than a national festival: it will be a feast of purest humanitarianism," *ein Fest reinster Humanität.*[7] Indeed, a very strange proposal by Goethe that the Battle of Leipzig in which according to official estimates 122,000 people lost their lives, should be celebrated as a *Fest reinster Humanität.*

Very much in line with this nationalist conception of the Reformation, the philosopher Hegel praises the Reformation as "the main revolution,"[...]"the banner under which we serve and which we carry", *die Hauptrevolution...die Fahne, unter der wir dienen und die wir tragen.*[8] In his work *Die Phänomenologie des Geistes,* Hegel declares: "The Protestants accomplished their revolution with the Reformation," while France has its revolution only now in 1789. In conclusion, Hegel distinguishes the Reformation from the tumultous French Revolution: "Where the freedom of the evangelical Church dominates, there reigns calm", *da ist Ruhe.*[9]

Between 1820 and 1850, in rather conservative reactions to the revolutions of 1789, 1830, and 1848 respectively, the Reformation is seen again as a revolution in the most negative sense of the word. The romanticist Joseph Görres and the conservative historian Karl Ernst Jarcke declare the Reformation to be the "second fall of man," the original sin of the modern world.[10] And in the words of the leader of the ultramontane party of Bavaria, Joseph Edmund Jörg, the period of the beginning Reformation a rebellion against the Catholic Church, the evil beginnings of all modern revolutions.[11] But shortly before the unsuccessful revolution of 1848, both liberal and nationalistic writers perceive the Reformation again as a positive, political, and German national revolution.

This sketchy outline allows the following conclusions: The conception of the Reformation as a revolution had become quite common in pre-revolutionary French enlightenment and is a part of the enlightened concept of *révolution d'esprit*. Catholics and conservatives value the revolutionary character of the Reformation negatively. Protestants, liberals, and German nationalists consider it positively. Shortly before and during the time of the French Revolution, the Reformation is viewed as a revolutionary national liberation.

The Marxist theory of the Reformation as a bourgeois revolution has its roots in the thinking of these liberal and nationalistic historians and philosophers of the early 19th century. If Hegel saw himself still fighting under the German-Lutheran banner of Luther's *Hauptrevolution*, Hegel's most effective student, Karl Marx, designated the Reformation "the only revolutionary past which Germany produced, at least theoretically, before the revolution of 1848." Marx, however, radically denies the spiritualism and any Christian reminiscences of his master Hegel and states: "Luther liberated the body from slavery, but he shackled the human heart."[12] In 1884 Friedrich Engels, the clairon of Marx, formulated the thesis: "The Reformation—the Lutheran as much as the Calvinist—is the first bourgeois revolution in which the Peasants' War constituted the critical episode."[13]

In 1850 Engels had written a pamphlet *Der deutsche Bauernkrieg* of the German Peasants' War of 1525. He had taken most of his ideas from the three-volume *Geschichte des großen deutschen Bauernkrieges,* written by the Swabian pastor and representative in the 1848 folk parliament,

Wilhelm Zimmermann. Engels sees the Reformation mainly from Zimmerman's Young-Hegelian point of view, by interpreting the Peasants' War and one of its revolutionary leaders, Thomas Müntzer, as the only focal point of this period, with no serious consideration to its general religious aspects or to Martin Luther himself. In addition, Engels looks at the Reformation in the same manner as Marx by comparing it with the bourgeois revolution of 1848. Taking the same anti-religious stand as Marx, he defines the Reformation as "the first brougeois revolution in religious guise."[14] Marx as well perceived the Reformation of 1517 from the viewpoint of the peasants' rebellion of 1525. He calls the Peasants' War "the most radical fact of German history, an undertaking which was wrecked by theology."[15]

It becomes evident from material such as this, that the fathers of Marxism see the Reformation exclusively from a socio-political standpoint without giving due consideration to the fact that Luther, Zwingli, Calvin, and Müntzer were men of the Church, priests and religious reformers whose proclaimed goal was a religious reform of Christianity. Marx and Engels derive their concept of the Reformation as a revolution form the subsequent Peasants' War, which in the opinion of many non-marxist historians had only partial reference to the Reformation and was brought about in tangible terms—and here East and West historians hold the same notion—by socio-economic causes. It is obvious that Marx' and Engels' concept of the Reformation as the Peasants' revolution has the ideological purpose of remodeling the Reformation into an important political event: as the beginning of, and first revolution by, early bourgeois-capitalism against the feudal class of the late Middle Ages. It is in this sense that Marx writes to Engels in 1856, the progress of the coming Proletarian revolution in Germany would depend on the opportunity to start another revolution like the Peasants' War. Or, if you will permit the original quotation in Karl Marx' charming hodge-podge of English and German: "The whole thing in Germany wird abhängen von der Möglichkeit to back the Proletarian revolution by some second edition of the Peasants' War."[16]

At the time when Marx and Engels declared the Reformation the first bourgeois revolution on the basis of the Peasants' War, the nationalist view of the Reformation as a revolution liberating Germany continued and was officially accepted in the Kaiserreich of 1871. Heinrich von Treitschke, the famous historian of the Wilhelminian era, considers Luther's Reformation "certainly a revolution,"[. . .]"more than any other political overthrow [*Umwälzung*] in modern history." This revolution has advanced the national unification of Germany. It was the first act of

Germany becoming one nation under the Prussian aegis.[17] In 1883, the four hundredth birthday of Martin Luther is celebrated in festivals, festive processions and even with military parades under the motto: "The German people owes to Luther its spiritual liberation and it national rebirth."[18] In 1917 the motto reads: "Germany's Sword, Consecrated by Luther," and next to Bismarck, the Iron Chancellor, stands Luther, the folk's man of iron.[19]

Nietzsche, in his earlier pro-German and pro-Lutheran period around 1873-74, sees Luther as a socio-political revolutionary. "If a Luther would arise today," he says in a one-time assertion, "he would revolt against the loathsome disposition of the capitalist classes, against their stupidity and thoughtlessness." But a few years later, Luther is for Nietzsche the backward leader of the Reformation as a mob rebellion in Germany and Northern Europe. In *Die fröhliche Wissenschaft* of 1883, Nietzsche explains the Reformation under the heading (§ 358): "The Peasant Revolt of the Spirit", *Der Bauernaufstand des Geistes.* Here he says: Luther, as a man from the lower clases, lacked all the hereditary qualities of a ruling caste, and all the instincts for power; so that his work, his intention to restore Christianity, merely became the commencement of a work of destruction. He unravelled, he tore asunder with honest rage, where the old spider [the Church] had woven longest and most carefully. His Reformation is also responsible for the degeneration of the modern scholar, with his lack of reverence, of shame, and of profundity. In short, he is responsible for the "plebeianism" of the spirit which is peculiar to the last two centuries. Even the "modern ideas" of the state [that is the socialist ideas] belong to this peasant revolution of the north against the cooler, more ambiguous, more suspicious spirit of the south [of the Renaissance].

Nietzsche totally reverses Marx' and Engels' stand on the Reformation as a bourgeois revolution of the exploited German peasantry, to the conception of a religious and anti-intellectual revolt, led by that one peasant, Martin Luther, whom he calls elsewhere "the Germanic barbarian," "the peasant," and "a boor."[20] We don't know whether or not Nietzsche was influenced by Marx and Engels in formulating his own and opposite conception of the Reformation. but his remarks and definition of the Reformation as "the peasant revolt of the spirit" could easily be read as an indication that he was well aware of the affinity *and* the difference between his own and Marx' view of the Reformation and that he intentionally used the punning expression "peasant revolt" for satirizing Luther's Reformation and poking fun at the socialism of his time, which he regarded "decadent" and "rabble" [*Gesindel*] and of which he says that it also "appeals to the Christian instincts."[21]

But not only Nietzsche seems to have used and misused the socialist conception of the Reformation for characterizing Luther's Reformation. The clarions from the anti-Lutheran Catholic camp also sounded in that new tone of class struggle and proletarian revolution. While conservative Catholic writers of the early 19th century declared the Reformation "a second fall of man" or a sinful rebellion against the Catholic Church, Johannes Janssen, Heinrich Denifle, Hartmann Grisar, and Albert Maria Weiß, the belligerent Jesuit fighters for the Catholic cause in the Wilhelminian era, used a pseudosocialist terminology and condemned Luther's Reformation as a "revolt of the proletariat," the "degeneration of aristocracy and the feudal system," and as "suppression of the lower classes."[22]

So far, our investigation has shown a long and antithetical process and pattern of viewing the Reformaion as a revolution, positively and negatively, alternating approval and condemnation, nationalism and socialism, triumph of the German empire and victory of a proletarian society. This dialectical process of conceiving Luther's Reformation as a revolution, this pattern of views brought forward by opposite literary, philosophical and political factions all along through the last three centuries, has hitherto been totally overlooked. But the same phenomenon is still present in our own days. In 1934, the *Deutsche Christen* movement within the Protestant Church of Germany greeted Hitler's seizure of power as "a German revolution in the aim of a Martin Luther."[23] In 1967, the prospectus of the State Travel Agency of the German Democratic Republic called Luther "the most courageous organizer of the most important revolution in German history before 1945."[24] In 1980, the East German state and party chief Erich Honecker opened the planning committee for the celebration of Luther's five hundredth birthday stating: "The Reformation and the German Peasants' War together constitute the first bourgeois revolution in Germany." Honecker tries to relate the revolution of the Reformation to the great German classics and their cultural heritage for the GDR. Schiller had pointed to the revolutionary spirit which had come forth from Luther's Reformation, Honecker believes. The classical German philosophy as well as Heine had recognized the Reformation as a revolution, Honecker remarks. But above all, Marx and Engels had perceived the revolutionary character of Luther and the Reformation and preserved the historical heritage for the socialist workers' class today.[25]

For the first time, a representative of the Protestant Church in East Germany, the Landesbischof Werner Leich, addressed the GDR State Council and spoke after Honecker at the same meeting. While praising the new cooperation between State and Church, Marxists and Christians, he declared that the Protestant churches and their Luther Committee nevertheless will go their own way and see Martin Luther and the Reformation, above all, under the aspects of reforming hte Church and of preaching the joyful tidings of Jesus Christ. There was not the slightest indication of a revolutionary, social or political conception of the Reformation in the Landesbischof's speech.

Honecker's statement, that the Reformation, together with the Peasants' War, constitutes the first bourgeois revolution in Germany, expresses also the official view of the Reformation in East German research and scholarship. Previously, Marxist scholars had been confronted with the problem that the so-called "bourgeois revolution" of Engels was carried out to 90 percent by rebelling peasants. Thus the Soviet historian A.D. Epstejn had felt compelled to classify the Reformation as "a bourgeois revolution without the bourgeoisie."[26] Shortly before Epstejn's statement in 1958, his colleague M.M. Smirin had maintained there had been a small radically bourgeois class in the early capitalist Germany of the fifteenth and sixteenth centuries, which by itself had an adequately revolutionary consciousness.[270] Smirin, at that time, could not offer any proof for his assertion. Recent East German historians are trying to demonstrate the Reformation in some important cities as a true political and social revolution of the bourgeois. However, some of these scholars are willing to admit that general conclusions about the revolutionary character of the Reformation as a whole would be premature at the present time.

While Engels' dictum of a "revolution in religious guise," so completely contradicting the historical religious and political realities of the sixteenth century, apparently has been dropped, East German historians of the Reformation are now searching the areas of humanism, religion, and theology for revolutionary ideas and assertions.

A few non-marxist historians in Germany between 1920 and 1950 had taken an ambivalent position. Gerhard Ritter and Richard Nürnberger speak of "revolutionary elements" and a "right-to-revolution" in Luther's theology.[28] For Rudolf Stadelmann and Eugen Rosenstock-Huessy the Reformation is—with certain restrictions—a revolution.[29] Karl Griewank sees "reformation and revolution" as two parallel but distinct movements. In that Griewank divides Luther's movement from the revolutionary element of his time, he also denies any revolutionary character to the Reformation itself.[30] West German historians, who recently have been dealing with the East German concept of the Reformation, admit that research of economical and social conditions of the Reformation had thus far been neglected in West Germany. Some still speak of the Reformation *and* revolution, or they consider, like Marxist scholars, the Reformation under the aspects of the Peasants' War.[31]

Since 1968, a few American historians as well have been considering some aspects of Luther's Reformation as "revolutionary," especially that of the printing press as a new medium in communicating revolutionary ideas on a massive scale.[32] From this point of view, Elizabeth Eisenstein speaks of the Reformation as of the "Protestant Revolt,"[33] while Robert M. Kingdon seems to be the first historian in this country and outside of Marxist historiography, who in 1974 came to the outright conclusion that "the Protestant Reformation was indeed a Revolution."[34]

Of course, everything depends on what one means by the word "revolution." The Marxist definition, as we have seen it applied to the Reformation, explains "revolution" as a basic change of society in which the forces of economic production conflict with the existing material economical conditions and in which the ruling class of oppressors is overthrown by the exploited class.[35] Modern historians, like Chalmers Johnson, Lawrence Stone, Hannah Arendt, and recently (1982) Perez Zagorin, speak very generally of a violent change in government and emphasize the complexity of causes which contributed to revolution.[36] For Karl Griewank, mentioned above (n. 30), a combination of three main conditions constitutes a revolution: first the violent change of political and legal conditions, second a social revolt of group or mass movements; and third the formulation of an idea or ideology with the goal of human reform or progress.[37] The American, German-born, political scientist Sigmund Neumann adds another fundamental change to these three main conditions: the change in economic property control.[38]

Mr. Kingdon adopts Mr. Neumann's definition of a revolution. He demonstrates how the Protestant Reformation, in the case of the city-state of Geneva between 1526 and 1559, provoked these fundamental changes which transformed Geneva from a rather backward episcopal principality, formerly allied to the duchy of Savoy, into an important secular state and the international focal point of Calvinism, now allied to the Swiss cantons.[39] The four fundamental changes which determine the revolutionary character of the Reformation in Geneva are: The renunciation of papal authority and abandonment of its legal system, the closing of all monastic communities and the confiscation of church property, as well as the significant change in the theological world view and myth of social order. These are the revolutionary changes which, according to Kingdon, always came with the Reformation and constitute an "anticlerical revolution,"[...]"indeed a revolution."[40] However, these fundamental changes in the religious, political, social, and economical organisation must occur as a usurpation of power in a sudden, radical, and forceful movement in order to be a true revolution in the sense of the word "revolution," eine Umwälzung, an overthrow. If these changes are brought forward in a slow and relatively peaceful movement and evolving process, we speak of an "evolution." For instance, the Reformation in the imperial city of Nürnberg seemed to have advanced, according to recent research, in such a non-violent and quietly progressing development, while the Reformation in Magdeburg burst forth as a violent and bloody revolt.

On the other hand, the fact that the Reformation in a particular city of territory was accomplished without any bloodshed or open rebellion, does not necessarily mean that the enforcement of the reformatory changes in that city or territory was not revolutionary. In 1977, I thoroughly investigated the Reformation of the Hanseatic city of Braunschweig between 1525 and 1529.[41] Here the Reformation was established without any violence, bloodshed, physical harm, or imprisonment, but nevertheless by force and suppression and by sudden basic changes in the structure of the society. The introduction of Johann Bugenhagen's *Der Erbarn Stadt Brunswig Christlike ordeninge* of 1528, which gave legal validity to the overthrow, exactly formulates, in the language of that time, the four fundamental changes which constitute the revolutionary character of the Reformation in the light of modern understanding and research.

The *ordeninge,* the new order, changed the *Dienst und das Amt der Kirche,* the service and the office of the Church, and instead of the law and hierarchy of the old Church, it installed its own *Ordnung* and *Prediger des Wortes Gottes,* its own preachers of the Word of God. Secondly, after all monasteries and religious institutions had been abolished, the city now established "good schools for everyone and social services for the ones who are in need." Thirdly, the confiscated property of the Church must be used for setting up *die gemeinen Kasten,* community chests or funds, for financing the new and worldly school, hospital, and social system. Fourthly, instead of "un-Christian ceremonies and godless mercantilism" in the Church, "the Word of God will be preached to the people purely and unadulteratedly" and everything will now be judged by the authority of, and service to, the Gospel, *alles wird als dienstlich dem Evangelium angesehen.*[42] These principles of the new *Christlike ordeninge* of the city of Braunschweig clearly express the four basic aspects of the Reformation as a revolutionary change. Except for one fourth of the city's councilmen who had been removed from office, the city government of Braunschweig had broadened its social and economical powers, but remained the same politically. The Reformation in Braunschweig apparently was a religious and social revolution.

From the slightly different results of the investigations in Braunschweig and Geneva and from the uncertain state of present historical and literary research, it is obvious that we cannot give a clear, univocal, and generally valid definition of the Reformation as a revolution at this time. There is ample evidence that the Reformation has not taken exactly the same course in all the cities and territories within and outside of Germany. Therefore, the same thorough investigation of religious, political, social, and economic changes, as in the cases of Geneva and Braunschweig, will have to be conducted for every territory or urban community which became Protestant during the time of the Reformation.

As far as literary studies are concerned, I have just published a lengthy *Forschungsbericht,* a first and comprehensive survey of the sociocritical and revolutionary literature of the time of the Reformation.[43] The survey demonstrates the increasing revolutionary tendencies at the time of the Reformation, expressed in satirical farces, rhyme songs, folk-books, fool-literature, flyers [*Flugschriften*], sermons, pamphlets, peasant songs, and rousing manifestos, rapidly distributed all over Germany by the mass medium of the newly invented printing press.

But let us turn to another significant—and closing aspect of our discussion: the question whether or not Luther and his contemporaries considered the Reformation a revolution. A discourse of this important problem has been conspicuously missing in recent scholarly investigations. Looking back at the various and contradicting conceptions of the Reformation from enlightened, nationalist, and socialist points of view, we must concede that the main concern of all these different estimations of a revolutionary Reformation was and still is, first of all, the historical legitimation of one's own cultural or political ideology, and only secondarily the cogency of evidence that the Reformation itself was revolutionary. The Reformation as a *révolution d'esprit* was supposed to give historical proof to enlightenment. The Reformation as a liberation of Germany has to legitimatize any kind of Chauvinism and nationalist power in Germany; while Nietzsche's conception of the Reformation as a revolt of that one German peasant Martin Luther has to explain the decline of the Renaissance. And finally, the Reformation as the first bourgeois revolution must establish the historical tradition and the heritage of a revolutionary socialist state in Germany. But Luther—as well as Zwingli and Calvin—saw themselves only as religious reformers and only wanted a religious Reformation of the Church. Therefore, a revolutionary selfconsciousness of Martin Luther can only be sought and found in his religious goals and convictions.

While Luther and the other reformers, as well as the contemporaries of the Reformation, were very aware of its violent character and of the worldly disturbances around them—they speak of *tumult* and *aufruhr*, uproar and riots—the Latin word *revolutio* did not have any political or social meaning yet. In Copernicus' treatise of 1543, *De orbium celestium revolutionibus*, the term *revolutio* means the inevitability of the revolving motion of a celestial body in its orbit and constant return to the place it has been before. Not until the end of the sixteenth century the term *revolutio* instead of *mutatio* is used—probably for the first time by Jean Bodin in 1586—to express changes in government.[44] Italian humanists and historians of the 14th and 15th centuries (Matteo Villani, Colluccio Salutati, and Leonardo Bruni) used the terms *mutare* and *mutazioni di stato* for the great political changes of states and governments. Machiavelli speaks of *mutazioni* as political changes which can also lead to a *renovazione* of a state. *Mutare* and *renovare* were the general terms for fundamental changes and reforms of the state since Joachim de Fiore before 1200, and Thomas Aquinas until the end of the sixteenth century.[45]

Luther makes use of the same termini *mutare* and *renovare* or *innovare* when he speaks of his reformation: *Sermo enim Dei mutaturus et innovaturus orbem, quoties venit.* "Indeed, the Word of God will change and renew the world in constant returns" [or: as often as it comes].[46] The forceful revolving motion of the renewing change in the later term "revolution" is here already indicated. But that revolutionary and reforming force is for Luther the Word of God. In the same pamphlet, Luther says: *Fortunam constantissimam verbi Dei, ut ob ipsum mundis tumultuetur* (*WA* XVIII, 218, 626). "The most permanent fate of the word God is that for its sake the world is put into an uproar." This is Luther's concept of a permanent revolution, as much as modern prophets, proclaiming a new, but political salvation of the world, have taught their worldly concept of a permanent revolution.

It seems to have gone unnoticed that Luther relates the concept of the Word of God, which changes and renews the world, to the term *auffruhr*, uproar and rebellion; so often and pejoratively used by Luther against Thomas Müntzer and the peasants, whom one should kill like mad dogs (XVIII, 358). In the same pamphlet *Wider die räuberischen und mörderischen rotten der Bauern, Against the Robbing and Murdering Hordes of Peasants* of 1525, he states: "There cannot be anything more poisonous, dangerous and more devilish than a rebellious man—*ein aufrurischer mensch"* (358). Three years earlier, in *Eyn trew vormannung Martini Luther tzu allen Christen, sich tzu vorhuten fur affruhr and emporung, Admonition to All Christians to Beware of Revolt and Insurrection* of 1522, he says about *auffruhr:* "No insurrection is ever right no matter how right its cause may be."

However in the same treatise, Luther makes an important distinction, to which hitherto only little attention has been given in Luther research. Luther distinguishes sharply between *leiblicher auffruhr,* "physical insurrection," and *geistlicher auffruhr,* "spiritual insurrection or revolt." While physical revolt is forbidden, spiritual revolt is right because it comes from the mouth of God. "Darum darfest du nit begehren einer leiblichen auffruhr. Es hat Christus selbst schon eine angefangen mit seinem Mund . . . Derselbige laß uns folgen und fortfahren." "Therefore there is no need for you to demand a physical revolt. Christ himself has already begun a revolt with his mouth . . . Let us take up and carry on that revolt." Luther continues: "It's the devil . . . who would like to stir up a physical revolt in order to foil and frustrate this spiritual revolt. But it's God's will that he shall not succeed. He must be destroyed not by taking up arms, but only by the [power of the] mouth" (VIII, 683-684).

The spiritual revolt with the mouth is, of course, the preaching of the Word of God. "Get busy now," Luther continues, "spread the holy gospel, and help others spread it; teach, speak, write, and preach that man-made laws are nothing, fight and give help . . . Let us do this for two years, and you shall see what will become of . . . all the swarming vermin of the papal regime. They will vanish like smoke!" The spiritual revolt of his followers, which Luther demands, is primarily directed against the Roman papacy. He grounds his conception of spiritual revolt by mouth on St. Paul's second letter to the Thessalonians 2: "And then shall be revealed the lawless-one, whom the Lord Jesus shall slay with the breath of his mouth and bring to nought by the manifestation of his coming."

On the basis of this biblical source Luther gives his spiritual revolt a significant eschatological aspect: "When the popish villainy has become fully evident and the breath of Christ's mouth is in full motion so that the pope with his lies means nothing anymore and is totally despised, then the Day of Judgement has come, and as Paul says, Christ will completely destroy him by the manifestation of his coming" (675-676). Here Luther expects his revolution by the preaching of the word of God to bring about the most radical change imaginable and the perfect utopia, the end of human history and eternal salvation for God's people.

One year later, in his treatise of 1523, *Von welltlicher Uberkeyt, wie weyt man yhr gehorsam schuldig sey, On Secular Authority: To what Extent It*

Should Be Obeyed, Luther demands that the power of worldly government be limited to jurisdiction over life, body and property. He rejects the notion—again on the basis of spiritual revolt by God's Word—that secular authority has any say in the spiritual realm of conscience and belief. "Where secular authority presumes to prescribe laws for the soul," he states, "it encroaches upon God's government and only misleads souls and destroys them." Even "heresy can never be prevented by force . . . that must be opposed and dealt with otherwise than with the sword. Here God's Word must strive" (XI, 261-262).

In his writing entitled *Dr. Martin Luthers Warnung an seine lieben Deutschen, Dr. Martin Luther's Warning to His Dear Germans,* published in 1531, after the Diet of Augsburg in 1530 when the possibility existed that the Emperor might go to war against the Protestants, Luther called for open defiance and bold resistance. Anyone fighting for the papists, he states, is helping in the destruction of Christ's Word and his whole kingdom. If such a war breaks out, Luther will not reprove those who defend themselves.

However, for Luther, spiritual revolt by the word of God is not limited to fighting the papacy, open resistance and self-defense. Worldly princes and rulers who govern like tyrants, oppress the common man and resist the course of the Word of God are threatened by willful disobedience, God's contempt. "The common man is learning to think," Luther asserts in his treatise *Von welltlicher Uberkeyt,* "and the prince's scourge, which God calls *contemptum,* is gathering force among the plebs and with the common man. . . . Men ought not, men cannot, men will not suffer your tyranny and wantonness much longer. Dear princes and lords . . . God will no longer tolerate it. The world is no longer what it was when you hunted and drove people like wild animals. Therefore drop your outrage and force, and remember to deal justly and let God's Word have its course, as it will and must and shall, nor will you prevent it" (XI, 270).

These and other inciting passages have lately been quoted in order to prove Luther's Reformation as a political revolution, leading to, and culminating in, the Peasants' War a few years later. However the characterization of the passages as spiritual revolt, their references to the power and the course of the Word of God have been conspicuously omitted.

Geistlicher auffruhr is not the only connotation which Luther associates with the Word of God and its revolutionary change and renewal of the world. In his *Trew vormannung . . . tzu allen Christen,* mentioned above, he speaks of the *selige auffruhr,* the "blessed revolt" of the Word of God: "Aber last unsz weysze sein, Gott dancken fur seyn heylig wort, und dyszer seligen auffruhr denn mund frisch dar geben." "But let's be understanding and thank God for His sacred Word and give our mouth freshly to its blessed revolt" (VIII, 684). In another pamphlet, Luther says: "It is a blessed strife, rebellion and uproar, which God's Word arouses." "Es ist ein seliger unfrid, auffruhr und rumor, den gottis Wort erweckt, da geht an rechter glaub und streytt widder den falschen Glauben." "There the right faith attacks and fights against the false beliefs" (VII, 281).

To be more specific, the preaching of the Word of God is Luther's revolutionary selfconsciousness. He blusters against the bishops who don't accept his message: "If they don't want to listen to the Word of God, what else is right for them than a strong rebellion (ein starcker auffruhr) which will root them out from this world" (X, II, 111). But with the same reference to the Word of God, he attacks the rebellious peasants: "Everyone who doesn't listen to, and accept the Word of God, must listen to the hangman. . . . We mean the Word of God who wants the king to be honored and the rebels be destroyed" (XVIII, 386). Luther distinguishes clearly between *auffruhr* against the worldly authority, a rebellion which he vehemently condemns, and the *seliger auffruhr* of his own preaching of the Word of God, which everyone has to accept or he will be attacked. His own *auffruhr* is not only permitted, but it is *his* preaching of the Gospel, his own reformation.

Luther's contemporaries were very much aware of this. One of his most active adversaries, Johannes Cochlaeus, reproaches him: "That the common man everwhere in Germany, except in Bavaria and Austria, is so mad and rebellious [*aufrürig*], is only the result of your own false and rebellious gospel. You have preached to the poor people so continously and falsely of God's Word and Christian freedom until they became totally rebellious and mad."[47]

But Luther is so convinced of the truth and rightness of his own interpretation and belligerent preaching of the Word of God that he includes fight and revolt and war in his reformation message. He closes his letter "About the rebellious spirit," addressed to the princes of Saxony: "This is now the summary, that your Highness should not resist the ministry of the Word [. . .]because the Word of God has to go to war and fight" (XVIII, 218). This, and only this, is Martin Luther's concept of the Reformation as a revolution.

Notes

1. Jean le Rond d'Alembert, *Oeuvres litteraires* (Paris, 1821), vol. I, p. 121-122.

2. Johann Gottfried Herder, *Sämtliche Werke,* ed. B. Suphan (Halle, 1891), vol. V, pp. 530-532. Johann Salomo Semler, *Lebensbeschreibung,* 2 vols. (Halle, 1781-82), vol. II, pp. 178-180.

3. "Einige Aehnlichkeit der Reformation und der Revolution," *Schleswigsches ehemals Braunschweigisches Journal,* Vol. II (Altona, 1792), p. 173.

4. Karl Marx, Friedrich Engels, *Werke,* ed. by the Institut für Marxismus-Lenismus beim ZK der SED, 39 vols. (Berlin, 1956-1968). In the following quoted as *MEW;* here *MEW,* vol. I, p. 385.

5. August Ludwig Schlözer, *Stats-Anzeigen,* vol. *XII* (1788), pp. 494-496.

6. Georg Forster, *Sämtliche Schriften,* 9 vols. (Leipzig, 1843), vol. VI, p. 84.

7. *Goethe. Berliner Ausgabe,* vol. *XVII* (Berlin, 1970), pp. 502-503.

8. Quoted after Heinrich Bornkamm, *Luther im Spiegel der deutschen Geistesgeschichte* (Heidelberg, 1955), p. 143.

9. Georg Wilhelm Friedrich Hegel, *Phänomenologie des Geistes,* ed. Johannes Hoffmeister, 5th ed. (Leipzig, 1949), p. 925.

10. Joseph Görres, *Deutschland und die Revolution* (Koblenz, 1820). Karl Ernst Jarcke, *Die französische Revolution von 1830* (Berlin, 1831).

11. Joseph Edmund Jörg, *Deutschland und die Revolutionsperiode 1522-1526* (Freiburg, 1851). For liberal and nationalistic views of the Reformation see: Johann Georg August Wirth, *Die politisch-reformatorische Richtung der Deutschen im 16. und 19. Jahrhundert* (Bellevue, 1841); Jean Joseph Louis Blanc, *Histoire de la Révolution française,* vol. I (Paris, 1847).

12. *MEW,* vol. I, pp. 385-386.

13. *MEW,* vol. XXI, pp. 402-403.

14. *MEW,* vol. XXVII, p. 274

15. *MEW,* vol. I, p. 386.

16. Marx, Engels, *Briefwechsel* (Moscow, 1934-38), vol. II, p. 166.

17. Heinrich von Treitschke, *Historische und politische Aufsätze,* vol. *IV* (Leipzig, 1897), p. 384.

18. Max L. Baeumer, "Lutherfeiern und ihre politische Manipulation," *Deutsche Feiern,* ed. Reinhold Grimm and Jost Hermand (Wiesbaden, 1977), p. 53. In the following quoted as Baeumer, "Lutherfeiern".

19. Baeumer, "Lutherfeiern," p. 54.

20. "If a Luther would arise today," Friedrich Nietzsche, *Werke,* Großoktav-Ausgabe (2), vol. II, p. 282. For this and the following quotations see also Max L. Baeumer, "Nietzsche and Luther: A Testimony to Germanophilia," forthcoming in *Studies in Nietzsche and the Judeo-Christian Tradition,* ed. J.C. O'Flaherty and others (Chapel Hill, North Carolina, 1983-84).

21. Nietzsche, *Die Götzen-Dämmerung,* sec. 37, *Der Antichrist,* sec. 57.

22. Winfried Becker, *Reformation und Revolution* (Münster, 1974), pp. 23-25; and Max L. Baeumer, "Sozialkritische und revolutionäre Literatur der Reformationszeit," *Internationales Archiv für Sozialgeschichte der deutschen Literatur,* 5 (1980), 212, 214-215. In the following quoted as Baeumer, "Sozialkritische und revolutionäre Literatur."

23. Leo Stern, *450 Jahre Reformation* (Berlin, 1967), p. 34.

24. The magazine *Der Spiegel*, vol. XXI (1967), no. 45.

25. Weekend edition of *Neues Deutschland* (June 14/15, 1980), and "Dokumentation," *Frankfurter Rundschau*, no. 156 (July 9, 1980), pp. 14-15.

26. A.D. Epstejn, "Reformation und Bauernkrieg in Deutschland als erste bürgerliche Revolution," *Sowjetwissenschaft, Gesellschaftswissenschaftliche Beiträge* (Berlin, 1958), pp. 362-392.

27. M.M. Smirin, "Wirtschaftlicher Aufschwung und revolutionäre Bewegung in Deutschland im Zeitalter der Reformation," *Sowjetwissenschaft, Gesellschaftswissenschaftliche Beiträge* (Berlin, 1958), pp. 243-265.

28. Gerhard Ritter, "Romantische und revolutionäre Elemente in der deutschen Theologie am Vorabend der Reformation," *Deutsche Vierteljahrsschrift für Literaturwissenschaft und Geistesgeschichte,* 5 (1927), 342-380. Richard Nürnberger, *Die Politisierung des französischen Protestantismus* (Tübingen, 1948), p. 24. Also Hans von Schubert, *Revolution und Reformation im XVI. Jahrhundert, Ein Vortrag* (Tübingen, 1927).

29. Rudolf Stadelmann, *Vom Geist des ausgehenden Mittelalters* (Halle, 1929); *Deutsche Vierteljahrsschrift für Literaturwissenschaft und Geistesgeschichte,* vol. 15). Eugen Rosenstock-Huessy, *Die europäischen Revolutionen und der Charakter der Nationen,* (Stuttgart, Köln, 1951).

30. *Der neuzeitliche Revolutionsbegriff,* 2nd ed. (Frankfurt, 1969; 1st ed. Weimar, 1955), pp. 70-101. In the following quoted as Griewank.

31. See the articles by Thomas Nipperdey, Otthein Rammstedt, Karl Dienst, and Rainer Wohlfeil in: *Reformation oder frühbürgerliche Revolution?,* ed. R. Wohlfeil (München, 1972). Bruno Gebhardt, *Handbuch der deutschen Geschichte,* 9th newly revised edition, ed. Herbert Grundmann, vol. VIII: Walther Peter Fuchs, *Das Zeitalter der Reformation* (München, 1973). Deutscher Taschenbuch Verlag, Wissenschaftliche Reihe, 4208), pp. 15-16. Richard van Dülmen, *Reformation als Revolution* (München, 1977). For a viewpoint of ecclesiastical history see Hans-Gerhard Koch, *Luthers Reformation in kommunistischer Sicht* (Stuttgart, 1967).

32. Margaret Aston, *The Fifteenth Century: The Prospect of Europe* (London, 1968), p. 76. Arthur G. Dickens, *Reformation and Society in Sixteenth-Century Europe* (New York, 1968), p. 51. Lowell H. Zuck, *Christianity and Revolution* (Philadelphia, 1975), p. 3, claims that the Reformation "produced a true revolution of religious consciousness."

33. "The Advent of Printing and the Protestant Revolt," *Transition and Revolution: Problems and Issues of European Renaissance and Reformation History,* ed. R.M. Kingdon (Minneapolis, 1974) pp. 235-270.

34. "Was the Protestant Reformation a Revolution? The Case of Geneva," *Transition and Revolution: Problems and Issues of European Renaissance and Reformation History,* ed. R.M. Kingdon (Minneapolis, 1974) pp. 53-77; in the following quoted as Kingdon, "The Case of Geneva."

35. *Marxistisch-Leninistisches Wörterbuch der Philosophie,* ed. G. Klaus and M. Bahr (Hamburg, 1972), vol. III, pp. 948-951. Karl Marx: *MEW,* XIII, p. 9.

36. Chalmers Johnson, *Revolutionary Change* (Boston, 1966), p. xi. Lawrence Stone, *The Causes of the English Revolution 1529-1642* (New York, 1972), Chapter One. Hannah Arendt, *On Revolution,* Third printing (New York, 1966). Arendt sees the Reformation not as a revolution because she believes the contents of Christian teachings could not constitute the origin of a revolution (p. 18). Perez Zagorin, *Rebels and Rulers, 1500-1660,* vol. I: *Society, States and Early Modern Revolution, Agrarian and Urban Rebellions* (Cambridge, 1982), emphasizes the use of violence.

37. Griewank, p. 21-22.

38. "The International Civil War," *World Politics,* vol. I (1948-49), p. 333, n. 1; also "The Structure and Strategy of Revolution: 1848 and 1948," *The Journal of Politics* (August 1949).

39. Kingdon, "The Case of Geneva," especially pp. 73-74.

40. Kingdon, "The Case of Geneva," pp. 60, 76.

41. Max L. Baeumer, "Ohn Tumult / ohn Schwermerey. Literarische Evidenz zum 'revolutionären' Charakter der Reformation in Braunschweig," *Wolfenbütteler Beiträge,* vol. IV (1981), pp. 59-110. In the following quoted as Baeumer, "Reformation in Braunschweig."

42. Baeumer, "Reformation in Braunschweig," pp. 96-97.

43. "Sozialkritische und revolutionäre Literatur der Reformationszeit," *Internationales Archiv für Sozialgeschichte der deutschen Literatur,* 5 (1980), 169-233.

44. Jean Bodin, *De Republica libri sex,* first ed. 1586, third ed. (Frankfurt, 1594), vol. IV, chap. 1 and 2. See also Griewank, pp. 146, 150, 173-174.

45. See Baeumer, "Sozialkritische und revolutionäre Literatur," pp. 216-217.

46. Martin Luther, *Werke,* Kritische Gesamtausgabe (Weimar, 1883-1966), vol. XVIII, p. 626. In the following quoted in the text as *WA* (Weimarer Ausgabe).

47. Quoted after *Flugschriften des Bauernkrieges,* ed. K. Kaczerowsky (Hamburg, 1970), pp. 174-174. See also Baeumer, "Sozialkritische und revolutionäre Literatur," p. 224.

LUTHER'S SOCIAL TEACHING
AND THE SOCIAL ORDER OF HIS AGE

Thomas A. Brady, Jr., *University of Oregon*

For when people first began to increase
Some gave themselves all to idleness,
And would not labour, but take by violence
That other men gat by labour and diligence.
Then they that laboured were gain to give
Them part of their gettings in peace to live,
Or else for their lands, money a portion;
So possession begun by extortion.[1]

John Rastell

... for in every city these two opposing parties exist ... the people desire not to be bossed and oppressed by the rich; the rich desire to boss and oppress the people.[2]

Niccolò Machiavelli

In the eyes of this world, it is true, one man is nobler than another because of his birth; one is smarter than another because of his intelligence; one is more comelier and stronger than another because of his body; one is richer and more powerful than another because of his wealth; and one is better than another because of his particular virtue. Such differences and such inequality must exist in this miserable, sinful and mortal life, if life and limb are to be preserved and the government maintained.[3]

Martin Luther

The "Luther-to-Hitler" thesis teaches that the idea of the authoritarian state forms the ideological spine of German history from Martin Luther to National Socialism. Its form was fixed by Thomas Mann in a lecture at the Library of Congress on May 29, 1945, only three weeks after the Allied victory in Europe. Mann said:

Luther was a liberating hero—but in the German style, for he knew nothing of liberty. I am not speaking now of the liberty of the Christian but of political liberty, the liberty of the citizen— this liberty not only left him cold, but its impulses and demands were deeply repugnant to him.

Four hundred years after his time the first president of the German Republic, a social Democrat, spoke the words: "I hate revolution like sin." This was genuinely Lutheran, genuinely German. In the same way Luther hated the peasant revolt which,... if successful, would have given a happier turn to German history, a turn toward liberty... Luther, the German man of the people, bears a good share of responsibility for the sad ending of this first attempt at a German revolution, for the victory of the princes, and for all its consequences.[4]

Mann seems here but to echo Luther's own boast that

If I had never taught or done anything else than that I had adorned and illuminated secular rule and authority, this alone should deserve thanks.... Since the time of the apostles no doctor or writer, no theologian or lawyer has confirmed, instructed, and comforted secular authority more gloriously and clearly than I was able to do through special divine grace.[5]

Mann's Luther, however, is not this bragging Luther of history but a Luther in modern dress, who was evoked out of the deep past to become "figure and symbol"—the words are Gerhard Ritter's—of the Second German Empire as a Protestant state of world-historical rank. After the Great War, this modern Luther became patron saint of a national counterrevolution, right down to what Paul Althaus called "the German hour of the Church" in January, 1933.[6] Our business today is not with this Luther of modern myth but with the Luther of the sixteenth century. If we are to understand his social teaching historically, we must first establish its context.

(1)

During the slightly more than two centuries between Thomas Aquinas' death and Martin Luther's birth, feudal monarchies based on vassalage and the identity of public function with personal power began to yield place to the ruler-and-estates governments typical of the late feudal age.[7] By the sixteenth century, the dynastic monarchies of Western Europe were assembling the arsenal of absolutist rule—standing armies, bureaucracies, taxation, trade and diplomacy—while the nobilities, their local power badly damaged by the agrarian crisis, were moving towards the monarch as, in Perry Anderson's phrase, "the new political carapace of a threatened nobility."[8] Late in Luther's century there also emerged the idea of the State as, in Quentin Skinner's words,

> a form of public power separate from both the rule and the ruled, and constituting the supreme political authority within a certain defined territory.[9]

The separation of personal and public power, corresponding to what one day would be called "society" and "the State," profoundly affected ideas of social order. The typical idea of social order between the twelfth and the sixteenth centuries presented a social hierarchy of estates, most commonly three: *oratores, bellatores, laboratores;* ecclesiastical, military, civil; Church, nobility, commons. This schema, though it had remote classical roots, seems to have originated in the Northern French heartland of feudalism after the year 1000.[10] Even then it arose to defend an existing social order against threatening forces; and with the rise of Christian Aristotelianism, it acquired all those anatomical metaphors over which modern readers chuckle.

The thirteenth and fourteenth centuries also witnessed the rise of communalism.[11] Whereas the monarchical State rested on the principle of sovereignty and grew through conquest, the commune rested on the principle of equality and grew through federation. Communal institutions and ideas sprang up at all social levels from the twelfth century onward, from the Church, where corporate rights and ideas confronted the neo-Augustinian papalists, to the cities, whose communes strove to become city-states, to the Alpine valleys, whose stockmen banded together to throw off their lords' yokes. The range of communal, federal, and corporate institutions was vast: urban communes, valley communes, mining communes, village communes, university faculties, religious orders, lay confraternities, guilds, associations of journeymen and of master artisans, and leagues of cities with one another, cities with nobles, and cities with rural communes. Wherever the progress toward centralized, dynastic monarchy was interrupted or weak, such institutions sprouted thickly and began to assume more or less state-like functions. It hardly surprises that this happened most dramatically in Europe's most highly urbanized regions: North and Central Italy, South Germany and the Netherlands.

The "equality" of the commune differed significantly from modern egalitarian equality. It contained two esential ideas: first, that no member of a commune might exercise direct, personal rule over another;[12] and secondly, that ordinary folk, persons who were not lords, could through solidarity and cooperation command their own affairs. This communal equality excluded neither oligarchy within the commune nor collective lordship of the commune over outsiders—e.g., rural subjects of urban communes—nor did it invade the patriarchal authority of heads of households, who alone, in most cases, could become full members of communes.

Beyond the realm of communal practice, which could be quite restrictive and conservative, late medieval society knew an egalitarian ideal, a rival to the notion of a hierarchy of estates based on the need for social inequality. The egalitarian ideal associated liberty with work, a proposition which flew in the face of classical notions, and saw in the *laboratores* the foundation of true social order.[13] Its radical forms drew on Christian monastic sources to teach that property is theft and that lords are parasites. Such notions seem to have flourished best—e.g., in England, Bohemia and Saxony—where communal institutions were weak or absent in everyday life.

Nowhere in Europe did communal and federal institution flourish more exuberantly than in South Germany, the southern tier of the German-speaking world between the High Alps and the Central Highlands. The movement's outstanding creation, the Swiss Confederacy, spread from the original Forest Cantons to the free cities in the valleys, clearing the social landscape of noble lordship and forging federal bonds between urban and rural communes.[14] On its borders formed "new Switzerlands," the League Above the Lake in Vorarlberg and the High Rhine Valley in 1407, the New League of the Swabian Allgäu in 1410, the three Rhaetian leagues during the fifteenth century, and the Alsatian Lower Union during the 1470s. The Confederacy became a true reference society or model for all the cities and rural subjects of South Germany, for whom "turning Swiss" became a phrase to describe the various ways of ridding themselves of noble domination.[15]

How far this politicization of ordinary people, the "Common Man"[16] in contemporary parlance, had moved by Luther's generation is illustrated by the rebels' programs during the Revolution of 1525.[17] Where consolidated territories already possessed dualistic regimes, as in Württemberg, Salzburg, and Tyrol, the peasants, miners, stockmen and some townsmen proposed to reform them into true assemblies of the reald [*Landschaften*]. Where, on the other hand, political fragmentation was the rule, as in Upper Swabia, the Upper Rhine Valley, and Franconia, the rebels ignored existing structures and projected communal-federal constitutions of their own. Notions of "ancient tradition" and "the common good" took on new and more radical meaning in Christianized forms, "the godly law" and "Christian common weal," lending force to the ideal fo a world without lords.

Two forces threatened to cripple and invade corporate and communal life in the German South around 1500, the dynastic state and large-scale business.[18] Emperor Maximilian (reigned 1493-1519) successfully built a system of clientage and federation, anchored on his Austrian lands, which halted the northward expansion of the Swiss Confederacy and blocked the expansionist plans of the Bavarian and Palatine Wittelsbachs and the House of Württemberg. Maximilian's centralist plans, beginning with a centralized Austrian government, on which the Imperial government was to have been made dependent, came to naught at the end of his reign; but they were briefly revived early in Charles V's reign by the Habsburg governor of the newly acquired duchy of Württemberg. The Revolution of 1525 then knocked the supports from under this Habsburg system and returned predominant police power in the German South to the other princely houses. But centralization there was, if not Habsburg then Bavarian or Hessian, to scotch the advance of the political alternative of communal-federalism.

The second invasive force, the urban bankers and big merchants, was allied to the princes through mining enterprises and other monopolies. The freedom of trade they sought, for which the Welser-connected Conrad Peutinger of Augsburg was an eloquent spokesman, threatened established commercial patterns, vested corporate privileges and protections and, in sum, all the institutions through which ordinary folk tried to protect their ways of life from the market. Their reaction to the growth of the great firms' power, called "the anti-monopoly movement," reached its peak during the early 1520s, when it added to the mounting pressure for change.

Wherever corporately constituted groups of ordinary folk gained political power, dynastic centralism, aristocratic rule and the freedom of big business suffered. The history of Basel illustrates perfectly just this point.[19] On the eve of the Swabian War of 1499, Basel was torn by conflicts between patricians and guilds and between Austrian and Swiss parties. Having reneged on its obligations and remained neutral during the war, Basel left the Habsburg system and "turned Swiss" in 1501. Fifteen years later the artisan guilds took over the government and ejected the patricians;

and in 1526 the guild regime passed a manufacturing ordinance which favored the artisan masters against the merchants. A few other free cities followed Basel's example—Mulhouse in 1511 and Rottweil in 1519—but by and large the oligarchies of the South German free cities preferred the security of the Habsburg system, at least until it was wrecked by the progress of the Reformation.

The commune, as Günther Vogler has recently reminded us, was not a universal institution in the German-speaking world.[20] It chiefly developed westward and especially southwestward of the great social fall line between the older Germany and the colonial East. This line deserves our attention for three reasons. First, the alliance of prince and nobles in a dualistic, ruler-and-estates regime, came very late to the East. In Luther's Saxony, for example, the nobles' corporate power was relatively slight.[21] Secondly, around 1500 the eastern peasantry, unprotected either by strong rural communes or by true political representation in territorial assemblies [*Landschaften*], stood on the brink of their descent into serfdom. The "new European division of labor," in Immanuel Wallerstein's phrase, pushed the East into a "coerced cash-crop economy" of dependence on western markets.[22] Saxony never quite became a classic eastern social landscape, but neither did its peasants escape the new domanial agriculture [*Gutsherrschaft*]. Thirdly, though Saxony urbanization far exceeded what we might imagine, based on the classic image of the German East as a land of forests and grainfields, the vigorous growth of towns and commerce did not produce, as it did in South Germany, the formation of communes and guilds and the social devolution of political power.[23] Taken together, these differences suggest that eastern society around 1500 was not more, but less structured than were the older social landscapes.

This impression is confirmed by the social effects of the tremendous growth of mining in the Saxon lands.[24] The silver mines of the Erzgebirge, dominated by the Saxon princes and their investing subjects, afforded sources of income which were safe respectively from territorial estates and urban commons. The mining districts themselves, notes Adolf Laube, exhibit "relatively progressive social relations with a transitional [i.e., to capitalism] character."[25] The sharp upswing of trade and investment after 1470 accelerated social change in the Saxon cities, where there were few entrenched districts, where high production costs and risks brought the mines into outside investors' hands.[26] Compared with the German Southwest, Saxony in Luther's day affords a picture of a fluid, dynamic social order, in which the territorial state presented the chief point of stability.

Martin Luther was a Saxon,[27] and the social context of his career was not "German society," which did not exist in his day, but the society of that Saxony from which westbound travellers in the sixteenth century said that they were headed "into the Empire."[28] Wittenberg, where he spent the last thirty-five years of his life, lies truly in the German East, as anyone can testify who has stood on the Elbe's bank there. Luther's earlier life shows a distinct lack of established social place. Born into a family which was rapidly moving upward away from its rural roots,[29] Luther spent his boyhood in one small Thuringian or Saxon town after another: Eisleben, Mansfeld, Magdeburg, Eisenach, and, finally, Erfurt. He had no true hometown.

It would be misleading, however, to draw too deep a contrast between Luther's Saxony and the German South. From the western Saxon lands, where Luther grew up, it was an easy passage over the Thuringian Forest, across the Upper Werra Valley and over the hills into the Franconian valleys that led southward towards Nuremberg, Bavaria, and Swabia. Elector Frederick the Wise and his brother, Duke John, were half-Bavarians; and from Luther's Erfurt the lines of political authority ran far westward to the Rhine. It was Luther, too, who helped to shackle the alien sounds of a southern tongue on the Protestant German North. All this warns against making the contrast between these lands too great or exaggerating the easternness of Luther's social milieu. He was nonetheless a child of the most fluid sector of a young, vigorous, colonial society, in which the strength of princely government combined with the weakness of local institutions.

If the social milieu of Luther's boyhood provided little experience of cooperation and solidarity beyond the family, his religious order does not seem to have made good the lack.[30] Luther's entire assault on monasticism suggests that, quite apart from the few good friendships he made within the order, he found there no strong feeling of fellowship or collegial well-being. His theological development supports this impression, for it reflects the centrality of the concept of experience to the *via moderna*.[31] All in all, Luther's early life and development as a reformer betray remarkably few contacts with communal values or corporate institutions.

The prevailing weakness of communal institutions in the everyday life of the German East may well supply an insight into the peculiarly radical positions taken by Luther and Thomas Müntzer during the Revolution of 1525. The Thuringian movement, under Müntzer's inspiration, was distinguished by its radical class consciousness, the ease with which it united peasants, miners and townsfolk, and the extremely strong Christian element in its program. It is possible—and this is merely a suggestion—that the weakness of cooperative institutions in everyday life and the extreme fluidity of social relations made the ideas of the more moderate Swabian and Rhenish programs in the year 1525, which built on familiar communal institutions, less credible in the East. It is worth adding that the Revolution's most radical programs came from the borderlands of the region in which communalism was properly at home.[32] The positions of Luther and Müntzer in 1525 have in common their fixing of social order in forms remote from the everyday experience of the common people, Luther in paternalistic princely authority, Müntzer in the egalitarian communism of the elect. In Luther's case the experience of 1525 helped to fix his commitment to a social teaching he had been developing since the Wittenberg disorders in the winter of 1521-1522.

(2)

Luther's social teaching is framed by most modern treatments into the doctrine of the Two Kingdoms, "the temporal," as he wrote,

> which is ruled by the sword and is seen with
> the eyes, and the spiritual, ruled by grace and
> the forgiveness of sins.[33]

This theme expressed one of the Augustinian antitheses into which Luther cast his theology during the 1510's, since his encounter with Augustine's division of creation into the *civitas dei* and the *civitas diaboli.* These two kingdoms or *Reiche,* in Luther's words, became one pair of a rich series of antitheses: spirit-flesh, eternal-temporal, heavenly-earthly, future-present, hidden-open, invisible-visible, inward-outward, and gospel-law.[34] Their union to the new doctrine of justification by faith alone produced by 1518 the explosive attack on the visible Church in the name of the invisible one,[35] which we read in the pamphlets of 1520, and Luther's confident "No!" to Charles V at Worms in 1521. From the *regnum dei* Luther evoked the image of the Church as the priesthood of believers, united in their equality *coram deo,* into this world, the *regnum diaboli,* to do battle with the papal monarchy, the sacramental system, and works-righteousness. In the process he swept away the status of the Church as an independent institution and, by implication at least—an implication the young Evangelical movement was not slow to realize—threatened the temporal social order as well. This explosive theology came wrapped in an eschatological expectation which let the order of this world appear paltry indeed *coram deo,* in the Gospel's shining light.[36]

Luther's concern for the order of this world began not with the

Revolution of 1525 but with the Wittenberg disorders of the winter of 1521-22.[37] It stunned him to find that the people, led by his own disciplines, had taken their reformation into their own hands, just as the Alpine stockmen had once taken control of their lives, and just as the urban commons in Swabia and on the Rhine would try during the mid-1520s and seize control of their own churches. Luther's reaction was immediate, his protest total. "But where is the order?" he asked the Wittenbergers,

> for everything has been done recklessly without any order, to the scandal of the neighbors; whereas one ought first to have prayed on the matter and then consulted the authorities. Then one might be sure that the reforms came from God.[38]

His own support for authority, as he admitted in 1525, was unswerving and unqualified.

> I have always been and always will be on the side of those against whom insurrection is directed, no matter how unjust their cause. I am opposed to those who rise in insurrection, no matter how just their cause, because there can be no insurrection without hurting the innocent and shedding their blood.[39]

These sentiments stand at the beginning of Luther's teaching on social order.

Luther's social teaching took its form from the doctrine of Three Estates, which came to him through his Christian-Aristotelian education and the medieval catechetical tradition. Before the Wittenberg disorders, Luther employed this doctrine in a traditional sense, meaning three different social groups, as he wrote in 1519:

> There are many who want to live as though they were devout and who say they would like to be devout. But there is no easier or shorter way than baptism and its fruits, suffering and death. For this purpose God established several estates [*stend*] in which one is to test oneself and learn to suffer: for some the matrimonial, for others the ecclesiastical, and for yet others the political estates.[40]

During the 1520s, however, he came to see the estates not as distinct social groups but as three webs of social relations, to each of which everyone belongs. "First of all," he wrote, you must be part of a family, a father or mother, a child, servant or maid. Secondly, you must live in a city or in the country as a citizen, a subject, or a ruler. Thirdly, you are part of the Church, perhaps a pastor, an assistant, a sexton, or in some other way a servant of the Church, if only you have and hear the Word of God.[41]

These estates, as he taught in 1528, were established by God:

But the holy order and true institutes founded by God are these three: the priestly office, the matrimonial estates, the temporal authority.... Therefore, such three institutes or orders are encompassed by God's Word and ordinance.

The individual relations that make up the estates are the famous "callings" [*Beruf, vocatio*], about which so much modern ink has been spilt.[43] By 1522 Luther was teaching that everyone is called by God to serve in his or her offices or callings. The long debate over how revolutionary was his attribution of (originally monastic) ethical significance to secular trades, professions, offices and familial roles, has ended in the prosaic recognition that Luther here completed a development which had been underway since the twelfth century.[44] *Coram mundo,* Luther taught, one stands not alone but only in social relations, for each is "bound in this life to another person."[45] The relations, then, into which God calls the individual, make up his or her social place.

During the decade of the 1520's Luther developed his teaching on the Three Estates in the diretion of centralized authority and clear-cut hierarchy. This process has been studied in detail only for government [*Obrigkeit*], on which Luther developed his teaching in the political pamphlets of the years from 1523 to 1526.[46] He came to unify political and paternal authority under a patriarchal image which sprang into full bloom in his catechisms of 1529. Following a long tradition, Luther placed this teaching under the rubric of the Fourth Commandment:

For all other forms flow from and are extensions of parental authority.... Thus all those who are called "lords" stand in the parents' stead and necessarily take their power and authority to rule from [the parental office]. Therefore the Bible calls them all "fathers," because they exercise in their rule the office of a father and ought to regard their folk with a fatherly heart. Just as, many

years ago, the Romans and others called the lords and ladies of
the household "patres et matres familias," that is, "fathers and
mothers of the household," so they called their princes and rulers
"patres patriae" or fathers of their country." It is shameful that we
Christians today don't call them by the same titles or at least
regard them and honor them as fathers.[47]

Each person thus has several fathers, "by blood, by household and by
country."[48]

Some years later, Luther reversed the direction of unification of
household and State by collapsing all "external" [*eusserlich*] institutions
into temporal authority.[49] If this has an absolutist ring, a sound reinforced
by Luther's continual harping on St. Paul's teaching on obedience to rulers
in Romans 13, it must be remembered that he did not allow the ruler to
invade the authority of the household's father.[50] Nevertheless, although
Luther sometimes recognized the household as a kind of cell of the social
order, he allowed the heads of household no claim of right or obligation on
the ruler. To patriarchalist conceptions of society Luther contributed, on
the one hand, the political argument from the Bible and, on the other,
obedience as the content of Biblical social teaching.[51] In the great
theoretical debate of the sixteenth century he stands clearly with the
patriarchalist forerunners of absolutism, and against the proponents of
popular sovereignty.

The ruler is father of his land; the father is ruler of his household. The
relationship between them is not one of dependence in either direction, and
each reflects God's rule over creation. They are thus related analogically, in
a kind of *analogia socialis,* and they belong strictly to the kingdom of this
world. However old-fashioned, even for his own day Luther's teaching on
the household and the State is symmetrical and clear. The same cannot be
said for his teaching on the third estate, the Church.[52] He started from the
distinction between temporal and spiritual churches, reflecting the
distinction between the Two Kingdoms.[53] The Church's unique connection
to the *regnum dei,* in its form as an egalitarian priesthood of believers,
made it impossible that the visible Church should take a form analogous to
those of the other two estates. This, after all, had been the point of Luther's
reformation, to destroy the visible Church as an institution of autonomous
social power. The lordship over the Church belonged to Christ alone.
"Christ can and will tolerate or suffer," he wrote,

no head or lordship in His Church, by virtue of which one person
might strive to be higher or better than another.[54]

One possibility was to the visible Church to take its form in analogy to the invisible, spiritual Church, and there are signs that during the early 1520s Luther did emphasize the priesthood [*sacerdotium*] of believers in a congregationalist direction. By 1523 at the latest, however, he veered toward a conception of the Church as a structure of offices [*ministerium*], founded by Christ, and this view held ecclesiological pride of place in his mature thought.[55] This shift agrees with the timing and direction of Luther's thought about the other two estates and about the Three Estates as a whole.

The Church became the point of incoherence between the Three Estates and the relationship between the two modes of the Church's existence, remained, in Wilhelm Maurer's words, "disputed and indeterminate."[56] The priesthood of believers, that is, the egalitarian union of true Christians in the *regnum dei*, retained just enough power to prevent the reconstruction of genuine authority in the visible Church, though not enough to determine the structure of that Church. The Church in the *regnum mundi* thus is no true estate at all, for it has not structure or authority of its own. This is the teaching behind all those queer institutional arrangements in the Luther territorial churches, bishops and superintendants, the prince as *Notbischof* and *praecipuum membrum ecclesiae*, and the princely *cura religionis, jus in sacra* and *jus circa sacra*. Luther's "emergency" placement of his church in the ruler's hands endured until the November Revolution and the Weimar Constitution.[57]

Through its modern history, Lutheranism has been dogged by Luther's refusal to give social substance to the priesthood of believers. Whatever his theological reasons, Luther's refusal to permit the communal principle to invade the Three Estates through a (congregationally organized) Church must be traced in part to his profound mistrust of the common people and his fear of social equality.[58] Contempt for "Lord Everybody" [*Herr Omnes*] and "the mob" [*der Pöfel*] is a leitmotiv of his social teaching from the Revolution of 1525 down to the Diet of Augsburg in 1530.[59] It was not that he held status, wealth, or birth to be marks of moral worth. *Coram deo*, he wrote,

> domestic servants and maids are just as Christian as other folk..., which is why God holds them in just as high esteem and as dearly as He does others.[60]

The *regnum mundi,* however,

> cannot endure where there is no inequality of persons, so that
> some are free and some bound, some are lords and some
> subjects.[61]

Where proper social subordination is disrupted, Luther once wrote,

> the mob [*der Pöbel*] is the Devil. God performs through it what he
> would otherwise do through the Devil to punish the wicked. Thus
> the people become rebellious when God removes from their
> hearts fear of and regard for authority.[61]

Behind this view lay the fear that swept into Luther's heart during the first
half of the 1520's, from the Wittenberg disorders to the Revolution of 1525.
"For what God wants," Luther preached in 1528,

> that He sufficiently ordains and commands. God does not sleep,
> He is no fool; and He knows quite well how to govern. Therefore,
> it it is not your task, leave it alone, and do not pick up the sword.
>   Against this it commonly happens that someone says: "There is
> violence and injustice and no good government. We must do
> something about it." When the mob [*der Pöbel*] hears such
> words, it takes them up and concludes: "So, let's do it." For the
> old Adam is so great a fool that he neglects and omits what is
> commanded, and he undertakes what is not commanded. What
> moved Müntzer if not the notion that government is bad, so we
> must make it Christian?
>   This is the bellows that puffs up and inflames the people's
> hearts. Thus, when the cry goes out, "Justice, justice! Injustice,
> injustice!" no one says to himself: "Is that your job?" You aren't
> the one who ought to establish justice and punish injustice. When
> some wrong is done in my house and my next door neighbor
> wants to break into my house and do justice there, what should I
> say to that?[63]

God always sides with the ruler, Luther continued, because He

> would rather sustain an unjust ruler than a people whose cause is
> just. The reason is that when Lord Everybody takes up the sword
> and makes war, under th pretext that justice is on his side,

everything is ruined. For a prince remains a prince, and he won't kill everybody, even though he does do some wrong and does kill some persons.[64]

From this position the later Luther never budged.

No deductions from his theology could express so well, as these passages do, Luther's deep and abiding fear of the Common Man. Princes and people are made by God, he thought, and to disrupt this order is to bring down upon society chaos, destruction, and death. Luther did not condemn the revolutionaries and rebels of 1525 only because they misused the gospel, his gospel; but he also was afraid because he had never seen ordinary people rule their own affairs, as did the guild masters of Basel, the stockmen of Uri, and the farmers on the Leutkircher Heide. Far away in remote corners of the Empire, in Switzerland and Ditmarsh, there existed, he acknowledged,

Democracy, where many of the Comman Man rule,[65]

but such oddities had nothing to do with the world as he knew it.

From the time of the Wittenberg disorders onward, therefore, Luther called on the doctrine of Three Estates to express his perceived need for a divinely established and conserved social order. The *regnum diaboli* sacrificed some of its demonic nature accordingly and became more and more a mere *regnum mundi;* and the Three Estates took on substance at the expense of the Two Kingdoms. Some, but not all, for the combination of Three Estates with Two Kingdoms, plus the troubled relationship between them, endured in his thought to the end. The Two Kingdoms helped to generate Luther's reforming fury during the years 1518 to 1522. Thereafter, his search for principles of social order in the *regnum diaboli* adopted the Three Estates—family, Church, and State—from the mainstream of Christian-Aristotelian thought. Where this structure joined the Two Kingdoms, in the dual nature of the Church, the logic of worldly social structure failed. The Church conformed neither to the social principle of the *regnum mundi,* hierarchical authority, nor to that of the *regnum dei,* Christian equality. Thus, what Bernhard Lohse has called Luther's "lack of an ecclesiological program" grew from the time when the chilling fear of social disorder collided with the reforming fury born of Luther's personal search for grace. This reaction, however, which froze his unfinished teaching on the Church as a social institution, reflects as well Luther's experience of his own social milieu and social place.

(3)

Luther holds no dominant place in the history of European social thought. He had little or no part in the major achievement of western European social thought during his century; the idea of the State "as an omnipotent yet impersonal power,"[66] beside which Luther's ideal of the ruler [*Obrigkeit*] seems archaic in its lack of distinction between rule and office. Though he taught a doctrine, which he grounded in St. Paul, of submission to established authority, he cannot be counted among the chief theorists of absolutism. Luther, who in Tawney's words "hated the economic individualism of the age not less than its spiritual laxity,"[67] aimed not to help build absolutism but merely to strengthen authority in an age threatened by social fluidity and disorder. His doctrines, suitably shaped by Melanchthon and other fathers of Orthodoxy, became comfortable companions of the typical prince-and-nobles state of the East, built on the Second Serfdom and the subjection of towns and churches.[68] However advanced social relations may have been in Luther's Saxony, the East as a whole was being pushed into the role of provider of primary products to western markets through cultivation by bound labor. Lutheran social teaching after Luther thus developed in lands which were being steadily underdeveloped, and which eventually entered the age of capitalism not on the "truly revolutionary path" of capitalists' seizure of power, but on what Marx called "the second way," in which capitalism is imported by the classes who already control the State.[69] This helps to explain the durability of classic Lutheran social teaching and the utility of the doctrine of Three Estates to the "throne-and-altar" ideology of nineteenth-century Germany.[70] The anomalous nature of the Church in Luther's teaching also helps to explain why ethical values and sentiments, which in Catholic and Calvinist lands attached to the churches, in German Lutheran lands tended to be sought in the State. No one ever characterized the mental world of the Three Estates and the Two Kingdoms after Luther better than did Ernst Troeltsch. His critics, above all Karl Holl, never denied this; they merely denied that this world faithfully represented the teachings of Luther. This question remains open, and so does the issue of whether Luther's social teaching belongs entirely to the mental apparatus of a world which was, in Yeats' words, "changéd, changéd utterly," when Communism swept through the European East.

As a closing word I must say something about the other, the ethical side of Luther's social teaching, the side that so exasperated R.H. Tawney:

Luther's utterances on social morality are the occasional explosions of a capricious volcano, with only a rare flash of light amid the torrent of smoke and flame, and it is idle to scan them for a coherent and consistent doctrine.[71]

True enough, but there is more to Luther's social teaching than his doctrine. In his sermons, Biblical commentaries and devotional writings, Luther transmitted to his descendants a profound sense of this bleak world's need for love. Love could not save the world, no more than could the law, but it could soften the harshness and cruelty of life in the Three Estates. In Pietism, the Lutheran Reformation's second (after Orthodoxy) and younger daughter, this belief contributed to the striving of those "German Puritans," who, in Carl Hinrichs' words, strove for

conversion and regeneration in the service of social improvement of the world and of humanity.[72]

Pietism strove to recover for Lutheran Christianity a belief in the power of Christian love to transform the world, and in so doing it reached back through Luther's Reformation to the piety of the pre-Lutheran age.

Notes

1. John Rastell, "Of Gentleness and Nobility," in *The Spider and the Fly,* ed. John S. Farmer (London, 1908) p. 453.

2. Niccolò Machiavelli, *The Prince,* chap. 9 (English: *The Chief Works and Others,* ed./transl. Allan H. Gilbert, 3 vols. (Durham, N.C., 1965), vol. I, p. 39.

3. "Von den Juden und ihren Lügen (1543)," in *WA* 53, 421, 30-36.

4. Thomas Mann, "Germany and the Germans," in *Thomas Mann's Addresses Delivered at the Library of Congress, 1942-1949* (Washington, D.C., 1963), pp. 53-54.

5. "Verantwortung der aufgelegten Aufruhr von Herzog Georg (1533)," in *WA* 38, 102, 30ff. (English here from George W. Forell, *Faith Active In Love: An Investigation of the Principles Underlying Luther's Social Ethics* (New York, 1954), p. 122 n.26. There is a nearly identical passage in "Ob Kriegsleute (1526)," in *WA* 19, 625, 15-17 (English in *LW* 46, 95).

6. On the Luther revival in the Second German Empire, see David W. Lotz, *Ritschl & Luther: A Fresh Perspective on Albrecht Ritschl's Theology in the Light of his Luther Study* (Nashville and New York, 1974); Otto Wolff, *Haupttypen der neueren Lutherdeutung*

(Tübinger Studien zur systematischen Theologie, 7; Stuttgart, 1938); and Ulrich Duchrow, "Zweireichelehre als Ideologie. Folgenreiche Umdeutungen Luthers im 19. Jahrhundert," *Lutherische Monatshefte,* 14 (June 1975), 296-300. On the "Luther Renaissance" of the interwar era, see Karl Kupisch, "The 'Luther Renaissance,'" *Journal of Contemporary History* 2, No. 4 (Oct. 1967), 39-49; Ernst Wolf, "Luthers Erbe?" and "Zur Selbstkritik des Luthertums," both in his *Peregrinatio,* vol. II (Munich, 1965), pp. 52-81, 82-103; and Klaus Scholder, *Die Kirchen und das Dritte Reich, Vorgeschichte und Zeit der Illusionen 1918-1934* (Berlin, 1977), pp. 125-30. *Luther. Gestalt und Symbol* is the title of Gerhard Ritter's Luther biography, published in 1925.

7. For literature and an introduction to this theme, see Heinz Rausch, ed., *Die geschichtlichen Grundlagen der modernen Volksvertretung. Die Entwicklung von den mittelalterlichen Korporationen zu den modernen Parlamenten,* I: *Allgemeine Fragen und europäischer Überblick* (Wege der Forschung, 196; Darmstadt, 1980), esp. Dietrich Gerhard, "Assemblies of Estates and Corporate Order", pp. 303-24; and Antonio Marongiu, "Das Prinzip der Demokratie und der Zustimmung (quod omnes tangit, ab omnibus approbari debet) im 14. Jahrhundert", pp. 183-211. See also Dietrich Gerhard, *Old Europe: A Study of Continuity, 1000-1800* (New York, 1981), esp. pp. 46-50.

8. Perry Anderson, *Lineages of the Absolutist State* (London, 1974), p. 18; and see the discussion of the resources of absolutist monarchy at pp. 29-39.

9. Quentin Skinner, *The Foundations of Modern Political Thought,* 2 vols. (Cambridge, 1978), vol. II, p. 353.

10. Georges Duby, *Les trois ordres ou l'imgainaire du féodalisme* (Paris, 1978) (English: *The Three Orders: Feudal Society Imagined,* transl. Arthur Goldhammer, Chicago, 1980). See Gerhard, *Old Europe* (note 7 above), pp. 46-50; and esp. Wilhelm Maurer, *Luthers Lehre von den drei Hierarchien und ihr mittelalterlicher Hintergrund* (Sitzungsberichte der Bayerischen Akademie der Wissenschaften, philosophisch-historische Klasse, 1970, No. 4; Munich, 1970), who cites the (depressingly scanty) literature, esp. pp. 67-118.

11. The best source for the idea of the commune is still Otto von Gierke's *Das deutsche Genossenschaftsrecht,* 4 vols. (Berlin, 1868-1913; reprinted, Graz, 1954), vol. I, pp. 300-637; vol. III, pp. 186-827. For the Church, see Antony Black, *Council and Commune: The Conciliar Movement and the Fifteenth Century Heritage* (London, 1979); and for the German-speaking world, see Peter Blickle, *Deutsche Untertanen. Ein Widerspruch* (Munich, 1981), pp. 23-60.

12. It is in this sense that Machiavelli speaks of "equality" in *Discorsi,* vol. I, p. 55, complimenting the German cities. See C.B. Macpherson, *The Political Theory of Possessive Individualism* (Oxford, 1962), pp. 122-29, 262ff., on the connection of this view with the origins of Liberal Democracy.

13. Perry Anderson, *Passages from Antiquity to Feudalism* (London, 1974), pp. 23-28. There is rich documentation for this point of view in Ruth Mohls's very useful *The Three Estates in Medieval and Renaissance Literature* (New York, 1933); and more in Norman Cohn's *The Pursuit of the Millennium,* 2nd ed. (New York, 1961), ch. 9-11.

14. Hans Conrad Peyer, *Verfassungsgeschichte der alten Schweiz* (Zürich, 1978), pp. 21-74.

15. This is based on my forthcoming book, *Between Commune and Caesar: Cities, Crown and Swiss in South Germany, 1450-1550.*

16. Robert H. Lutz, *Wer war der gemeine Mann? Der dritte Stand in der Krise des Spätmittelalters* (Munich and Vienna, 1979), though I agree with Peter Blickle's critique in *Die Revolution von 1525,* (Munich and Vienna, [2]1981), p. 194, n. 30 (English: *The Revolution of 1525: The German Peasants' War from a New Perspective,* transl. Thomas A. Brady, Jr., and H.C. Erik Midelfort, Baltimore 1981, p. 220, n. 43). See, however, the critique of Blickle's

views by Tom Scott, "The Peasants' War: A Historiographical Review," *The Historical Journal*, 22 (1979), 693-720, 953-74, here at 957, 966.

17. Peter Blickle, *Die Revolution von 1525*, pp. 196-223 (English: *The Revolution of 1525*, pp. 124-45).

18. This and the next paragraph are based on my forthcoming study (note 15 above).

19. Hans Füglister, *Handwerksregiment. Untersuchungen und Materialien zur sozialen und politischen Struktur der Stadt Basel in der ersten Hälfte des 16. Jahrhunderts* (Basler Beiträge zur Geschichtswissenschaft, 143; Basel, 1981); and for a broader perspective, see Hans R. Guggisberg, *Basel in the Sixteenth Century: Aspects of the City Republic Before, During, and After the Reformation* (St. Louis, 1982), pp. 4-7.

20. Günther Vogler, in *Archiv für Reformationsgeschichte, Literaturbericht* 11 (1982), p. 10, reviewing Blickle's *Deutsche Untertanen* (note 11 above).

21. Karlheinz Blaschke, *Sachsen im Zeitalter der Reformation* (Schriften des Vereins für Reformationsgeschichte, 185; Gütersloh, 1970), pp. 53-54.

22. Immanuel Wallerstein, *The Modern World-System*, 1: *Capitalist Agriculture and the Origins of the European World-Economy in the Sixteenth Century* (New York, 1974), ch. 2.

23. Blaschke (note 21 above), pp. 68-79.

24. *Ibid.*, pp. 38-43; and see, above all, Adolf Laube, *Studien über den erzgebirgischen Silberbergbau von 1470 bis 1546*, (Forschungen zur mittelalterlichen Geschichte, 22; Berlin, ^{2}1976).

25. *Ibid.*, p. 281.

26. *Ibid.*, pp. 83-86.

27. Martin Brecht, *Martin Luther. Sein Weg zur Reformation 1483-1521* (Stuttgart, 1981), p. 21.

28. Quoted by Blaschke (note 21 above), p. 126.

29. Brecht (note 27 above), p. 32, judges Luther's background to have been bürgerlich-städtisch"; and Heiko A. Oberman, *Luther. Mensch zwischen Gott und Teufel* (Berlin, 1982), p. 91, considers Luther's social milieu to have been "neuzeitlich."

30. See Brecht (note 27 above), pp. 70-82, for a very good account of Luther's life as a monk; Heinz-Meinolf Stamm, *Luthers Stellung zum Ordensleben* (Veröffentlichungen des Instituts für europäische Geschichte Mainz, 101; Wiesbaden, 1980), pp. 95-126.

31. Oberman (note 29 above), pp. 126-127.

32. Of the four "utopian" programs analyzed by Blickle (note 16 above, pp. 145-54), the possible exception is Balthasar Hubmaier's "Draft of a Constitution," which, however, "borrowed heavily from Thomas Müntzer," p. 228 (English p. 148).

33. "Ueber das 1. Buch Mose, Predigten (1523-24)," in *WA* 24, 6, 1-3. For orientation to the literature, consult W.D.J. Cargill-Thompson, "The 'Two Kingdoms' and 'Two Regiments': Some problems of Luther's 'Zwei-Reiche-Lehre'," *Journal of Theological Studies*, n. F. 20 (1969), pp. 164-185; and esp. Martin Honecker, "Zur gegenwärtigen Interpretation der Zweireichelehre," *Zeitschrift für Kirchengeschichte*, 89 (1978), 150-162.

34. Ulrich Duchrow, *Christenheit und Weltverantwortung. Traditionsgeschichte und systematische Struktur der Zwei-Reiche-Lehre* (Forschungen und Berichte der Evangelischen Studiengemeinschaft, 25; Stuttgart, 1970), p. 447. Oberman (note 29 above), pp. 170-171, dates Luther's engagement with Augustine to 1509, first as an ally against Aristotle, then as interpreter of St. Paul. On the use of antitheses, see Marjorie O'Rourke Boyle, "Stoic Luther: Paradoxical Sin and Necessity," *ARG*, 73 (1982), 69-93, who argues that they are of Stoic origin.

35. I intend here no commitment to one or another date for Luther's discovery, as I agree on the whole that the search for a single date is fruitless. See Heiko A. Oberman, "'Iustitia

Christi' and 'Iustitia Dei.' Luther and the Scholastic Doctrines of Justification," *Harvard Theological Review,* 59 (1966), 1-26; and see, for the state of the question, Bernhard Lohse, *Martin Luther. Eine Einführung in sein Leben und sein Werk* (Munich, 1981), pp. 157-160.

36. Ulrich Asendorf, *Eschatologie bei Luther* (Göttingen, 1967). See, for recent reflections on the escatalogical aspects of Luther's thought, Oberman (note 29 above), chap. 9; and *idem,* "Martin Luther, Vorläufer der Reformation," in *Verifikationen. Festschrift für Gerhard Ebeling zum 70. Geburtstag,* eds. Eberhard Jüngel, *et al.* (Tübingen, 1982), pp. 91-119, here at 97-102.

37. Heinrich Bornkamm, *Martin Luther in der Mitte seines Lebens. Das Jahrzehnt zwischen dem Wormser und dem Augsburger Reichstag,* ed. Karin Bornkamm (Göttingen, 1979), pp. 72-75.

38. "Invocavitpredigten (1522)," at 9 March 1522, in *WA* 10.3, 9, 10-13. See Lohse (note 35 above), pp. 62-64, though I cannot share his view that "So sehr Luther in der Auseinandersetzung mit den Wittenberger Reformern seine früheren Auffassungen näher entfaltete..., so handelt es sich dabei doch im ganzen nicht um eigentliche Weiterentwicklungen, sondern eher um Präzisierungen."

39. "Eine treue Vermahnung zu allen Christen (1522)," in *WA* 8, 690 (English: *LW* 45, 63). See Mark U. Edwards, Jr., *Luther and the False Brethren* (Stanford, 1975), ch. 1-2.

40. "Ein Sermon von dem Sakrament der Taufe (1519)," in *WA* 2, 734, 20-28. See Maurer (note 10 above), the fundamental work; Duchrow (note 34 above), pp. 495-512; and Reinhard Schwarz, "Luthers Lehre von den drei Ständen und die drei Dimensionen der Ethik," *Luther-Jahrbuch,* 45 (1978), 15-34. As will become apparent, I do not share the view of Jürgen Küppers, "Luthers Dreihierarchienlehre als Kritik an der mittelalterlichen Gesellschaftsauffassung," *Evangelische Theologie,* 19 (1949), 361-74, that the doctrine of Three Estates is an alternative to the Two Kingdoms.

41. *WA TR* 6, No. 6913, p. 266, 16-27 (English by Forell, note 5 above, p. 123). See F. Edward Cranz, *An Essay on the Development of Luther's Thought on Justice, Law, and Society* (Harvard Theological Studies, 19; Cambridge, Mass., 1959, pp. 153-50). Cranz's argument, that the pre-Luther doctrine of Three Estates turned on the contrast between the ecclesiastical and the worldly estates (pp. 173-78), is quite mistaken, and therefore he judges to be a radical innovation by Luther what was in fact a turning back towards medieval positions. The same mistake is made by Gerhard Gloege, "Politia divina. Die Überwindung des mittelalterlichen Sozialdenkens durch Luthers Lehre von der Obrigkeit," reprinted in his *Theologische Traktate,* vol. II: *Verkündigung und Verantwortung* (Göttingen, 1967), pp. 69-108; and by Küppers (note 40 above). The only reliable guide to this question is Maurer (note 10 above), who studies the medieval texts, whereas the other commentators rest content with inferences.

42. "Vom Abendmahl Christi. Bekenntnis (1528)," in *WA* 26, 504, 31-505, 10.

43. The basic work is Gustaf Wingren's Swedish monograph of 1942, translated into German as *Luthers Lehre vom Beruf* (Munich, 1952), and into English as *Luther on Vocation* (Philadelphia, 1957).

44. Werner Conze, "Beruf," in *Geschichtliche Grundbegriffe. Historisches Lexikon zur politisch-sozialen Sprache in Deutschland,* vol. I (Stuttgart, 1972), pp. 490-507, here at p. 402. What is said about the doctrine of Three Estates (note 41 above) applies as well to this topos.

45. "Auslegung der Bergpredigt (1530-32)," in *WA* 32, 390, 33-34.

46. Walther von Loewenich, "Luthers Stellung zur Obrigkeit," reprinted by Gunther Wolf, ed., *Luther und die Obrigkeit* (Wege der Forschung, 85; Darmstadt, 1972), pp. 425-32; Eike Wolgast, *Die Wittenberger Theologie und die Politik der evangelischen Stände. Studien zu Luthers Gutachten in politischen Fragen* (Quellen und Forschungen zur Reformationsgeschichte, 47; Gütersloh, 1977) pp. 40-74.

47. "Deudsch [Grosser] Catechismus (1529)," in *WA* 19, 152, 20-35. See Maurer (note 10 above), pp. 19-24; and Wolgast (note 46 above), p. 76.

48. *WA* 30.1, 147, 22ff.

49. "Der 127. Psalm ausgelegt (1532/33)," in *WA* 40.3, 202ff. See Loewenich (note 46 above), p. 433.

50. This step came only much later. See Otto Brunner, "Das 'ganze Haus' und die alteuropäische 'Oekonomik,'" in his *Neue Wege der Verfassungs- und Sozialgeschichte.* (Göttingen, ²1968), pp. 103-27. See, on the Reformation and the household, Michael Mitterauer and Reinhard Sieder, *The European Family: Patriarchy to Partnership from the Middle Ages to the Present*, transl. by Karla Oosterveen and Manfred Hörzinger (Chicago, 1982), pp. 7-10. It is puzzling that this subject is not treated at length by Joyce Irwin, "Society and the Sexes," in *Reformation Europe: A Guide to Research*, ed. Steven Ozment (St. Louis, 1982), pp. 343-60.

51. Skinner (note 9 above), vol. II, chap. 1, esp. pp. 12-19; Sheldon S. Wolin, "Luther: The Theological and the Political," in *Politics and Vision: Continuity and Innovation in Western Political Thought* (Boston, 1960), pp. 141-161, esp. pp. 142-44. Skinner's demonstration, that the roots of the doctrine of popular sovereignty lie not in Protestantism but in the Thomist revival of the sixteenth century, finds the Catholic neo-Thomists and Calvinist monarchomachs on one side of the debate and Luther and the fathers of absolutist theory on the other. This fits with the current position on Luther's long-alleged "secularization" of the State and society, vigorously upheld by Reinhold Seeberg as recently as 1933 (see Lohse, note 35 above), pp. 192-93). The argument that Luther affirmed the "autonomy" [*Eigengesetzlichkeit*] of the State was developed by those who hoped to save Luther's relevance to the modern world from the intellectual wreck of Orthodoxy, and who hoped to prove thereby that the passing of the idea of the "Christian magistrate" did not invalidate Luther's thought. This entire argument was so gravely compromised by the militant Christian nationalists in Germany that it is seldom heard today. Cranz (note 41 above, p. 177) tries to save its essence through the notion of "a Christian secularization," with little success. The present state of the question is well formulated by Wolgast (note 46 above), p. 46: "Indem die Obrigkeit in Gottes Ordnung steht, ist sie zugleich gesichert gegen jeden Autonomismus."

52. The most important recent literature is listed by Lohse (note 35 above), pp. 206-07. I have relied on Wolfgang Stein, *Das kirchliche Amt bei Luther*, (Veröffentlichungen des Instituts für europäische Geschichte Mainz, 73; Wiesbaden, 1974); and Gert Haendler, *Amt und Gemeinde bei Luther im Kontext der Kirchengeschichte* (Arbeiten zur Theologie, 63; Stuttgart, 1979; English: *Luther on Ministerial Office and Congregational Function*, ed. Eric Gritsch, transl. Ruth Gritsch, Philadelphia, 1981), though I believe that Haendler exaggerates the survival of congregational tendencies in Luther's thought after the mid-1520s. Haendler is surely correct, however, to assert that: "Luther could not seriously conceive of the possibility of a rural congregation capable of functioning independently and also electing its own pastor."

53. *WA* 6, 296, 38-297, 5. See Stein (note 52 above): esp. pp. 202-13.

54. "Matthäus 18-24 in Predigten ausgelegt (1537-40)," in *WA* 47, 233, 6-8. See "Von weltlicher Obrigkeit (1523)," in *WA* 11, 271, 1ff., though there is a contrary suggestion in "Sommerpostille (1526)," in *WA* 10.2, 246, 21-22.

55. Lohse (note 35 above): 187, summarizes the state of the question.

56. Maurer (note 10 above): 124.

57. Martin Heckel, "Zur Entwicklung des deutschen Staatskirchenrechts von der Reformation bis zur Schwelle der Weimarer Verfassung," *Zeitschrift für evangelisches Kirchenrecht*, 12 (1966/67), 1ff. See Johannes Heckel, *Cura religionis, ius in sacra, ius circa sacra* (Darmstadt, ²1962); Lewis W. Spitz, "Luther's Ecclesiology and his Concept of the

Prince as 'Notbischof,'" *Church History,* 22 (1953), 113ff. See, too, the comment by Wolgast (note 46 above), p. 66: "In reale Aufgaben wurde die geistliche Funktion der christlichen Obrigkeit erst nach 1525 umgesetzt."

58. There is nothing newer on this theme than Friedrich Lezius, "Gleichheit und Ungleichheit. Aphorismen zur Theologie und Staatsanschauung Luthers," in *Greifswalder Studien, Theologische Abhandlungen, Hermann Cremer zum 25 jährigen Professoren-jubiliäum dargebracht* (Gütersloh, 1895), pp. 285-326.

59. "Ob Kriegsleute (1526)," in *WA* 19, 536, 7-16; "Predigt 1527," in *WA* 24, 6767, 14ff., and 677, 3-4; "Predigt vom 5. Dezember 1528," in *WA* 28, 250, 8; Martin Luther to the "Jakobigemeinde" of Goslar, 31 May 1529, in *WA Br* 5, No. 1432, p. 93, 21-22; "Predigt vom 31. Oktober 1529," in *WA* 29, 600, 5; *WA* 32, 485, 1-3; *WA TR* 1, No. 758, p. 360, 20-24; *WA TR* 2, No. 2082, p. 314, 24-30.

60. "Epistel S. Petri gepredigt und ausgelegt (1523)," in *WA* 12, 336, 16-18.

61. "Ermahnungen zum Frieden (1525)," in *WA* 18, 327, 6-8.

62. *WA TR* 2, No. 2982, p. 314.

63. "Wochenpredigten über Johannis 16-20," at 5 December 1528, in *WA* 28, 246, 35-36, and 247, 1-10.

64. *WA* 28, 250, 27-32.

65. *WA TR* 4, No. 4342, p. 240, 43-44 (1529). And see "Ob Kriegsleute (1526)," in *WA* 19, 635, 17-18.

66. Skinner (note 9 above), vol. II, p. 358. See Wolgast (note 46 above), pp. 43-47.

67. R.H. Tawney, *Religion and the Rise of Capitalism. A Historical Study* (London, 1926), p. 89.

68. Anderson (note 8 above), p. 195-98.

69. Karl Marx, *Capital,* vol. III, chap. 20, entitled "Merchant Capital." See the discussions in R.H. Hilton, ed., *The Transition from Feudalism to Capitalism* (London, 1978).

70. Ernst Wolf, "Politia Christi. Das Problem der Sozialethik im Luthertum," reprinted in his *Peregrinatio,* vol. I (Munich, 1954), pp. 214-42; Duchrow (note 6 above).

71. Tawney (note 67 above), p. 88.

72. Carl Hinrichs, *Preussentum und Pietismus. Der Pietismus in Brandenburg-Preussen als religiös-soziale Reformbewegung (Göttingen, 1971),* p. 12.

THREE KINDS OF "CHRISTIAN FREEDOM": LAW, LIBERTY, AND LICENSE IN THE GERMAN REFORMATION

Gerald Strauss, *Indiana University at Bloomington*

Anniversaries of the famous make serious problems for the historian, especially the social historian. We want not only to commemorate, we want to magnify our hero; on the other hand, the professional judgment, reinforced by our experience of life, tells us that individuals—even extraordinary individuals—leave no more than a shallow impression on the course of human affairs. Before a notable life is over or a distinguished career has wound down, the real person has ceased to be and the image, or the myth, has taken over. And it is the myth that determines historical afterlife. Certainly this has been true of Luther. His powerful image dominates the German Reformation, but this may be because we have learned to see the event from the eminence of his personal stature. Once we switch viewpoints, things look very different: not correspondence, but the divergence between the Reformer and the Reformation strikes us as we survey the scene. Such a shift is increasingly being effected now in Reformation scholarship, and this does no dishonor to Luther who never wanted to be, or thought it would be possible to be, the creator of a Reformation. For the historian, this shift in viewpoint means asking the only kinds of questions we now consider adequate to the reality of human existence in the world—questions about the always complex and usually ambiguous interactions between an individual and the human collectivity within which he lives and acts.

I want to focus the remarks that follow on the subject of freedom, because whether proposed as ideal, as criterion, or as program, or sounded as slogan, "freedom" and "free" are words that turn up so regularly in the documents that I'm persuaded we have in them a useful clue to the reception, at all levels of society, of the central issues of the Reformation as these were declared from the lectern and the pulpit, and as they were understood below. The issue of freedom, more specifically of Christian freedom, seems to me to go to the heart of Reformation concerns; in an important sense it is what the Reformation was about. And there is an additional advantage to be gained from a consideration of Christian freedom: it brings us face to face with a problem not only foremost in the age of the Reformation, but of concern also in our own day. The best compliment we can pay Luther as we celebrate him this year is to conclude that what he thought and wrote about is still a live issue in our world. The extent of our agreement with him matters less here than the fact that we are still involved with him.

Let me begin with the best known use of the word "free," in the third of the Twelve Articles of the peasants of southwestern Germany of March 1525. For in the space of three short sentences in this passage, the condition of freedom is invoked in a number of different senses, pointing us to the overlapping meanings of the word in secular and religious discourse. "We find in the Bible," the familiar phrases go, "that we are free and want to be so. Not that we wish to be altogether free, to have no ruling authority over us; God doesn't teach us that. We are taught to live by commandments, not in free fleshly license, but to love God, recognize him as our Lord in our neighbor, and to do all things as we would have them done to us, as God commanded us at the Last Supper."[1]

The careful distinctions drawn here between the state of personal freedom and actions taken in consequence of it, between legitimate and illegitimate uses of freedom, reflect the unsettled position of the word in the political and legal literature of the time, an instability already given in the New Testament reference cited in the margin of the article, 1 Peter 2:16 (on which Luther had preached a cautionary sermon during the troubled months of 1522-23)[2] and very evident in the ambivalent and often contradictory—at least in practice contradictory—uses of the term "freedom" in contemporary political documents. Its most often encountered sense lies in the plural, "freedoms," meaning stated rights and privileges granted to a group or an individual, specifying something that may be done or may not be done. But "free" meant also that something was "free for the taking;" thus, the insurrectionaries in the 1520s argued that birds, fish, and the wild game of the forest should be "free" to all, that hunting and trapping should be free, and so on.[3] Others claimed that they were "free" to do as they pleased with their goods and persons; "the laws of all the nations," they said, "suppose and assume that every person and his belongings are free and untrammelled."[4] This is affirmed as a right. In the face of denials of this right, to be free comes to mean being one's own lord and master,[5] a proposition readily turned into a political slogan, as in the common adage "To be free like the Swiss," or in the insistent reminders of the lost freedom of the German nation given in the writings of Ulrich von

Hutten, who begins his first letter to Martin Luther, in 1520, with the motto *"Vive Libertas"*.[6]

If we can fill these and similar catchwords with some political content, they might lead us to an understanding of the common view of what a "Reformation" was expected to accomplish in the early decades of the sixteenth century, for "freedom," or more precisely "Christian freedom," was the issue. Concretely, then, what did "free" and "fair," "just" and "right," "Christian" and "godly" mean in 1525 when these words were used by people in a hurry to see them put into practice? The goal, to put it first in general terms, was "Christian freedom" or, rather, its realization in an equitable, cooperative, brotherly, communitarian society to replace the present state of affairs with its ethic of egoism resulting from the substitution of man's law for God's law, human ambitions for the gospel. Christian freedom, in this view of it, was emancipation from the indignities and insecurities of life lived under the yoke of *Aigennutz,* of self-seeking. It avowed instead the principle and practice of the common good, *Gemeiner Nutz, res publica,* which was expected to follow from the restoration of the New Testament to its proper positon as law giver. It was recognized that attitudes and behavior result from social patterns. The virtues or faults of the latter govern the quality of the former. Hence the need for a thorough-going reconstruction of church and state, "so that the common man will be no longer defrauded of his Christian freedom," to quote from one of the plans.[7] This view of the Kingdom of God as attainable on Earth gave powerful ideological and rhetorical force to demands for a rearrangement of customs and institutions. Nearly all these demands had been made before, in the past. But they had never been drawn together into reform programs on so large a scale or with so wide an appeal as those aired in the years around 1525.

Actualizing Christian freedom in practical terms in society[8] meant above all other things the establishment of equal justice for all, that is to say a new condition of legal equality resulting from the shift from partisan and vested "human laws," now enthroned, to "godly natural laws in accord with Christian freedom." Next, everyone's basic needs were to be met, and each was required to do what he could, and no more. Those who had little to offer, or had suffered misfortune, would be cared for: the sick nursed, the old housed and fed, orphans raised and trained in useful occupations, the needy supported. The minimum mandated by Christian conscience was a fair sharing of the wealth and a redirection of social effort toward supportive caring. the maximum—disappearance of all distinctions between mine and thine—was proposed in schemes like Johann Hergot's

Impending Transformation of Christian Life of 1526, whose language is apocalyptic in the style of much of the social criticism of the time, but whose suggestions for reconstituting Christian society are solidly grounded in contemporary expectations. Hergot's appeal to conscience can stir us even today. "There are three tables in the world," he wrote in the concluding sentences of his *Impending Transformation,* "the first set sumptuously with great abundance of good things to eat; the second modestly, neither too much nor too little; the third meagerly, providing only scraps. And those feasting at the bountiful table came intending to take the bread away from the poorest table. From this arose the struggle [a reference to the events of 1525] and now God will smash the table of surfeit and the table of privation and make broad the table of moderation."[9]

To the Christian reformer intent on bringing about the Kingdom of God on Earth, there was nothing utopian about the grand turnabout announced here in prophetic tones. Thomas Müntzer said much the same thing: "All things should be in common" he insisted in his testimony, "and should be divided up among people according to their needs." His revolt, he maintained, was undertaken "so that all Christians might be made equal."[10] There is some controversy over how faithfully Müntzer's words, which were obtained under torture, reflected his real thoughts. However, what the scribe wrote down as Müntzer's confession in May 1525 could be heard almost everywhere at about the same time. In the spring of 1524, Johann Schilling, lecturer in the Franciscan monastery in Augsburg, began to preach vigorously against church and municipal authorities in that city, particularly against Jacob Fugger, saying, according to one who heard him, "that all things should be held in common, and with this and similar ideas he gathered a great crowd of people together."[11] In Augsburg, a large population of struggling weavers furnished a ready-made audience for this egalitarian message. But elsewhere the appeal was much the same. In Cologne, the slogan was "equal sharing," with reference to both wealth and the special privileges traditionally enjoyed by the rich.[12] In Frankfurt, in April 1525, the leaders of a guild revolution asked for the right of communal consent to taxation and for greater concern for the poor in setting prices of grain and wood.[13] In towns and cities from Ulm to Danzig and Königsberg, the communal idea of Christian freedom was translated into demands for, and of the action toward, a diminution of social and political differences among citizen groups to keep pace with the Reformation's equalization of clergy and laity. R.W. Scribner has recently summed up the underlying principle and its application in these and many similar actions. In the political events taking place in German cities in the early Reformation, he writes, "there is the sense of a considered collective decision, firmly taken and justified by the yardstick of Scripture."[14] "Christian freedom" and Holy Writ demanded no less than this: an equitable sharing among brothers of what life had to offer to all.

Most reform programs, however, were less grandiose in what they hoped to achieve, attending chiefly to matters for immediate improvement.[15] Serfdom was to disappear altogether; excessive and conspicuous wealth was to be channelled to the poor and needy; a host of regulations were to keep merchants honest. At the same time the plans show a conscious drive toward rationalization of economic and administrative procedures: standardization of weights and measures within territories; abolition of road taxes and other impediments to free-moving trade; better control of coinage; streamlining of administrative arrangements; and so on. Governments were asked to reduce cronyism, the tendency of entrenched functionaries to favor their friends and relations in judging, governing, financing. And one notices in these manifestoes, as in so much of the literature of the time, a pronounced suspicion of men of academic learning, and of the enlarged authority lately given them and their book knowledge in the councils of church and state. The strongest animus was against lawyers, deeply rooted by now in political administrations and courts of territorial and municipal governments. A kind of backlash against these unwelcome modernizers (as they were perceived) was one of the forces behind the push to do away, as much as possible, with so-called "worldly laws," and to substitute for them the binding code of the "godly and natural law." A few radical reformers—Gaismair for example—even moved to restrict all academic teaching to the Bible.[16] Man-made statutes not directly drawn from the Bible were reclassified as *Neuerungen*, innovations, a word with strongly pejorative associations in the sixteenth century. *Neuerungen* were held responsible for the corruption of life, and the repair of such perversions was always seen as a return to the past, above all to Scripture. This is the perspective from which we should judge the prominent place given in almost every statement of grievances to the request for freely elected pastors to "preach to us"—that is to every community or congregation—"the holy Gospel purely and clearly, without human additions, human doctrines, or human precepts."[17] "Human additions" were *Neuerungen*. They were deviations from true doctrine and were held responsible for the loss of that Christian freedom whose recovery was the chief ideological objective of the revolutionaries of 1525.

This, then, is what *"Reformation"* meant to a large segment of the German population in the 1520s: a trasformation of secular and religious life to bring it into line with Scripture. A Christian's freedom was his right to live in such a christianized society. It was also his right to help bring it about. To scruples about people's license to alter laws and social arrangements the reformers had a short answer: if their plans were in harmony with Scripture, well and good. The divine law gave them more than adequate authority. Acts 5:29: "We must obey God rather than men." 1 Cor. 7:21: "If a chance of liberty should come, take it." These passages were often cited.[18] But it would be wrong to let them stand for the whole movement. Christian freedom and Christian justice did not insist on insurrection. Only the most rigid apocalyptics advocated violence and destruction as a means to a desirable end. Most leaders had absorbed too much Christian quietism to endorse a code of violence. With the authors of the Twelve Articles they believed that "The Gospel does not cause rebellion and uproars, because it tells of Christ, the promised Messiah, whose words and life teach nothing but love, peace, patience, and unity."[19] On the other hand, though violent overthrows were not usually intended, the reformist movement did develop a true revolutionary momentum, a dynamism given in its belief in God's irresistible purpose, of which human wills were the instruments. "If God deigns to hear the peasants' earnest plea that they may be permitted to live according to His word," the Twelve Articles threatened, "who will dare deny His will? Who indeed will dare question His judgment? Who will dare oppose His majesty?"[20] The insurrection of 1525 thus derived its revolutionary power not so much from a commitment on the part of its leaders to violent overthrow, as from the conviction that their cause was one with the will of God manifesting itself in history and tending to the establishment of the right order in society.

Now, this was a most unLutheran reading of both history and Scripture: an utterly different sense from Luther's of what Reformation meant and what the Reformation was about. On Christian freedom and its responsibilities, Luther and the reformers talked past each other. Scorning all efforts to alter the status quo in the world, Luther condemned every attempt to make of Christian liberty a material kind of freedom. "Christ doesn't want to change worldly states," he said, "nor does he want to do away with serfdom. What does he care how princes and lords govern? It's nothing to him how you plow, sow, make shoes, build houses, pay interest, or take dividends.... Christ speaks of no such external matters. He concerns himself with a freedom that is beyond and above outward things, namely, how you are redeemed from sin, from death, from God's wrath, from devil and hell and eternal damnation.... This Christian freedom comes to a free man and also to a serf, to a man in prison as well as to one who takes a prisoner, to women and to men, to a serving man or maid and to master and mistress. We speak here of a freedom before God, who frees us from sin...."[21] The promise of this spiritual freedom is one of the root doctrines of evangelical Christianity, and Luther described it often and was tireless in distinguishing it from the other, vulgar, carnal freedom after which, he said, the mob hankers, and which it pursues with, he thought, misguided perseverance.[22] After the mid-1520s, and in reaction to the events of those years, his contrasting of the two freedoms against each other grew more polarizing and his excoriation of those who wanted the fleshly sort much more strident. "The freedom of the flesh is the devil's freedom," he said in *Lectures on Galatians* of 1535, "through which Satan rules the world. Those who claim this kind of freedom obey neither God nor the laws; they do as they please. This is the sort of freedom the rabble is after nowadays."[23] It was not for this that Christ had come into the world, he says, adding with some bitterness, "though people would seem to prefer it that way."[24] Luther had few illusions, and he was a close and, by-and-large understanding, observer of the human scene. "Most men interpret the doctrine of faith in a material way," he admitted "and want to make spiritual freedom out to be a freedom of the flesh. You can see this every day," he adds, confessing that he has found himself wishing that "such swine who trample pearls under their feet were still living under the tyranny of the Pope."[25]

Luther, then, had no sympathy with the reformers' struggle for a more just world drawn from the New Testament understood as a gospel of liberation. "Laws don't make you free," he said to the reformists; "Christian freedom has nothing to do with the body or with your ordinary lives. It has to do with the soul."[26] In sentences such as these—and there are many of them—Luther's meaning is unmistakable. On the other hand, his writings do contain passages in which this message is blurred, and these are sure to have led many of his followers along a path Luther came to consider, in the light of later events, fatally wrong. Justus Maurer, who has made a study of over two hundred evangelical preachers active in the years leading up to the revolution of 1525, attributed their success as crowd gatherers and crowd pleasers to the *"Befreiungserlebnis"* their sermons conveyed to their audiences, a sense of exhilaration arising from the newly uplifted status of the pious lay person vis-à-vis the clergy. Maurer concludes that "Freedom was the cue word" for this raising up of the laity with its claim that ordinary people, by their faith, were placed as high as the clerical estate.[27] Now, this is a proposition that, while not original with Luther, owes everything to the force with which he preached it and wrote about it in the early years of the Reformation. In some of his most widely propagated publications, the idea had a distinctly libertarian cast. In *To the Christian Nobility of the German Nation,* for example, "free" and "freedom" are used so often and, for evident propaganda purposes, given such an emotional charge, that some scholars have suspected the pamphlet of misleading its readers into giving Christian freedom a falsely political and social meaning.[28] It is hard to imagine that Luther was not at the time alert to this ambiguity. Everything we know about how people read and listen suggests that they insert words and ideas into their own frames, making sense of them by aligning them with their own familiar social landmarks, and no doubt this is what happened in the 1520s. Luther's contemporaries are not likely to have made tidy distinctions, as he did, between religious and worldly needs and obligations. Nor did they place the former above the latter; nor did they agree that a good Christian is bound to do so. To Luther, reformation was all inward (although he was, of course, all for doing away with any structure that constrained the freedom of the Gospel to form consciences); its central thrust was the acceptance of Christian freedom as emancipation from sin and promise of eternal life. The material reformers had totally misconceived this meaning, with—so Luther thought—disastrous consequences. He did not deny the accuracy of their description of the real world or the justice of their criticism of the inhumanity and rapaciousness of the powerful men who dominated it. But he thought such criticism pointless, and those who made it, misguided. His sense of being implicated in this misunderstanding no doubt explains the forcefulness of his repudiation of all revolutionary aims in 1525 and thereafter, and his decisive denial of the image of reformation as an ideology of political and social freedom.

I have restated some familiar facts and speculations. A more interesting question arises from them. Why are we so willing to accept Luther's strictures of the reformist platform while holding on to our generous view of him as a sympathetic judge of the human scene? The world was, for most people, a cruel place. They had little to expect from their God, from nature, from their fellow men. Was it helpful to tell them that it didn't really matter, that—as he put it in his response to the Twelve Articles—"these things don't concern a Christian, and he cares nothing about them"?[29] Clearly, to most people, rightly or wrongly, worldly cares were precisely what mattered. How could Luther tell them that Christians should be martyrs on Earth, and why does this advice not destroy Luther's image for us?

The answer is, of course, that centuries of Luther scholarship have convinced us of the total honesty of Luther's central outlook: his unshakable acceptance of the absolute priority of otherworldly concerns, the consequences of which he was as ready to apply to himself as to others. The depth of Luther's commitment to taking God's view rather than man's, and the cost to him in human terms of this obligation, has recently been brought out dramatically in Heiko Oberman's warm and compassionate new biography. Professor Oberman's book bears the subtitle: "Mankind between God and Devil." In the tug of war between these two cosmic forces, the only thing that counted for the human individual was the outcome. What were a few years of pain and trouble compared to the promise of bliss everlasting? Life mattered only to the extent that it affected what came thereafter. Luther really believed this, and we believe that he believed it.

But our view of these things is surely swayed also by the knowledge that they relate to history, to the past, in this case the quite distant past. Do we not make automatic discriminations in our value judgments according to whether we appraise events far or near in time and space? Obviously we do; we do it all the time; and our distinctions often trouble us in our conscience, although we don't seem to be able to do much about our tendency to make them. With respect to the past, our frequently cavalier way of presenting it must be due to the fact that it *is* past: done and gone. Elaborate, often strained, demonstrations are needed to link it to the present. We wish only to *understand* the past, no more. When it comes to our own time, on the other hand, we want much more than that: not merely to understand it, but to live in it as well. A very different set of standards is brought into play to serve this much more demanding objective. Understanding in its two-fold sense—not only to grasp or apprehend, but also to gain a sympathetic and tolerant attitude toward something or someone—is routinely awarded in history, from which the passage of time has insulated us. In our dealings with the present it is much more reluctantly given. Were he writing today, in reaction to events in our own time, Luther would be studied with a much colder eye, and judged by much less accommodating standards, than is the historical figure in his safely remote sixteenth century.

Let me make a test of this supposition. Not long ago I picked up a paperback published in 1982 by the Ethics and Public Policy Center in Washington, called *The Pope and Revolution: John Paul II Confronts Liberation Theology.*[30] The book opens with a brief foreword by Richard J. Neuhaus, a Lutheran pastor prominent in conservative circles in the United States. Reading this foreword, a Reformation historian at once finds his attention seized because of the striking way in which its author has repeated the gist of Luther's response to the revolutionaries of his own day. Throughout Christian history, Neuhaus writes, there have been individuals and movements ready to settle for less than the Kingdom of God. Trying to make the world a better place is settling for less because it means confusing the Kingdom with our own programs for making things the way we think they ought to be. Liberation theology is the latest of these confusions. As preached in the Third World, particularly in Latin America, it substitutes short-term gratification for long-term deliverance. "Almost as in a mirror image of earlier illusions," Neuhaus says, "it is often posited that demolishing the social, economic, and political orders . . . is necessary to establish the Kingdom of God." Neuhaus thinks this is understandable, but wrong. We get tired of waiting for the promise, he contends. We long for the fleshpots of Egypt—in this case, for the satisfaction of a cause or a movement to make us feel important and powerful in the world. We want the Gospel to be useful to this cause. "Useful" is settling for less. "When we are no longer sure that the Gospel is true," he writes, "we are eager to prove that it is useful." "What is at stake," he concludes, "is the integrity of the Gospel." The Gospel is truly revolutionary. Compared to its thorough-going radicalism, our little plans for quick and partial changes are conventional, mere accommodations, and Neuhaus dismisses them as such. Instead of dreaming of a few changes we think we can make, we should learn patience and rest content to wait for the promise to be fulfilled. Any other attitude is human presumption; any other action is folly.[37]

I don't know about other readers of this preface,[32] but I find it distasteful in its reasoning and extremely disturbing in its implications. But it is also clear to me that I judge it to be so chiefly because I am much more keenly alert to these implications—specifically to their effect on real men and women in real places—than I would be if they related to events I study in history. The former, the lives of my contemporaries, touch me in a way in which the latter—figures in the past—do not. What Neuhaus says upsets me for this reason, and no amount of scene setting and interpretation can take the callousness out of his remarks. What bothers me about them is their hypocrisy. He tries to have it both ways. He doesn't justify the status quo, he will even admit criticism of it; but he won't have it altered: things must stay as they are while we await the time of the promise. The Bible's absolute truth and utter radicalism preclude any lesser means with which the lot of our fellow men might be eased. Meanwhile people suffer, in concrete ways brought graphically home to all but the most resolutely ivory-towered among us. Witnessing their suffering, I wonder not about the meaning of it, but only about whether it can be lessened, and how this might be done, and how soon. Neuhaus's posture strikes me as both cruel and dishonest. Surely the long wait for the promise to be fulfilled is more tolerable for some of us, favored in the circumstances of our lives, than it is for others, who are not. I do not even want to understand a man who can't or won't see the moral flaw in this position and seems so indifferent to its consequences. Needless to say, this is an emotional reaction on my part. I am free to indulge it in response to what I read in the daily press. But the criteria of our scholarly discipline dictate that it has no place in my study of the past, where it would seriously compromise my understanding of it. And I agree that this is so. What results is a double standard, one which I imagine we all practice, and which has direct and, I think, serious bearing on the character of our work. But I believe it is useful on occasion to exchange the respective attitudes governing our activities. The results can be instructive.

Liberation theology and the opposition to it are interesting to Reformation historians precisely because they let us test the give and take of sixteenth-century arguments in a tangible, present, living situation. Language differs, but arguments are much the same then and now. A few aphoristic fragments must suffice here to show the correspondence.[33] Liberation theology, Gutierrez says, is "critical reflection on Christian praxis in the light of the Word."[34] It admits no distinctions between world and faith.[35] According to Leonardo Boff, it sees the Kingdom of God as expressing "man's utopian longing for liberation from everything that alienates him . . . : anguish, pain, hunger, injustice, death . . . ",[36] and accepts as an article of faith the utopian belief in the possibility of constructing a qualitatively different society.[37] It addresses its rhetoric to a society primarily religious, not yet fully secularized[38] and based not on individuals, but on communities.[39] It sees Jesus as a liberator, as one who broke barriers and opposed legalism in all its forms.[40] Above all, it concerns itself with consequences, with the practical results of what is preached and taught. Christianity is considered as action, not merely as doctrine. A serious view of the Christian faith sees it as an instrument not only of individual change, but also of social transformation.[41]

In all essentials, these are the base positions from which the revolutionaries of the 1520s argued their grievances and stated their demands. And the rejection of these positions on the ground of their mere worldliness is also Luther's denial of the Gospel as a charter of secular freedom. We need not, of course, decide for one and against the other of these postulates as we try to make out what happened in 1525. Historians have long maintained—perhaps not always honestly—their right to a posture of impartiality, although others would argue instead the very impossibility of speaking or writing without judging. But when we see Luther's arguments restated in a setting so near, so timely, and so emotionally charged for us, we cannot help but judge them. *How* should we judge them? There is only one fair and sensible way—or so it seems to me: by their consequences in the real world. I have no doubt of the superiority of Gutierrez, Boff, Segundo, et al. over Neuhaus when their respective ideas are tested on this ground. As for the Reformation of the sixteenth century, we might return to it by asking the same question: what were the results of the theologians' denial of the reformist claim that Christian freedom has radical secular applications? Let us remind ourselves that Luther was only the most prominent of the many pastors and preachers who rejected the liberationist position after 1525; among them were men like Johann Eberlin, Jakob Strauss, Christoph Schappeler who had helped direct, lead, or inspire the revolutionary movement in the early 1520s. Now they did their part in showing the way to a passive ethic of acceptance.[42] Luther himself did not indicate his sense of what the consequences might be, beyond suggesting a bad end for unrepentant rebels. But Philip Melanchthon, to whom the events of 1522 to 1525 were even more traumatic and foreboding than they were to Luther, drew a deeply antagonistic lesson from what he had seen. "It would be well," he wrote in his own response to the Twelve Articles, "if so wild and unruly a people as the Germans had even less freedom than they now have." The insurrection had shown, he thought, what happens when you relax the reins. He was all for tightening them now.[43]

And this is exactly what happened. Backing up the preachers' moral authority, Lutheran states made the correct understanding of Christian freedom a matter of legal obligation on all their subjects. From the late 1520s, every German *Kirchenordnung* made the orthodox definition of Christian freedom one of the fundamental laws of state. The object was to discredit the liberationist interpretation of the gospel and to link Christian freedom with the citizen virtues of political loyalty and compliance. Pastors were required to give frequent sermons on Christian freedom, preaching, they were cautioned, not "out of your own heads," but correctly, out of St. Paul and the officially formulated creed. Bible passages were given on which to base homilies on this subject: 1 Peter 2:16 and Galatians 5:13 on the abuse of freedom; Exodus 20 and 22, Matthew 22:21 on the necessity of civil obedience; Romans 13, Titus 3:1, and 1 Peter 2:13-17 on submission to authority.[44] These passages, it was said, "show clearly and sufficiently that Christian freedom does not consist of being free of rents, interest, tithe, tax, service, or any other external burdens and grievances, as subjects call them, but is instead an inner, spiritual thing alone, and that in all external matters and laws, subjects owe their superiors obedience and submission."[45] The established social order is explicitly affirmed. "Christian freedom," the *Kirchenordnung* of Rothenburg states, "is not in conflict with our classes, orders, or Estates . . . ; on the contrary, it upholds them and demands loyalty to the laws that protect them."[46] The authorized view of Christian freedom is presented as the best hope for peace and harmony in society, for instance by Veit Dietrich, in his Agenda book for rural pastors in Nuremberg, in which Dietrich told his colleagues that "if you preach and teach in this way about Christian freedom, you will not only hold down rebellion in the populace . . . but will also encourage people to be dutiful to their worldly authorities and do whatever is best for peace and well being. . . . For Scripture is our witness to this," he continued, "that worldly governments are founded by God, who commands us as their subjects to obey them in all that touches worldly matters."[47] Not all pastors gave the political rationale such a blank check; but many did, and a preliminary and unscientific attempt on my part to plot these on a map of Germany suggests that sternly conservative definitions of Christian freedom tended to appear in governmental pronouncements wherever the revolution of 1525 had been most painfully felt. Indoctrinating their subjects in these definitions became a paramount concern of church and state authorities after 1525. In the process, most of the reform demands that had earlier been deduced from Christian freedom were dropped from the orthodox statement of it. Most notable in its omission from these post-1525 authorized definitions was any and all reference to the right of communities or congregations to choose their own pastors. This change illustrates what was probably the chief lesson taken by church and state authorities from the events of 1525. Everywhere in Germany, governments now devised administrative and educational procedures designed to centralize and control the job of instructing the public. From the point of view of the ruling elites in church and society, this strengthening of their authority, and of the means of exerting it, is what the 16th-century Reformation was all about.

With this dénouement Luther had virtually nothing to do. He was far from approving of, or associating himself with, or sharing the rationale of, the conservative reaction. By his lights, governments policies in the backlash of 1525 were as wrong-headedly carnal, as opposed to Gospel and true Christian freedom, as had been the trouble-making of the rebels. To be sure, Luther accepted and welcomed the need for discipline, and therefore for laws, including restrictive laws, and their enforcement. But the resulting political and judicial order had no claim to being a Christian polity. Its ethos of coercion and involuntary acquiescence, of reciprocal mistrust, revealed it as archetypically worldly. In a true Christian society, association is voluntary, not compulsory. Its bond and drive is love, not force. "A Christian," said Luther, "lives not for himself, but for Christ and his fellow man, for Christ through faith, for his fellow man through love.[48] There was little faith and less love in the crass new society then abuilding. Luther saw this as clearly, and I think as sorrowfully, as the reformers had seen it in the early 1520s. It must have been a consolation to him to know that it would not last much longer.

Notes

1. The German text is printed in Adolf Laube and Hans Werner Seiffert eds., *Flugschriften der Bauernkriegszeit* (Berlin [East], 1975), p. 28. English translation in Peter Blickle, *The Revolution of 1525*, tr. Thomas A. Brady, Jr., and H.C. Erik Midelfort (Baltimore, 1981), p. 197.

2. *WA* 12, 331-333.

3. E.g. Articles of peasants of Allgäu, February 1525, in Günther Franz ed., *Quellen zur Geschichte des Bauernkrieges* (Munich, 1963), No. 35, p. 164.

4. From reply of *Gotteshausleute* of Kempten to complaints of their prince-abbot, September 1525 in *ibid.* No. 27, p. 128.

5. E.g. Articles of peasants of Stühlingen and Lupfen, 1525 in *ibid.*, No. 25, p. 121; articles of Memmingen peasants, February-March 1525 in *ibid.*, No. 40, p. 169; also *ibid.*, No. 34b, p. 153; No. 30, p. 141; No. 29, p. 136.

6. Hutten to Luther, June 4, 1520, *WA Br*, vol. 2, No. 295. On the issue of freedom in early modern German law and politics see Herbert Grundmann, "Freiheit als religiöses, politisches und persönliches Postulat im Mittelalter," *Historische Zeitschrift*, 183 (1957), 23-53; Karl Bosl, "Die alte deutsche Freiheit. Geschichtliche Grundlagen des modernen deutschen Staates" in: *Frühformen der Gesellschaft im mittelalterlichen Europa* (Munich, 1964), pp. 204-219; *id.*, "Freiheit und Unfreiheit. Zur Entwicklung der Unterschichten in Deutschland und Frankreich während des Mittelalters," in: *ibid.*, pp. 180-203; Joseph Schlumbohm, *Freiheitsbegriff und Emanzipationsprozess. Zur Geschichte eines politischen Wortes*, Göttingen, 1973. (especially 14-20).

7. From a reform plan submitted to the Assembly of Franconian peasants, May 1525: Günther Franz, *op. cit.* No. 124, p. 375.

8. For sources of this paragraph, see the following reform plans and manifestos: *An die Versamlung gemayner Pawerschaft* (1525) ed. Siegfried Hoyer, Leipzig, 1975; reform plan by Wendel Hipler and Friedrich Weygandt (1525)—the so-called Heilbronn Program—printed in Laube and Seiffert eds., *Flugschriften*, 75-79 and in Klaus Arnold, "Damit der arm man unnd gemainer nutz iren furgang haben...," *Zeitschrift für historische Forschung*, 9.3 (1982), 288-311; Johann Hergot, *Von der newen Wandlung eynes christlichen lebens* (1526 or 1527) in Laube and Seiffert, eds., *op. cit.*, 547-557; the Meran Articles of Tirol (1525) in Günther Franz, *op. cit.*, No. 91, pp. 272-285; *Michael Gaismairs Landesordnung* (1526) in *ibid.*, No. 92, pp. 139-143; the Franconian plan mentioned in note 7 above.

9. Johan Hergot, *Von der newen Wandlung...* in Laube and Seiffert eds., *op. cit.*, p. 557.

10. "Bekenntnis" in Thomas Müntzer, *Schriften und Briefe*, ed. Günther Franz (Gütersloh, 1968), 548. On the problems connected with this "confession," see Walter Elliger, *Thomas Müntzer. Leben und Werk* (Göttingen, 1975), 797-798.

11. Wolfgang Zorn, *Augsburg* (Munich, 1976), pp. 169-173.

12. From the testimony of Tilman Rebein, one of the ringleaders of the Cologne revolution: Hugo Stehkämper, *Revolutionen in Köln* (Cologne, 1973), p. 57.

13. Sigrid Jahns, *Frankfurt, Reformation und Schmalkaldischer Bund* (Frankfurt am Main, 1976), pp. 34-42.

14. R.W. Scribner, "Practice and Principle in the German Towns: Preachers and People" in P.N. Brooks, ed., *Reformation Principle and Practice. Essays in Honour of Arthur Geoffrey Dickens* (London, 1980), p. 98. On political and social instability in German cities, see Rudolf Endres, "Zünfte und Unterschichten als Elemente der Instabilität in den Städten," in: Peter

Blickle, ed., "Revolte und Revolution in Europa," *Historische Zeitschrift, Beiheft 4,* Neue Folge, (1975), 151-170.

15. This paragraph rests on my reading of the printed sources listed in notes 1, 3-5, and 7.

16. Michael Gaismair in Laube and Seiffert, eds., *op. cit.,* pp. 286-287.

17. From the first of the Twelve Articles, English translation in Peter Blickle, *op. cit.,* p. 196.

18. Two examples: "46 Artickel, so die gemeyn einem ersamen rath der...stat Franckenfurt...fürgehalten" (April, 1525) in Laube and Seiffert eds., *op. cit.,* p. 59; "An die Versamlung gemayner Pawerschaft" (1525) ed. Siegfried Hoyer, p. 108.

19. "Twelve Articles" in Blickle, *op. cit.,* p. 195.

20. *Ibid.,* p. 196.

21. From Sermons on John (1530-32); on 8:34-38, *WA* 33, 659-60.

22. Exegesis of First Epistle of Peter (1523), *WA* 12, 331; Second Sermon on Jeremiah 23:5-8 (1526), *WA* 20, 579; Lectures on Galatians (1535), on 5:13, *WA* 40.2, 60.

23. Lectures on Galatians (1535), *WA* 40.2, 2-3.

24. Sermons on John 6-8 (1530-32), *WA* 33, 668.

25. Lectures on Galatians (1535), *WA* 40.2, 60.

26. Second Sermon on Jeremiah 23:5-8 (1526, *WA* 20, 579.

27. Justus Maurer, *Prediger im Bauernkrieg* (Stuttgart, 1979), pp. 34-35.

28. Wilhelm Maurer, *Von der Freiheit eines Christenmenschen. Zwei Untersuchungen zu Luthers Reformationsschriften 1520/21* (Göttingen, 1949), p. 43.

29. "Ermahnung zum Frieden auf die zwölf Artikel der Bauerschaft...," *WA* 18, 328.

30. Quentin L. Quade ed., *The Pope and Revolution. John Paul II Confronts Liberation Theology,* Washington, D.C., 1982.

31. *Ibid.,* vii-x.

32. Neuhaus's preface reiterates the positions framed in the so-called "Hartford Declaration" of 1975 by a conference of scholars, theologians, and pastors of which Neuhaus was one of the conveners. It was answered in 1976 by "the Boston Affirmations" drafted by the Boston Industrial Mission Task Force. Its publication led to a spirited correspondence in the pages of the *Andover Newton Quarterly* (16.4) of March, 1976, pp. 235-270. See especially the "Hartford Declaration's refutation of Theme 12: "The struggle for a better humanity will bring about the Kingdom of God" and the "Boston Affirmations" section "Present Witnesses," as well as correspondents' discussion of these points.

33. Some general works on Liberation Theology are: Francis P. Fiorenza, "Latin American Liberation Theology," *Interpretation,* 28 (1974), 441-457, with excellent bibliography; J. Andrew Kirk, *Liberation Theology. An Evangelical View from the Third World,* Atlanta, 1979; Thomas M. McFadden, ed., *Liberation, Revolution, and Freedom. Theological Perspectives. Proceedings of the College Theology Society,* New York, 1975; Dermot Lane, eds., *Liberation Theology. An Irish Dialogue* (Dublin, 1977); Charles R. Strain, "Liberation Theology: North American Perspectives," *Religious Studies Review,* 8.3 (July, 1982), 239-244; *idem,* "Ideology and Alienation: Theses on the Interpretation and Evaluation of Theologies of Liberation," *Journal of the American Academy of Religion* 45 (1977), 473-490.

34. Gustavo Gutierrez, *A Theology of Liberation. History, Politics, and Salvation,* tr. and ed. by Sister Caridad Inda and John Eagleson (Maryknoll, N.Y., 1973), pp. ix, 13.

35. J. Andrew Kirk, *op. cit.,* pp. 31-32.

36. Leonardo Boff, "Salvation in Jesus Christ and the Process of Liberation" in Claude Geffré and Gustavo Gutierrez, eds., *The Mystical and Political Dimension of the Christian Faith. Concilium: Religion in the Seventies* (New York, 1974), pp. 80-81.

37. J. Andrew Kirk, *op. cit.,* pp. 33-34.

38. Francis P. Fiorenza in: *loc. cit.,* p. 443.

39. Mary I. Buckley, "Freedom as Personal and Public Liberation" in Thomas M. McFadden ed., *op. cit.,* p. 40.

40. Leonardo Boff in *loc. cit.,* pp. 83-84.

41. Claude Geffré and Gustavo Gutierrez, eds., *op. cit.,* pp. 10-11.

42. Johann Eberlin, *Ein getrewe warnung an die Christen in der Burgauischen Mark, sich auch füre hin zu hüten vor aufrur...* (1526) in Ludwig Enders, ed., *Johann Eberlin von Günzburg, Sämmtliche Schriften* vol. III (Halle, 1902), pp. 279-280. Cf. Justus Maurer, *op. cit.,* p. 426. Jakob Strauss, *Christliche... Antwort... auf das ungütige Schmähbüchlein D. Johannis Coclei* (1526) quoted in Hermann Barge, *Jakob Strauss* (Leipzig, 1937), pp. 125-132. Christoph Schappeler to Zwingli, May 1525 in *Huldreich Zwinglis Sämmtliche Werke,* vol. VIII (Leipzig, 1914), pp. 324-326. On the about-face executed by many preachers during and after 1525, see Justus Maurer, *op. cit.,* pp. 263-275. For a general account of the reactions of Lutheran pastors and theologians to the revolt, see Robert Kolb, "The Theologians and the Peasants: Conservative Evangelical Reactions to the Peasant Revolt," *Archiv für Reformationsgeschichte,* 69 (1978), 103-130.

43. Philip Melanchthon, *Eyn schrifft... widder die artikel der Bawrschaǳfft* (1525) in Laube and Seiffert, eds., *op. cit.,* p. 234.

44. These citations from *Der Durchleuchtigen Hochgebornen Fürsten... Casimirn and... Georgen..., Marggraven zu Brandenburg... anzeygen, wie die gewesen empörung und aufrurn... auss ungeschickten predigen entstanden sind...* (1525) in: Emil Sehling, continued by the Institut für evangelisches Kirchenrecht der Evangelischen Kirche in Deutschland, eds., *Die evangelischen Kirchenordnungen des XVI. Jahrhunderts,* vol. 11 (Tübingen, 1961), p. 86.

45. *Ibid.,* p. 87.

46. *Ordnung der Kirchen... der Stat Rothenburg ob der Tauber* in *ibid.,* p. 576.

47. Veit Dietrich, *Agendbüchlein für die Pfarrherrn auff dem Land* (1545) in *Ibid.,* p. 552.

48. "Von der Freiheit eines Christenmenschen" (1520), *WA* 7, 38.

Index of Names